A Stairway Taken by the Lucid
Tsong kha pa's Study of Noble Beings

ŚATA-PIṬAKA SERIES

INDO-ASIAN LITERATURES

Volume 643

Reproduced in original scripts and languages
Translated, annotated and critically evaluated by
specialists of the East and the West

Founded by
Prof. RAGHUVIRA *M.A., Ph.D., D.Litt. et Phil.*
Continued by his son
Prof. LOKESH CHANDRA

आचार्य—रघुवीर—समुपक्रान्तं

जम्बुद्वीप-राष्ट्राणां
(भारत-नेपाल-गान्धार-शूलिक-तुरुष्क-पारस-ताजक-भोट-चीन-मोंगोल-मञ्जु-
उदयवर्ष-सिंहल-सुवर्णभू-श्याम-कम्बुज-चम्पा-द्वीपान्तरादीनां)

एकैकेषां समस्रोतसां संस्कृति—साहित्य—समुच्चय—
सरितां सागरभूतं

शतपिटकम्

A Stairway Taken by the Lucid

Tsong kha pa's Study of Noble Beings

Introduced and Translated
by
James B. Apple

ADITYA PRAKASHAN
New Delhi

First published: 2013

ISBN 978-81-7742-131-6

Published by Aditya Prakashan, 2/18 Ansari Road,
New Delhi – 110 002.

email: contact@adityaprakashan.com
website: www.adityaprakashan.com

Printed at Thomson Press, Delhi - 110 020.

Contents

INTRODUCTION	**1**
1. TSONG KHA PA AND HIS WORKS ON THE TWENTY SAṂGHAS	**14**
2. THE EARLY YEARS OF THE LIFE OF TSONG KHA PA	**19**
3. WRITING OF *THE STAIRWAY TAKEN BY THOSE OF LUCID INTELLIGENCE*	**24**
4. *THE STAIRWAY TAKEN BY THE LUCID*	**32**
BIBLIOGRAPHY	**198**
INDEX	**216**

Abbreviations

AA	*Abhisamayālaṃkāra*
AAĀ	*Abhisamayālaṃkārālokā* of Haribhadra (ed. Wogihara, 1932-1935)
AASPh	*Abhisamayālaṃkārasphuṭārthā* (ed. Amano, 2000)
AAV	*Abhisamayālaṃkāravṛtti* of Ārya Vimuktisena (ed. Pensa, 1967)
ACIP	Asian Classics Input Project
AK	*Abhidharmakośakārikā* (ed. Gokhale, 1946)
AKBh	*Abhidharmakośabhāṣya* (ed. Pradhan, 1967. Reprint, 1975)
AKV	*Abhidharmakośabhāṣyavyākhyā* (ed. Śāstrī, 1971)
AN	*Aṅguttaranikāya* (ed. Morris and Hardy, 1885-1900)
AS	*Abhidharmasamuccaya* (ed. Pradhan, 1950)
ASBh	*Abhidharmasamuccayabhāṣya* (ed. Tatia, 1976)
Aṣṭa	*Aṣṭasāhasrikāprajñāpāramitāsūtra*
BEFEO	Bulletin de l'Ecole Française d'Extrême-Orient
BHSD	Buddhist Hybrid Sanskrit Dictionary (Edgerton, 1953. Reprint, 1977)
BSOAS	*Bulletin of the School of African & Oriental Studies* (London)
EOB	*Encyclopedia of Buddhism* (G.P. Malalasekara, 1973)
D	*Blo gsal bgrod pa'i them skas* (Delhi 1975-1979)
DN	*Dīghanikāya* (Rhys-Davids and Carpenter, Reprint, 1960-1967)
GBBN	*Sgra sbyor bam po gnyis pa* (ed. Ishikawa, 1990)
Golden Garland	*Legs bshad gser phreng* of Tsong kha pa (1970/1977)
IIJ	Indo-Iranian Journal
JAOS	*Journal of the American Oriental Society*
JIABS	*Journal of the International Association for Buddhist Studies*
JIBS	*Indogaku Bukkyō Kenkyū* [Journal of Indian and Buddhist Studies]
JIP	*Journal of Indian Philosophy*
LVP	La Vallée Poussin's (1923) French translation of AK and AKBh
M	*Blo gsal bgrod pa'i them skas* (Mtsho sngon mi rigs dpe skrun khang, 1986)
MHTL	*Materials for a History of Tibetan Literature* (Chandra, 1985)
MN	*Majjhimanikāya* (ed. Trenckner and Chalmers, Reprint, 1960-1964)
MSA	*Mahāyānasūtrālaṃkāra* (ed. Lévi, 1907-1911)
MVP	*Mahāvyutpatti* (1916-1925)
MW	Monier-Williams Sanskrit English Dictionary (1899)
Pañcaviṃśati	*Pañcaviṃśatisāhasrikāprajñāpāramitāsūtra* (ed. Dutt, 1934)

P	*Blo gsal bgrod pa'i them skas* (Peking Edition, ed. Suzuki, 1956-1961)
Pk	Peking edition of the Tibetan Tripiṭaka (ed. Suzuki, 1956-1961)
PP	*Prajñāpāramitā*
PSPh	*Abhisamayālaṃkāraprasphuṭapadā* of Dharmamitra
Pugg	*Puggala-paññatti* (ed. Morris, *P*1972)
Pugg-A	*Puggala-paññatti-atthakathā* (ed. Landsberg and Davids, 1972)
Rjes gnang	*Dge 'dun nyi su bsdus pa rjes gnang ba dang zhugs gnas* of Tsong kha pa (1977)
Rnam rgyal	Blo bzang 'phrin las rnam rgyal (1967)
Śgs	*Śūraṃgamasamādhisūtra* (Lamotte 1998)
SN	*Saṃyuttanikāya* (ed. L. Feer, Reprint, 1973-1990)
Stairway	*Blo gsal bgrod pa'i them skas* of Tsong kha pa (1977)
T	*Taishō Shinshū Daizōkyō*
Taipei	Taipei edition of Tibetan Tripiṭaka bka' 'gyur (ed. Barber, 1991)
Traité	*Le Traité de la Grande Vertu de Sagesse de Nāgārjuna* (Lamotte, 1944-1980)
Vks	*Vimalakīrtinirdeśasūtra* (Lamotte, 1976)
WZKSO	Wiener Zeitschrift für die Kunde süd-und Ostrasiens

INTRODUCTION

The text edited and translated here is the *Zhugs pa dang gnas pa'i skyes bu chen po rnams kyi rnam par bzhag pa blo gsal bgrod pa'i them skas* (literally, *The Stairway taken by the Lucid-A Presentation of the Great Beings who Enter and Abide* [*in the Four Fruitions*], hereafter *Stairway*) by the Tibetan Buddhist scholar Tsong kha pa (1357-1419). This text consists of a detailed investigation into the enumeration of Noble beings or Noble individuals (*'phags pa'i gang zag, āryapudgala*) that constitute the spiritual community (*dge 'dun, saṃgha*) that Tibetan Buddhists venerate, as well as emulate, in practicing Buddhist pathways to awakening. The following pages introduce the translation by discussing the importance of enumerating Noble beings in Tibetan Buddhism, describing Tsong kha pa's written works related to Noble beings, and providing a historical account of the circumstances for his writing of the *Stairway*. This translation complements my previous work on this subject (Apple 2003, 2004, 2008) and readers may wish to consult those sources for further analysis and explanation of this topic in the works of Tsong kha pa as well as in Tibetan Buddhist scholasticism.

The following work consists of a critical Tibetan edition of the *Stairway* with an annotated English translation on facing pages. The aim of this critical edition and annotated translation is to provide access to the earliest extant individual Tibetan work that describes the characteristics, attainments, and cosmological locations of Noble beings in Tibetan forms of Buddhism. The edition and translation indicate the meaning and syntax of Buddhist technical terms for the categories and definitions of Noble beings in Tibetan and their correlations found in Sanskrit, as well as in Pāli, canonical sources. In this way the work serves as handbook for a comprehensive Tibetan account of Noble beings in traditional Buddhism based on an important primary source in Tibetan.

ENUMERATING NOBLE BEINGS IN TIBETAN BUDDHISM

Early Buddhist textual sources as preserved in the Nikāyas and Āgamas contain numerous instructions and advice that the Buddha Śākyamuni gave to his disciples over the long course of his teaching career to indicate their progress on the path to spiritual liberation, what they had achieved, and their future destiny to achieve spiritual liberation. The Buddha most commonly outlined four levels of spiritual progress: the levels of Stream-enterer, Once-returner, Non-returner and Arhat (described below). These levels of spiritual progress were tersely described by the Buddha and sublevels within the four standard levels were also mentioned. In these accounts, the Buddha, for the most part, outlined a profoundly gradualistic, step-by-step progress in spiritual development that could often take more than one lifetime to reach the liberated goal of Awakening (*nirvāṇa*). Over the centuries after Śākyamuni's life, scholarly disciples who followed his teachings reformulated and systematized these accounts of spiritual progress in technical digests and commentaries.

In Tibetan forms of Buddhism, the scholarly accounts of spiritual progress that were received from India came in the form of technical digests such as the *Abhidharmakośa*, the *Abhidharmasamuccaya*, and the *Abhisamayālaṃkāra*. The exegesis and elucidation of Noble beings developed in Tibetan Buddhist scholastic traditions by way of commenting upon the *Abhisamayālaṃkāra* and the related Indian and Tibetan Buddhist commentarial literature surrounding the *Prajñāpāramitā* (Perfection of Wisdom, hereafter PP) corpus. The exegesis of Noble beings in Tibetan forms of Buddhism developed as a special topic within the Tibetan monastic curriculum for a number of centuries and descended from lineages of Indian and Tibetan Buddhist commentators of the *The Ornament for Clear Realization* (AA; *abhisamayālaṃkāra* ≈ *mngon par rtogs pa'i rgyan*) tradition. This commentarial scholastic topic became known as the "Twenty *Saṃgha*s" (Skt. *viṃśatiprabhedasaṃgha*, Tib. *dge 'dun nyi shu*). The "Twenty *Saṃgha*s" in Tibetan forms of Buddhism refers to the stages through which

Noble Beings (Skt. *ārya*, Tib. *'phags pa*) may pass in their progress toward *nirvāṇa* through various lifetimes in various cosmological realms.

In medieval Indian Buddhist and Tibetan Buddhist commentaries up to the present day, the subject matter of the "Twenty *Saṃgha*s" encompasses a comprehensive list of the stages through which Noble Beings (*ārya*) may pass in their progress toward *nirvāṇa*. This typological list of twenty does not provide a description of any one individual's path to awakening; rather, it enumerates all of the possible stages through which any given individual might pass, depending upon factors such as that individual's cosmological circumstances and the acuity of her or his faculties. The Twenty *Saṃgha*s therefore presents the defining characteristics of these individuals, providing a complete picture of all possible states on the path to awakening. Indian and Tibetan Mahāyāna Buddhist scholars regard this topic as crucially important, and its importance is reflected in the inclusion of the Twenty *Saṃgha*s in the ten topics of special instruction (*avavāda*) mentioned in the body of literature surrounding the systematic study of the AA. The exegetical system of the AA stipulates that bodhisattvas must train in these topics of special instruction in order to attain complete omniscience (*sarvākārajñatā*).

Although an extremely complex subject, the topic's title, the "Twenty *Saṃgha*s" (*dge 'dun nyi shu*), is well known to Tibetan Buddhists. The topic serves as a Mahāyāna Buddhist instruction that centers on one of the three essential components of Tibetan Buddhism: the Buddha, the Dharma, and the Saṃgha. In a public discourse on the Stages of the Path (*lam rim*), the Fourteenth Dalai Lama explains the meaning of these "Three Jewels" (Tib. *dkon mchog gsum*, Skt. *triratna*):

> When one meditates on taking refuge in the Three Jewels, one should first generate a recollection of their individual qualities and potencies.... ...[T]aking refuge in the Buddha means that one should meditate on the qualities, wisdoms and powers of a Buddha's body, speech, and mind;

> refuge in Dharma means that one meditates on all the paths and practices leading to the truth of cessation, or the peace of Nirvāṇa; and refuge in the Saṃgha requires an awareness of the twenty types of Saṃgha.... (Mullin, 1985: 108)

The key term in this citation from the Dalai Lama is *saṃgha* (Tib. *dge 'dun*), which in its South Asian context generally refers to an assembly, crowd, group or community. The term has a long history in South Asia, as it was used in pre-Buddhist India to refer to a merchants' or artisan's guild, the ruling council of a royal family, or to a religious community. The term *saṃgha* also referred to a group of seekers who gathered around a master in order to attain, with his help, spiritual knowledge and realization of the highest truth. Śākyamuni Buddha was sometimes described as the leader and teacher of a body of monks and his "saṃgha" consisted of at first monks (*bhikṣu*), novices (*śrāmaṇera*), lay followers (*upāsaka*), and later on nuns (*bhikṣuṇī*). Since the way of life of the Śākyamuni's *saṃgha* was determined by rules established in the Vinaya code, the term *Saṃgha* in this context meant a religious body adhering to particular views and rules of discipline (*diṭṭhisīlasāmaññasaṃghātabhāvena saṅgho*).

Śākyamuni Buddha's *saṃgha*, or community of followers, took part in certain disciplines that set them apart, including keeping certain precepts, living the homeless life, and the begging of food. Early on at some point in the course of Buddhism's development, the community became known as "worthy of worship, worthy of offerings, etc." and the term "*saṃgha*" came to refer an object of veneration and a "place of refuge." The *saṃgha* evolved into one of the three essential components, along with Buddha and Dharma, of Śākyamuni's doctrine, and together these were known as the "three jewels" (*triratna*, *ratnatraya*). An early standard definition of the *saṃgha* as one of the three jewels, according to the Nikāya tradition, was as follows:

> Well-directed is the Saṅgha of the Lord's disciples, of upright conduct, on the right path, on the perfect

> path; that is to say the four pairs of persons, the eight kinds of individuals. The Saṅgha of the Lord's disciples is worthy of offerings, worthy of hospitality, worthy of gifts, worthy of veneration, an unsurpassed field of merit in the world.[1]

The *saṃgha*, often called the congregation, is compared to the nurses or medical assistants of the Buddha. They are meant to have successfully taken in the Buddha's teaching and to be faithfully administering it to other beings. Tibetan scholars classify the *saṃgha* into two general categories: the conventional *saṃgha* (Tib. *kun rdzob pa'i dge'dun*) and the *saṃgha* in the highest sense (Tib. *don dam pa'i dge'dun*). The conventional *saṃgha* usually signifies a group or five or more monks (Skt. *bhikṣu*, Tib. *dge long*) who perform rituals and recite the Pratimokṣa vows together. The saṃgha in the highest sense signifies individuals who have achieved the Path of Seeing (*darśanamārga*) and are actualizing the Truth of Cessation (*nirodhasatya*) and the Truth of the Path (Skt. *mārga*, Tib. *lam*).

In the *Stairway*, as well as in his *Golden Garland* (220.12) commentary to the *Abhisamayālaṃkāra*, Tsong kha pa examines the *saṃgha* in its highest sense from a Tibetan perspective in which various Indian Buddhist sources are compiled together to form a unified exposition. Tsong kha pa classifies the definition of the *saṃgha* jewel into two parts in the *Golden Garland*, the system according to the *śrāvaka* vehicle and that according to the greater vehicle, the Mahāyāna. The definition for the *śrāvaka* vehicle is our focus here, as it is the enumeration of *śrāvaka* Noble beings that is found in the following translation of the *Stairway*. Tsong kha pa draws from the *Abhidharmakośa* (AK iv.32) to

[1] *Majjhimanikāya* 7.7 *Vatthūpamasutta*: *saṅghe aveccappasādena samannāgato hoti: supaṭipanno bhagavato sāvakasaṅgho, ujupaṭipanno bhagavato sāvakasaṅgho, ñāyapaṭipanno bhagavato sāvakasaṅgho, sāmīcipaṭipanno bhagavato sāvakasaṅgho, yadidaṃ cattāri purisayugāni aṭṭha purisapuggalā, esa bhagavato sāvakasaṅgho āhuneyyo pāhuṇeyyo dakkhiṇeyyo añjalikaraṇīyo anuttaraṃ puññakkhettaṃ lokassāti.* For similar statements in the Nikāyas see *Dīghanikāya, Sangītisutta* (III.28.33), *Aṅguttaranikāya* (III.286, III.313, III.316, V.331), *Saṃyutta Nikāya, Sakkasaṃyutta* (I.11).

define the highest sense of *saṃgha* in the *śrāvaka* vehicle,

> One who takes the triple refuge takes refuge in the dharmas of the Aśaikṣa which produce the Buddha, in the dharmas of both types which produce the saṃgha, and in nirvāṇa."[2]

In taking the saṃgha as a refuge, the *saṃgha* is composed of the qualities of those who are training on the path (*śaikṣa*) and those who are no longer training (*aśaikṣa*), not including the Buddha. This refers to the qualities that are acquired by the eight Noble individuals (*aṣṭāryapudgala*) who, by being unbreakable from the path, are called "saṃgha."[3] In Tsong kha pa's understanding, one takes refuge in the uncontaminated continuity of the eight holy individual's five aggregates, but any remnant left over from that is not a refuge since it is not a part of the saṃgha in its definitive sense.

As the distinguished Theravādin Buddhist scholar, Walpola Rahula (1978: 55) has noted, it is important to clearly understand the distinction between what is termed the "spiritual" saṃgha and the "institutional" saṃgha. The "institutional" saṃgha is considered to be the Buddhist community that consists of monks (bhikṣu), nuns (*bhikṣuṇī*), and lay followers (upāsaka) who follow a code of behavior given in the monastic laws of the Vinaya. Custodians of the Dharma, they are the organized, visible, representative body of the Saṃgha Jewel and are responsible for its transmission and perpetuation. To understand the "spiritual" saṃgha requires an awareness of the types of individuals who are considered to be Noble Beings (ārya). Noble Beings are those who have

---

[2]AK iv.32: *buddhasaṃghakarāndharmānaśaikṣānubhayāṃśca saḥ /nirvāṇaṃ ceti śaraṇaṃ yo yāti śaraṇatrayam /*

[3]The sense of *saṃgha* as being "unbreakable" is expressed by Haribhadra in his AAA (8.27-9.2) following Candrakīrti's *Triśaraṇagamanasaptati* (Sorenson, 1986: 34-35): *buddhadharmau tathā saṃgho mārakoṭiśatair api / bhettuṃ na śakyate yasmàt tasmāt saṃgho 'bhidhīyate //* (Since even one hundred ten million Māra-devils are incapable of breaking apart the Buddha, his Dharma, and the Community, therefore it is called "Community"). Asaṅga, in his *Saṃghānusmṛtivyākhyā* (Pk5484: 19.5), notes that "saṃgha" means to be firm in faith which is unbreakable (*mi phyed pa'i dad pa brtan po dang ldan pa'i phyir dge 'dun*).

developed a cognitive and meditative understanding of reality (*tattva*) through following the practices of the Buddhist path. The insight gained in this understanding has soteriological value and advances an individual toward *nirvāṇa*. As the renowned Tibetan scholar Geshe Sopa (1985: 156) has mentioned, when an individual attains this level of insight into reality, a stage known as the Noble Path (āryamārga), that individual begins to develop all the spiritual and noble qualities of the saṃgha in the highest sense within his or her own person.

The saṃgha in the highest sense refers to the various types of Noble Beings who are making progress toward spiritual liberation. Therefore, Tibetan Buddhists conceive of the saṃgha both as an outer object of refuge and as a community of people who follow the values taught by the Buddha, a community to which they can look for guidance and fellowship. Tibetan Buddhists also understand the *saṃgha* to represent "ideal figures as the embodiment and proof of the path" (Buswell and Gimello, 1992: 10). The *saṃgha* in this sense represents those qualities of an ideal figure that provide the structure and worldview in which soteriological results of the path take place. Dreyfus has demonstrated (1997) that the study of the path is the central concept of the Tibetan Buddhist tradition. As Buswell and Gimello (1992: 6) suggest, the path "incorporates, underlies, or presupposes everything else in Buddhism, from the simplest act of charity to the most refined meditative experience and the most rigorous philosophical argument. [It]… directs attention…to a general pattern of discipline encompassing both the whole life of the individual and corporate life of the whole Buddhist community." Thus, the topic of the Twenty Saṃghas is a soteriological model that is intimately related with the study of the path to *nirvāṇa*.

While soteriologically significant, the objectified, codified, and detailed scholastic descriptions of these ideal figures do not serve as practical guides to Buddhist practice, nor do they provide details of actual spiritual experience. Rather, the topic of the Twenty Saṃghas serves as an archetypal pattern of the worldview in which spiritual liberation is possible for the individual practitioner. What Dreyfus (1997: 62) states for the *Abhisamayālaṃkāra* in general, can also be applied to the special topic of the Twenty Saṃghas, namely, that it "provides the Tibetan tradition with the framework that makes a narrative of spiritual progress possible and introduces an element of closure without which the commitment required by Buddhist practices cannot be sustained." The topic of the Twenty Saṃghas has this kind of direct soteriological meaning for the Tibetan Buddhist.

The special topic of the Twenty Saṃghas is found in the twenty-third and twenty-fourth verses of the *Abhisamayālaṃkāra*. These verses may be translated as follows:

> There are Twenty [categories]: the [(1) Stream-enterer enterer] with dull and [(2) Stream-enterer enterer] with sharp faculties, [(3) the Stream-enterer abider,] the [(6) Once-returner and (9) Non-returner enterer] who have attained faith and vision, [the Stream-enterer abider] born from family to family [(4) among gods and (5) among humans], (7) one born with an interval, [(8) the Once-returner abider,] (10) those who are born in the intermediate state, (11) those who are born, (12) with effort and (13) effortlessly, those who proceed to Akaniṣṭha the (14-16) three who leap, those who go to the upper limit of the world destroying attachment to the form realm being the (17) one who pacifies in the present and the (18) bodily witness,[(19) the arhat enterer,] and the (20) one who is like the horn [of a rhinoceros].[4]

[4] The Sanskrit is: [AA 23a-b] *mṛdutīkṣṇendriyau śraddhādṛṣṭiprāptau kulaṃkulau* / [c-d.] *ekavīcyantarotpadya kārākārākaniṣṭhagāḥ* // [24a-b.] *plutās trayo bhavasyāgraparamo rūparāgahā* / [c-d.] *dṛṣṭadharmaśramaḥ kāyasākṣī khaḍgaś ca viṃśatiḥ* // Although the Twenty Saṃghas always consists of a list of twenty, various interpretations can lead to various lists of twenty (See Apple 2004, 2008:148-180). While one can point to other scholastic lists in Buddhism

I have provided a thorough analysis of these verses in my previous publications and readers may consult these works for more details (Apple 2004, 2008). Hopkins and Sopa (1989: 212) give a brief description of this topic as follows:

> The twenty members of the spiritual community represent a classification of the location and number of lives remaining for practitioners on the way to attaining the fruits of Stream-enterer (*srota-āpanna*, *rgyun du zhugs pa*), Once Returner (*sakṛdāgamin*, *lan gcig phyir 'ong*), Never Returner (*anāgāmin*, *phyir mi 'ong*), and Arhat (*dgra bcom pa*).

As previously mentioned, classification into the one of the four results–Stream-enterer, Once-returner, Non-returner, and Arhat–is one of the oldest categorical lists found in the history of Buddhism. The topic is well-known to Buddhist Studies, particularly in relation to the Pāli and the Theravādin tradition (see for instance Horner, Eimer). The list of four results organizes a sequence of progressive attainments based on moral virtue, meditative cultivation, and cognitive insight through practicing the Noble Eightfold Path (*ārya-aṣṭāṅga-mārga*). In general, a Stream-enterer has fully integrated the stream of the Buddha's teaching (dharma) and is a Noble Being who will never be reborn in a lower cosmological realm as a hell-being, ghost, or animal. A Once-returner will be reborn once more in the desire realm, the ordinary world dominated by sensual gratification. A Never Returner, or Non-returner, will never be born in the desire realm, but will attain liberation among the form realm heavens. Arhats have completely overcome karma and mental afflictions (*kleśa*) and are liberated from *saṃsāra*, the unending cycle of

---

with fixed numbers but varying contents, the Twenty Saṃghas differs from many of these lists, inasmuch as one cannot provide any easy formula to compute its possible contents. This lack of regularity indicates the complexity of the topic. However, Tsong kha pa's *Stairway* focuses on the definitions and characteristics of the individuals within the *śrāvaka saṃgha* and not on the exegesis of verses from the *Abhisamayālaṃkāra*.

birth and death.

Tsong kha pa's elucidation of Noble beings in the Stairway is based on a combination of Abhidharmic scholasticism and *Prajñāpāramitā* exegesis. He provides a detailed examination through his investigation of Abhidharma digests that were available to him, namely the *Abhidharmakośabhāṣya* and its *Vyākhyā,* along with the *Abhidharmasamuccaya* and its *Bhāṣya*. Tsong kha pa's enumeration of Noble beings therefore represents a classification of Noble Beings that was fairly well established by the sixth century in India. The South Asian traditions that upheld the Nikāyas know of eight types of Noble Beings (*aṣṭāryapudgala*) grouped into four pairs (AN, II: 56; IV: 373): the candidates for and those who abide in the four main results. In particular, the *Aṅguttaranikāya* (I: 220-221) enumerates nine different classes of Noble Beings according to their removal of fetters (*saṃyojana*). Another sutta of the *Aṅguttaranikāya* (IV: 379) enumerates nine individuals (*puggala*) worthy of worship (*dakkhiṇeya*). The individuals who are worthy of worship were understood to be the Noble Community of disciples (*ariyasāvakasaṅgha*). This Community may be divided in two classes: those still in training (*śaikṣa*) and those who have no more to train in (*aśaikṣa*). Another list from the *Madhyamāgama* (T 26, ch.40, 616a) distinguishes eighteen kinds of *śaikṣa*s. These lists found in the Nikāyas are not fully articulated or systematized. That was the task of later South Asian commentators. As we have mentioned, for Tsong kha pa and the Tibetan scholarly traditions that followed him, the enumeration of Noble beings was comprised of the types of *saṃgha* found in the first chapter of the *Abhisamayālaṃkāra* and correlated with accounts found in the *Abhidharmakośa* and *Abhidharmasamuccaya*. This tradition of exegesis primarily follows the views of the Sarvāstivāda Nikāya lineage in terms of the number of categories that comprise the list of Noble beings as well as the characteristics of such beings (Apple 2008:94-95).

Tsong kha pa's exegesis of *śrāvaka* Noble beings parallels the *Sarvāstivāda* account of *śaikṣa* and *aśaikṣa* found in the *Abhidharmakośa* and its commentaries. For Tsong kha pa, a *śrāvaka* progresses to the goal of *nirvāṇa* through successively abandoning defilements that are associated with an established sequence of cosmic realms and meditative stages. A result of practice is a stage on the way to *nirvāṇa* that is defined in accordance with the abandonment of specific defilements associated with specific realms. For example, in order to become a Once-returner one must abandon the sixth path of cultivation defilement of the desire realm. The variety of defilements are correlated with three cosmic realms-the realm of desire (*kāmadhātu*), the realm of form (*rūpadhātu*), and the formless realm (*ārūpyadhātu*). Each defilement in each realm is specified according to whether it is to be abandoned by the path of seeing (*darśanamārga*) or the path of cultivation (*bhāvanāmārga*). Abandonment occurs by progressing through successive stages of seeing the Nobles' Four Truths in the path of seeing and then repeated practice in the path of cultivation of what was seen in the path of seeing. Therefore, comprehensive realization (*abhisamaya*) of the Nobles' Four Truths characterize both the path of seeing and teh path of cultivation in this system.

The path of seeing involves sixteen thought-moments (*cittakṣaṇa*) in which sixteen aspects of the Nobles' Four Truths are cognized. The path of cultivation involves a removal of defilements through a repeated familiarization with the Nobles' Four Truths. The defilements of the path of cultivation are calculated as eighty-one: each of the nine stages of the cosmic realm—i.e., the realm of desire, the four concentration levels of the realm of form, and the four spheres in the form realm, possess nine varieties of defilements (coarse-coarse, coarse-moderate, coarse-subtle, etc.). The first nine path of cultivation defilements are important to note because they exist in the desire realm and mark the boundary to progressing into the form and formless realms. The paths of seeing and cultivation are demarcated by the character of the defilements to be abandoned, the frequency of practice each path requires, and the type of individual engaged in the path.

In general, there are two types of individuals: ordinary people (*pṛthagjana*) and Noble Beings (*ārya*). These two types of individuals are differentiated in relation to the sixteen moments of the path of seeing. Generally, at the beginning of the first sixteen moments of the path of seeing one becomes a Noble Being (*ārya*) and various results of spiritual praxis can be attained, depending on the categories of defilements that have been, or still need to be, abandoned through practicing the path of cultivation. One has to pass through the moments of the path of seeing only once, whereas one must pass through the stages of the path of cultivation repeatedly. Ordinary individuals (*pṛthagjana*) practice only the mundane path of cultivation, while Noble Beings (*ārya*) may practice both the path of seeing and the supermundane path of cultivation. When ordinary persons abandon certain defilements by practicing the path of cultivation, it is referred to as a mundane path (*laukikamārga*). Abandoning defilements as an ordinary person on the mundane path obviates the need to abandon them once again as a Noble Being (*ārya*) on the path of seeing. Defilements removed by a Noble Being after completing the path of seeing occur in the supermundane path of cultivation (*lokottarabhāvanāmārga*).

At the sixteenth moment of the path of seeing, a Noble Being achieves the result known as Stream-enterer, one will never be reborn again as a hell-being, hungry ghost, or animal. While making effort to abandon the first six of the nine desire realm defilements, one is a candidate for the result of Once-returner. At this point a practitioner is approaching or entering into the next result. In the following translation the term "enterer" is applied to those individuals who are approaching or entering into a given result. When the sixth desire realm defilement is removed, an individual obtains or abides in the result of Once-returner. I use the translated term "abider" to an individual who is "staying in a certain status" (*phalastha*), that is, residing or abiding (*viharati*) in a given result on the way to *nirvāṇa.* A Once-returner will return to the desire realm by the force of unabandoned defilements one more time, will then strive to abandon the three remaining defilements of the desire realm, and will become an enterer to the result of Non-returner. At the time when an individual has removed the ninth defilement of the desire realm, he is known as an abider in the result of Non-returner. A Non-returner will never take rebirth in the desire realm again and has removed all the path of cultivation defilements associated with the desire realm. However, a Non-returner may take birth in various form or formless realm heavens depending on defilements that need to be abandoned. At this point one takes rebirth in the form and formless realms to remove the remaining seventy-two defilements of the path of cultivation. When an individual makes effort to abandon the remaining seventy-two defilements of the form and formless realms, he or she becomes an enterer to the result of Arhat. One becomes an abider in the result of Arhat with the removal of all eighty-one defilements of the path of cultivation, and this result is synonymous with the *śrāvaka* goal of *nirvāṇa*—i.e., emancipation from the suffering of *saṃsāra*.

Tsong kha pa mentions both in the *Stairway* (268) and *Golden Garland* (224) that these four principal results of Stream-enterer, Once-returner, Non-returner, and Arhat compose the allegorical saṃgha. These four results are also known as the four pairs of persons (*skyes bu zung bzhi*). When enumerating the allegorical saṃgha according to entering into and abiding in the four principal results, the saṃgha is referred to as the eight great individuals (*gang zag chen ya brgyad, mahāṣṭapudgala*):[5] the enterers to (*pratipannakāḥ, zhugs pa rnams*) and abiders in (*phalasthā, gnas pa rnams*) the results of the Stream-enterer (*srota-āpanna, rgyun du zhugs pa*), the Once-returner (*sakṛdāgāmin, lan cig phyir 'ong*), the Non-returner (*anāgāmin, phyir mi 'ong*), and the Arhat (*dgra bcom pa*). Tsong kha pa will also include the Pratyekabuddha (*rang sangs rgyas*) in this *saṃgha*.

---

[5]May, *Prasannapadā* 281, f.n. 740: *catvāraþ pratipannakāþ pudgalāḥ catvāraḥ ca phalasthā ity ete 'ṣṭau paramadakṣiṇārhā mahāpuruṣapudgalā bhagavatā saṃgho bhavantīty uktāþ* / Poussin 1970:486.8. We will not discuss the definition of the Noble beings according to Candrakīrti in the *Prasannapadā* as well as Tsong kha pa's *Rtsa shes ṭik chen* (1973: 395-399) since this represents a different system of interpretation.

Within Tibetan monastic traditions, the Twenty Varieties of the Saṃgha is considered a special topic of investigation among the 173 topics addressed in the study of the *Abhisamayālaṃkāra* and the related *Prajñāpāramitā* (*phar phyin*) literature. Within these 173 topics there are four which are regarded as distinctive and difficult to comprehend (*rtogs dka' ba*): the teaching concerning dependent-origination (*rten 'brel*), the teaching related to the hermeneutics of distinguishing between definitive and interpretable scriptures (*drang nges*) along with the difference between Madhyamaka and Yogācāra interpretations of the *Prajñāpāramitā* literature, the teachings concerning form and formless realm meditative absorption (*bsam gzugs*), and finally the topic presented in Tsong kha pa's *Stairway* outlining the types of Noble beings that constitute the Twenty Varieties of the Saṃgha (*dge 'dun nyi shu*).

TSONG KHA PA AND HIS WORKS ON THE TWENTY SAṂGHAS

Tsong kha pa's *Stairway* is the earliest extant independent work in Tibetan forms of Buddhism that outlines the characteristics of Noble beings. As we will see, Tsong kha pa wrote this text while still a young developing scholar. Tsong kha pa would later go on to become one of the most profoundly influential and innovative minds in the history of Tibetan Buddhism. Born as the fourth child to an ordinary nomadic family, Tsong kha pa would later become such a prominent figure in Tibetan Buddhist scholarship that the later Gelukpa (*dge lugs pa*) tradition would call him "the Second Buddha" (*sang rgyas gnyis pa*). Tsong kha pa, an erudite and thoroughly trained scholar, was also an accomplished practitioner who blended together theory and practice, utilizing both an emphasis on monastic discipline and the techniques of Tantric meditation. He is most widely known as the founder of the Dga'-ldan pa school, which later evolved into the present day Gelukpa school. He is recognized for his innovative establishment of a definitive understanding of Prāsaṅgika Madhyamaka philosophy within Tibet that utilized an integration of the

Pramāṇa traditions of epistemology with the middle way view of the Madhyamaka. Tsong kha pa wrote over two hundred works in eighteen volumes but his definitive interpretation of Madhyamaka philosophy was presented within four major treatises: the Great Stages on the Path to Enlightenment (*lam rim chen mo*); the Illumination of the Thought (*dgongs pa rab gsal*); the Ocean of Reasoning (*rigs pa'i rgya mtsho*); and the Essence of True Eloquence (*legs bshad snying po*). His scholastic genius that articulated subtle distinctions of Prāsaṅgika Madhyamaka was only superseded by his acknowledgement as an embodiment of the Buddha of Wisdom himself, Mañjuśrī. As van der Kuijp (1983: 45) notes, Tsong kha pa's great contribution to Tibetan Buddhist thought was his re-evaluation of Indian Buddhist *sūtra*s and *śāstra*s that not only substantiated his views in regards to Madhyamaka philosophy but also elaborated a new hermeneutical system of differentiating definitive and interpretable meaning found in scripture. Besides his innovative contributions to Tibetan scholarship, Tsong kha pa also performed "four great deeds" that shaped Tibetan Buddhist culture: the refurbishing of the Maitreya image at 'Dzing ji (1395), the teaching of the Vinaya at Gnam-rtse-ldeng (1400), establishing the Great Prayer Festival in Lhasa (1409), and the founding of Dga'-ldan monastery (1410). The great scholastic and cultural activity that occurred after Tsong kha pa had passed the age of forty is attributed to a transformative enlightenment experience he is said to have had in 1398. As van der Kuijp mentions (1985: 47), this year of 1398 "separates the old from the new Tsong-kha-pa. His enormous literary output from that time up to his demise in 1419…set into motion a series of momentous controversies among his contemporaries and immediate successors. These contributed greatly to the further fragmentation of the Sa-skya-pa school and ultimately resulted in the establishment of the more or less autonomous Dga'-ldan-pa doctrinal entity."

Before this great transformation occurred in Tsong kha pa's life, in which he had a vision of Mañjuśrī and began to construct his special understanding of Madhyamaka philosophy, Tsong kha pa went through a period of training and study in which he studied under many teachers and developed his hermeneutical skills. This time of formative training in Tsong kha pa's life is considered to be the first period of his intellectual development and is referred to as the "*Prajñāpāramitā* study period" which culminates with his writing of the *Golden Garland* (*gser phreng*) commentary to the *Abhisamayālaṃkāra* in May or June of 1389. It is this early period of Tsong kha pa's life in which he composed works on the Twenty Saṃghas, specifically *The Stairway taken by the Lucid.*

Tsong kha pa lived during an unique period of Tibetan Buddhist history for the study of the AA cycle of literature. Ruegg (1980: 278) distinguishes four periods in the development of Buddhism in Tibet: (a) preliminary assimilation (eighth-ninth century), the early propagation (snga dar); (b) full assimilation (tenth-fourteenth centuries), during which doctrines were systematized; (c) the classical period (fourteenth-sixteenth centuries); and (d) the scholastic period (sixteenth-twentieth centuries), during which textbooks were systemized in an effort to reach definitive exegesis of previous interpretations. Tsong kha pa matured as a scholar at a pivotal point in the history of Buddhist doctrinal development in Tibet, namely the cusp between the full assimilation of Indian Buddhism and its systemization. This was a period of Tibetan Buddhist development in which all the major Indian commentaries of the AA had been translated and several generations of indigenous Tibetan AA commentaries had been composed. As such, it was a period where it was possible for the first time to examine all the important AA commentaries in a standardized religious language (*chos skad*) that allowed for new intellectual developments to take place.

The Tibetan scholastic cultural purview that was inherited from India was modeled upon the study, reflection, and exegesis of Indian Buddhist *śāstra*s (i.e., *Madhyamakāvatāra*, *Pramāṇavārttika*, *Abhidharmakośa*, etc.) that had been translated primarily during the second wave (*phyi dar*) of scriptural importation into Tibet several hundred years earlier. More specifically, the commentarial lineage that centers around the Indian Buddhist śāstra of the AA is known as the lineage of "extensive deeds" (*udārācāraparamparā*, *rgya chen spyod pa'i brgyud*). This lineage focuses on the soteriological structure of the path and the activities that are necessary to accomplish Buddhahood. The Indian Buddhist scholar Dharmamitra (ca.800-850 C.E.) appears to be the first writer to set out this tradition based on the exegesis of the *Prajñāpāramitā sūtra*s, for it is Dharmamitra who is possibly the first to make reference to a "profound" (*gambhīra*) and "vast" (*vistara*) tradition of interpreting these sūtras.[6]

The "profound" tradition comments on the explicit content of the PP sūtras through philosophical analysis and exegesis of emptiness (*śūnyatā*), the profound nature of reality (*tathatā*). The Indo-Tibetan tradition views this lineage as beginning with the Bodhisattva Mañjuśrī and as having a foundation in the human realm with the "Six Collections of Reasoning" (*rigs tshogs drug*) of Nāgārjuna (ca. 150-250). This lineage is considered to pass down through Buddhapālita (ca. 500), Candrakīrti (ca. 650), and Śāntideva (ca. 695-743).

The "vast" or "extensive" lineage articulates the hidden meaning of the PP *sūtra*s, the stages of realization leading to full awakening. It is considered to begin with Maitreyanātha and continue on through Asaṅga (ca. fourth century C.E.), Vasubandhu (ca. fourth to fifth century C.E.), Ārya Vimuktisena, and so on. This is the lineage of teaching and textual study that Tsong kha pa follows to articulate the Twenty Saṃghas as well as to elucidate the Noble beings found in the Stairway.

Tsong kha pa inherited this tradition which traces itself back to the fourth or fifth century of the common era in India with the appearance in the human realm of the AA. The lineage is considered to continue unbroken on into Tibet through Tsong kha pa in the fourteenth century and up until the present day.

---

[6]*Prasphuṭapadā*, Pk 5194, vol. 91, 65.2.8-66.3.2: *de la snying po'i don ni mdo sde zab mo 'am gsal par bstan cing 'phags pa klu sgrub kyi zhal snga nas dbu ma rtsa ba'i shes rab la sogs par... gang du mngon par rtogs pa'i don bstan pa ni rab tu rgyas pa dang zab par ldan pas... don 'di nyid 'phags pa byam pa..../*

This lineage begins with the *Abhisamayālaṃkāra*, a verse summary of the hidden meaning of the *Prajñāpāramitā* (PP) that emerged between the fourth to six centuries of the common era. The later Indian tradition (8th century c.e.) attributed this text to Maitreyanātha. The first chapter's twenty-third and twenty-fourth stanzas of this śāstra succinctly presented a list of Noble beings known as the Twenty Saṃghas. At an early time in India this verse summary text was correlated with the 25,000-verse PP which resulted in a standardized revised 25,000-verse PP utilized in conjugation with the AA. The most influential Indian commentators were Ārya Vimuktisena and Haribhadra who presented different systems of interpreting the Twenty Saṃghas. The tradition of commenting on Haribhadra's *Sphuṭārthā* was brought to Tibet by Rngog lo tsā ba (1059-1109 c.e.) in the eleventh century. Rngog lo's work began a tradition of commenting on the AA which resulted in an enduring lineage of successive generations of more expansive Tibetan commentaries. The tradition of expansive AA commentaries became especially apparent with the *Lung gi nye ma* of Bu ston rin chen grub (1290-1364). In this commentary we find subdivisions and detailed descriptions of the Twenty Saṃghas substantiated with citations of Indian *śāstra*s. This style of commenting on the Twenty Saṃghas expanded exponentially with the work of Nya dbon kun dga' dpal and many of his Sa skya pa contemporaries like Bla ma dam pa bsod nams rgyal mtshan (1312-1375). The expanded AA exegesis of fourteenth century Tibetan commentators provided detailed examinations of particular topics in the AA. The expansion of investigating AA topics resulted in the topic of the Twenty Saṃghas being investigated independently of the AA. The earliest known evidence of this genre of literature is the *Dge 'dun nyi shu'i mtshan nyid 'phreng ba* by Nu mgo rgyal ba rin chen (1328-1386), an extraordinary scholar from Mi-nyag rab-sgang who is usually identified as a Sa skya pa.[7] However,

[7] I would like to acknowledge and thank E. Gene Smith would provided me with this information in October, 1999.

this work is not available and the earliest extant independent treatise on the Twenty Saṃghas is the work that is translated here, *The Stairway taken by the Lucid* (*blo gsal bgrod pa'i them skad*) of Tsong kha pa. The following sections will describe the early years of Tsong kha pa's life and the context for when he wrote the *Stairway*.

THE EARLY YEARS OF THE LIFE OF TSONG KHA PA

Blo bzang grags pa (1357-1419) was born in the northeastern area of Tibet known as A-mdo, in the province of Tsong-kha, "the land of onions," and hence his better known title of Tsong kha pa, "the man from onion valley." Tsong kha pa was born the fourth of six sons amid many alleged wondrous signs and miraculous events. He received *upāsaka* vows as an infant from the Karmapa bla ma Rol pa'i rdo rje and was given his first name of Kun dga' snying po. At the young age of two, Tsong kha pa was entrusted to a Ka-dam-pa monk who would be his first teacher and abbot, Chos rje don grub rin chen, also a native of A-mdo who stayed at Bde-ba-can near Snye-thang. Tsong kha pa received several tantric consecrations of *Hevajra*, *Vajrapāṇi*, and *Cakrasaṃvara*, and received the tantric name Don yod rdo rje. At the age of six, he took the novice (*śrāmaṇera*) commitments under Don grub rin chen and Gzhon nu byang chub. At this time, he was given the name that he is also commonly known under, Blo bzang grags pa'i dpal.

With the intention to give this bright young student the proper education, Don grub rin chen, his teacher, encouraged Tsong kha pa to travel to central Tibet. At the age of fifteen, Tsong kha pa was ready to leave for the study centers of Dbus and Gtsang. Don grub rin chen gave Tsong kha pa some final instructions on the principal course of study, instructions that Obermiller (1934: 323) refers to as a *versus memorialis* and which is found in all the Tibetan biographies. The statement emphasizes the importance of the five texts of Maitreya (*byams chos sde snga*) and most likely reflects the educational sentiments of Don grub rin chen that influenced Tsong kha pa before he even left for central Tibet. The first stanza of what Don grub rin chen is purported to have advised Tsong kha pa is important for our purpose here:

> First study with zeal the *Abhisamayālaṃkāra*, which is like an ornament of the three, the Great (*Śatasāhasrikā*), Middle (*Pañcaviṃśatisāhasrikā*), and Abridged (*Aṣṭasāhasrikā*) great Mother (*Prajñāpāramitā sūtras*).[8]

This injunction to study first the AA, and consequently the AA's special topic of the Twenty *Saṃgha*s, is one of the contributing factors explaining why the first works Tsong kha pa composed were on the Twenty *Saṃgha*s.

Arriving in central Tibet, Tsong kha pa traveled to 'Bri-khung and underwent the ritual for generating the *Mahāyāna* altruistic thought for highest Enlightenment (*bodhicittotpāda*). He likewise heard from the master Sbyan ngas rin po che chos kyi rgyal po various Tantric teachings, such as the *Vajramālā*, Five sections on *Mahāmudrā*, and Six Yogas of Nāropa. Then Tsong kha pa studied the healing arts and the eight subjects of medicine under a medical scholar from the district of Tshal called Dpon dkon mchogs skyabs. However, this period of medical study did not last long and Tsong kha pa went on to the monastic college of Bde-ba-can.

At Bde-ba-can, Tsong kha pa would take to heart the advice of his teacher and put his efforts into mastering the AA and its commentaries. He studied AA commentaries under Bkra shis Seng ge, a native of Snye-thang, the reading master Yon tan rgya mtsho, and U rgyan pa. It is said that by the age of seventeen Tsong kha pa had mastered the words of the AA commentarial cycle and by relying on the Sa skya pa commentary of 'Jam skya Nam mkha dPal, a

---

[8] *Dam pa'i 'jug ngog* (1966: 18): *yum chen rgyas 'bring bsdus gsum gyi / rgyun du gyur pa'i mngon rtogs rgyan / thog mar bslab cing nan han bya .... /* The advice continues for a couple of pages. A paraphrase of the statement is in Obermiller (1934: 323). These statements are also found in the *Rnam thar chem mo* (1967: 112-113) and *Lam rim bla ma brgyud pa'i rnam thar* (1990: 321-322).

teacher of Bu ston, he understood the essential meaning of the AA. He would also study the rest of the five books of Maitreya, particularly the *Mahāyānasūtrālaṃkāra* under a Blama of Bde-ba-can named 'Jam Rin pa. Tsong kha pa completed the initial course of *Prajñāpāramitā* studies within two years. It is at this time that Tsong kha pa is said to have mastered the introductory "coursework" associated with the AA: the cycle of teachings concerned with the levels of concentration in the form and formless realms (*bsam gzugs*), and more importantly, the cycle of teachings concerning the Twenty *Saṃgha*s (*dge 'dun nyi shu*).[9] At the age of eighteen, he took part in philosophical debate and examinations on the *Prajñāpāramitā* at the great monastic colleges of Gsang-phu and Bde-ba-can.

Tsong kha pa then completed travels in the areas of Gtsang: Snar-thang, Sa-skya, Stod-byang, Jo-mo-nang, Bo-dong, Mar-res-spyi-po-lhas, and Nyang-stod. At many of these places he received teachings or participated in debates concerning difficult matters of doctrine, particularly on the *Prajñāpāramitā*. At Sa-skya and Nyang-stod, Tsong kha pa participated in debates focusing on the subject matter of the *Prajñāpāramitā.* He studied under Chos rje phyogs las rnam rgyal at Jo-mo-nang and received the Bka' gdams pa precepts concerning the gradual stages to Enlightenment at Mar-res-spyi-po-lhas. Tsong kha pa also took part in debate activities at Er and went on to Snar-thang.

Up until this time, Tsong kha pa had focused his studies exclusively on the *Prajñāpāramitā.* However, the AA commentary of 'Jam skya Nam mkha dPal of Sa-skya that Tsong kha pa had studied earlier contained numerous citations of the *Abhidharmakośa*. Wishing to learn the details of the *Abhidharma*, Tsong kha pa requested and received *Abhidharma* teachings from a master at Snar-thang, the teacher-translator Don bzang pa. While at Snar-thang, Tsong kha pa saw the AA commentary of Nya dbon kun dga' dpal

[9]Kaschewsky (1971: III, 6r.5-6): *de ltar lo gnyis kyi nang du phar phyin gyi tshigs don kun la shin tu mkhas par gyur nas / de'i nang nas dge 'dun nyi shu'i skor dang bsam gzugs kyi skor las brtsams ba'i zin bris kyang mdzad do /*

(1285-1379; van der Kuijp, 1985: 52) being carried in the arm of one of the Kalyāṇamitras. This commentary gave a clearer articulation of the subject matter than that of 'Jam skya Nam mkha dPal and also contained many passages from the *Abhidharmakośa*. Tsong kha pa generated a strong yearning to study the *Prajñāpāramitā* and *Abhidharma* with Nya dbon and set out to study with him. Tsong kha pa was welcomed in Nya-stod (Rnam rgyal 1967: 121, mKhas grub 1966: 23) and completed a debate cycle of the *Prajñāpāramitā* in Gnas-rnying. In his nineteenth year, during the summer of the Fire-Dragon year (1376), Tsong kha pa went to Rtse-chen and met with the great master Nya dbon, receiving a new explanation of the AA from the old master. However, with respect to the study of the *Abhidharmakośa*, Nya dbon indicated that his health was not that good and that Tsong kha pa should go and study under one of Nya dbon's brightest students, Red mda' ba gzhon nu blo gros (1349-1412). Tsong kha pa met Red mda' ba at Rtse chen and at that time began with him a systematic study of the *Abhidharmakośa* and its *Bhāṣya*.

Besides Don grub rin chen, Red mda' pa would prove to be a great influence on Tsong kha pa and the two became great colleagues, traveling together for many years. After a summer at Rtse-chen, the student and teacher went to Nyan-stod-bsam-gling where Tsong kha pa would study the *Madhyamakāvatāra* which was being taught by Red mda' pa. Tsong kha pa traveled on to Dbus, where he studied the *Abhidharmasamuccaya* with the translator Byang chub rtse mo at Po-ta-la. He would go on to Bde-ba-can and then to Skyor-mo-lung. At Skyor-mo-lung, Tsong kha pa met and studied the *Vinaya* and *Abhidharma* under the famous master Bka' bzhi blo gsal. This teacher was a great disciple of a Dge bshes Thag ma. Tsong kha pa was able to gain a complete understanding of the *Vinaya* and its root commentaries. At this time, Tsong kha pa had an extraordinary religious experience concerning the meaning of the *Prajñāpāramitā* while participating in a ritual recitation of the *Heart Sūtra* at the Skyor-mo-lung monastery. He allegedly had a profound realization on the nature of emptiness (*śūnyatā*), the lack of inherent nature in the appearances of all things, and was absorbed in meditative concentration throughout the nine levels of *dhyāna*. This experience relates the intensity of Tsong kha pa's study in the PP at this stage in his life. It shows, at least for his biographers, that his efforts utilized both theory and practice.

Tsong kha pa would study intensely fourteen volumes of commentaries related with the *Vinaya* and *Sūtras*. At this time, Tsong kha pa also traveled in Gtsang and spent time in Gnas-rnying. In Gnas-rnying it is said that he gave his first teachings on the *Abhidharmasamuccaya.*

In his twenty-first year, the Earth-Male-Horse year (1378), Tsong kha pa met again with Red mda'pa at Sa-skya (Rnam rgyal 1967: 132). They stayed there for eleven months, during the course of which Tsong kha pa, besides hearing the path and its fruit teachings (*lam 'bras*), studied the *Abhidharmasamuccaya*, *Pramāṇavārttika*, and *Madhyamakāvatāra*, and received several Tantric teachings as well. From Sa-skya, the student and teacher went through Stod and Byang and stayed in Ngam-ring during the spring and summer. At this time Red mda' pa wrote his commentary to the *Abhidharmasamuccaya*.

After traveling to Dbus, Tsong kha pa planned a trip back to his homeland in Mdo-smad, based on a request from his ailing mother. He went to Mal-gro-lha-lung. However, Tsong kha pa changed his mind; he decided not to go back to his home and reaffirmed a dedication to his studies. As for his mother, it is said that he sent a painted image of himself which spoke to her when she received it, giving her immeasurable joy and happiness (Rnam rgyal 1967: 133-134).

While staying at Mal-gro-lha-lung, Tsong kha pa began an intensive study of Dharmakīrti's *Pramāṇavārttika* under the Sa skya pa scholar Bson nams grags pa. Tsong kha pa had a profoundly moving spiritual experience while following the *Pramāṇavārttika* commentary of 'U yug pa Rigs pa 'i seng ge (ca. 1190-after 1267: van der Kuijp, 1999: 650), specifically in regards to the *Pramāṇasiddhi* chapter. Mkhas grub (1966:36-37) gives a description of this experience:

> On account of his study and insight into [Rigs pa'i seng ge's] *Rigs mdzod* articulation of the *Pramāṇavārttika* and clearly perceiving the section on the second chapter which demonstrates the arrangement of the path, he was overcome with an insuppressible intense force of immeasurable faith in the doctrinal system and reasoning method of Dharmakīrti. During his stay [at Mal gro lha lung] that autumn, merely seeing the *Pramāṇavārttika* text would generate faith such that the hairs on the back of his neck would stand up and he could not hold back his tears.[10]

As we will show, this religious awe for the *Pramāṇavārttika* serves as factor for the circumstantial evidence of when Tsong kha pa composed the *Stairway taken by those of Lucid Intelligence*, his foundational work on the Twenty *Saṃgha*s.

WRITING OF *THE STAIRWAY TAKEN BY THOSE OF LUCID INTELLIGENCE*

After his stay at Mal gro lha lung, Tsong kha pa went back to Bde-ba-can and stayed there for the winter. It is at this time that he composed *Stairway taken by those of Lucid Intelligence* (*Blo gsal bgrod pa'i them skas*). Of all Tibetan biographies, only Blo bzang tshul khrims cha har dge bshes states this time of composition:

[10]Mkhas grub (1966: 36-37): *rnam 'grel gyi rnam bshad rigs mdzod la gzigs rtogs mdzad cing / le'u gnyis pa'i skabs kyi lam gyi rnam gzhag ston pa'i skabs la legs par gzigs pa'i rkyen byas nas / chos kyi grags pa'i gzhung lugs dang rigs pa'i srol la dpag du med pa'i dad shugs drag po mnan pas mi non pa 'khrungs shing / ston der bzhugs kyi ring la rnam 'grel gyi gzhung la gzigs tsam nas dad pa'i spu ling g.yos te spyan chab kyi rgyun bcad par mi nus pa rtag tu 'ong zhig byung gsung ngo /* Op. cit. 'Brug rgyal 1967: 139, Thurman 1984: 75.

> That winter he stayed in Bde-ba-can having gained insight into many texts. On account of being requested by many seekers, he composed a *śāstra* called *Blo gsal bgrod pa'i them skas* being a presentation of [the types of Noble Beings such as] the Stream-enterer, Once-Returner, and so forth.[11]

Working from the colophon of the *Stairway*, Blo bzang tshul khrims quotes a stanza that Tsong kha pa wrote with regard to the importance of study and casting away desire for fame and profit (*Stairway* 1977: 354). Can we adhere to Blo bzang tshul khrims' claims that Tsong kha pa composed texts related to the Twenty *Saṃgha*s at Bde-ba-can monastery when he was twenty-one years old? I believe the internal literary evidence gives enough circumstantial evidence to substantiate this claim.

First, the colophon of the *Stairway* itself mentions that it was composed at Bde-ba-can. Tsong kha pa states,

[This text] was written at the great college Bde-ba-can in the face of being urged on by some possessing clear mindedness searching for meaning.[12]

The place being established, there are several factors that make it most likely that he composed this text after coming to Bde-ba-can from Mal-gro-lha-lung. First, Tsong kha makes exclusive praise to Red mda' pa, unlike the *Golden Garland* where he praises both Red mda' pa and Don grub rin chen. This exclusive praise is significant in that it relates the importance of Red mda' to the subject matter presented in the *Stairway*. The majority of the material in the *Stairway*, although correlated to the special topic of the Twenty *Saṃgha*s, is based on research from the *Abhidharmakośa* and *Abhidharmasamuccaya* and their respective subcommentaries. As we have shown above, Red mda' pa was

---

[11] Kaschewsky (1971: III,16v-III,17r): *de'i dgun bde ba can du bzhugs nas gshung mang po la gzigs rtog mdzad / don gnyer can du mas zhus pa la / rgyun zhugs phyir 'ong sogs kyi rnam gzhags bstan blo gsal bgrod pa'i them skas zhes bya ba'i bstan bcos mdzad /*

[12] *Stairway* (1977, D 355): *...blo gsal don gnyer dang ldan 'gas bskul ba'i ngor chos grwa chen po bde ba can du sbyar ba'o /*

Tsong kha pa's main teacher of *Abhidharma* and was writing and teaching on the *Abhidharmasamuccaya* in the period of time right before coming back to Bde-ba-can. Tsong kha pa purportedly even taught this text before coming back to Sa-skya to study with Red mda' pa. Another important piece of internal evidence is that in the middle of the *Stairway*, Tsong kha pa displays a youthful enthusiasm and knowledge of the *Pramāṇavārttika's* second chapter. He quotes two sets of stanzas from the *Pramāṇasiddhi* chapter to demonstrate that a Noble trainee (*ārya śaikṣa*), as opposed to an Arhat, has the possibility to backslide from his abandonment (*Stairway* 1977: 331-332). In one of the citations Tsong kha pa combines stanzas in a unique manner that demonstrates that he had acquired a firm knowledge of the *Pramāṇasiddhi* chapter through intensive study.[13] As we have mentioned above, his intensive study of the *Pramāṇavārttika* occurred at Mal-gro-lha-lung right before he came back to Bde-ba-can. Finally, the last paragraph of the *Stairway's* colophon provides almost an autobiographical summation of the years from meeting Red mda' pa, to studying the *Vinaya* at Skyor-mo-lung, up to his study of *Pramāṇa* at Mal-gro-lha-lung. Praising Red mda' pa, Tsong kha pa states:

> [I] obtained illumination of [my] mind in regard to the meaning of all the upper and lower texts of the *Abhidharma* and was able to examine what is correct and incorrect with special confidence in the

[13] Tsong kha pa's combination of verse sections of the *Pramāṇavārttika* occurs at *Stairway* (1977, D 332): *sdug bsngal brten min phyir legs yin zhes dang / bdag lta'i sa bon spangs pa'i phyir / slar mi gshegs pa nyid yin no / zhes dang / goms phyir ma lus spang pa yin /* This is a combination of *pramāṇasiddhi* chapter, verses 139-142a, as listed in Vetter's *Der Buddha und Seine Lehre in Dharmakīrtis Pramāṇavārttika* (Vienna, 1984). The bold print is Tsong kha pa's reference: (139) *hetoþ prahāṇaṃ triguṇaṃ sugatatvam* ***aniśrayāt / duþkhasya śastaṃ*** *nairātmyadṛṣṭes tad yuktito 'pi vā* (140) *punarāvṛttir ity uktau janmadoṣasamudbhavau /* ***ātmadarśanabījasya hānād apunarāgamaþ*** (141) *tadbhūtabhinnātmatayā śeṣam akleśanirjvaram / kāyavāgbuddhivaiguṇyaṃ mārgoktyapaṭutā Õpi vā* (142a) ***aśeṣahānam abhyaasād…***. I have translated the verse combination as "because [the Buddha's abandonment] is not a basis of suffering it is good….because [the Buddha's abandonment] abandons the seed of the view of self it is irreversible…" and "it is complete abandonment because of habituation."

methods of logical reasoning (*pramāṇa*), and in the piṭakas of *Sūtra* and *Vinaya*.[14]

From the above circumstantial and internal literary evidence I propose that Tsong kha pa did indeed write the *Stairway* at Bde-ba-can monastery when he was twenty-one years old.

After his winter stay at Bde-ba-can monastery, Tsong kha pa would spend the next eleven years travelling to various monasteries in central Tibet, taking part in doctrinal debates and study concerning the topics of *Prajñāpāramitā*, *Pramāṇa*, and *Madhyamaka*. It is recorded that he began his main volume on the *Prajñāpāramitā*, the *Golden Garland* (*Legs bshad gser phreng*), during this period when he traveled to Tshal.[15] At the age of thirty-one in 1389, Tsong kha pa finished the *Golden Garland* at Tshal and marking the end of his *Prajñāpāramitā* study period. According to current an oral tradition, at a later time, Tsong kha became dissatisfied with his presentation in the *Golden Garland* and requested his disciple Rgyal tshab dar ma rin chen (1364-1432) to write a study of the *Prajñāpāramitā* from his newly found perspective. One should see van der Kuijp (1985: 52-54) for a discussion of the problems with this oral tradition.

Tsong kha pa most likely utilized his research on the Twenty *Saṃgha*s in the *Stairway* to assist in his compilation of the *Golden Garland*. This is because the first chapter of the *Golden Garland* contains over one hundred pages on the Twenty *Saüghas*. However, a close look at the material on the Twenty *Saṃgha*s from the *Stairway* and *Golden Garland* reveals that the two texts are complementary. In other words, the subject matter on the Twenty *Saṃgha*s that

---

[14]*Stairway* (1977, D 355) *...chos mngon pa'i gzhungs gongs 'og thams cad kyi don la / blo'i snang ba thob cing mdo sde dang 'dul ba'i sde snod dang / gtan tshigs rig pa'i tshul la yang spops pa dge bas rigs pa dang / mi rigs pa rnam par dpyod par nus pa.../*

[15]Mkhas grub (1966: 43): *tshal du bzhugs nas / bka' dang bstan bcos bod yul du 'gyur ro 'tshal la gzigs rtogs zhib par mdzad / gsung rab mtha' dag gi don la rnam par dpyod pa'i sgo du ma zhig thugs la 'khrungs / mngon par rtogs pa'i rgyan 'grel ba dang bcas pa'i rnam bshad chen mo de yid kyi rtsom pa'ang mdzad /* Also Tshe mchog ye shes (1990: 330).

was not included in the *Stairway* is given in the *Golden Garland* such that the *Golden Garland* completes the topic of the Twenty *Saṃgha*s. For example, the *Stairway* gives a presentation solely on the allegorical (*tshon byed dpe)* or *śrāvaka saṃgha.* The presentation found in the *Golden Garland* offers complementary material on the *śrāvaka saṃgha*, but then it also gives a complete presentation of the actual (*tshon bya don*) or *bodhisattva saṃgha* not found at all in the *Stairway*. In fact, with regards to the *śrāvaka saṃgha* described in the *Golden Garland*, Tsong kha pa advises that one should look in the *Stairway* for detail on this type of *saṃgha*. In the *Golden Garland* regarding his presentation of the *śrāvaka saṃgha*, Tsong kha pa states:

> These *Saṃgha*s have been merely roughly described and since I have specifically composed an extensive essay on this topic, one should look there.[16]

Therefore, a complementary relationship exists between the *Stairway* and *Golden Garland* with regards to the topic of the Twenty *Saṃgha*s.

I have identified the location where Tsong kha pa wrote the *Stairway* and given my hypothesis as to the time of its composition. The next major question is: why did Tsong kha pa focus on the topic of the Twenty *Saṃgha*s and write the *Stairway*? I have already noted that Tsong kha pa states in the colophon that he was "urged on by others" to address this topic. Tsong kha pa also states at the beginning of the *Stairway* (1977:267-268), aside from the necessary soteriological importance of understanding the essential nature of the *saṃgha*, that:

> [I] have applied myself only to the presentation of the great individuals who enter and abide [in the four fruitions] because those who claim to be greatly learned in the teachings from the *Abhidharma*

[16] *Golden Garland* (1970: 244): *dge 'dun 'di dag ni che long tsam ste rgyas par ni wi ge logs shig tu bris yor pas der lta'o* /

> scriptures on the many divisions within these [great individuals] are seen to be mistaken.[17]

I can only conjecture about the actual scholars Tsong kha pa is referring to: he may be making reference to Nu mgo rgyal ba rin chen or another Sa skya pa scholar. Nevertheless, from this statement we can infer that Tsong kha pa is indirectly stating, not only the lack of knowledge among fellow students in his PP debating cycles (*phar phyin gyi grwa skor*), but also and more importantly, the lack of understanding about the teachings of *Abhidharma* among previous Tibetan AA scholars.

With Tsong kha pa's Tibetan scholastic predecessors, beginning with Gnyal zhig 'jam pa'i rdo rje (fl. ca. 1200), we see a trend toward the expansion of AA commentary supplemented with an articulation of doctrine based on Indian *śāstra* citation in regards to the topic of the Twenty *Saṃgha*s. I also noted that in the commentaries of Bu ston and Nya dbon the citation and correlation of *Abhidharma* texts is used to define the distinguishing characteristics of the individuals within the Twenty *Saṃgha*s. In the commentaries of Tsong kha pa's predecessors we see a progression of development in which each successive generation cites a wider range of available *Abhidharma* texts. For instance, in his section on the Twenty *Saṃgha*s Bu ston utilizes citations from the *Abhidharmakośa* and *Abhidharmakośabhāṣya* and Nya dbon utilizes, in addition, citations from the *Abhidharmasamuccaya* and its *Bhāṣya*. Tsong kha pa's work on the Twenty *Saṃgha*s is more developed than these predecessors from a textual standpoint in his use of the *Abhidharmakośavyākhyā.* We will see that Tsong kha pa clarifies doctrinal problems that he sees in previous scholarship on the Twenty *Saṃgha*s, such as concerning the Arhat, utilizing this commentary. Along these lines, we can postulate that Tsong kha pa, having been exposed to the

---

[17]*Stairway*, 1977, D 267-268: *...zhugs pa dang gnas pa'i skyes bu chen po rnams kyi rnam par bzhag pa nyid lhur blangs te / 'di dag gi nang gses kyi dbye ba du ma ma mo'i sde snod nas gsungs pa rnams la mang du thos pa'i sha tshugs can rnams 'khrul par mthong ba'i phyir ro /*

commentaries and subcommentaries of the *Abhidharmakośa* and *Abhidharmasamuccaya* by Red mda' pa, noticed detailed descriptions of the individuals within the Twenty *Saṃgha*s that he had not seen in other AA commentaries which he had previously studied. Also, because the AA is traditionally the first textbook studied in the monastic curriculum, the study and debate of controversial points concerning the Twenty *Saṃgha*s may have been a topic of discussion in his early PP debating rounds. Another possible scenario is that along with the AA being the first textbook studied in the monastery, the topic of the Twenty *Saṃgha*s may have been a specialized class within the first year of coursework. Tsong kha pa may have been reacting to monastic textbooks that he studied which were devoted to the Twenty *Saṃgha*s composed by various Sa skya pa scholars that are no longer extant.

Summary

I have documented the scholastic purview that Tsong kha pa inherited from his predecessors and the historical circumstances that were influential in his writing about the Twenty *Saṃgha*s. I have demonstrated that Tsong kha pa matured as a scholar at a pivotal point in Tibetan history of AA commentarial transmission, a period of time in which the evolution of scholastic commentary had progressed to allow for the possibility of the Twenty *Saṃgha*s being addressed as an independent topic of composition. Within these circumstances, Tsong kha pa's *Stairway* is the earliest extant independent text that we have concerning the Twenty *Saṃgha*s. Along with the *Stairway*, Tsong kha pa addressed the topic of the Twenty *Saṃgha*s in his own AA commentary, the *Golden Garland*. The following annotated translation consists of Tsong kha pa's *Stairway* providing an early primary source for how Tibetan scholars enumerated Noble beings in their understanding of Buddhist traditions.

The Tibetan Edition of *The Stairway taken by the Lucid*

The critically edited Tibetan text is based on the Mtsho sngon mi rigs dpe skrun khang edition (1986:1291-1360) (=M) of the *Zhugs pa dang gnas pa'i skyes bu chen po rnams kyi rnam par bshag pa blo gsal bgrod pa'i them skas shes bya bya* (Tohoku Catalogue 5413. Volume Tsha 1-42). This version was checked against the edition in the *Khams gsum chos kyi rgyal poa tsong kha pa chen po'i gsung bum*, volume 27, folio 265-309 Delhi: dGe ldan gsung rab mi nyams rgyun phel series 79-105, published by Nga dbang dge legs bde mo, 1975-79 (=D) as well as the block print edition in the Peking Tripiṭaka, No. 6146, folio 100b2-139b1 (=P). I have placed in the margin text numerals indicating the pagination of these editions to facilitate cross-referencing between the translaton and the Tibetan text.

D 265 ཞུགས་པ་དང་གནས་པའི་སྐྱེས་བུ་ཆེན་པོ་རྣམས་ཀྱི་རྣམ་པར་བཞག་པ་

བློ་གསལ་བགྲོད་པའི་ཐེམ་སྐས་ཞེས་བྱ་བ་བཞུགས་སོ་

D 266 ༄༅། །རྒྱལ་བ་སྲས་དང་སློབ་མར་བཅས་པ་ལ་གུས་པས་ཕྱག་འཚལ་ལོ།

|P100b །སྨྲ་བའི་དམ་པ་སྨྲ་བ་ངན་འཇོམས་སྲིད་གསུམ་འདི་ན་སྲིད་ལས་བརྒལ་[1]བ་ཤཱཀྱའི་ཏོག།ལྷ་ཡི་ལྷར་གྱུར་ལྷ་མིའི་འདྲེན་པ་མི་མཉམ་མཉམ་པ་མེད་པ་དེའི་གསུང་བདུད་རྩིའི་རྒྱུན།།ཆའི་ཆ་ཙམ་མྱངས་པ་དེས་ཀྱང་དངོས་འཛིན་གདོན་གྱི་སྲི་བཀོང་[2]ལྟ་ངན་གཡུལ་ལས་རྒྱལ།།ཐུབ་བསྟན་འདོད་དགུའི་འབྱུང་གནས་གང་དེ་ཞེན་ལྟའི་དྲི་ཡིས་ནམ་ཡང་སྒྲིབ་པར་མ་གྱུར་ཅིག།

།སྟོན་པའི་རིང་ལུགས་ལུང་དང་རྟོགས་པ་དག།རབ་ཡངས་ཆོས་ཀྱི་སྤྱན་གྱིས་ཀུན་གཟིགས་ནས།།།རྣམ་དག་བསྟན་པའི་རྒྱལ་མཚན་སྒྲེང་མཛད་པའི།།།འཕགས་མཆོག་རྣམས་ཀྱིས་བདག་ལ་བརྩེ་བར་དགོངས།

---

[1]brgal M P] rgal D | [2]bkong D M] skong P

---

[1] "*blo gsal bgrod pa'i them skas* ." Tsong kha pa undoubtedly draws the analogy of a stairway (them skas, skt./pāli. "*sopāna* " {sa + upāyana}) from Yaśomitra's AKV (Śāstrī pp.927-928) citation of three *sadṛṣṭāntāni sūtrāni* found in the *Saṃyuktāgama* (T 99, ch.16, p.113a-b) on the Buddha's solemn assertion that the comprehension of the four Noble Truths are progessive and not simultaneous (*caturṇām āryasatyānām anupūrvābhisamayo na tv ekābhisamayaḥ*). These three comparisons are of a storied mansion (*kūṭāgāra*), a stairway with four flights (*catuṣkadevara sopāna*), and a ladder with four rungs (*catuṣpadikā niḥśreṇī*). Cf. *Saṃyuttanikāya* (V). See also *Dīgha Nikāya*, II.178; *Dhammapada* v.239, Aṅguttara *Nikāya*, IV, pp.200-1. In Tibetan Buddhist artwork this is depicted as a four runged ladder.

D265 **The Stairway taken by the Lucid**[1]

A Presentation of the Great Beings who enter and abide [in the Four Fruitions].[2]

D266 Homage with reverence to the Buddha along with his sons and disciples!

The crown ornament of the Śākya clan, who passes over existence in these three worlds, destroyer of harmful speech, holy speaker, the god beyond gods, unequaled guide among gods and men, whose speech is unequaled, like a stream of nectar; even by tasting a mere part of a drop, frightens the demon of substantialism (*dngos 'dzin*), giving victory over the battle of wrong view (*lta ngan*). May Śākyamuni's teaching, the source of all wishes, never at any time be obscured by the view of attachment's odor.

The holders of the teaching, those with scriptural knowledge and spiritual realization, who see all with the vast eye of dharma, who raise high the victory banner of the pure teaching, the supreme Noble ones, please consider me with compassion![3]

---

[2] "Great Beings who Enter and Abide [in the four fruitions]" (skt. *pratipannakaphalasthaḥ catvāraḥ mahāpuruṣāḥ*). Here the title indicates that the subject to follow is a presentation of the Noble *śrāvaka saṃgha*, the enterers to and abiders in the stages of Stream-enterer, Once-returner, Non-returner up to Arhat, and the divisions within these four stages.

[3] In this verse of request, Tsong kha pa is drawing from the Abhidharma literature. AK, viii.39a-b, comments that the Good Law (*saddharma*) of the Teacher is made up of scriptural knowledge (*āgama*) and spiritual realization (*adhigama*). In general the *āgama* is the three baskets (*tripiṭaka*) of *Sūtra*, Vinaya and Abhidharma. Haribhadra in his AAĀ 29.6, list twelve limbs (*aṅgas*) of scripture. These are set forth in the *Pañcaviṃśati*, 95-116 and exhaustively discussed by Lamotte, Traité, 2279-2305. Poussin (AKBH, tome v, 219) notes that *adhigama* signifies "penetration, intelligence" and is synonymous with "clear realization of the truth" (*satyābhisamaya*). Those who see with the "eye of dharma" is a reference to scholars who study the Abhidharma (infra, fol. 280)

D 267 །གང་ཡང་མུ་མཐའ་བྲལ་བའི་སྲིད་པའི་མཚོ་ལས་བརྒལ་ཏེ་ཐར་པ་བླ་
ན་མེད་པའི་སྐབས་ལ་གནས་པར་འདོད་པ་དེ་དག་ནི་གདོན་མི་ཟ་བར་རྣམ་
པ་ཀུན་ཏུ་མི་བསླུ་བའི་སྐྱབས་ལ་བརྟེན[3]་ན་འགྱུར་གྱི།།གཞན་དུ་ན་འདམ་དུ་
ཆེར་བྱིང་བའི་སྐྱེས་བུ་སྟོབས་དམན་པ་གཞན་དྲིང་མི་འཇོག་པར་ཕ་རོལ་ཏུ་
འགྲོ་བར་འདོད་པ་ལྟར་འདོད་པའི་ཕྱོགས་སུ་མི་ཕྱིན་པར་ངལ་བ་འབའ་
ཞིག་ཏུ་འགྱུར་ཏེ།

།སྟོན་པ་དང་དེའི་ཉན་ཐོས་ཀྱིས་བསྟན་པའི་ལམ་ལས་གཞན་པའི་
P101a ཐབས་ཀྱིས་སྲིད་པ་ཉིད་འདྲེན་པར་བྱེད་ཀྱི་སྲིད་པའི་རྩ་བ་བཟློག་པར་མི་
1292 ནུས་པའི་ཕྱིར་ཏེ།།འདི་ལྟར་ཆོས་འདི་ལས་ཕྱི་རོལ་ཏུ་གྱུར་པ་རྣམས་ནི་བདག་
མེད་པ་རྟོགས་པ་དང་བྲལ་ལ་བདག་ཏུ་ལྟ་བ་ཡང་ལུས་ཅན་སྲིད་པར་
འཆིང་བའི་རྩ་བ་ཡིན་པའི་ཕྱིར་རོ།།དེའི་ཕྱིར་བློ་དང་ལྡན་པ་དག་གིས་སྐྱབས་
གསུམ་གྱི་རང་བཞིན་ཅི་འདྲ་བ་དེ་ནི་བསམ་པར་བྱ་བ་ཁོ་ན་ཡིན་ལ།དེ་ལས་
ཀྱང་འདིར་ནི་ཞུགས་པ་དང་གནས་པའི་སྐྱེས་བུ་ཆེན་པོ་རྣམས་ཀྱི་རྣམ་པར་
བཞག་པ་ཉིད་ལྷུར་བླངས་ཏེ།འདི་དག་གི་ནང་གསེས་ཀྱི་དབྱེ་བ་དུ་མ་མ་
མོའི་སྡེ་སྣོད་ནས་གསུངས་པ་རྣམས་ལ་མང་དུ་ཐོས་པའི་ཤ་ཚུགས་ཅན་
D 268 རྣམས་འཁྲུལ་པར་མཐོང་བའི་ཕྱིར་རོ།།

དེ་ལྟ་ན་ཞུགས་པ་དང་གནས་པའི་གང་ཟག་དེ་དག་ཀྱང་དུ་ཞིག་ཅེ་
ན།རྒྱུན་དུ་ཞུགས་པའི་འབྲས་བུ་ལ་ཞུགས་པ་དང་འབྲས་བུ་ལ་གནས་པ་
དང་།ལན་ཅིག་ཕྱིར་འོང་བའི་འབྲས་བུ་ལ་ཞུགས་པ་དང་འབྲས་བུ་ལ་གནས་
པ་དང་།ཕྱིར་མི་འོང་བའི་འབྲས་བུ་ལ་ཞུགས་པ་དང་འབྲས་བུ་ལ་གནས་པ་
དང་།དགྲ་བཅོམ་པའི་འབྲས་བུ་ལ་ཞུགས་པ་དང་འབྲས་བུ་ལས་གནས་པ་
སྟེ།དེ་ལྟར་ན་ཞུགས་པ་བཞི་དང་གནས་པ་བཞི་སྟེ་བརྒྱད་དུ་འགྱུར་རོ།རྒྱུན་
དུ་ཞུགས་པའི་འབྲས་བུ་ལ་ཞུགས་པ་གང་ཞེ་ན།འདི་ལ་རྒྱུན་དུ་ཞུགས་པའི་
ཞུགས་པ་གང་ནས་ཞུགས་པར་འཇོག་པར་འདོད་པ་ལ་ནི་ཆོས་མངོན་པ་བ་
རྣམས་ནི་མི་མཐུན་པའི་ཚུལ་གཉིས་ཏེ།འདི་ལྟར་ཆོས་མངོན་པ་པ་བྱེ་བྲག་ཏུ་
སྨྲ་བ་དང་།སློབ་དཔོན་འཕགས་པ་ཐོགས་མེད་དོ།།དེ་ལ་བྱེ་བྲག་ཏུ་སྨྲ་བ་
རྣམས་ནི།ཞུགས་གནས་བརྒྱད་པོ་ཐམས་ཅད་འཕགས་པར་འདོད་པས་

[3] brten D M] bstan P

Those who desire to abide on the dry land of unsurpassable
D267 emancipation and pass over the ocean of boundless *saṃsāra* undoubtedly will do so if relying on a refuge which is undeceiving in all aspects. Otherwise, the individual who greatly sinks in the mud [of *saṃsāra*], not leaving behind dependence on other inferior forces while desiring to go to the other shore, will only become exhausted in not reaching the desired side.

The means other than the path that is taught by the Teacher and his disciples are unable to reverse the root of *saṃsāra* but leads to *saṃsāra* itself. Accordingly, those outside of this doctrine are separated from the realization of selflessness, and a view for the self (*ātmadarśana*) is the root that binds sentient beings in saṃ*sāra*. Therefore, only those who are wise will examine, "What is the essential nature of the three refuges?" Here, from among these [three], [I] have applied myself only to the presentation of the great individuals who enter and abide [in the four fruitions] because I have perceived as mistaken those who claim to be greatly learned in the teachings from the Abhidharma scriptures on the many classifications
D268 within these [great individuals].

So, who are those individuals (*pudgala)* who enter and abide [to the resultant fruitions?] [There is] the enterer to the result and abider in the result of Stream-enterer, the enterer to the result and abider in the result of Once-returner, the enterer to the result and the abider in the result of Non-returner, and the enterer to the result and abider to the result of Arhat; therefore, there are four enterers and four abiders making eight. Who is an enterer to the result of Stream-enterer? Regarding this, from which [definition of] Stream-enterer enterer do we accept to posit as an enterer, as *Ābhidhārmikas* have two discordant methods, that is, the *Vaibhāṣika* and the Ācārya Ārya Asaṅga. Concerning this, the *Vaibhāṣika*s hold the boundary of the first [result] from the persevering receptivity for knowing the doctrine (*dharma*) in regards to the [truth] of suffering (*duḥkhe dharmajñānakṣānti*), because they accept all eight enterers and abiders

ཞུགས་པ་དང་པོ་ཡང་སྡུག་བསྔལ་ལ་ཆོས་བཟོད་ནས་དང་པོའི་མཚམས་
འཛིན་པ་ཡིན་ཏེ།ཇི་སྐད་དུ་མཛོད་ལས

P101b །དེ་ལ་སྐད་ཅིག་བཅོ་ལྔ་ནི།།མ་མཐོང་མཐོང་ཕྱིར་མཐོང་བའི་
ལམ།།དབང་པོ་རྣོ་རྟུལ་དེ་དག་དུ།།དད་དང་ཆོས་ཀྱི་རྗེས་འབྲངས་
པ།།སྒོམ་[4]པས་སྤང་བྱ་མ་སྤངས་ན།།འབྲས་བུ་དང་པོ་ལ་ཞུགས་
པ།།ཞེས་གང་གསུངས་པ་ཡིན་ནོ།

1293 །འོན་ཀྱང་ཐ་མའི་མཚམས་ལམ་ལ་རྗེས་སུ་ཤེས་པའི་བཟོད་པ་ནས་
D 269 འཛིན་པ་ལ་ནི་མི་མཐུན་པ་མེད་དེ་བཅུ་དྲུག་པ་ཐོབ་པ་ན་མཐོང་སྤང་[5]མ་
ལུས་པར་སྤངས་པའི་ཕྱིར་དང་དེ་ཙམ་གྱིས་[6]རྒྱུན་ཞུགས་ཀྱི་འབྲས་བུ་ཡང་
ཐོབ་པའི་ཕྱིར་རོ།

།སློབ་དཔོན་ཐོགས་མེད་ནི།སྦྱོར་ལམ་ནས་དང་པོའི་མཚམས་འཛིན་
པར་བཞེད་དེ། ཀུན་ལས་བཏུས་སུ།

རྒྱུན་དུ་ཞུགས་པའི་འབྲས་བུ་ལ་ཞུགས་པ་གང་ཞེ་ན།གང་ངེས་པར་
འབྱེད་པའི་ཆ་དང་མཐུན་པ་ལ་གནས་པ་དང་མཐོང་བའི་ལམ་གྱི་
སེམས་ཀྱི་སྐད་ཅིག་བཅོ་ལྔ་ལ་གནས་པའི་གང་ཟག་གོ།ཞེས་སོ།

།དེ་ཡང་སྟན་གཅིག་ལ་སྦྱོར་ལམ་དང་མཐོང་ལམ་གཉིས་བར་མ་ཆད་
དུ་བསྐྱེད་པའི་སྦྱོར་ལམ་ཡིན་ལ།ཚེ་བརྗེས་ནས་མཐོང་ལམ་སྐྱེད་པའི་སྦྱོར་
ལམ་པ་དག།ཚེ་འདི་ཉིད་ལ་མཐོང་ལམ་སྐྱེད་ཀྱང་སྟན་གཅིག་ལ་མི་སྐྱེད་པའི་

[4] sgom M] bsgom D P | [5] spang M] spangs D P | [6] de tsam gyis M] de tsam gyi D P

as Noble Beings (*ārya*), even the first enterer. As is said in the *Abhidharmakośa*:

> Fifteen moments are that [path of seeing], because of seeing that which has not been seen, it is the path of seeing...in these [moments], the ascetics of weak and sharp faculties are the ones who follow by faith (*śraddhānusārin*) and the ones who follows by doctrine (*dharmānusārin*), if they have not abandoned the defilements to be abandoned through cultivation, they are enterers to the first result.[4]

Moreover, the last boundary, that which is held from the persevering receptivity of subsequent knowledge on the truth of the
D269 path (*mārge anvayajñānakṣānti*), that is not discordant for when one attains the sixteenth [moment] one abandons without exception all the obstacles to be removed by the path of seeing, and one obtains the result of Stream-enterer by merely that.

The Ācārya Āsaṅga maintains the boundary of the first [result] from the path of preparation (*prayogamārga*), in the *Abhidharmasamuccaya*:

> Who is the enterer to the result of Stream-enterer? It is the individual who abides in the "preparatory analytical factors"(*nirvedhabhāgīya*) and on the fifteenth moment of thought of the path of seeing.[5]

Namely, in one sitting, it is the path of preparation that generates uninterruptedly both the path of preparation and the path of seeing. The path of preparation is that which generates the path of seeing during future lives, and even in this life itself, the path of seeing is generated. It is evidently not asserted for the path of preparation which paths of preparation are not generated in a single

---

[4]AK(G) 94, vi.29c-d to 30c-d, AKBH, Pradhan, vi.28c-d to 29c-c, 352-353: *adṛṣṭadṛṣṭer dṛṅmārgas tatra pañcadaśa kṣaṇāḥ / mṛdutīkṣṇendriyau teṣu śraddhādharmā`nusāriṇau ahīnabhāvanāheyau phalādyapratipannakau/*

[5] AS, Rahula,152, #6; Pradhan, 88: *srotāpattiphalapratipannakaḥ katamaḥ / nirvedhabhāgīyeṣu pañcadaśasu darśanamārgacittakṣaṇeṣu yaḥ pudgalaḥ /*

སྦྱོར་ལམ་པ་རྣམས་ཀྱི་སྦྱོར་ལམ་ལ་མི་བཞེད་པར་མངོན་ཏེ།ཀུན་བཏུས་འགྲེལ་པར་

> ངེས་པར་འབྱེད་པའི་ཆ་དང་མཐུན་པ་སྟན་གཅིག་པ་ནས་བཟུང་སྟེ་དང་པོའི་འབྲས་བུ་མ་ཐོབ་པའི་བར་དུའོ།།ཞེས་འབྱུང་བའི་ཕྱིར་རོ།

།འོ་ན་སྟན་གཅིག་པ་ལ་དགོས་པ་ཅི་ཞེ་ན།གང་ལ་ཞུགས་པའི་འབྲས་བུ་དེའི་ཐུན་མོང་མ་ཡིན་པའི་སྤང་བྱ་སྤོང་བའི་ཕྱིར་མི་བརྩོན་ན་དེ་ལ་ཞུགས་པ་མ་ཡིན་ཏེ།ཞུགས་པའི་དོན་འབྲས་བུ་ཐོབ་པའི་འགལ་རྐྱེན་སེལ་བ་དང།མཐུན་རྐྱེན་སྒྲུབ་པ་ཡིན་པའི་ཕྱིར་རོ།དེས་ན་སྤང་བྱ་སྤོང་བ་ལ་མི་
བརྩོན་པ་ནི་ཞུགས་པར་མི་འགྱུར་བས་སྤང་བྱ་སྤོང་བའི་སྦྱོར་བ་རྒྱུན་ཆགས་
P102a པ་དགོས་ལ་དེ་ཡང་སྟན་གཅིག་པ་ལ་འབྱུང་གི་གཞན་ལ་ངེས་པ་མེད་པའི་
|D 270 ཕྱིར་རོ།འདིའི་དོན་གཞན་གྱིས་མ་དཔྱད་མོད་འོན་ཀྱང་དེ་ཙམ་ཞིག་ནི་
འཐད་པར་ཁོང་དུ་ཆུད་དོ།

།དེ་ལྟར་ལུགས་དེ་གཉིས་ཀ་འཐད་པ་ནི་མི་རིགས་ཏེ་དཔྱད་པར་བྱ་བའི་གཞི་རྒྱུན་ཞུགས་ཞུགས་པ་གཅིག་པུའི་སྟེང་དུ་མི་མཐུན་པ་གཉིས་དམ་བཅས་པའི་ཕྱིར་རོ།།གཉིས་ཀ་མི་འཐད་ན་གང་ངེས་པའི་དོན་དུ་འདོད་པར་
1294 བྱ་ཞེ་ན།ཅི་སྐད་བཤད་པའི་སྐྱོན་དུ་འགྱུར་བའི་ཕྱིར་ཕྱོགས་དང་པོ་ནི་ཁས་མི་
ལེན་ནོ།།དེ་ལྟར་ན་ཡང་ཀུན་ལས་བཏུས་ཀྱི་ལུགས་དེ་ཁོ་ན་རྨ་མེད་པ་ཡིན་ཏེ

།ཕྱི་ཐག་ཏུ་སྨྲ་བའི་པཎྜི་ཏ་དག་ནི་རང་དགར་མདོའི་དོན་ལ་གཟུ་ལུམ་

---

[6] Tsong kha pa is questioning which factors of the "preparatory analytical factors" is generated during the "one sitting" as the texts do not clearly state the matter. The "preparatory analytical factors" (*nirvedhabhāgīya*, *nges 'byed cha mthun pa*) is a synonym for the path of preparation *(prayogamārga*, *sbyor lam*). This path consists of four divisions which are also known as "cultivating the good roots leading to penetration" (*nirvedhabhāgīya kūśalamūla*). The four are heat (*ūṣmagata*, *drod*), summit (*mūrdhan*, *rtse mo*), forbearance (*kṣānti*, *bzod pa*), and highest mundane dharma (*laukikāgradharma*, *'jig rten pa'i chos kyi mchog*). AK vi.24 mentions that the Buddha and Pratyekabuddha go as far as *bodhi* "in one sitting", (AKBH) implying not arising from absorption. AKBH, Śāstrī, 920: *ekatraivāsane caturtham eva dhyānaṃ niśrityāniñjyapaṭu samādhitvān nirvedhabhāgīyānyārabhya yāvad bodhirūtpadyate*.

[7] ASBh, Tatia, 119: [*srotāpattiphalapratipannaka*] *ekāsanikaṃ nirvedhabhāgīyam ārabhya yāvad ādyaṃ phalaṃ na prāpnoti* /

session of meditative equipoise.[6] In the *Abhidharmasamuccayabhāṣya*, it states that:

> ...holding from a single session meditative equipoise of the "preparatory analytical factors" up to the first result there is no attainment.[7]

Well then, what is necessary for the single session meditative equipoise? If one does not make an effort for the purpose of abandoning the defilements that are in common with that result of enterer, [there] is not an enterer to that [result], because the meaning of enterer is [one who] achieves the harmonious conditions and clears away the impeding conditions of attaining the result. Therefore, since [one] will not be an enterer if not making effort for abandoning defilements, it is necessary to have a continual application that abandons defilements. In addition, this occurs for one in a single session of meditative equipoise but it is not true for others. Although
D270 this meaning may not be examined by others, just this much is pleasing to press upon one's mind.

Accordingly, on account of proposing two discordant [systems] in terms of a single locus of analysis, the enterer to the result of Stream-enterer, it is not reasonable for both systems to be correct. If both [systems] are incorrect what is the definite meaning to be accepted? Because it will be damaging to the explanation, the first opinion is not to be admitted. Accordingly it is just that system of the *Abhidharmasamuccaya* that is not flawed.[8]

Since the Vaibhāṣika paṇḍitas freely examined the meaning of the *sūtra*[s] in their own way and having reflected on the meaning of

---

[8] The view that Tsong kha pa establishes here is different than his *Madhyamakāvatāra* commentary, the *Dgongs pa rab gsal*. The reason being that the Vaibhāṣika and Mādhyamika-prāsaṅgika viewpoint toward the approacher to Stream-enterer is similar, and that differs from the Mādhyamika-svātantrika-yogācāra viewpoint which is presented here and correlated to the lineage system of the path which Tsong kha pa follows after Haribhadra. *Dgongs pa rab gsal* (1992:37) : *nyan thos kyi sbyor lam stan gcig pa nas bzung ste / 'bras bu dang po ma thob pa'i bar rnams rgyun zhugs par mngon pa kun las btus las bshad pas / dpe ma grub bo snyam na / rgyun zhug zhugs pa 'phags lam thob pa nyid la 'jog par mngon pa mdzod las bshad la / kun las btus las snga ma ltar yang bshad pas/ lugs mi mthun pa gnyis byung ba la slob dpon 'di mngon pa mdzod ltar bzhed do /* See also Hopkins 1985:139.

[7]གྱི་དཔྱོད་པས་དེ་དག་གི་མཛོད་ལ་སོགས་པར་མདོའི་དོན་དུ་བསམས་ནས་ཐེག་པ་གསུམ་གྱི་གང་ཟག་རྣམས་ཀྱི་མངོན་རྟོགས་རྒྱུད་ལ་བསྐྱེད་པའི་ཚུལ་ལ་སོགས་པའི་རྣམ་གཞག་བྱས་པ་ཕལ་མོ་ཆེ་ལ།སངས་རྒྱས་གཉིས་པས་རིགས་པའི་གནོད་པ་ཡང་དག་པ་བརྗོད་ནས་མདོའི་དོན་དུ་སྨྲ་བ་བཀག་པའི་ཕྱིར་དང།སློབ་དཔོན་ཐོགས་མེད་ནི་མདོའི་དོན་འབྱེད་[8]པའི་སྣ་འཛིན་དམ་པར་དེ་བཞིན་གཤེགས་པ་ཉིད་ཀྱིས་ལུང་བསྟན་པའི་ཕྱིར་རོ།

།གལ་ཏེ་བྱེ་བྲག་ཏུ་སྨྲ་བ་རྣམས་ལ་ཞུགས་པ་དང་པོ་ཐམས་ཅད་མཐོང་ལམ་ལ་གནས་པར་གསུངས་པའི་མདོའི་ཁུངས་རྣམ་པར་དག་པ་ཡོད་ན་ཡང་མི་གནོད་དེ་ཕལ་ཆེ་བའམ་འཕགས་པའི་ཞུགས་པ་ལ་དགོངས་པར་བརྟག་པར་ནུས་སོ།།གང་དག་ཀུན་བཏུས་ཀྱི་ལུགས་མདོ་སྡེ་པའི་ཡིན་ནོ་ཞེས་པ་ལ་ཤེས་པར་བྱེད་པ་ཙུང་ཟད་ཀྱང་མེད་དོ།།ཡང་མདོ་སྡེ་པའི་ལུགས་སློབ་
D 271 དཔོན་གྱིས་བཟུང་ནས་མཐོང་ལམ་སྐད་ཅིག་བཅོ་ལྔ་ལ་གནོད་པ་བརྗོད་ཅིང་ཞུགས་པ་དང་པོ་འཕགས་པ་ཡིན་ཏེ

P102b །དེ་ལྟ་ན་འདོད་པའི་སྒོམ་སྤང[9]་གཏན་མ་སྤངས་པའམ།གཅིག་ནས་ལྔའི་བར་དུ་སྤངས་ཀྱང་དྲུག་པ་མ་སྤངས་ཤིང།རྒྱུན་ཞུགས་ཀྱི་འབྲས་བུ་ཐོབ་པའི་ཕྱིར་དུ་བརྩོན་པའི་ཐེག་དམན་ནི་སྔར་བཤད་པ་ལྟར་སྟན་གཅིག་པའི་སྦྱོར་ལམ་ནས་བཟུང་སྟེ་ལམ་ལ་རྗེས་བཟོད་ཀྱི་བར་ལ་གནས་པ་ན་རྒྱུན་དུ་ཞུགས་པའི་འབྲས་བུ་ལ་ཞུགས་པ་ཡིན་ནོ།

།དེ་ལ་ཡང་རང་གིས[10]་བདེན་པ་རྣམས་མངོན་པར་རྟོགས་པར་བྱེད་པ་གཞན་གྱིས་བསྟན་པ་ཁོ་ནའི་རྗེས་སུ་འབྲངས་པ་དད་པའི་རྗེས་འབྲངས་དང།ངེས་པར་གཞན་གྱིས་བསྟན་པ་ལ་མི་ལྟོས་པར་རང་ཉིད་ཀྱི་རྣམ་དཔྱོད་ཀྱིས་བདེན་པའི་ཆོས་ཀྱི་རྗེས་སུས་འབྲངས་ནས་རྟོགས་པར་བྱེད་པ་ཆོས་ཀྱི་རྗེས་འབྲངས་གཉིས་སུ་འགྱུར་ཏེ།ཇི་སྐད་དུ་ཀུན་བཏུས་ལས།

1295 དད་པའི་རྗེས་སུ་འབྲངས་པ་གང་ཞེ་ན།གང་ཚོགས་བསགས་པ་

[7]gzu lum M] gzu lums D; gzu lugs P | [8]'byed D M] byed P | [9]sgom spang M] bsgoms spangs D P | [10]rang gis M] rang gi D P

*sūtra*s [mentioned] in the *Abhidharmakośa* and so forth; it is greater to make the explanation of the method that generates in the continuum a clear realization for the individuals of [all] three vehicles. The second Buddha [Vasubandhu] refuted what [the Vaibhāṣikas] said for the meaning of [those] *sūtra*s through eloquently stating the faults with reasoning, and the Ācārya Asaṅga, as a sacred keeper of the doctrine who opens up the meaning of the *sūtra*s, was prophesied by the Tathāgata himself.

If it is the case that the Vaibhāṣikas have justified the source of the *sūtra*s which teach as abiding on the path of seeing all first enterers, then in that which is generally flawless, one can examine the intention with regard to the Noble (*ārya*) enterer. All those who say "the system of the *Abhidharmasamuccaya* is Sautrāntika" are without even a small [textual] source. Furthermore, the Sautrāntika system belittles [both] the first fifteen moments of the path of seeing that is
D271 held by the Ācārya [Asaṅga] and the first enterer being a Noble Being (*ārya*).

Thus, a person of the inferior vehicle who makes effort for the sake of attaining the result of Stream-enterer either does not abandon the series of obstacles to be removed by the path of cultivation in the desire realm or abandons the first up to the fifth but does not [abandon] the sixth [defilement]; as previously explained, an enter to the result of Stream-enterer is one who abides from the path of preparation of one meditative session up until the time of abiding in the subsequent intellectual receptivity of the path.

For that, there are two, the follower, who merely taught by others, clearly realizes for himself the nature of the truths, the follower of faith (*śraddhānusārin*) and the follower of doctrine (*dharmānusārin*), who realizes having followed after the dharma of the truth by investigating oneself, definitely not relying on being taught by others. As is said from the *Abhidharmasamuccaya*:

> Who is the follower of faith? One who, having acquired the provisions, having weak faculties,

དབང་པོ་རྟུལ་པོ་[11]ཕ་རོལ་གྱིས་བསྟན་པའི་རྗེས་སུ་འབྲངས་ནས་
བདེན་པ་མངོན་པར་རྟོགས་པར་བྱ་བའི་ཕྱིར་སྦྱོར་བའོ།

།ཆོས་ཀྱི་རྗེས་སུས་འབྲངས་པ་གང་ཞེ་ན།གང་ཚོགས་བསགས་པ་
དབང་པོ་རྣོན་པོ་བདག་ཉིད་ཀྱི་བདེན་པའི་དབང་དུ་བྱས་པའི་
ཆོས་ཀྱི་རྗེས་སུ་འབྲངས་ནས་བདེན་པ་མངོན་པར་རྟོགས་པར་བྱ་
བའི་ཕྱིར་སྦྱོར་བའོ།།ཞེས་དང
།མཛོད་འགྲེལ་ལས་ཀྱང་།

དད་པ་དང་ཆོས་ཀྱི་རྗེས་སུ་འབྲངས་པ[12]་དེ་དག་ཉིད་གལ་ཏེ་སྔོན་
D 272 འཇིག་རྟེན་པའི་ལམ་གྱིས་བསྒོམས་པས་སྤང་བར་བྱ་བ་མ་སྤངས་
པ་འཆིང་བ་མཐའ་དག་དང་ལྡན་པ་ཞིག་ཡིན་ན་ནི།དེ་གཉིས་རྒྱུན་
དུ་ཞུགས་པའི་འབྲས་བུ་ལ་ཞུགས་པ་ཞེས་བྱའོ།

།གལ་ཏེ་སྔོན་འཇིག་རྟེན་པའི་ལམ་གྱིས་བསྒོམ་པའི་སྤང་བར་བྱ་བ་
འདོད་པ་ན་སྤྱོད་པ་རྣམས་ལས་རྣམ་པ་ལྔའི་བར་དུ་སྤངས་པ་ཞིག་
ཡིན་ན་ཡང་དེ་ཁོ་ན་བཞིན་དུ་དང་པོའི་འབྲས་བུ་ལ་ཞུགས་པ་
དག་ཅེས་བྱའོ
P103a །ཞེས་འབྱུང་ཞིང་དད[13]་འབྲང་དང་ཆོས་འབྲང་གི་དོན་ཡང་སྔར་ལྟར་
སྔོན་གསུང་རབ་ཀྱི་དོན་འཆེད་པ་གཞན་དྲིང་ལ་ལྟོས་མི་ལྟོས་ལ་བཤད་དོ།

།འདོད་ཉོན་དྲུག་པ་མ་སྤངས་པར།སྦྱོར་ལམ་སྐན་གཅིག་ནས་
བཟུང་སྟེ།།ལམ་ལ་རྗེས་བཟློད་པར་དག་ལ།།གནས་པ་དེ་ནི་རྒྱུན་
ཞུགས་ཞུགས།

[11]rtul po M] brtul po D P | [12]pa D M] ba P | [13]dad D M] dang P

[9] AS, Pradhan, 88: *śraddhānusārī pudgalaḥ katamaḥ/ saṃbhṛtasaṃbhāro mṛdvindriyaḥ paropadeśam anusmṛtya yaḥ satyābhisamayāya /* Cf. MN (I, 479).

[10] AS, Pradhan, 88: *dharmānusārī katamaḥ / saṃbhṛtasaṃbhāras tīkṣṇendriyaḥ svayam eva satyādhipateyaṃ dharmam anusmṛtya yaḥ* [*satyā*bhi]*samayāya prayujyate /* Cf. MN I, 479.

> practices for the sake of clearly realizing the truth having recollected the teaching [given] by others.[9]

> Who is the follower of the doctrine? One who, having acquired the provisions, having sharp faculties, practices the clear realization of the truth having recollected the doctrine dominated by the truth by himself.[10]

Moreover, the *Abhidharmakośabhāṣya* states:

> If it is the case that those followers of faith and doctrine have not previously, by a mundane path, abandoned the defilements to be abandoned by cultivation, they are one who is "bound by all the bonds" (*sakalabandhana*); therefore both of them are called "enterers to the result of Stream-enterer. "[11]

> If it is the case, previously, by a mundane path, [those two] abandon the obstacles to be removed by the path of cultivation, those in the desire realm up to the fifth category, they are the same as the enterers to the first result.[12]

Furthermore, the meaning of the follower of dharma and the follower of faith, according to the former [quote], is the previously beneficial scriptural passage [that] explains [whether one] relies or does not rely in dependence on others. In a condensed verse:

> One who abides from the single session meditative period of the path of preparation up to the subsequent persevering receptivity of the path and has not abandoned the six obstacles of the desire realm is an enterer [to the result] of Stream-enterer.

---

[11]AKBh, Pruden, 953, Śāstrī, 933:...*yadi pūrvaṃ laukikena mārgeṇāprahīṇabhāvanāheyau bhavataḥ sakalabandhanau tau srotaāpattiphalapratipannakāv ucyate* /

[12] AKBh, Pruden, 953, Śāstrī, 933: *yadi pūrvaṃ laukikena mārgeṇa kāmāvacarāṇāṃ bhāvanāheyānāṃ yāvat pañca prakārāḥ prahīṇā bhavanti tathaiva prathama phalapratipannakāv ucyate* /

།ཞེས་བྱ་བ་ནི་བསྡུ་བའི་ཚིགས་སུ་བཅད་པའོ།།རྒྱུན་དུ་ཞུགས་པའི་འབྲས་བུ་ལ་ཞུགས་པ་བཤད་ཟིན་ཏོ།།

།།རྒྱུན་དུ་ཞུགས་པའི་འབྲས་བུ་ལ་གནས་པ་གང་ཞེ་ན།འདོད་པའི་སྒོམ་སྤང་དྲུག་མ་སྤངས་ཤིང་བཅུ་དྲུག་པའི་རྟོགས་པ་ལ་གནས་པའི་ཐེག་དམན་པའོ།།དེ་ཡང་སྤང་བྱ་རིམ་གྱིས[14]་སྤོང་བའི་དབང་དུ་བྱས་པ་སྟེ་ཅིག་ཅར་བ་ནི་འོག་ཏུ་བཤད་པར་བྱའོ།

འདི་ལ་རྒྱུན་ཞུགས་ཀྱི་འབྲས་བུ་ཙམ་ལ་གནས་པ་དང།འབྲས་བུ་ཁྱད་
པར་ཅན་ལ་གནས་པ་གཉིས་སུ་ཡོད་དོ།།དེ་ལ་རྒྱུན་ཞུགས་འབྲས[15]་གནས་
1296 གང་འདོད་པའི་སྒོམ་སྤང་[16]གཏན་མ་སྤངས་པ་ད་ལྟ་སྤོང་བའི་སྦྱོར་བ་ལ་མི་
D273 བརྩོན་པའམ་གཅིག་ནས་ལྔའི་བར་གང་ཡང་རུང་བ་སྤངས་ཀྱང་ད་ལྟ་སྤོང་
བའི་སྦྱོར་བ་ལ་མི་བརྩོན་པ་རྒྱུན་ཞུགས་འབྲས་གནས་ཙམ་པོ་ཉིད་དུ་འགྱུར་
རོ།།དེ་ལྟར་ཡང་མཛོད་འགྲེལ་ལས།

> འབྲས་བུ་ལ་གནས་པ་ཇི་སྲིད་དུ་ཁྱད་པར་དུ་བྱ་བའི་ཕྱིར་འབྲས་བུ་གཞན་ཐོབ་པ་ལ་མི་བརྩོན་པ་དེ་སྲིད་དུ་ཞུགས་པ་ཞེས་མི་བྱ་སྟེ་དེ་བཞིན་དུ་འབྲས་བུ་གཞན་ལ་ཡང་སྦྱར་བར་བྱའོ།

།ཞེས་དང།དེ་འགྲེལ་བཤད་དུ།

> ཉོན་མོངས་པ་མ་སྤངས་པ་སྤོང་བའི་ཕྱིར་འབྲས་བུ་གཞན་ཐོབ་པའི་ཆེད་དུ་སྦྱོར་བ་མི་བྱེད་པ་དེ་སྲིད་དུ་ཞུགས་པ་ཞེས་མི་བྱའོ།ཤུགས་ཀྱིས་ན་གང་གི་ཚེ་རབ་ཏུ་སྦྱོར་བ[17]དེའི་ཚེ་ནི་ཞུགས་པ་ཡིན་ནོ།

།ཞེས་བཤད་པར་འགྱུར་ཏེ་ཞེས་རྒྱུན་ཞུགས་འབྲས་གནས་སྤོང་བའི་
P103b སྦྱོར་བ་ལ་མི་བརྩོན་ན་འབྲས་བུ་གོང་མ་ལ་མ་ཞུགས་པ་དང།འབྲས་བུ་ཁྱད་
པར་ཅན་ལ་མི་གནས་པར་བསྟན་ཏོ།།དེ་ལྟ་བུའི་འབྲས་གནས་ཙམ་པོ་སྒོམ་

[14]rim gyis D M] rigs kyis P | [15]'bras D M] 'bas P | [16]sgom spang M] bsgom spangs D P | [17]rab tu sbyor ba D P] rab tu ston pa

[13] AKBh, Pruden, 955, Śāstrī, 935-936: *phale hi labhyamāne phalaviśiṣṭo mārgo na*

The explanation of the enterer to the result of Stream-enterer is finished.

Who is the abider in the result of Stream-enterer? One of the inferior vehicle who abides on the realization of the sixteenth [moment] and does not abandon the sixth obstacle to be removed by the path of cultivation in the desire realm. Along these lines, we are concerned [here] with the one who abandons defilements gradually, the simultaneous [abandoner] will be explained [further below].

For this [result] there are two: the abider in the mere result of Stream-enterer and the abider in the result who has distinction. Regarding this, whatever abider in the result of Stream-enterer that has not completely abandoned the obstacles to be removed by the path of cultivation in the desire realm and likewise does not make effort in the application of abandonment or, although abandoning whichever
D273 [defilements] from one to five, does not make effort in the application of [further] abandonment will be a mere abider in the result of Stream-enterer. In this way the *Abhidharmakośabhāṣya* explains:

> The abider in a result, as long as not making effort in attaining other results for the sake of making progress, for that long cannot be called an "enterer" and likewise does not even acquire other fruitions.[13]

The *Abhidharmakośabhāṣyavyākhā* states:

> In order to abandon unabandoned afflictions, [if] not making application for the sake of obtaining other results, for that long, one may not be called "enterer." Whenever there is superior application with force, then at that time [one] is an enterer."[14]

The abider in the result of Stream-enterer, if not making effort in the application of abandonment, does not enter to the upper fruitions and is indicated to not abide in the distinctive [Stream-enterer] result. Such is the manner of the mere abider in the result, not

---

labhyata ityeṣu niyamaḥ / ataḥ phalastho yāvan na viśeṣāya prayujyate phalāntaraprāptau tāvat pratipannako nocyate evam anyatrāpi phale veditavyam //

[14] AKV, Śāstrī, 936: *yāpannāprahīṇākleśaprahāṇāya phalāntaraprāptinimittaḥ prayogaṃ karoti tāvatpratipannako nocyate yadā prayujyate tadā pratipannak ityarthāduktaṃ bhavati /*

སྤང་[18]གཏན་མ་སྤངས་པ་སོ་སོ་སྐྱེ་བོའི་ཚེ་སྲིད་པ་བདུན་སྟོང་ངེས་ཀྱི་ལས་བསགས་པ་ནི་སྲིད་པ་ལན་བདུན་པ་ཞེས་བྱ་ལ་འདི་འདྲ་བ་དེས་ནི་ངེས་པར་སྐྱེ་བ་བདུན་ལེན་པར་ངེས་པ་ཡིན་ཏེ།མཛོད་འགྲེལ་དུ་

> མཆོག་ཏུ་ཐོགས་ན་ལན་བདུན་པ་གཞན་ཡང་ཡོད་མོད་ཀྱི་མ་ངེས་པས་མ་བརྗོད་དོ་ཞེས།འབྲས་གནས་སྒོམ་སྤང་[19]་བྱ་མ་ཟད།།རི་ལྟར་ཐོགས་ན་ལན་བདུན་པ།

།ཞེས་པའི་སྐབས་སུ་བཤད་པའི་ལན་བདུན་པ་འདི་བདུན་ལེན་ངེས་པས་བརྗོད་ཀྱི་རི་ལྟར་ཐོགས་ན་ལན་བདུན་པ་གཞན་ཡོད་ཀྱང་འདིར་མ་
D 274 བརྗོད་པ་ནི་བདུན་ལེན་པ་མ་ངེས་པས་འདིར་མ་བསྟན་ཅེས་འབྱུང་བའི་ཕྱིར་དང་།

ཅིའི་ཕྱིར་སྲིད་པ་བརྒྱད་པ་མངོན་པར་མི་འགྲུབ་ཅེ་ན།དུས་དེ་སྲིད་ཀྱིས་གདོན་མི་ཟ་བར་རྒྱུད་ཡོངས་སུ་སྨིན་པའི་ཕྱིར་ཏེ།ལམ་དེ་ནི་དེ་འདྲ་སྟེ་སྦྲུལ་གོམ་པ་བདུན་པས་ཟིན་པ་ལྟ་བུ་དང་རིམས་ཉིན་བཞི་པ་བཞིན་ནོ་ཞེས་པའི་འགྲེལ་བཤད་དུ།

> དཔེར་ན་སྦྲུལ་གོམ་པ་བདུན་པ་ཞེས་བྱ་བ་དེས་ཟིན་ན་གོམ་པ་
> 1297 བདུན་པོར་ནས་འཆིའོ།།ཕན་ཆད་དུ་ཡང་མ་ཡིན་ལ་ཚུན་ཆད་དུ་
> ཡང་མ་ཡིན་ཏེ།

ཞེས་འབྱུང་བའི་ཕྱིར་དང་།ཚེ་བདུན་གྱི་བར་དུ་སྐྱེ་བས་ན་ལན་བདུན་པའོ།།ཐམས་ཅད་ནི་མ་ཡིན་པས་རི་ལྟར་ཐོགས་ན་ཞེས་བྱ་བ་ནི་ཐམས་ཅད་ཀྱི་ཐ་ཤལ་པའོ་ཞེས།འབྲས་གནས་སྒོམ་སྤང་བྱ་མ་ཟད་ཀྱིས་བསྟན་པའི་ལན་བདུན་པ་ལན་བདུན་ལེན་པས་ལན་བདུན་པ་རྣམས་ཀྱི་ཐ་ཤལ་དུ་གསུངས་པའི་ཕྱིར་རོ།།དེ་ལྟ་ན་སྔར་བཤད་པའི་འབྲས་བུ་ལ་གནས་པ་དང་།སྒོམ་སྤང་[20]་གཏན་མ་སྤངས་པ་དང་།སོ་སྐྱེའི་དུས་སུ་འདོད་པར་སྐྱེ་བ་བདུན་སྟོང་ངེས[21]་

[18]sgom spang M] bsgom spangs D P | [19]sgom spang M] bsgom spangs D P | [20]sgom spang M] bsgom spangs D P | [21]nges D M] des P

[15] AKBh, Pk ṅu 24b.2, Pruden, 962, L.V.P., 206, Śāstrī, 944: *anyo 'pi vā syāt*

abandoning any of the obstacles to be removed by the path of cultivation, [one] accumulates the karma of definitely experiencing seven existences at the time of each rebirth and is called "one who takes existence seven-times." Like this, that [one] is certain to definitely take seven rebirths. In the *Abhidharmakośabhāṣya*,

> There are other seven-times-at-the-most, but [they] are not mentioned since they are not definite. The abider in the result who does not exhaust that to be abandoned through [the path of] cultivation is "one who takes rebirth seven-times at the most (*saptakṛtparama*)." [15]

One that takes seven times who is explained in this section is called such by definitely taking seven times but there are also others who take seven-times-at-the-most not proclaimed here and since those do not definitely take seven times they are not indicated here.

D274 Why not achieve realization in an eighth existence? This is because at that time of the [seventh] existence the mental continuum is undoubtedly fully matured. That path is exhausted similar to a seven-footed serpent or like the four-day fever. The *Abhidharmakośabhāṣyavyākhā* explains:

> For example, if bitten by the "seven-footed snake" one dies having taken seven-steps, not more than nor less than that. "[16]

Through being reborn up to seven times one is a seven-timer. Since all [seven times] may not be [taken], it is called "at the most." A seven-timer who is identified by being an abider in the result that has not exhausted the obstacles to be removed by the path of cultivation is called "lowest of all" since he is said to be the lowest of the seven-timers by taking seven times. Therefore, only those possessing the three distinctions of being an abider in the result explained previously, not firmaly abandoning the defilements to be abandoned by the path of cultivation, and accumulating the karma which definitely

---

saptkṛtvaḥ paramo ha tu niyata iti nocyate. Abhidharmakośa verse 34a-b, Pk ṅu 23a.4, Pruden, 958, L.V.P, 200, Śāstrī, 939: *akṣīṇabhāvanāheyaḥ phalasthaḥ saptakṛt paraḥ* /

[16] AKV, Śāstrī, 942: *saptapadāśīviṣeṇa tena dṛṣṭo yathā saptapadāni gatvā mriyate na pareṇa nārvāk* /

P104a ཀྱི་ལས་བསགས་པའི་ཁྱད་པར་གསུམ་ལྡན་དེ་ཉིད་ཕོ་ན་ལན་བདུན་ལེན་པར་ངེས[22]་ཀྱི་རྒྱུན་ཞུགས་འབྲས་གནས་གཞན་རྣམས་རེ་ལྟར་ཐོགས་ན་ལན་བདུན་པ་ཡིན་ཡང[23]་བདུན་ལེན་ངེས་མེད་པ་ལ་དགོངས་ནས་འོག་ཏུ་

> གོང་དུ་འཕོ་བ་དེ་དག་བར་སྐབས་སུ་ཡང་མྱ་ངན་ལས་འདའ་བར་ཉུང་བར་ལྟའོ།།འོག་མིན་དང་སྲིད་པའི་རྩེ་མོའི་མཐར་ཐུག་པར་འགྲོ་བ་ཉིད་ནི་ཕན་ཆད་དུ་འགྲོ་བ་མེད་པའི་ཕྱིར་ཏེ།དཔེར་ན་རྒྱུན་དུ་ཞུགས་པ་མཆོག་ཏུ་ཐོགས་ན་ལན་བདུན་པ་བཞིན་ནོ།

D 275 །ཞེས་དང་དེའི་འགྲེལ་བཤད་དུའང་

> དཔེར་ན་རྒྱུན་དུ་ཞུགས་པ་མཆོག་ཏུ་ཐོགས་ན་ལན་བདུན་པ་ཉིད་བཞིན་དེ་དེ་ལ་སྲིད་པ་གཉིས་སམ་གསུམ་མངོན་པར་གྲུབ་ནས་ཡོངས་སུ་མྱ་ངན་ལས་འདའ་བ་མི་སྲིད་པ་མ་ཡིན་མོད་ཀྱི་དེ་ཕན་ཆད་སྲིད་པ་བརྒྱད་པ་མངོན་པར་འགྲུབ་པར་མི་བྱེད་པས་མཆོག་ཏུ་ཐོགས་ན་ལན་བདུན་པ་ཞེས་བཤད་དོ།

།ཞེས་གང་གསུངས་པ་ཡིན་ནོ།།དེ་ལྟར་བྱས་ན་གོང་དུ་བདུན་ལེན་ངེས་སུ་གསུངས་པ་དང།འོག་ཏུ་ལེན་ངེས་མེད་པར་བསྟན་པ་ལ་འགལ་བ་ཅུང་ཟད་ཀྱང་མེད་དོ།།རེ་ལྟར[24]་ཐོགས་ན་ལན་བདུན་པ་ཞེས་པ་འདི་འཕགས་པ་ཕོ་ནར་ཡང་མ་ངེས་པར་གསལ་ཏེ་ལན་བདུན་པ་གཞན་ཡང་ཡོད་མོད་ཀྱི་ཞེས་པའི་འགྲེལ་བཤད་དུ།

> གཞན་ཡང་ཞེས་བྱ་བ་ནི་སོ་སོ་སྐྱེ་བོ་རྒྱུད་ཡོངས་སུ་སྨིན་པའོ།།མ་
> 1298 ངེས་པ་ཞེས་བྱ་བ་ནི་གལ་ཏེ་ན་འདི་ཉིད་དམ་སྲིད་པ་བར་མ་དོ་ལ་སོགས་པར་ཡོངས་སུ་མྱ་ངན་ལས་འདའ་བར་འགྱུར་བས་འདིར་མ་བརྗོད་དོ།

[22]nges D M] des P | [23]yang D M] kyang P | [24]re ltar D M] da ltar P

[17] AKBh, Pk ṅu 26b.7-8, Pruden, 969, Śāstrī, 953: *antarāpi tu parinirvāṇamūrdhvasrotaso yujyamānaṃ paśyāmaḥ / akaniṣṭabhavāgraparamatvaṃ tu pareṇa gatyabhāvād / yathā saptakṛtvaḥ paramatvaṃ srotaāpannasyeti //*

experiences seven rebirths in the desire realm at the time of each rebirth is an abider in the result of Stream-enterer which definitely takes seven times; others are also seven-times-at-the-most with the intention being that they do not definitely take seven times. [The *Abhidharmakośabhāṣya* states:]

> In the period for those *ūrdhvaṃsrotas* also we view as suitable for *nirvāṇa* because the transmigrators to Akaniṣṭha heaven and the Peak of Existence are without transmigrating [necessarily] up to those [realms]. For example, like the *Saptakṛtvaparama* Stream-enterer.[17]

D275 or as the *Abhidharmakośabhāṣyavyākhā* says:

> "For example, like the *Saptakṛtvaparama* Stream-enterer," it is not impossible to achieve *parinirvāṇa* having come into existence two or three rebirths but since there is no cause to come into existence beyond eight rebirths, it is explained as "seven-times-at-the-most" (*saptakṛtvaparama*).[18]

If construed accordingly, it firmly indicates to take seven in the upper realms and there is not even a little contradiction in indicating that there is not [rebirth] taken in the lower realms. This one called "*Saptakṛtvaparama*" is not definite as exclusively being a Noble Being (*ārya*), "there are others taking seven times"[19] as said in the *Abhidharmakośabhāṣyavyākhā*:

> Stating "others" means the ordinary individual's fully ripened mind-stream. "Not definite" is in the case that in this life itself or in an intermediate existence and so forth [one] will achieve *parinirvāṇa*. Consequently, we do not speak of this here.[20]

---

[18] AKV, Pk chu 223b.8-224a.2, Śāstrī, 953: *tadyathā srotaāpannasya saptakṛtvaḥ paramatvam na hi tasya dvau trīn vā bhavānabhinirvartya parinirvāṇa na sambhavatīti / tataḥ pareṇa tvaṣṭaṃ bhavaṃ nābhinirvartayatīti saptakṛtvaḥ parama ukta iti /*

[19] AKBh, Pk ṅu 24b.2, Pruden, 962, Śāstrī, 944: *anyo 'pi vā*

[20] AKV, Pk chu 218a.8-218b.1, Śāstrī, 944: *anyo 'pi veti / pṛthagjanaḥ paripakvasantānaḥ / na tu niyata iti / kadācid ihaiva parinirvāyāt antarābhāveṣu cetyato nocyate /*

།ཞེས་ འབྱུང་ བས་ ན།སོ་ སྐྱེ་ རེ་ ལྟར་ ཐོགས་ ན་ ལན[25]་ བདུན་ པ་ དང་
འཕགས་ པ་ རྒྱུན་ ཞུགས་ ལན་ བདུན་ པ་ གཉིས་ སུ་ འགྱུར་ ལ།དང་ པོ་ ནི་ སྦྱོར་
ལམ་ པ་ ཚེ་ དེའམ་ བུལ་ ཡང་ སྲིད་ པ་ བརྒྱད་ པ་ མི་ འགྲུབ་ པར་ མྱུར་ འདས་
མངོན་དུ་བྱེད་ངེས་རྣམས་ཡིན་ཞིང།གཉིས་པ་ལ་ནི་གོང་དུ་སྨོས་པ་ལྟར་ངེས་
P104b པ་ དང་ མ་ ངེས་ པ་ གཉིས་ སོ།འདིར་ ཁ་ ཅིག་ འབྲས་ གནས་ སྒོམ[26]་ སྤང་ བྱ་ མ་
ཟད་ དབྱེ་ གཞིར་ བྱས་ ནས་ དེ་ ལ་ སྐྱེ་ བ་ གཅིག་ དང་ གཉིས་ ལ་ སོགས་ པ་ ལེན་ པ་
D 276 དང།རེ་ལྟར་ཐོགས་ན་ལན་བདུན་པ་གཅིག་ཀྱང་ཡོད་ཅིང་[27]དེ་ཡང་དང་པོ་
རྣམས་ མ་ ངེས་ པ་ དང་ ཕྱི་ མ་ ལན་ བདུན་ པ་ ངེས་ པ་ ཡིན་ ཞེས་ ཚིག་ ཀང་
གཉིས་ པ་ དབྱེ་ བའི་ ཡ་ གྱལ་ དུ་ བྱས་ ནས་ གཞུང་ གི་ དགོངས་ པ་ དཔྱིས[28]་ ཕྱིན་
པར་ འདོད་ པ་ ནི་ ཚིག་ ཤེས་ པ་ རྣམས་ དགའ་ བར་ བྱེད་ ཀྱི་ དོན་ ཤེས་ པ་ ནི་ མ་
ཡིན་ ཏེ།འདིར་ ལྟར་ འབྲས་ བུ་ ལ་ གནས་ པ་ སྒོམ་ སྤང་[29]མ་ སྤངས་ པ་ རེ་ ལྟར་
ཐོགས་ ན་ ལན་ བདུན་ པ་ གསུམ་ གས[30]་ གང་ ཟག་ གཅིག་ སྟོན་ པའི་ ཕྱིར་ རོ།།དེ་
ལྟར་[31]ཡང་འགྲེལ་པར་

> འབྲས་ བུ་ ལ་ གནས་ པ་ གང་ ཞིག་ བསྒོམས་[32]པས་ སྤང་ བར་ བྱ་ བའི་ ཉོན་ མོངས་ པ་ མ་ སྤངས་ པ་ དེ་ ནི་ རྒྱུན་ དུ་ ཞུགས་ པ་ ཡིན་ ལ་ ཚེ་ བདུན་གྱི་བར་དུ་སྐྱེ་བས་ན་ལན་བདུན་པའོ་

ཞེས་དང།དོན་བསྡུར་ཡང་

> རེ་ཞིག་བསྒོམས་པས་སྤང་བར་བྱ་བ་མ་སྤངས་པ་མཆོག་ཏུ་ཐོགས་ན་ལན་བདུན་པ་ནི་དེ་ལྟ་བུ་ཡིན་ནོ།།ཞེས་འབྱུང་བའི་ཕྱིར་རོ།

།ཡང་ ཤར་ ཕྱིན་ པ། ་གཞན་ དག་ སྐྱེ་ བ་ གཉིས་ དང་ གསུམ་ ལ་ སོགས་ པ་ བླངས་ པའི་ ཚེ་ཡང་ ལན་ བདུན་ པར་ འདོད་ པ་ ཡང་ ལྷ་ རྣམས་ དགའ་ བར་ བྱེད་ པ་ སྟེ།ལན་ བདུན་ པ་ ངེས་ པ་ ཅན་ དེ་ སྒོམ་ སྤང་ གཅིག་ ཀྱང[33]་ མ་ སྤངས་ པར་ བཤད་ ལ་ སྐྱེ་ བ་ བརྗེས་ ནས་ ཉོན་ མོངས་ གཅིག་ ཀྱང་ མ་ སྤངས་ པར་ མི་

[25] lan D M] lam P | [26] sgom M] bsgom D P | [27] cing D M] cang P | [28] dpyis D M] phyis P | [29] sgom spang D M] sgom sangs P | [30] gsum gas D M] gsum kas P | [31] de ltar D M] da ltar P | [32] bsgoms M] bsgom D P | [33] kyang D M] gyang P

The ordinary individual seven-times-at-the-most and the Ārya Stream-enterer seven-times-at-the-most are the two types. The first type in that life's path of preparation or on a childish (i.e., mundane) path definitely manifests *nirvāṇa* while not achieving an eighth existence and the second [type], as stated above, is of two divisions: definitely or not definitely taking seven rebirths. Here someone says: "the abider in the result that does not exhaust the defilements of the path of cultivation is construed as the divisional basis, that one who
D276 takes one, two, and so forth rebirths and there is also one "seven-times-at-the-most" that, the first ones are not definite and the latter are definitely seven timers" thus the two lines are accepted as the complete intention of the text having construed only one part of the division; the understanding of these words is not a meaning that is pleasing. So, in this manner, the abider in the result, not abandoning the obstacles of the path of cultivation, the seven-times-at-the-most, those three [characteristics] indicate a single individual. Moreover, the *Abhidharmakośabhāṣya* says:

> Whoever abides in the result that does not abandon the afflictions that are to be abandoned by the path of cultivation is a Stream-enterer and by being born up to seven lifetimes [one] is called a "seven-timer."[21]

And the condensed meaning,

> Like thus, so long as not abandoning that to be abandoned by cultivation one is a "seven-times-at-the-most".[22]

Furthermore, those other [Prajñāpāramitā scholars] who also accept one as a seven-timer at the time of taking a second or third rebirth and so on, please the deities. One who definitely has seven times is said to not abandon even a single obstacle to be removed by path of cultivation, and in achieving the abandonment of even a single

---

[21] AKBh, Pk ṅu 23a.4-5, Pruden, 958, L.V.P., 200, Śāstrī, 939: *yasya hi phalasthasyaiko 'pi bhāvanāheyaḥ prakāro'prahīṇaḥ sa srotaāpannaḥ saptajanmāni karoti saptakṛt paraḥ sarvāntyaḥ / na hi sarvasaptakṛditi /*

[22] AKBh, Pk ṅu 24b.2-3, Pruden, 962, L.V.P, 206, Śāstri, 944: *evaṃ tāvadakṣīṇabhāvanāheyaḥ phalasthaḥ saptakṛtvaḥ paramo bhavati /*

འགྲུབ་སྟེ་ཕྱིར་འོང་དང་ཕྱིར་མི་འོང་དུ་ཡང་འགྱུར་བའི་ཕྱིར་རོ།།དེ་ལྟར་ཡང་འགྲེལ་པར་

བར་སྐབས་[34]སུ་ཡང་འཕགས་པའི་ལམ་མངོན་དུ་བྱེད་ཅིང་མྱ་ངན་
1299 ལས་མི་འདའ་སྟེ[35]་དེ་སྲིད་དུ་སྲིད་པ་སྤྱོད་པར་འགྱུར་བའི་ལས་ཀྱི་
སྟོབས་བསྐྱེད་པའི་ཕྱིར་རོ།
D 277 །ཞེས་གང་གསུངས་པ[36]་ཡིན་ནོ།།ཚིག་ཕྱི་མ་འདིས་ནི་སྔོན་སོ་སོ་སྐྱེ་
P105a བོའི་དུས་སུ་སྲིད་པ་བདུན་སྤྱོད་ངེས་ཀྱི་ལས་བསགས་པ་ཞེས་བྱ་བའི་ཁྱད་
པར་བསྟན་པ་ཡིན་ནོ།།དེས་ན་འདི་དང་རིགས་ནས་རིགས་སྐྱེ་གཉིས་ཀ་ཡང་
སྐྱེ་བ་བདུན་དང་ཚེ་གཉིས་ད་གཟོད་[37]ལེན་ངེས་ལ་འདོད་ཀྱི་སྐྱེ་བ་ལྷགས་
ནས་ནི་རིགས་ནས་རིགས་སྐྱེ་ཡང་མ་ཡིན་ཏེ་[38]འོག་ཏུ་དཔྱད་པར་བྱའོ།།ཅི་
སྲིད་པ་ལན་བདུན་པ་ཞེས་པ་འགྲོ་བ་གཅིག་ཏུ་སྲིད་པ་ལན་བདུན་ལེན་
པའམ་འོན་ཏེ་གཞན་ལེན་ཞེ་ན།འདི་ལ་མི་མཐུན་པ་གཉིས་ཏེ།ཁ་ཆེ་བྱེ་བྲག་
ཏུ་སྨྲ་བ་དང།དེ་ལས་གཞན་པའི་སྡེ་པ་འགའ་ཞིག་གོ

དེ་ལ་བྱེ་བྲག་ཏུ་སྨྲ་བ་ནི་ལྷའི་རྟེན་ལ་རྒྱུན་ཞུགས་ཐོབ་པ་དེ་ཚེ་འཕོས་ནས་མིར་སྐྱེ་སྲིད་ལན་བདུན་བར་སྲིད་ལན་བདུན་ལྷགས་ནས་སླར་ཡང་འདོད་ལྷའི་ནང་དུ་སྐྱེ་སྲིད་བདུན་བར་སྲིད་བདུན་ལྷགས་ནས་སླར་ཡང་འདོད་ལྷའི་ནང་དུ་སྐྱེ་སྲིད་བདུན་བར་སྲིད་བདུན་ལྷགས་ནས་ལྷའི་རྟེན་ལ་མྱ་ངན་ལས་འདའ་ལ་མིའི་རྟེན་ལ་ཐོབ་པ་ཡིན་ན་དེ་ལས་བཟློག་པའོ།

།འོ་ན་སྐྱེ་བ་ཉེར་བརྒྱད་ལེན་པས་ལན་བདུན་པར་[39]མི་འགྱུར་རོ་ཞེ་ན་དེ་ལྟ་ཡིན་ཡང་[40]ལན་བདུན་པ་མ་ཡིན་པར་མི་འགྱུར་ཏེ་བདུན་ཚན་[41]དུ་འདྲ་བའི་ཕྱིར་རོ།།དེ་ལྟ་བུ་ཐ་སྙད་ལ་ལར་བྱས་པ་ཡོད་དམ་ཞེ་ན་ཡོད་པ་ཁོ་ན་སྟེ[42]།དཔེར་ན་འཇིག་རྟེན་གྱི་ཐ་སྙད་ལ་ཤིང་འགའ་ཞིག་ལ་འདབ་མ་བརྒྱ་ཕྲག་མང་པོ་ཡོད་ཀྱང་ལོ་མ་རེ་རེ་ལའདབ་མ་བདུན་པ་ཞེས་པ་དང་།གསུང་རབ་ཀྱི་ཐ་སྙད་ལ་ཡང་

[34]skabs D M] slabs P | [35]ste D M] sta P | [36]pa D M] ma P | [37]gzod D M] bzod P | [38]te D M] de P | [39]P inserts yang | [40]yang D M] kyang P | [41]tshan D M] chen P | [42]ste D M] te P

affliction in subsequent births, one will become a Once-returner or Non-returner. In this way the *Abhidharmakośabhāṣya* states:

> Manifesting the *Āryan* path even in the intermediate state one does not achieve *nirvāṇa*, because as long as one generates the force of karma [one] will experience existence. ”[23]

D277 These latter words indicate in particular that “in the previous time of being an ordinary individual (*so so skye bo*, *pṛthakjana*) one accumulates karma which definitely experiences seven existences.” Therefore, both this one and the individuals [who go] family to family (*kulaṃkula*) definitely take at this time now [respectively] seven rebirths and two existences and through taking a desire-realm rebirth there cannot be one who goes family to family; this will be investigated further below. “What is a seven-times existence?”–one who takes seven times in existence as a single transmigrator or if not, are other [existences] taken? Regarding this there are two discordant [systems]: the Kashmiri Vaibhāṣika, and some schools other than them.

With regard to the Vaibhāṣika: having died at the time of attaining the result of Stream-enterer in a gods embodiment, through taking seven rebirths in existence as a human, taking seven intermediate state existences, and again taking seven rebirths in existence among desire realm gods, and taking seven intermediate state existences, one achieves nirvāṇa in the embodiment of a god, it is opposite from that if [the result of Stream-enterer] is attained in the embodiment of a human.

(Objection) Well then, how can this be seven times since one takes twenty-eight rebirths? (Response) It is like that even if not [exactly] seven times because it is similar to the series seven. Such as when someone merely says or makes an expression, for example: the worldly convention for a certain tree, although it has many hundreds of petals with seven petals on each leaf, [because the leaves are] produced in series of sevens [the tree] is called a “seven petaled tree” and [this applies] also for conventions of instruction:

---

[23] AKBh, Pk ṅu 24a.3-4, Pruden, 961, L.V.P, 204, Śāstrī, 942: *antareṇāpyāryamārgaṃ sammukhīkurvāṇo na parinirvāti tāvad bhavavedanīyasya karmaṇo balādhānāt* /

དགེ་སློང་དག་ཇི་ལྟར་[43]ན་དགེ་སློང་གནས་བདུན་ལ་མཁས་པ་
ཡིན་ཞེ་ན།གཟུགས་ཡང་དག་པ་ཇི་ལྟ་བ་བཞིན་དུ་རབ་ཏུ་ཤེས་
D 278 སོ།།གཟུགས་ཀུན་འབྱུང་བ་དང།གཟུགས་འགོག་པ་དང།གཟུགས་
འགོག་པར་འགྲོ་བའི་ལམ་དང།གཟུགས་ཀྱི་རོ་མྱོང་བ་དང།ཉེས་
དམིགས་དང།ངེས་པར་འབྱུང་བ་ཇི་ལྟ་བ་བཞིན་ཏུ་རབ་ཏུ་ཤེས་
སོ།།ཞེས་ཕུང་པོ་ལྔ་ཆར་ལ་གསུངས་པས་ན་བདུན་ལྔ་སུམ་ཅུ་སོ་ལྔ་
ལ་ མཁས་པ་ཡིན་ཡང་བདུན་ཚན་དུ་འདུ་བས་གནས་བདུན་ལ་
|P105b མཁས་པ་ཞེས་འབྱུང་བ་བཞིན་ནོ་ཞེས་འདོད་དོ།

།སྡེ་པ་[44]གཞན་དག་ནི་

གང་ཞིག་མི་རྣམས་ཀྱི་ནང་དུ་བདེན་པ་མཐོང་བ་དེ་ནི་ལྷ་རྣམས་ཀྱི་ནང་དུ་ལན་གསུམ་འཕོར་ལ་མི་རྣམས་ཀྱི་ནང་དུ་ཡང་ལན་གསུམ་ཁོ་ན་འཕོར་ནས་དེ་ནས་ལྷ་རྣམས་ཀྱི་ནང་དུ་འོངས་ནས་ཡོངས་སུ་མྱ་ངན་ལ་འདའོ།།གང་ཞིག་ལྷ་རྣམས་ཀྱི་ནང་དུ་བདེན་པ་མཐོང་བ་དེ་ཡང་དེ་ཁོ་ན་བཞིན་དུ་མི་རྣམས་ཀྱི་ནང་དུ་ལན་གསུམ་འཕོར་ལ་ལྷ་རྣམས་ཀྱི་ནང་དུ་ཡང་ལན་གསུམ་འཕོར་ནས་དེ་ནས་མི་རྣམས་ཀྱི་ནང་དུ་འོངས་ནས་ཡོངས་སུ་མྱ་ངན་ལ་འདའོ།།གང་ཞིག་ལྷ་རྣམས་ཀྱི་ནང་དུ་བདེན་པ་མཐོང་བ་དེ་ཡང་དེ་ཁོ་ན་བཞིན་དུ་མི་རྣམས་ཀྱི་ནང་དུ་ལན་གསུམ་འཕོར་ལ་ལྷ་རྣམས་ཀྱི་ནང་དུ་ཡང་ལན་གསུམ་འཕོར་ནས་དེ་ནས་མི་རྣམས་ཀྱི་ནང་དུ་འོངས་ཏེ་ཡོངས་སུ་མྱ་ངན་ལས་འདའོ་ཞེས་སྨྲས་སོ།

།ཞེས་འགྲེལ་བཤད་དུ་འབྱུང་བ་ལྟར་འདོད་དོ།

།ཤེས་བྱེད་ནི་མདོ་ལས་ལྷ་དང་མི་རྣམས་ཀྱི་ནང་དུ་ལན་བདུན་འཕོར་ཞེས་འབྱུང་གི་སོ་སོར་འཕོར་ཞེས་མི་འབྱུང་བའི་ཕྱིར་དང།གཞན་ཡང་མདོ་ལས་གང་ཟག་འཕགས་པ་རྣམས་སྲིད་པ་བརྒྱད་མི་འགྲུབ་པར་གསུངས་པས་

43ji ltar D M] ci ltar P | 44sde pa D M] sbe pa P

[24] In AKBh see Pruden, 959, Śāstrī, 939. AKV preserves Sanskrit, 940: *kathaṃ ca bhikṣavo bhikṣuḥ saptasthānakuśalo bhavati / rūpaṃ yathābhūtaṃ prajānāti rūpasamudayaṃ rūpanirodhaṃ rūpanirodhagāminīṃ pratipadaṃ rūpasyāsvādamādīnavaṃ niḥsaraṇaṃ yathābhūtaṃ prajānāti / evaṃ vedanāṃ saṃjñāṃ*

> "How is it Monks, that a monk is wise in seven objects? [One] understands form exactly how it is, one understands exactly the arising of form, the cessation of form, the path of going to the cessation of form, the taste of form, the punishing fault of form, and arising of form." If speaking with regard to the five skandhas, since one is wise in seven [sets of] five, or thirty-five [objects], they are similar in being series of seven, [and the expression occurs] as "one who is wise in seven objects." [24]

Other schools say:

> That seeing the truth among human one transmigrates three times among the gods and having transmigrated just three times among humans then having gone among the gods one achieves *parinirvāṇa*. One that sees the truth among gods, just like that, transmigrates three times among humans and having transmigrated three times among the gods, from that, one goes among humans and achieves *parinirvāṇa*.

Thus it is asserted according to the occurrence in the *Abhidharmakośabhāṣyavyākhyā*.[25] (Objection) The proof (*shes byed*) from the *sūtra* occurs when stating "transmigrating seven times among gods and humans" but it does not say "transmigrating in each one." Moreover, since it teaches from the *sūtra* that Noble beings

---

saṃskārān vijñānaṃ yathābhūtaṃ prajānāti / vijñānasamudayaṃ vistareṇa yāvanniḥsaraṇaṃ yathābhūtaṃ prajānāti iti / evamanena nyāyena pañcasaptakāni pañcatriṃśaditi pañcatriṃśat kuśalaḥ prāpnoti / Distant comparison with Saṃyutta, iii.160-1.

[25] AKV, Śāstrī, 941: *taduktaṃ bhavati- yo manuṣyeṣu dṛṣṭasatyaḥ sa deveṣu triṣkṛtvaḥ saṃsṛtya manuṣyeṣu ca triṣkṛtva eva tato devānāgamya parinirvātīti / yo vā deveṣu dṛṣṭasatyaḥ sa tathaiva / sa manuṣyeṣu triṣkrvo deveṣu ca triṣkṛtva eva saṃsṛtya tato manuṣyānāgamya parinirvātīti /*

ཉེར་བརྒྱད་ལེན་པ་ལ་གནོད་ལ་གལ་ཏེ་མདོ་དེའི་དགོངས་པ་འགྲོ་བ་གཅིག
ཏུ་སྲིད་པ་བརྒྱད་མི་ལེན་པ་ལ་འདོད་ན་ཡང་མི་རུང་སྟེ།

སྲིད་མཐར་ཐུག་འགྲོ་ཚངས་རིས་ནས་ཚངས་ཆེན་མ་གཏོགས་པའི་
D 279 འབྲས་བུ་ཆེ་བའི་བར་དུ་སྐྱེ་བར་བྱེ་བྲག་ཏུ་སྨྲ་བ་རང་ཉིད་འདོད་པས་ན་
ལྷའི་འགྲོ་བ་གཅིག་ཏུ་སྲིད་པ་བརྒྱད་ལེན་པའི་ཕྱིར་རོ།

།འདོད་པ་ཁམས་ཀྱི་འགྲོ་བ་གཅིག་ཏུ་སྲིད་པ་བརྒྱད་མི་འགྲུབ་པ་ལ་
དགོངས་པ་བླང་བར་ཡང་མི་ནུས་ཏེ།འདི་ལ་ཤེས་བྱེད་མེད་པས་ལྷ་མི་གཉིས་
ཀའི་ནང་དུ་བསྡོམས་པའི་ལན་བདུན་མིན་པར་སོ་སོར་ལན་བདུན་པ་ལ་
ཡང་ཤེས་བྱེད་མེད་དེ་སྔར་མདོ་དྲངས་པ་ལྟར་ཐུན་མོང་དུ་ལན་བདུན་ཞེས་
འབྱུང་གི་སོ་སོར་མི་འབྱུང་བའི་ཕྱིར་རོ་སྙམ་དུ་བསམས་པའོ།

P 106a །དེ་ལྟར་སྔེ་བ་གཞན་གྱིས་བྱེ་བྲག་ཏུ་སྨྲ་བའི་སྲིད་པ་ཉེར་བརྒྱད་ལེན་
པར་འདོད་པའི་ཕྱོགས་ཐེ་ཚོམ་དུ་བྱས་པ་དང།སློབ་དཔོན་སངས་རྒྱས་གཉིས་
པས་བྱེ་བྲག་ཏུ་སྨྲ་བའི་ཕྱོགས་འཐད་པར་གཟིགས་ནས་དེའི་གཞུང་འཛུགས་
1301 པའི་ཕྱིར་འོད་སྲུངས་སྔེ་པའི་ལུང་ལས།ལྷ་རྣམས་ཀྱི་ནང་དུ་ལན་བདུན་མི་
རྣམས་ཀྱི་ནང་དུ་ལན་བདུན་ཞེས་སོ་སོར་འབྱུང་བ་ཡོད་པས་ལྷ་མི་བསྡོམས་
པའི་ལན་བདུན་ལ་ཞེན་པར་མི་བྱ་ཞེས་གསུངས་པས་ན་སྔེ་པ་གཞན་གྱི་བྱེ་
བྲག་ཏུ་སྨྲ་བ་ལ་འདོད་ཁམས་ཀྱི་འགྲོ་བ་གཅིག་ཏུ་སྲིད་པ་བརྒྱད་མི་ལེན་པ་
དང།སོ་སོར་བདུན་མིན་གྱི་ཐུན་མོང་དུ་བདུན་ཡིན་པ་ལ་ཤེས་བྱེད་མེད་ཅེས་
སྨྲས་པ་ཡང་བསལ་བ་ཡིན་ནོ།

།དེ་ལྟར་མིན་པར་ལྷ་དང་མི་རྣམས་ཀྱི་ནང་དུ་ལན་བདུན་ཞེས་པ་སྤྲ་
སོར་བཞག་བྱེད་ན་སྐྱེ་སྲིད་ཉི་ཚེ་ལན་བདུན་ལེན་པར་འགྱུར་གྱི།བར་སྲིད་མ་
D 280 སྨོས་པས་བར་སྲིད་མེད་པར་འགྱུར་ན་དེ་ཡང་མི་འཐད་དེ།གཟུགས་ཅན་གྱི་
ཁམས་ན་སྐྱེས་བ་ལེན་པ་ལ་བར་སྲིད་མེད་པ་མི་སྲིད་པའི་ཕྱིར་རོ་སྙམས་དུ་
བྱེ་བྲག་སྨྲ་བ་རྣམས་སེམས་སོ།

།འདིར་སློབ་དཔོན་རྒྱལ་པོ་སྲས་ཀྱིས་ལྷ་མི་སོ་སོར་ལན་བདུན་ཞེས་
པའི་ལུང་འདོད་པའི་འགྲོ་བ་གཅིག་ཏུ་སྲིད་པ་བརྒྱད་མི་འགྲུབ་པ་ལ་ཤེས་
བྱེད་དུ་འགྲོ་བའི་རྒྱུ་མཚན་གཟུགས་དང་གཟུགས་མེད་ཀྱི་འཕགས་པ་ཕྱིར་མི་

(*āryan*) do not achieve an eighth existence, to take twenty-eight is damaging. (Response) If that is the case, one should accept the intention of that *sūtra* to be that one does not take an eighth existence as a single transmigrator, otherwise it is not suitable.

(Objection) The *Ūrdhvaṃśrotas* who transmigrates up to the Peak of Existence, from the *Brahmakāyikayas* heaven up to the
D279 *Bṛhatphala* heaven, not counting the *Mahābrahma* realm, is accepted by the Vaibhāṣika themselves as taking an eighth existence as a single transmigrator of the gods.

(Response) Again, this is not possible; the intention is that [one] does not achieve an eighth existence as a single type of transmigrator within the desire realm. Regarding this, since there is no proof for this–there not being seven times taken together among both gods and humans and also there is no proof to take seven times in each one. Reflecting on the thought drawn out from the previous *sūtra*, concordantly "seven times"occurs but "for each one" does not occur.

Accordingly, other schools doubt the Vaibhāṣika's position which accepts twenty-eight existences and the Ācārya Second Buddha [Vasubhandhu] having correctly perceived the Vaibhāṣika position, for the sake of setting out their text, [quotes] from the scripture of the Kāsyapīyas where it states that "seven times among gods, seven times among humans" occurs for each one and stating "seven times taken together among gods and humans" is not acceptable. Other schools among the Vaibhāṣika's clearly state that one does not take an eighth existence for one transmigrator of the desire realm and that there is no proof in saying that there is not seven in each one but there is seven harmoniously.

In this way, a rebirth–existence is not construed for each word when stating "seven times among gods and humans." Simply seven times will be taken but, since intermediate states are not mentioned,
D280 there will not be intermediate state existences, and that is incorrect. The thought of the Vaibhāṣika is that there is an intermediate state existence when taking rebirth in the realm of form.

Here, Ācārya Jinaputra [gives] a reason that serves as proof for not achieving an eighth existence as a single transmigrator of the desire [realm] in a scripture which says "seven times in each among gods and humans" because by being a Non-returner Noble being of

འོང་ཡིན་པས་དེ་ད་གཟོད་[45]མིར་མི་སྐྱེ་བའི་ཕྱིར།ལྷ་དང་མི་རྣམས་སུ་སོ་སོར་
ལན་བདུན་འཁོར་ཞེས་པ་མི་འཐད་གསུངས་པ་ནི་དམ་པའི་ཆོས་མངོན་པ་
ལ་ཆོས་ཀྱི་སྤྱན་ལྡན་ཆེན་པོའི་གསུང་ཡིན་ཡང་དཔྱད་ན་འཐད་པར་མི་
མངོན་ཏེ།

།དེ་ལྟར་མིན་པར་ལྷ་དང་མི་རྣམས་ཀྱི་ནང་དུ་ལན་བདུན་ཞེས་པ་སྔ་
སོར་བཞག་བྱེད་ན་སྐྱེ་སྲིད་ཉི་ཚེ་ལན་བདུན་ལེན་པར་འགྱུར་གྱི།བར་སྲིད་མ་
སྨོས་པས་བར་སྲིད་མེད་པར་འགྱུར་ན་དེ་ཡང་མི་འཐད་དེ།གཟུགས་ཅན་གྱི་
ཁམས་ན་སྐྱེས་བ་ལེན་པ་ལ་བར་སྲིད་མེད་པ་མི་སྲིད་པའི་ཕྱིར་རོ་སྐམས་དུ་
བྱེ་བྲག་སྨྲ་བ་རྣམས་སེམས་སོ།འདོད་པའི་འགྲོ་བ་གཅིག་ལ་དགོངས་པ་ཡིན་
པའི་མདོ་ནི་གང་ཟག་ལྟ་བ་ཕུན་སུམ་ཚོགས་པ་སྲིད་པ་བརྒྱད་པ་མངོན་པར་
འགྲུབ་པ་གང་ཡིན་པ་དེ་ནི་གནས་མེད་ཅེས་པ་འདི་ཡིན་ལ་འདིའི་དགོངས་
P 106b པ་དེ་ལྟར་ཡིན་པའི་རྒྱུ་མཚན་ཡང་འོད་སྲུངས་སྡེ་པ་རྣམས་ལྷ་མི་སོ་སོར་
ལན་བདུན་ཅེས་འབྱུང་བས་འཕགས་པས་སྲིད་པ་བརྒྱད་ལེན་པར་བསྟན་ལ་
སྲིད་རྩེ་མཐར་ཐུག་འགྲོས་ཀྱང་ལྔའི་འགྲོ་བ་གཅིག་ཏུ་སྲིད་པ་བརྒྱད་ལ་
སོགས་པ་ལེན་པས་ན་ཁམས་འདོད་ཁམས་པ་དང་།འགྲོ་བ་རིགས་མཐུན་
གཅིག་ཏུ་བརྒྱད་མི་ལེན་པ་ལ་མདོ་སྡེ་མའི་དགོངས་པ་མི་ལེན་པར་སྔ་རང་
1302 སོར་བཞག་ན་དེ་གཉིས་མི་འཐད་པར་འགྱུར་བའི་ཕྱིར་རོ།།དེས་ན་འདོད་
པའི་འགྲོ་བ་རིགས་གཅིག་ལ་དགོངས་པའོ་ཞེས་བཤད་ན་འགྲེལ་པའི་རྩོད་
D 281 ལན་སྔ་ཕྱི་[46]ཐམས་ཅད་འབྲེལ་པར་འགྱུར་རོ།།སྔར་བཤད་པ་དེ་དག་གི་ཤེས་
བྱེད་ཡང་ཇི་སྐད་དུ་མཛོད་འགྲེལ་ལས།

།བྱེ་བྲག་ཏུ་སྨྲ་བ་རྣམས་ན་རེ།དེ་ནི་དེ་ལས་གཞན་པའི་སྐྱེ་བའི་སྲིད་པ་བདུན་དང་།སྲིད་པ་བར་མ་བདུན་དུ་མི་རྣམས་ཀྱི་ནང་དུ་ཉིང་མཚམས་སྦྱོར་བར་བྱེད་ལ་དེ་བཞིན་དུ་ལྷ་དག་གི་ནང་དུ་ཡང་ཉིང་མཚམས་སྦྱོར་བར་བྱེད་དེ།དེ་ལྟར་སྲིད་པ་ཉི་ཤུ་རྩ་བརྒྱད་ཀྱི་བར་དུ་ཉིང་མཚམས་སྦྱོར་བར་བྱེད་དོ།།སྲིད་པ་བདུན་ཚན་དུ་འདྲ་བའི་ཕྱིར་མཆོག་ཏུ་ཐོགས་ན་ལན་བདུན་པ་ཞེས་བཤད་དེ།གནས་བདུན་ལ་མཁས་པ་ཞེས་བྱ་བ་དང་།འདབ་མ་བདུན་པ་ཞེས་བྱ་བ་བཞིན་ནོ།།ཞེས་ཟེར་རོ།

[45] gzod D M] bzod P | [46] snga phyi D M] snga kyi P

the form and formless [realms] they are not reborn as a human.[26] It is wrong to say "transmigrating seven individual times in the realms of gods and humans." For, when examining the holy Abhidharma which is a teaching possessing the great eye of the doctrine, it is not evidently admitted.

The *sūtra* has the intention for a single transmigrator of the desire [realm], stating "the individual possessing views that achieves an eighth existence is unsuitable" is also a proof for the intention of this. The Kāsyapīyas, with the occurrence "seven times in each of the gods and humans," teach a Noble being (*ārya*) as taking eight existences, and even the *Ūrdhvasrotas* who goes up to the peak of existence, by taking eight existences and so forth in a single transmigrator of the devas realm will become a desire realm being, and when construeing the words in one's own way and not accepting the intention of the former *sūtra* as not taking an eighth existence as a single homogeneous lineage transmigrator, the two assertions become incorrect. Therefore, when explaining that the intention is for a single lineage transmigrator of the desire [realm], all former and later
D281 arguments and objections of the commentary become coherent. The previously explained proofs are stated in the *Abhdharmakośabhāṣya*:

> The Vaibhāṣikas say: Other than the present existence, one takes up seven existences among humans and seven intermediate state existences, and in the same manner takes birth among the gods. Accordingly [one] is reborn up to twenty-eight existences. Since it is like the series of seven existences, it is explained as "reborn at the most seven times" as like [a monk] "wise in seven objects" (*saptasthānakuśala*) and like [a tree] called "seven-petaled" (*saptaparṇa*).

[26] Discussion in AKV, Pk chu 216b.1-3, Śāstrī, 942: *....yaccoktam iva caiva kiṃ jñāpakam pratyekaṃ devamanuṣyeṣu saptakṛtvaḥ iti / pratyekamarthaparigrahenaiva hi kāmadhātvabhisandhirapi sūcito bhavati / na hi rūpārūpyadhātvoḥ saptakṛtvo devamanuṣyeṣu saṃsaraṇaṃ yujyate tatropannānāmanāgāmināṃ manuṣyānāgamanāt / yuktirapyata eva gamyate /*

།འོ་ན་ཡང་མདོ་ལས།གང་ཟག་ལྟ་བ་ཕུན་སུམ་ཚོགས་པ་སྲིད་པ་
བརྒྱད་པ་མངོན་པར་གྲུབ་པ་གང་ཡིན་པ་ནི་གནས་མ་ཡིན་ཞིང་
[47]གོ་སྐབས་མེད་དེ།འདི་ནི་གནས་མེད་དོ་ཞེས་གསུངས་པ་ཇི་ལྟ་བུ་
ཞེ་ན།

འགྲོ་བ་གཅིག་ཏུ་དགོངས་པ་ཡིན་ནོ།འོན་ཏེ་སྨྲ་ཇི་བཞིན་དུ་བཏག་
ན་ནི།སྲིད་པ་བར་མ་ཡང་ཡོད་པར་མི་འགྱུར་རོ།།དེ་ལྟ་ན་ཡང་
སྲིད་པའི་རྩེ་མོའི་བར་དུ་གོང་དུ་འཕོ་བ་འགྲོ་བ་གཅིག་ཏུ་སྐྱེ་བའི་
སྲིད་པ་བརྒྱད་པར་མི་འགྱུར་རོ་ཞེ་ན[48]།འདོད་པའི་ཁམས་ལ་
P 107a དགོངས་ཏེ་གསུངས་པའི་ཕྱིར་ཉེས་པ་མེད་དོ།།འདི་ལ་ཤེས་པར་
བྱེད་པ་མདོ་འམ་རིགས་པ་ཅི་ཞིག་ཡོད།ལྷ་དང་མི་རྣམས་ཀྱི་ནང་
ན་སོ་སོར་ལན་བདུན་སྐྱེའི།གཉིས་ཀའི་ནང་དུ་ནི་ལན་བདུན་མ་
ཡིན་པ་ཉིད་དོ།།ཞེས་གསུང་པ་འདི་ལ་ཤེས་པར་བྱེད་པ་ཅི་ཞིག
D 282 ཡོད་དེ།འདི་སྐད་དུ་ལྷ་རྣམས་དང་མི་རྣམས་ཀྱི་ནང་དུ་ལན་བདུན་
ཞེས་འབྱུང་ངོ་ཞེ་ན།འོད་སྲུངས་པ་རྣམས་ལྷ་རྣམས་སུ་ལན་བདུན་
མི་རྣམས་སུ་ལན་བདུན་ཞེས་སོ་སོར་ཡང་འདོན་པས་འདི་ལ་
མངོན་པར་ཞེན་པར་མི་བྱའོ།།གང་ཞིག་མི་དག་གི་ནང་དུ་རྒྱུན་དུ་
ཞུགས་པར་གྱུར་པ་དེ་ནི་དེ་ཁོ་ནར་འོངས་ནས་ཡོངས་སུ་མྱ་ངན་
1303 ལས་འདའ་ ལ།གང་ཞིག་ལྷ་དག་གི་ནང་དུ་རྒྱུན་དུ་ཞུགས་པར་
གྱུར་པ་དེ་ནི་དེ་ཁོ་ནར་འོངས་ནས་ཡོངས་སུ་མྱ་ངན་ལས་འདའོ།
།ཞེས་གང་གསུངས་པ་ཡིན་ནོ།།དེ་ལྟར་ལུགས་གཉིས་ལས་སངས་རྒྱས་
གཉིས་པ་ནི་ཉེར་བརྒྱད་ལེན་པའི་ཕྱོགས་བཞེད་པར་འགྲེལ་བཤད་དུ་འབྱུང་
ལ།ཀུན་ལས་བཏུས་སུ་ཡང་

---

[47]zhing M] cing D P | [48]zhe na D M] ce P

---

[27] AKBh, Pk ṅu 23b.1-24a.2, Pruden, 959-960, Śāstrī, 940-941: *sa eva tasmād anyān saptopapattibhavān manuṣyeṣu pratisandadhāti saptāntarābhavān / evaṃ deveṣvityaṣṭāviṃśatibhavān pratisandadhāti / saptakasāmānyattu saptakṛtvaḥ parama uktaḥ/ saptasthānakauśalasaptaparṇavaditi vaibhāṣikāḥ /* (see also *Kathāvatthu*, xii.5 and distant *Saṃyutta*, iii.160-1) *yattarhi sūtra uktam asthānamanavakāśo yad*

(Objection) Well then, when the *sūtra* states: "the individual possessing views (*dṛṣṭisaṃpanna*) to be one who attains clearly an eighth existence," how is that unsuitable and inapplicable?

(Reply) This be understood as unsuitable. It is the intention as a single transmigrator, but holding to the letter of the teaching, there also will not be any intermediate state existences. Again, how it is that the *Ūrdhvasrotas* who is a *Bhavāgraparamas* will not produce an eighth existence of birth as a single transmigrator? It is the intention for the realm of desire and so there is no fault. What is the reasoning or text that proves this? What is the proof for this teaching, among gods and humans seven times in each one but not seven times [in all] among both? Why does the text read "appearing seven times among humans and among gods"? Since the Kāśyapīyas also read for each one "seven times among gods, seven times among humans,"one should not be too devoted to this [question]. One who becomes a Stream-enterer among humans, returns to just that for *parinirvāṇa*. One who becomes a Stream-enterer among the gods, returns to just that for *parinirvāṇa*.[27]

Accordingly, from the two systems, the Second Buddha [Vasubandhu], as it appears in the *Abhidharmakośabhāṣyavyākhā*, asserts the opinion of taking twenty-eight existences. The *Abhidharmasamuccaya* says:

---

dṛṣṭisampannaḥ pudgalo 'ṣṭtamaṃ bhavamabhinirvartayiṣyati / nedaṃ sthānaṃ vidyate iti / ekasyāṃ gatāvityabhiprāyaḥ / yathārūtaṃ vā kalpyamāne 'ntarābhavo'pi na syāt / [941] *evamapyūrdhvaṃsrotaso bhavāgraparamasyaikasyāṃ gatāvaṣṭama upapattibhavo na prāpnoti / kāmadhātvabhisandhi-vacanādadoṣaḥ / kimatra jñāpakam sūtram yuktirvā / iha caiva kiṃ jñāpakaṃ pratyekaṃ devamanuṣyeṣu saptakṛtvo na punarūbhayeṣveva saptakṛtva iti / evaṃ hi paṭathate saptakṛtvo devāṃś ca manuṣyāś ca iti pratyekam api tu kāśyapīyāḥ paṭanti saptakṛtvo devān saptakṛtvo manuṣyān iti / nātrābhiniveṣṭavyam / yaś ca manuṣyeṣu sotaāpanno bhavati sa tānevāgamya parinirvāti yo deveṣu sa taneva /*

རེ་ལྟར་ཐོགས་ན་ལན་བདུན་པ་གང་ཞེ་ན།རྒྱུན་དུ་ཞུགས་པའི་གང་ཟག་ཉིད་ལྷ་དང་མིར་ཡན་མན་དུ་ལན་བདུན་དུ་སྲིད་པར་འཁོར་བར་བྱས་ནས་སྡུག་བསྔལ་གྱི་ཐ་མ་ཐོབ་པའོ་

ཞེས་འབྱུང་བས་གཅིན་ཡང་སྐྱེ་བ་ཉེར་བརྒྱད་ལེན་པ་བཞིན་པར་བརྟག་ནུས་ཏེ།ལྷ་མི་ཡན་མན་ནི་ཕན་ཚུན་སོ་སོར་གྱི་དོན་དུ་བཤད་པར་ནུས་པའི་ཕྱིར་དང་།འདོད་པར་སྐྱེ་བ་ལ་ཡང་བར་སྲིད་ལེན་པས་ཁྱབ་པའི་ཕྱིར་རོ།

།ལན་བདུན་པ་ལ་སྐྱེ་འཕགས་གཉིས།།འཕགས་པ་ལ་ཡང་ངེས་མ་ངེས།།རྣམ་གཉིས་ཉེར་བརྒྱད་སྐྱེ་ན་ཡང་།།བདུན་ཚན་འདྲ་ཕྱིར་བདུན་ཞེས་དང་།།དང་པོར་ཐོབ་པའི་རྟེན་དེ་ལ།།མྱང་འདས་མངོན་དུ་བྱེད་པ་སྟེ།
P 107b གོང་འོག་གཉིས་ཀྱི་གཞུང་རྣམས་ཀྱིས[49]།།སྐུ་མཆེད་གཉིས་ཀྱི་དགོངས་པར་བསྒྲུབས།

D 283 །ཞེས་བྱ་བ་ནི་བསྡུ་བའི་ཚིགས་སུ་བཅད་པའོ།།རྒྱུན་དུ་ཞུགས་པའི་
འབྲས་བུ་ཙམ་ལ་གནས་པའི་རྣམ་པར་བཞག་པ་བཤད་ཟིན་ཏོ།། ༈
།།རྒྱུན་དུ་ཞུགས་པའི་འབྲས་བུ་ཁྱད་པར་ཅན་ལ་གནས་པ་གང་ཞེ་
ན།རྒྱུན་དུ་ཞུགས་པའི་འབྲས་བུ་ལ་གནས་པ་གང་འདོད་པའི་སྒོམ་སྤང་དང་
པོ་ནས་དྲུག་པའི་བར་གང་ཡང་རུང་བ་སྤོང་བའི་སྦྱོར་བ་ཅན་ནོ།།དེ་ལ་ཡང་
ལྷའི་རིགས་ནས་རིགས་སུ་སྐྱེ་བ་དང་།མིའི་རིགས་ནས་རིགས་སུ་སྐྱེ་བའོ།།འོན་
ཀྱང་དེ་ཙམ་དུ་གྲངས་ངེས་པ་ནི་མ་ཡིན་ཏེ།འདི་ལྟར་རྒྱུན་ཞུགས་འབྲས་
གནས་ཀྱི་རྟེན་དེ་ཉིད་ལ་ཕྱིར་འོང་དང་ཕྱིར་མི་འོང་མངོན་དུ་བྱས་ཏེ་དེ་ཚེ་
འཕོས་ནས་ཁམས་གོང་མར་སྐྱེ་བ་ཡོད་ལ་རིགས་ནས་རིགས་སྐྱེ་ནི་ཚེ་དེ་ལ་
1304 འབྲས་བུ་བར་པ་ གཉིས་མི་བསྐྱེད་ཅིང་ཁམས་གོང་མར་ཡང་འགྲོ་བ་མི་
སྲིད་པའི་ཕྱིར་རོ།།དེ་ལ་སྤྱིར་རིགས་ནས་རིགས་སུ་སྐྱེ་བ་ལ་ཁྱད་པར་གསུམ་

[49] kyis D M] kyi P

[28] AS, Rahula, 155, Pradhan, 90.5: *saptakṛdbhavaparamaḥ katamaḥ / srotaāpanna eva*

> Who is an individual [that is born] "seven-times-at-the-most"? Oneself a Stream-enterer who, having transversed in existence seven times above and below among devas and humans attains the end of suffering. [28]

Since it appears this way, even Older Brother [Asaṅga] is able to be examined as teaching to take twenty-eight rebirths because of the ability to explain as the meaning of each one mutually transmigrating above or below among gods and humans and because [it is that which] is pervaded by taking existence again as a rebirth in the desire [realm]. Set forth in condensed verse:

> Regarding the seven-timers, there are two: ordinary beings and Noble beings. Also with regard to the Noble Being there are two types: definite and the not definite. Although born twenty-eight times, they are called "seven" because of being similar to sets of seven. They actualize *nirvāṇa* in that embodiment in which it is initially attained and the texts of the two, the upper and lower [Abhidharmas], establish this as the intention of the two brothers.

The explanation of the arrangement of the mere abider in the result of Stream-enterer is finished.

Who abides in the distinctive result of Stream-enterer? The upper abider in the result of Stream-enterer applies himself to abandoning whichever of the first up to the sixth desire realm obstacles to be removed by the path of cultivation. Regarding this, there are those born from family to family among the gods and those born from family to family among humans.

However, one does not ascertain the enumeration as merely that. Accordingly, that very embodiment of the abider in the result of Stream-enterer when actualizing the result of Once-returner or Non-returner is reborn in the upper realms when passing away and a *Kulaṃkula* in that life is not reborn in the two middle results and does not transmigrate in the upper realms. For this generally, one born from

---

pudgalaḥ saptakṛtvo 'pi miśromiśra devamanuṣyeṣu bhavāt samṣrtya yo duḥkhasyāntamanuprāpnoti /

དང་ལྡན་པ་ཞིག་[50]དགོས་ཏེ།དེ་ཡང་གང་ཞེ་ན།མཛོད་དུ།

> རྣམ་ གསུམ་ རྣམ་ བཞི་ ལས་ གྲོལ་ བ།།ཚེ་ [51]གཉིས་ གསུམ་ དུ་ རིགས་ ནས་ རིགས།

།ཞེས་འབྱུང་བ་ལྟར་ཉོན་མོངས་སྤངས་པའི་ཁྱད་པར་དང།སྐྱེ་བ་ལེན་ཚུལ་གྱི་ཁྱད་པར་དང།གཉེན་པོ་ཐོབ་པའི་ཁྱད་པར་རོ།།དེ་ལ་འདོད་པའི་སྒོམ་[52]སྤང་གསུམ་པ་ངེས་པར་སྤངས་བཞི་པ་མ་སྤངས་ཀྱང་ལྔའི་ལྔ་པ་ངེས་པར་མ་སྤངས་པ་ཞིག་[53]དགོས་ཏེ།།འགྲེལ་པར།

> ཉོན་ མོངས་ པ་ སྤངས་ པ་ ལས་ ནི་ ཉོན་ མོངས་ པའི་ རྣམ་ པ་ གསུམ་
> D 284 མམ་ བཞི་ སྤངས་ པའི་ ཕྱིར་ རོ།

།ཞེས་གསུམ་དང་བཞི་ལ་འདམ་ག་[54]ཅན་མཛད་ལ་གཉིས་དང་གཅིག་
P 108a མ་སྨོས་པའི་ཕྱིར་དང།ལྔ་པ་སྤངས་ན་དྲུག་པ་ཡང་ངེས་པར་སྤོང་བས་ཕྱིར་འོང་དུ་འགྱུར་ལ།དེ་ལྟར་ན་འགྲོ་བ་རིགས་མཐུན་གཅིག་ཏུ་སྐྱེ་བ་གཉིས་ལེན་མི་སྲིད་པའི་ཕྱིར་དང།རིགས་ནས་རིགས་སྐྱེ་མ་ཡིན་པར་ཐལ་བའི་ཕྱིར་རོ།།གལ་ཏེ་དེ་ལྟ་ན་ཕྱིར་འོང་བར་ཆད་གཅིག་པ་ཡང་བརྒྱད་པ་སྤངས་པ་ན་དགུ་པ་ཡང་ངེས་པར་སྤོང་བས་ཕྱིར་མི་འོང་དུ་འགྱུར་ལ།དེ་ལྟ་ན་ཚེ་གཅིག་བར་མི་འགྱུར་རོ།།ཞེ་ན་མི་མཚུངས་ཏེ།སྒོམ་[55]སྤང་དགུ་པ་སྤོང་བ་ལ་ཁམས་ལས་འདའ་དགོས་པས་དཀའ་ལ་དྲུག་པ་སྤོང་བ་[56]ལ་དེ་ལྟ་མིན་པའི་ཕྱིར་རོ།།དེ་ལྟར་ཡང་ཇི་སྐད་དུ།མཛོད་འགྲེལ་ལས།

> ཅིའི་ ཕྱིར་ རྣམ་ པ་ ལྔ་ སྤངས་ པའི་ ཕྱིར་ མ་ ཡིན་ ཞེ་ ན།དེ་ སྤངས་ ན་ དྲུག་ པ་ ཡང་ གདོན་ མི་ ཟ་ བར་ སྤོང་ བའི་ ཕྱིར་ཏེ་ དེའི་ རྣམ་ པ་ གཅིག་

---

[50]zhig M] cig D; gcig P | [51]tshe D M] che P | [52]sgom M P] bsgom D | [53]zhig M] cig D; gcig P | [54]'dam ga D M] 'dam kha P | [55]sgom M] bsgom D P | [56]spong ba D M] speng ba P

---

[29] AK vi.34c-d, Pk ṅu 24b3, Pruden, 962, Pradhan, 357, Śāstrī, 944: *tricaturvidhamuktastu dvitrijanmā kulaṃkulaḥ /*

family to family needs to have three distinctive [qualities]. What are these [three]? The *Abhidharmakośa* states:

> Delivered from three or four categories, destined for two or three rebirths, is one who goes family to family (*Kulaṃkula*)[29]

According to this statement one who goes family to family has the distinction of abandoning afflictions, distinction in the manner of taking birth, and the distinction of obtaining a relative. Regarding this, one needs to definitely abandon the third obstacle to be removed by the path of cultivation, although one may abandon the fourth, one definitely does not abandon the fifth obstacle. The *Abhidharmakośabhāṣya* states:

> From the point of view of abandoning afflictions, three or four aspects of the afflictions are to be abandoned.[30]

D284 One makes the option with three or four because it does not say two or one and if abandoning the fifth, one also definitely abandons the sixth and becomes a Once-returner. Along these lines, it is not possible for the transmigrator to take two rebirths in a single homogeneous lineage because of the consequence of not being one who is born family to family (*kulaṃkula*).

(Objection) If this is the case then even an *Ekavīcika* Once-returner, if abandoning the eighth, then definitely will abandon the ninth and become a Non-returner. Therefore it will not be as one life. Why is it not similar?

(Reply) It is difficult to abandon the ninth obstacle to be abandoned by the path of cultivation since one needs to pass over the desire realm, but it is not like that in abandoning the sixth obstacle. The *Abhidharmakośabhāṣya* says:

> Why does one who goes family to family not abandon the fifth category? Because in abandoning that fifth category, the sixth is undoubtedly also abandoned; one category of that defilement is not

---

[30] AKBh, Pruden, 962, Pradhan, 357, Śāstrī, 944: *kleśaprahāṇatas tricatuḥprakāraprahīṇatvāt /*

གིས་ནི་བར་ཆད་གཅིག་པ་བཞིན་དུ་འབྲས་བུ་ལ་གེགས་བྱ་བར་མི་
ནུས་ཏེ་ཁམས་ལས་མི་འདའ་བའི་ཕྱིར་རོ་

ཞེས་གང་གསུངས་པ་ཡིན་ནོ།།སྐྱེ་བ་ལེན་ཚུལ་གྱི་ཁྱད་པར་ནི།འདོད་
པའི་འགྲོ་བ་གཅིག་ཏུ་སྐྱེ་བ་གཉིས་ངེས་པར་ལེན་དགོས་ཏེ་རིགས་ནས་
རིགས་སྐྱེའི་དོན་བཟློས་པ[57]འམ་འདབས་པའི་དོན་ཡིན་པའི་ཕྱིར་དང།འདོད་
པའི་འགྲོ་བ་མི་གཅིག་པ་ གཉིས་སུ་ལན་གཉིས་སྐྱེ་བ་ཕྱིར་འོང་[58]ལ་ཡང་
ཡོད་པའི་ཕྱིར་རོ།།སྐྱེ་བ་གསུམ་ནི་བླངས་ཀྱང་བླ་ལ་མ་བླངས་ཀྱང་བླའི།བཞི་
D 285 ངེས་པར་མ་བླངས་པ་ཞིག[59]དགོས་ཏེ།འགྲེལ་པར་

ཚེ་གཉིས་སམ་གསུམ་ལུས་པའི་ཕྱིར་རོ།

།ཞེས་ཚེ་གསུམ་ཡན་ཆད་ལས་འདམ་ག[60]མ་མཛད་པའི་ཕྱིར་
རོ།།གཉེན་པོའི་ཁྱད་པར་ནི།སྔར་བཤད་པའི་ཉོན་མོངས་སྤང་བའི་གཉེན་པོ་
ཟག་མེད་ཀྱི་ལམ་ཐོབ་པའོ།།དེ་ནི་རྣམ་གསུམ་རྣམ་བཞི་ཞེས་པའི་རྐང་པ་
P 108b གཉིས་སུ་དངོས་སུ་མ་སྨོས་པ་ནི་རྒྱུན་ཞུགས་ཕྱིས་ཉོན་མོངས་པའི་རྣམ་པ་
གཅིག་ལ་སོགས་པ་སྤོང་བ་ནི་དེ་དག་གི་གཉེན་པོ་ཟག་མེད་ཀྱི་ལམ་ཐོབ་པ་
དེ་མ་སྨོས་ཀྱང་རྟོགས་པར་འགྱུར་ཏེ་གཉེན་པོ་མེད་པར་ཉོན་མོངས་སྤོང་
[61]མི་སྲིད་པའི་ཕྱིར་དང།འཕགས་པ་ཡིན་པས་ཟག་མེད་ཀྱི་ལམ་གྱི་ཐོབ་པ་
[62]ཡང་སྐྱེ་བའི་ཕྱིར་རོ།།གལ་ཏེ་འཇིག་རྟེན་པའི་ལམ་གྱིས་སྤོང་[63]ན་ཡང་ཟག་
མེད་འཐོབ་སྟེ[64]ཇི་སྐད་དུ།མཛོད་ལས།

འཕགས་པ་བྲལ་བའི་ཐོབ་རྣམ་གཉིས།

།ཞེས་འཕགས་པས་འཇིག་རྟེན་པའི་ལམ་གྱིས་ཉོན་མོངས་སྤོང་བ་ལ་
ཟག་བཅས་ཟག་མེད་ཀྱི་ཐོབ་པ་གཉིས་ཀ་སྐྱེ་བར་གསུངས་པའི་ཕྱིར་རོ།།དེ་
ལྟར་ཡང་མཛོད་འགྲེལ་ལས།

---

[57]zlos pa D M] bzlos pa P | [58]phyir ’ong D M] phyir ’ongs P | [59]zhig M] cig D; gcig P | [60]’dam ga D M] ‘dam kha P | [61]spong D M] spongs P | [62]lam gyi thob pa D M] lam thob pa P | [63]spong D M] spongs P | [64]ste D M] te P

---

[31]AKBh, Pk ṅu 24b6, Pradhan, 357, Pruden, 963, Śāstrī, 945: *kasmān na*

> able to create an obstacle to the result, as is the case for one separated by a single birth (an *Ekavīcika*), because one does not pass into another realm of existence.[31]

The distinction of the manner of taking birth is as follows: it is definitely necessary to take two rebirths in a single transmigration sequence within the desire realm because it is the conventional or expressed meaning of one who is born from family to family (*Kulaṃkula*) and because to take rebirth two times in two, not one transmigration sequence, is the characteristic for a Once-returner.

It is also easy to take or not take three rebirths but definitely not
D285 necessary to take four rebirths because the *Abhidharmakośabhāṣya* says:

> ...because of two or three lives remaining,[32]

Therefore an option is not made for above three lives. The distinction of antidote: [the *Kulaṃkula*] attains the uncontaminated path antidotes of abandoning the afflictions explained formerly. That is not actually spoken in the two stanzas which say "three categories, four categories"; after the Stream-enterer abandons one category of the defilements and so forth, the antidote of those, the attaining of the uncontaminated path, although not mentioned will be realized because there is not abandoning afflictions without an antidote and because the individual also attains the uncontaminated path since one is a Noble being. For instance, if abandoning by the mundane path one also attains the uncontaminated. The *Abhidharmakośa* states:

> A Noble being attains two types of separation through a mundane path.[33]

Thus, it is taught that a Noble being generates both a contaminated and uncontaminated attainment for abandoning the afflictions by a mundane path. The *Abhidharmakośabhāṣya* says:

---

pañcaprakāraprahaṇāt / tat prahāne ṣaṣṭasyāvasyaṃ prahāṇāt / nahi tasyaikaḥ prakāraḥ phalaṃ vighnayittuṃ samarthaḥ ekavīcikasyeva dhātvanatikramāt /

[32] AKBh, Pruden, 962, Śāstrī, 944, Pradhan, 357: (*janmato*)*dvitrijanmāvaśeṣatvāt* /; Pk ṅu 24b4 mistakenly says "one or two rebirths remaining." Tsong kha pa text agrees here with the Sanskrit readings. | [33] AK, vi.46a-b, Pruden, 986, Śāstrī, 974 :" *laukikenāryavairāgye visaṃyogāptayo dvividhā*."

ཚོགས་སུ་བཅད་པའི་ནང་དུ་གཉིས་ཤིག་སློས་པ་ནི་རྒྱུན་དུ་ཞུགས་པ་ཕྱིས་ཉོན་མོངས་པ་སྤོང་བར་བྱེད་པ་ན་དེ་གཉེན་པོ་ཟག་པ་མེད་པའི་དབང་པོ་ཐོབ་པ་ནི་མ་སློས་ཀྱང་འགྲུབ་པའི་ཕྱིར་རོ། །ཞེས་སོ། །དེ་ལྟར་ན་འདོད་པའི་སྒོམ[65] སྤང་དྲུག་པ་མ་སྤངས་པ་ལམ་ལ་རྗེས་ཤེས་ལ་གནས་པ་ཉོན་མོངས་སྤོང་བའི་སྦྱོར་བ་དང་ལྡན་པ་འདོད་པའི་འགྲོ་བ་གཅིག་ཏུ་སྐྱེ་བ་
D 286 གཉིས་ངེས་པར་བླངས་ནས་འདའ་བ་དེ་ནི་རྒྱུན་ཞུགས་རིགས་ནས་རིགས་སྐྱེ་
ཡིན་ནོ།

།དེ་ལ་ལྷའི་རིགས་ནས་རིགས་ནས་སྐྱེ་དང་།མིའི་རིགས་ནས་རིགས་སྐྱེ་
གཉིས་ཡོད་དོ།།དང་པོ་ནི།འདོད་ལྷ་དྲུག་པོ་གང་རུང་གི་རྟེན་ལ་རྒྱུན་ཞུགས་
ཐོབ་པ་དེ་ལྟར་ལན་གཉིས་སྐྱེས་ནས་དང་པོའི་ལྷ་རིགས་དེའམ་གཞན་ལྔ་པོ་
1306 གང་རུང་ལ་མྱ་ངན་ལས་ འདའོ།།གཉིས་པ་ནི།འཛམ་བུ་གླིང་པ་ལྟ་བུའི་རྟེན་
ལ་རྒྱུན་ཞུགས་ཐོབ་པ་དེ་མིར་ལན་གཉིས་སྐྱེས་ནས་གླིང་དེ་ཉིད་དམ་ཤར་
P 109a ནུབ་ གང་ རུང་ དུ་ སྐྱེས་ ནས་ མྱ་ ངན་ ལས་ འདའོ།།དེ་ ལྟར་ ཡང་ ཇི་ སྐད་
དུ།མཛོད་འགྲེལ་ལས།

> རིགས་ནས་རིགས་སུ་སྐྱེ་བ་ནི་རྣམ་པ་གཉིས་ཏེ།ལྷའི་རིགས་ནས་རིགས་སུ་སྐྱེ་བ་ནི་ལྷ་དག་གི་ནང་དུ་རིགས་གཉིས་སམ་གསུམ་དུ་འཕོར་ནས་ལྷའི་རིགས་དེའམ་གཞན་དུ་ཡོངས་སུ་མྱ་ངན་ལས་འདའ་བའོ།མིའི་རིགས་ནས་རིགས་སུ་སྐྱེ་བ་ནི་མི་དག་གི་ནང་དུ་རིགས་གཉིས་སམ་གསུམ་དུ་འཕོར་ནས་གླིང་དེའམ་གཞན་དུ་ཡོངས་སུ་མྱ་ངན་ལས་འདས་པ་གང་ཡིན་པའོ།

།ཞེས་གང་གསུངས་པའོ།།འདིར་འགྲེལ་བཤད་དུ།

[65] sgom M] bsgom D P

> Within the verse only two are mentioned, for when abandoning the afflictions after attaining the result of Stream-enterer, one obtains the antidote of that result, the faculty of the uncontaminated, although not spoken, is achieved. [34]

Accordingly, one is a family to family Stream-enterer (*kulaṃkula srotaāpanna*) if not abandoning the sixth obstacle of the desire realm to be removed by the path of cultivation, applies oneself to the abandoning of afflictions while abiding on the subsequent knowledge on the truth of the path, and passes beyond sorrow having definitely taken two births in a single transmigration of the desire
D286 realm.

For this there are two: one born family to family among gods and one born family to family among humans. First, having attained the status of Stream-enterer in a suitable embodiment from among the six types of desire realm gods, having been born two times, that lineage of the first class of gods or whatever suitable other five classes of desire realm gods one then achieves parinirvāṇa. The second is one who attains the status of Stream-enterer in an embodiment within Jampudvīpa, having been born two times as a human, having been born in that continent itself or a suitable eastern or northern [continent] achieves *parinirvāṇa*. This explanation is also taught in the *Abhidharmakośabhāṣya*:

> A *Kulaṃkula* is of two types: a *Devakulaṃkula* who, having transmigrated in two or three families among the gods, attains *nirvāṇa* in that lineage of gods or in another and a *Manuṣyakulaṃkula* who, having transmigrated in two or three families among humans, attains *nirvāṇa* in this continent or in another.[35]

The *Abhidharmakośabhāṣyavyākhā* says:

---

[34] AKBh, Pk024b.6, Pruden, 963, Śāstrī, 945: *sloke tu dvayograhaṇam srotaāpannasya paścāt prahīṇe sati tatpratipakṣānāsvendriyasyānuktasiddhatvāt* /

[35] AKBh,Pruden, 963, Śāstrī, 946: *sa eva kulaṃkulo dvividhaḥ / devakulaṃkulaḥ yo deveṣu dve trīṇi vā kulāni saṃsṛtya parinirvāti tatra vā'nyatra vā devanikāye / manuṣyakulaṃkulaḥ yo manuṣyeṣu tatra vā'nyatra vā dvīpe parinirvāti* /

གང་ཞིག་རྣམ་པ་གཅིག་གམ་གཉིས་ལས་གྲོལ་བ་དེ་ཅི་ཞིག་ཡིན་
ཞེ་ན།ཁ་ཅིག་ན་རེ་རིགས་ནས་རིགས་སུ་སྐྱེ་བ་ཡིན་ཏེ།རྣམ་པ་
གསུམ་དང་བཞི་ལས་གྲོལ་བ་སྨོས་པ་ནི་དཔེར་བརྗོད་པའི་ཕྱིར་
རམ།དེ་ཕན་ཆད་དུ་ནི་མ་ཡིན་ནོ་ཞེས་ཚད་དུ་བྱས་པའི་ཕྱིར་
རོ།།ཞེས་ཟེར་རོ།།གཞན་དག་ན་རེ་རྣམ་པ་གཅིག་གམ་གཉིས་ལས་
D 287 གྲོལ་བ་དེ་ནི་ཚེ་ལྔའམ་དྲུག་པ་ཡིན་ཏེ་རྣམ་པ་གསུམ་མམ་བཞི་
ལས་གྲོལ་བ་ཞེས་ཁྱད་པར་སྨོས་པའི་ཕྱིར་རོ།།།ཞེས་ཟེར་ཏེ་འདི་ནི་
བཤད་པ་བྱེད་པ་རྣམས་ཀྱིས་མ་དཔྱད་པས་འདི་དཔྱད་དགོས་པ་
ཡིན་ནོ་ཞེས་འབྱུང་ངོ་།

།དེ་ལ་ལུགས་སྔ་མ་ནི།སྒོམ་སྤང་རྣམ་པ་གསུམ་མམ་བཞི་ལས་གྲོལ་
བའི་རིགས་སྐྱེ་འདོད་པ་བཞིན་དུ་རྣམ་པ་གཅིག་གམ་གཉིས་ཙམ་ལས་གྲོལ་
བའི་རིགས་སྐྱེ་ཡོད་ལ་རིགས་སྐྱེ་ལ་གསུམ་མམ་བཞི་སྤང་དགོས་པར་བསྟན་
པ་ནི།རིགས་སྐྱེའི་ཕྱོགས་གཅིག་མཚོན་པའམ་བཞི་མན་ཆད་མ་སྤངས་པ་
ཞིག་[66]དགོས་ཞེས་ཕ་མཐའི་ཚད་བསྟན་པ་ཙམ་ཡིན་ནོ།།ཞེས་པའི་དོན་
ནོ།།ལུགས་གཉིས་པའི་དོན་ནི།རྣམ་པ་གསུམ་མམ་བཞི་ལས་གྲོལ་བ་ལ་ཚེ་
P 109b གཉིས་སམ་གསུམ་ལུས་པའི་ཁྱད་པར་བསྟན་པ་ནི། རྣམ་པ་གཅིག་གམ་
1307 གཉིས་ལུས་པར་ཡང་གོང་མའི་གནད་ཀྱིས་ཚེ་ལྔའམ་དྲུག་ལུས་པ་ ཡིན་
ནོ།།ཞེས་པའི་དོན་ནོ།

།དེ་ལྟར་གཉིས་པོ་དེ་ལ་སློབ་དཔོན་རྒྱལ་པོ་སྲས་ཀྱིས་[67]ནི།སྔོན་གྱི་ཆོས་མངོན་པའི་འཆད་པ་པོ་རྣམས་ཀྱིས་འདི་ལྟ་བུ་མ་དཔྱད་པས་དཔྱད་དགོས་པར་འདུག་ཅེས་ཐེ་ཚོམ་བསྐྱུར་བ་ཙམ་ལས་མི་སྣང་ཡང་མི་འཐད་པར་མངོན་ཏེ།

སློབ་དཔོན་ཀྱིས་[68]རིགས་སྐྱེའི་སྤངས་པའི་[69]ཁྱད་པར་འཆད་པ་ན་
གསུམ་མམ་བཞི་ལས་གྲོལ་བ་བསྟན་པ་དེ་འདི་ཙམ་སྤངས་པ་དགོས་ཞེས་
པའི་དོན་ཡིན་གྱི་འདི་ཕན་ཆད་མ་སྤངས་པ་ཞིག་[70]དགོས་ཞེས་བསྟན་ན་མ་
D 288 འབྲེལ་བར་འགྱུར་ཏེ།རིགས་སྐྱེས་ཉོན་མོངས་གཅིག་གཉིས་སོགས་གང་

---

[66]zhig M] cig D; gcig P | [67]kyis D M] kyi P | [68]kyis D M] gyi P | [69]spangs pa'i D M] spang pa'i P | [70]zhig M] cig D; gcig P

---

[36] AKV, Śāstrī, 945: (*dvitrijanmā kulaṃlula iti niyamārtham vicārthate ya*)

> Someone asks: 'Who is that person liberated from one or two aspects?' Someone says: 'It is one the born from family to family. Devoting oneself to be liberated from three or four aspects is for the sake of an illustration or for the sake of measuring that but not for the sake beyond that.' Others say: "[one] liberated from one or two aspects has five or six rebirths and saying, 'liberated from three or four categories' is a distinguishing expression. Since it is not examined by these explanations, it is necessary to discuss this." [36]

Regarding this, [in] the first system, while asserting a lineage-born (i.e.-*kulaṃkula*) who is liberated from three or four aspects of the obstacles to be removed by the path of cultivation, there is a lineage-born liberated merely from one or two aspects and the lineage-born is necessarily taught to abandon three or four aspects. This illustrates one side of the lineage-born or is merely showing the measure of the limit saying "[the lineage-born] necessarily does not abandon more than four aspects." That is the meaning of saying as such. The meaning of the second system is that liberated from three or four aspects shows the quality of two or three lives remaining; also for one or two aspects remaining, because of the above reason, there is five or six lives remaining. That is the meaning of saying as such.

Accordingly, for both those systems, the Ācārya Jinaputra stated that since opinions such like this were not examined by previous analyzers of the Abhidharma, it is necessary to examine, although the occurrence's incorrectness does not appear other than merely casting doubt on these opinions.

When the Ācārya explained the distinction of the lineage-born's abandonment, indicating to be liberated from three or four aspects means "this much needs to be abandoned" but if teaching "more than
D288 this does not need to be abandon" it will be unrelated. In stating "not abandoning more than four aspects" in order to explain the lineage-

---

ekadvividhamuktaḥ sa kiṃ bhavati / kulaṃkula ityeka / tricaturvidhamukta grahaṇaṃ tu udāharaṇārtham parimāṇārtha vā nātaḥ pareṇeti ekadvividhamuktaḥ pañcaṣatjanmetyapare / tricaturvidhamukta iti viśeṣaparigrahāt naitad vyākhyānakārairvicāritamiti vicāryametat /

སྤྱངས་འཆད་པ་ལ་བཞི་ཕན་ཆད་མ་སྤྱངས་པ་ཞེས་བརྗོད་པས་གཅིག་ནས་
བཞིའི་བར་གང་སྤྱངས་མི་ཤེས་པའི་ཕྱིར་དང་།རྣམ་གསུམ་རྣམ་བཞི་ལས་
གྲོལ་བ།།ཞེས་པས་རིགས་སྐྱེ་རྣམས་ཀྱི་ཕྱོགས་ཙམ་དཔེར་བརྗོད་ནས་དེས་
མཚོན་པའི་དོན་འགྲེལ་པར་གསུངས་པར་རིགས་ཏེ།དེའི་འགྲེལ་པར་དེ་ལས་
གལ་ཆུང་བ་རྣམས་ཀྱང་དཔྱད་པ་[71]མཛད་འདུག་པའི་ཕྱིར་དང་།།སྐྱེ་བ་
ལྔའམ་དྲུག་ཙམ་བླངས་པ་ཡང་རིགས་སྐྱེར་འགྱུར་ན་ལན་བདུན་པ་ལ་ཡང་
ཐལ་ཆེས་པ་དང་།འགྲེལ་པར་རིགས་སྐྱེའི་ཚེ་ཅི་ཙམ་ལུས་ཐུན་མོང་དུ་དཔྱད་
པ་[72]དང་།སོ་སོར་དཔྱོད་པའི་སྐབས་གཉིས་ཀར་ཡང་ཡ་མཐའ་གཉིས་དང་མ་
མཐའ་གསུམ་པོ་ནར་མཛད་འདུག་པའི་ཡང་ཕྱིར་རོ།

།ཁ་ཅིག་ཉོན་མོངས་མོངས་གསུམ་སྤྱངས་ན་གསུམ་པ་བཞི་སྤྱངས་ན་
གཉིས་ལེན་ཅེས་པ་ཡང་གསོག་ཉིད་དུ་མཐོང་སྟེ།དེ་ལྟ་ན་ཡང་ལན་བདུན་
པ་ཡང་ལན་དགུ་པར་འཇོག་པར་འགྱུར་བ་དང་།།དྲུག་པ་ཙམ་སྤྱངས་པའི་
ཕྱིར་འོང་ཡང་གསུམ་ངེས་པར་ལེན་པར་ཐལ་བར་འགྱུར་རོ།

P110a །དེས་ན་གསུམ་དང་བཞི་ལས་གྲོལ་བ་དང་ཚེ་གཉིས་དང་གསུམ་ལེན་
པ་གཉིས་ཀ་ལ་འགྲེལ་པར་འམ་གྱི་སྒྲ་འབྱུང་བ་འདམ་ག་[73]ཅན་ཡིན་ལ་དེ་
ཡང་སྔར་བཤད་པ་ལྟར་རིགས་སྐྱེ་ལ་གསུམ་སྤྱངས་པ་ངེས་པར་དགོས།ཡང་
ན་བཞི་སྤྱངས་ཀྱང་བླ་[74]ཚེ་གཉིས་ལུས་པ་དགོས།[75]གསུམ་ལུས་ཀྱང་བླ་ཞེས་
པའི་དོན་ནོ།

1308 །དེ་ལྟར་ན་སྤྱངས་པ་དང་སྐྱེ་བ་གཉིས་ཀ་ལ་འདམ་ག་[76]ཅན་མཛད་
|D 289 ཀྱང་[77]གསུམ་སྤྱངས་པ་དང་།ཚེ་གཉིས་ལུས་པ་སོར་བཞག་པས་ན་ཁོ་བོས་
བཤད་པ་འདི་རྒྱ་མེད་པའོ།།རིགས་སྐྱེ་ལ་སྐྱེ་བ་གཉིས་ལེན་ངེས་སུ་བསྟན་པ་
འདིས་ནི་རིགས་སྐྱེ་ཚེ་འཕོས་པ་རིགས་སྐྱེར་ཁ་ཅིག །ཕར་ཕྱིན་པ།འདོད་པ་
དང་།རིགས་སྐྱེ་ཚེ་ཡོངས་སུ་གྱུར་པའི་འཕགས་པར་འདོད་པ་རྣམས་ཀྱང་སུན་
ཕྱུང་བ་ཡིན་ཏེ།[78]འདོད་པར་ཚེ་གྱུར་གྱི་འཕགས་པ་ནི་འཕགས་ཆོས་ཚེ་

[71]dpyad pa D M] dbyad pa P | [72]dpyad pa D M] dpyod pa P | [73]'dam ga M] 'dam kha D P | [74]om. / D M] insert / P | [75]insert / D M] om. / P | [76]'dam ga M] 'dam kha D P | [77]kyang D M] khyang P | [78] / D M] om. / P

born abandoning whichever of the first, second, and so forth afflictions, because of not knowing whichever is abandoned from one up to four and having proclaimed as an example merely one side of the lineage-born by saying "liberated from three or four aspects," the meaning which is shown by that is incorrect as spoken in the *Abhidharmakośabhāṣya*. Because in that commentary even insignificant small questions are to be examined and if one will be a lineage-born also by taking merely five or six rebirths, that applies even for a Seven-timer and because the *Abhidharmakośabhāṣya*, in both occasions of a common examination and specific analysis as to the number of lives remaining for the lineage-born, makes that to be only two lives at the least and three at the most.

Someone says also: "If abandoning three afflictions, one takes three rebirths; if abandoning four afflictions, one takes two rebirths," likewise so forth and so on. In this way, a Seven-timer will also be established as a Nine-timer and even the Once-returner who abandons merely six categories has the consequence of definitely taking three rebirths.

Therefore, there is an option occurring in the word of "or" in the *Abhidharmakośabhāṣya* for both: being liberated from three or four aspects and for taking two or three rebirths. Also that, as formerly explained, the lineage-born definitely needs to abandon three aspects yet it could easily abandon four aspects. Two rebirths necessarily remain although three rebirths could easily remain. This is the meaning of [*Abhidharmakośabhāṣya*] saying as such.

Accordingly, although an option is made for both abandonment
D289 and rebirth, since it is definitely set out to abandon three aspects and that at least two rebirths remain, our explanation is not flawed. By definitely showing two rebirths for the lineage-born, some [*Prajñāpāramitāyins*] assert that one who dies as a lineage-born is reborn as a lineage-born and these assertions for the Noble being who is reborn as a lineage-born are also refuted because the Noble being who is reborn in the desire realm will have the virtuous quality of a

གཉིས་སུ་བརྟེན་ཟིན་པ་ཡིན་པའི་ཕྱིར་རོ།། །དེ་ཡང་སྐབས་ཅི་ལྟ་བ་བཞིན་དུ་བཤད་པར་བྱའོ།

།དེ་ལྟར་རིགས་ནས་རིགས་སྐྱེ་ལ་ངེས་པར་ལན་གཉིས་འཁོར་བ་ནི་སློབ་དཔོན་ཐོགས་མེད་ཀྱང་བཞེད་པ་ཡིན་ཏེ།ཀུན་ལས་བཏུས་ལས་

> རིགས་ནས་རིགས་སུ་སྐྱེ་བ་གང་ཞེ་ན།ལྷ་འམ་མི་རྣམས་ཀྱི་ནང་དུ་
> རིགས་ནས་རིགས་སུ་སོང་ནས་སྡུག་བསྔལ་གྱི་ཐ་མ་འཐོབ་པའོ་
> ཞེས་འབྱུང་ལ་འགྲེལ་པར་ཡང་
>
> ངེས་པར་གཉིས་འཁོར་ཞེས་འབྱུང་བའི་ཕྱིར་རོ།
> །དོན་འདི་ལ་ཁ་ཅིག་མཛོད་འགྲེལ་དུ་
>
> སྐྱེ་བ་ནི་གལ་ཏེ་ན་གོང་མའི་སྐལ་བ་དང་ལྡན་པའི་ཕྱིར་ཆེས་ཉུང་ངུར་ཡང་འགྱུར་བས་དེའི་ཕྱིར་འདི་སྨོས་སོ།

།ཞེས་པས་རིགས་ནས་རིགས་སྐྱེ་སྐྱེ་བ་གཉིས་ལས་ཀྱང་ཉུང་བར་
འགྱུར་བར་བསྟན་པར་བསམས་ནས་ཀུན་བཏུས་ཀྱི་འགྲེལ་པར་ངེས་པར་
P110b གཉིས་འཁོར་བར་བཤད་པ་མི་ལེགས་པར་ཚེ་གཉིས་ལེན་པ་བ་མཐའ་
བསྟན་པར་བཞེད་པ་ནི།[79]མཛོད་འགྲེལ་གྱི་ལུང་དེའི་དོན་གཏན་མ་རྟོགས་
D 290 པར་མངོན་ཏེ[80]།དེའི་ལུང་དོན་ནི་རིགས་སྐྱེ་ལ་ཁྱད་པར་གསུམ་ཡོད་པ་
ལས།རྣམ་གསུམ་རྣམ་བཞི་ལས་གྲོལ་བ་དང།[81]།ཚེ་གཉིས་གསུམ་དུ་རིགས་
ནས་རིགས།།ཞེས་པས་སྐྱེ་བའི་ཁྱད་པར་དང།ཉོན་མོངས་སྤང་བའི་ཁྱད་
[82]པར་གཉིས་བསྟན་ལ།[83]གཉེན་པོ་ཐོབ་པའི་ཁྱད་པར་ནི་ཤུགས་ལས་གོ་བས་
མ་བསྟན་ཅེས་སྨོས་པ་ན།

79/ D M] om. / P | 80te D M] ste P | / D M] om. / P | 82khyad D M] nyung P | 83/ D M] om. / P

[37] Skt. *āryadharma*, Tib. *'phags chos*. This term refers is glossed as a genitive *tatpuruṣa*, "the quality (*chos*) of an *ārya* (*'phags*)," *'phags'i chos*. In this context *āryadharma* refers to the virtous qualities (*śuklāḥ dharmāḥ*) that one has obtained after the path of seeing (*darśanamārga*). See AKBh, 355.

Noble being[37] for two rebirths. We will further explain this point while examining a later section.

Likewise, transmigrating two times definitely for the *Kulaṃkula* is also maintained by the Ācārya Āsaṅga because the *Abhidharmasamuccya* states:

> Who is one reborn as a *Kulaṃkula*? One who obtains the end of suffering having gone from family to family among deities and humans. " [38]

The *Abhidharmasamuccayabhāṣya* also says:

> ....transmigrates definitely two times....[39]

Regarding this meaning, someone thinks that since the *Abhidharmakośabhāṣya* states:

> "For the number of rebirths, since there is the capability of obtaining the quality of upper fruitions then the rebirths will also be fewer, this is established because of that,"[40]

shows that the *Kulaṃkula* will have fewer than two rebirths, and the explanation in the *Abhdharmasamuccayabhāṣya* is also incorrect, since it maintains that the *Kulaṃkula* is demonstrated to take no more than two rebirths. Here, the meaning of that section of the *Abhidharmakośabhāṣya* is not firmly comprehended. The meaning of
D290 that section is that, through the lineage-born having three qualities, stating "delivered from three or four categories, destined for two or three rebirths, one is a *Kulaṃkula*,"[41] shows two qualities, the quality of abandoning afflictions and the quality of taking rebirth, while the quality of obtaining the antidote to the afflictions is established as being implicitly understood.

---

[38] AS, Pradhan, 90: *kulaṃkulaḥ katamaḥ / deveṣu vā kulātkulaṃ gatvā (manuṣye)ṣu vā yo duḥkhasyāntamanuprāpnoti /*

[39] ASBh, Tatia, 120, bold print representing Tsong kha pa's emphasis: *kulaṃkulaḥ kulaḥ srotāpanna eva sakṛdāgāmiphalapratipannako deveṣu vā manusyeṣu vā niyamena dvau bhavau saṃsṛtya parinirvāti /*

[40] AKBh, Pk 24b5-24b6, Pruden, 963, Pradhan, 357: *janma tu kadācidalpīyaḥ syāt. pareṇa bhavyatvād / ato' sya grahaṇam /*

[41] AK, vi.34c-d, Pk ṅu 24b3, Pruden,p. 962, Śāstrī, 944: *tricaturvidhamuktastu dvitrijanmā kulaṃkulaḥ.*

འོ་ན་སྐྱེ་བའི་ཁྱད་པར་ཡང་ཤུགས་ལ་བསྟན་པས་ཚིག་མོད་སྐམ་དུ་
དོགས་པ་[84]ལ་རྒྱུན་ཞུགས་སྲིད་པ་གཉིས་ལེན་ཐུང་འགའ་ཞིག་གོང་མ་ཕྱིར་
1309 འོང་ནས་དགྲ་བཅོམ་གྱི་བར་སྐྱེ་བ་འདིའམ་སྐྱེ་བ་ཕྱི་མ་ཉིད་ལ་འཐོབ་པ་
ཡོད་པས་དེ་རྣམས་ནི་སྐྱེ་བ་ཉུང་བར་འགྱུར་ལ་རིགས་ནས་རིགས་སྐྱེའི་ཚེ་དེ་
ལྟ་བུ་མ་ཡིན་པར་ཚེ་གཉིས་སམ་གསུམ་ངེས་པར་ལེན་པར་བསྟན་པའི་ཕྱིར་
རིགས་སྐྱེའི་སྐྱེ་བའི་ཁྱད་པར་རྩ་བར་དངོས་སུ་སྨོས་ཞེས་པ་ཡིན་པའི་ཕྱིར་
རོ།།དེ་ལྟར་ཡང་ལུང་དེའི་འགྲེལ་བཤད་དུ།

> དེའི་ཕྱིར་འདིའི་ཚེ་ནི་ཚེ་གཉིས་གསུམ་སུ་[85]རིགས་ནས་རིགས་ཞེས་
> ངེས་པར་བྱ་བའི་ཕྱིར་སྨོས་པ་ཡིན་ནོ།

།ཞེས་འབྱུང་བས་ན་ཁོ་བོ་ཅག་ནི་ལུང་དེ་[86]རིགས་སྐྱེ་སྲིད་པ་གཉིས་
ངེས་པར་ལེན་པའི་ཁུངས་སུ་འགྲོ་བར་འདོད་པ་ཡིན་ནོ།།དེ་ལྟ་ན་དེ་དང་དེ་
ལྟ་བུའི་རིགས་གཞན་བསྟན་བཅོས་སམ་གཙུག་ལག་གི་དགོངས་པར་མ་སོན་
པ་རྣམས་གཟུ་བོའི་བློས་བཀག་པ་ན་བཤེས་གཉེན་ངན་པའི་ངན་རྟོག་གིས་
བློ་གྲོས་བསླད་པ་དང༌།ཆོས་ལ་མི་རྟོན་པར་གང་ཟག་ལ་རྟོན་པ་[87]དག་ཕྲག་
དོག་གིས་རྣ་བ་མི་གཏོད་མོད།།འོན་ཀྱང་བློ་དང་ལྡན་པ་དག་གིས་ཕྱོགས་
D 291 འཛིན་དོར་ཏེ་ཚུལ་བཞིན་བརྟགས་ན་རིགས་པ་དང་མི་རིགས་པ་དག་གི་
P111a རྣམ་པར་དབྱེ་བ་ཁོང་དུ་ཆུད་པར་འགྱུར་རོ།།འདིར་སྨྲས་པ།

> ཡང་དག་ལྟ་བ་འོད་སྟོང་ལྡན་པ་ནུབ།།གནས་ལུགས་འདོམས་པའི་
> མཁས་རྣམས་ཕལ་ཆེར་གཤེགས།།[88]ལོག་པའི་ལམ་སྟོན་ཚོངས་པ་
> ཀུན་གྱིས་བཀུར།ཀྱི་མའོ་ཐུབ་བསྟན་སུ་ཡིས་གནས་པར་ནུས།ཡིན་

[84]dogs D M] dog P | [85]su D M] du P | [86]de D M] di P | [87]rton pa D M] brton pa P | [88]/ / D M] om. / / P

[42] AKV, Śāstrī, 945: *dvitrijanmā kulaṃkulaḥ iti niyamārthamidamiha….*/ | [43]Tsong kha pa is referring to the opposite of the first of the four reliances *(rten pa bzhi, catvāri pratisaraṇāni*): "Rely not on the individual (*gang zag, pudgala*), but on the doctrine (*chos, dharma*); Rely not on words (*tshig `bru, vyañjana*), but on meaning (*don, artha*); Rely not on *sūtra*s of interpretable meaning (*drang don gyi mdo*, *neyārthasūtra*), but on *sūtra*s of definitive meaning (*nges don gyi mdo, nītārthasūtra*); Rely not on [dualistic]

Well then, there is doubt as someone thinks it is permitable to show also the quality of rebirth to be implicit, since it is suitable for some Stream-enterers to take two rebirths and upper fruitions of Once-returner up to Arhat to be attained in this life or later lives. Those fruitions will take fewer rebirths, but the rebirths of the *Kulaṃkula* is not such like that, because in order to show that two or three rebirths are definitely taken, the rebirth quality of the lineage-born is explicitly established in the root text. In that way also, with the occurrence of the *Abhidharmakośabhāṣyavyākhyā* on that section saying,

> "Therefore, the rebirths of this are established because of definitely saying, 'destined for two or three rebirths one is a Kulaṃkula.' "[42]

We accept that scripture as being a source of the *Kulaṃkula* definitely taking two existences. In this way, the incorrect intentions of texts or *śāstra*s which discuss other lineages of the *Kulaṃkula* or such like it, when I reject with a straightforward understanding, those who have deluded understanding through the wrongful thoughts of deficient teachers and those who rely on the individual instead of relying on the doctrine,[43] with envy, will not listen. Yet, those who possess discriminating intelligence cast away attachment to opinions
D291 and, when properly examining, will understand the distinctions between what is correct and incorrect. Here I say:

> The right view that shines like a thousand lights has set. Those great scholars who teach the nature of reality have gone. Those who show the wrong path slander with complete ignorance. Alas, who is able to persevere in the doctrine of Śākyamuni? If

---

consciousness (*rnam par shes pa, vijñāna*) but on [nonconceptual] wisdom (*ye shes, jñāna*)." These are set forth by the Buddha in the *Catuḥpratisaraṇasūtra*, the Sanskrit is preserved in Yaśomitra's *Abhidharmakośavyākhyā* : *catvārīmāni bhikṣavaḥ pratisaraṇāni/ katamāni catvāri/ dharmaḥ pratisaraṇaṃ na pudgalaḥ arthaḥ pratisaraṇaṃ na vyañjanam nītārthaṃ sūtraṃ pratisaraṇaṃ na neyārtham jñānaṃ pratisaraṇaṃ na vijñānam/* See Etienne Lamotte, "La critique d'interprétation dans le bouddhisme," *Annuaire de l'Institut de philologie et d'histoire orientales et slaves*, Vol. IX (Brussels: UniversitÇ Libre de Bruxelles, 1949), 341-361, for discussion of this *sūtra*. For a creative discussion of the four reliances see Robert Thurman, *Essence of True Eloquence*, 1984:114-130.

ཚུལ་བཤད་ན་མཁས་འདོད་ཅན་དུ་མཐོང༌།།ལོག་པར་བསྟན་ན་ལྷ་
ངན་ཕྱི་ཕྱིར་འཕེལ།།མི་སྐྱིའི་བརྟུལ་ཞུགས་བཟུང་ན་དོན་མི་
འགྲུབ།།ཀྱེ་མའོ་ཐུབ་བསྟན་ཅི་ལྟར་གཟུང་བར་བྱ།

།ཞེས་བྱ་བ་ནི་བར་སྐབས་ཀྱི་ཚིགས་སུ་བཅད་པའོ།

།ཉོན་མོངས་གསུམ་དང་སྐྱེ་བ་གཉིས།།རིམ་བཞིན་ངེས་[89]སྤྱང་ངེས་
པར་ལེན།།བཞི་པ་སྤངས་དང་སྐྱེ་བ་ནི།།།གསུམ་པ་བླངས་དང་མ་
བླངས་འདྲ།།སྤང་བྱ་ལྔ་པ་སྐྱེ་བ་བཞི།།ངེས་པར་མ་སྤངས་མ་བླངས་
པ།།རིགས་ནས་རིགས་སྐྱེའི་ཁྱད་ཆོས་སུ།།མཁས་པ་རྣམས་ཀྱིས་
རྟོགས་པར་བྱ།

1310 །ཞེས་བྱ་བ་ནི་བསྡུ་བའི་ཚིགས་སུ་བཅད་པའོ།

།རྒྱུན་ཞུགས་འབྲས་གནས་ཁྱད་པར་ཅན་གྱི་རྣམ་པར་བཞག་པ་བཤད་
ཟིན་ཏོ།།

།།ལང་ཅིག་ཕྱིར་འོང་བའི་འབྲས་བུ་ལ་ཞུགས་པ་གང་ཞེ་ན།འདི་དང་
ཕྱིར་མི་འོང་གི་ཞུགས་གནས་བཞི་ག་[90]ལ་འབྲས་བུ་ཐོབ་རྒྱལ་བ་དང་འབྲས་
བུ་རིམ་གྱིས་པ་གཉིས་ཡོད་པ་ལས་རེ་ཞིག་འབྲས་བུ་རིམ་[91]གྱིས་པ་ཉིད་
བཤད་པར་བྱ།

D 292 ངེས་ན་བཅུ་དྲུག་པ་ཐོབ་ཅིང་འདོད་ཉོན་དྲུག་པ་མ་སྤངས་ལ་དང་པོ་
ནས་དྲུག་པའི་བར་གང་ཡང་རུང་བ་སྤོང་བ་ལ་བརྩོན་པའི་གང་ཟག་དེ་དག་
ནི་ཕྱིར་འོང་གི་འབྲས་བུ་ལ་ཞུགས་པ་ཞེས་བྱ་སྟེ།འདི་ནི་རྒྱུན་ཞུགས་འབྲས་
གནས་ཁྱད་པར་ཅན་དང་རྫས་གཅིག་པའོ།།དེ་ལྟར་ཡང་འགྲེལ་པར་ཞུགས་
P11b པ་ལྷག་མ་རྣམས་[92]ནི་འབྲས་བུ་ལ་གནས་པ་གསུམ་ལས་ཐ་མི་དད་པའི་ཕྱིར་
རོ།།ཞེས་མཐར་གྱིས་པའི་སྐབས་སུ་ཞུགས་པ་དང་པོ་མ་གཏོགས་པ་ཞུགས་པ་
ཕྱི་མ་གསུམ་རིམ་པ་བཞིན་དུ་རྒྱུན་དུ་ཞུགས་པ་དང་ཕྱིར་འོང་དང་ཕྱིར་མི་
འོང་འབྲས་ནས་ཁྱད་པར་ཅན་དུ་གསུངས་པའི་ཕྱིར་རོ།།སློབ་དཔོན་ཐོགས་
མེད་ནི་ཕྱིར་འོང་ཞུགས་པ་ལ་འདོད་ཉོན་ལྔ་པ་སྤངས་ནས་དྲུག་པ་སྤོང་བའི་

[89] nges D M] des P | [90] bzhi ga M] bzhi ka D P | [91] rim D M] rims P | [92] rnams D M] rnam pa P

> explaining how things are, a scholar is seen as ambitious. If incorrectly teaching, wrong view expands outward. If holding to the practice of silence, the aim is not achieved. Alas, how should one uphold the doctrine of Śākyamuni?

Thus some verses of intermission have been composed.[44]

> Definitely abandoning three afflictions and definitely taking two rebirths gradually, the fourth abandonment and the third rebirth may or may not be abandoned or taken. Four rebirths and five abandonments are definitely not taken nor abandoned. This particularity of the *Kulaṃkula* should be realized by the wise in the doctrine.

These are the summary verses. This finishes the explanation setting forth the aspect of the distinctive abider in the result of Stream-enterer.

Who is the enterer to the result of Once-returner? There are four enterers and abiders within this and the Non-returner result, from that there are two fruition skippers and gradual progressors, briefly, I should explain the gradual progressor in the result itself.

Here, those individuals, having obtained the sixteenth moment
D292 and not abandoning the sixth desire realm affliction, who make effort at abandoning the first through the sixth desire realm afflictions are called "an enterer to the fruit of Once-returner." This is synonymous with possessing a distinction in abiding in the result of Stream-enterer. Likewise, in the *Abhidharmakośabhāṣya*, the remaining enterers are differentiated from the three abiders in a result. Thus, not counting the first enterer in the period of liberation, the three later enterers, gradually, are spoken of as possessing distinction in abiding in the fruit of Stream-enterer, Once-Returner, and Non-returner. Ācārya Asaṅga appears to accept that the Once-returner enterer, having

[44] At this point, Tsong kha pa seems to be lamenting over the lack of decisive understanding from previous scholars, e.g Jinaputra, on the definitional characteristics of the Kulaṃkula and has expanded this sentiment to the understanding of Śākyamuni's doctrine in general. On the function of intermission stanzas see K. Mimaki, "Sur le role de l'antaraśloka ou du saṃgrahaśloka," *Indianisme et Bouddhisme, Mélanges offerts à Mgr Etienne Lamotte* (Louvain-la-Neuve: 1980), 233-244.

སྦྱོར་བ་ལ་བརྩོན་པ་ཞིག་[93]བཞེད་པར་མངོན་ཏེ།ཀུན་ལས་བཏུས་སུ་

> །ལན་ཅིག་ཕྱིར་འོང་བའི་འབྲས་བུ་ལ་ཞུགས་པ་གང་ཞེ་ན།གང་བསྒོམ་པའི་ལམ་ལ་འདོད་པ་ན་སྤྱོད་པའི་ཉོན་མོངས་པ་རྣམས་པ་[94]ལྔ་པ་སྤངས་པའི་ལམ་ལ་གནས་པའི་གང་ཟག་གོ་

།ཞེས་གསུངས་སོ།།དེ་ལྟར་བཞེད་པའང་ཕྱིར་འོང་གི་ཞུགས་པ་ནི་ཕྱིར་
འོང་གི་ཉེ་བའི་སྦྱོར་བ་ལ་ཞུགས་པ་ལ་བྱའི་ཕྱིར་འོང་གི་རྒྱུ་ཙམ་ལ་ཞུགས་པ་
ཡང་ཡིན་ན་ཧ་ཅང་ཐལ་བར་འགྱུར་ལ།དེའི་ཕྱིར་གང་སྤངས་པ་ཙམ་གྱིས་
ཕྱིར་འོང་གི་འབྲས་བུ་ཐོབ་པའི་སྤང་བྱ་དེ་ཉིད་སྤོང་བ་ལ་བརྩོན་པ་ནས་
ཞུགས་པར་བཞག་རིགས་ལ་དེ་ཡང་ལྔ་པ་མན་ཆད་སྤོང་བ་ལ་མེད་པའི་ཕྱིར་
1311 རོ།།མངོན་པ་བ་འགའ་ཞིག་ལྔ་པ་སྤངས་པ་ཞེས་འབྱུང་བ་ཐ་མའི་མཚམས་
D 293 བཟུང་བ་ཡིན་ཞེས་འཆད་པ་ཡང་ཡོད་མོད་ཀྱི་འོན་ཀྱང་འདི་དང་ཕྱིར་མི་
འོང་ཞུགས་པ་གཉིས་ཆར་ལ་ལྔ་པ་སྤངས་པ་དང་བརྒྱད་པ་སྤངས་པ་ངེས་
པར་སྨོས་པའི་ཕྱིར་བཤད་པ་སྔ་མ་ཉིད་དགོངས་པ་ཡིན་པར་འཐད་པར་
རྟོགས་སོ།

> །དྲུག་པའི་བར་སྤོང་བརྩོན་པ་དང་།ངེས་པར་དྲུག་པ་སྤོང་བརྩོན་པ།།ཕྱིར་འོང་ཞུགས་ཡིན་ཞེས་པ་ནི།།གང་འོག་གཉིས་ཀྱི་ལུགས་སུ་བཤད།

།ཅེས་བྱ་བ་ནི་བསྡུ་བའི་ཚིགས་སུ་བཅད་པའོ།།ཕྱིར་འོང་ཞུགས་པ་
P112a བཤད་ཟིན་ཏོ།། །།ལན་ཅིག་ཕྱིར་འོང་བའི་འབྲས་བུ་ལ་གནས་པ་གང་ཞེ་
ན།བཅུ་དྲུག་པ་ཐོབ་ལ་འདོད་ཉོན་དྲུག་པ་སྤངས་ཤིང་དགུ་པ་མ་སྤངས་པའི་
ཐེག་དམན་ནོ།།དེ་ལ་ཡང་འབྲས་བུ་ཙམ་ལ་གནས་པ་དང་།འབྲས་བུ་ཁྱད་
པར་ཅན་ལ་གནས་པ་གཉིས་སི་འགྱུར་རོ།།དེ་ལ་ཕྱིར་འོང་འབྲས་གནས་གང་
འདོད་ཉོན་དྲུག་པ་ལས།གོང་མའི་ཉོན་མོངས་སྤོང་བ་ལ་མི་བརྩོན་པ་དེ་ནི་

[93] zhig M] cig D; gcig P | [94] rnams pa D M] rnam pa P

abandoned the fifth desire realm affliction, makes effort to abandon the sixth. The *Abhidharmasamuccaya* states:

> Who is one that enters to the fruit of Once-returner? This is the person who, in the path of cultivation, abides in the path of abandoning the five aspects of the afflictions pertaining to the desire [realm].[45]

Accordingly, the Once-returner enterer, if entering to the proximate application of Once-returner also enters into the mere cause of Once-returner, and there will be an excessive consequence. Therefore, in making the effort for abandoning the defilements which attains the result of Once-returner, one in the lineage established as an enterer does not abandon lower than five afflictions. Some Ābhidhārmikas also explain that "the lower border is held with the
D293 occurrence "abandoning the fifth." However, for both this Once-returner enterer and the Non-returner enterer, because the text definitely states they abandon the fifth aspect and the eighth aspect respectively, the former explanation itself is correctly realized to be the intention. A summary verse:

> Those who strive to abandon up to the sixth aspect,
> and those who stive to definitely abandon the sixth
> are called "an Once-returner enterer" as explained in
> the system of the two, upper and lower [, Abhidharmas].

The Once-returner enterer explanation is finished.

Who is the abider in the fruit of the Once-returner? The lesser vehicle person who abandons the sixth desire realm affliction and does not abandon the ninth affliction on attaining the sixteenth moment [of the path of seeing]. For that, there are two: the abider in the mere result and the abider who has distinction in the result. One who abides in the Once-returner result, who does not make effort in abandoning the upper realm afflictions, other than the sixth desire realm affliction, is one that merely abides in the result. The *Abhidharmakośa* states:

---

[45] AS, Rahula, 153, Pradhan, 89: *sakṛdāgāmiphalapratipannakaḥ katamaḥ / bhāvanāmārge kāmāvacarāṇāṃ pañcaprakārāṇāṃ kleśānāṃ prahāṇamārge yaḥ pudgalaḥ /*

འབྲས་བུ་ཙམ་ལ་གནས་པ་སྟེ།ཇི་སྐད་དུ་མཛོད་ལས།

རྣམ་པ་དྲུག་པ་ཟད་གྱུར་པ།།དེ་ནི་ལན་ཅིག་ཕྱིར་འོང་བ།

།ཞེས་གང་གསུངས་པའོ།།ཕྱིར་འོང་འབྲས་གནས་གང་བདུན་པ་ནས་
དགུ་པའི་བར་སྤོང་བ་ལ་བརྩོན་པ་ནི་འབྲས་བུ་ཁྱད་པར་ཅན་ལ་གནས་པ་
སྟེ།ཕྱིར་མི་འོང་ཞུགས་པ་དང་གནད་གཅིག་གོ།ཕྱིར་འོང་འབྲས་གནས་ཁྱད་
པར་ཅན་བར་ཅད་གཅིག་པ་ཞེས་འབྱུང་བ་དེ་ཇི་ལྟ་བུ་ཞེ་ན།[95] ཕྱིར་འོང་
འབྲས་གནས་ཁྱད་པར་ཅན་གང་འདོད་ཉོན་བདུན་ནམ་བརྒྱད་སྤངས་པས་
D 294 [96]ཕྱིར་མི་འོང་གི་འབྲས་བུ་ཐོབ་པ་ལ་ཉོན་མོངས་གཅིག་གིས་བར་དུ་ཆོད་ལ་
སྐྱང་འདས་འཐོབ་པ་ལ་ཚེ་གཅིག་གིས་བར་དུ་ཆོད་པ་གང་ཡིན་པ་སྟེ།ཇི་
སྐད་དུ་མཛོད་ལས།

ཉེས་ཆ་བདུན་དང་བརྒྱད་ཟད་པ།།ཚེ་གཅིག་བར་ཆད་གཅིག་པ་
དང་།།གསུམ་པ་ལ་ནི་ཞུགས་པའང་ཡིན།

།ཞེས་པས་སོ།།དེ་ལ་ཉོན་མོངས་བརྒྱད་ཟད་ན་ཚེ་གཅིག་པ་དང་བར་
1312 ཆད་གཅིགཔ་གཉིས་ཆར་ཡིན་ལ།བདུན་ཟད་ན་ཚེ་གཅིག་པ་ཡིན་ཀྱང་བར་
ཆད་གཉིས་པ་ཡིན་ཞེས་འགའ་ཞིག །མངོན་པ་བ།འདོད་ལ་ཁ་ཅིག

།བདག་གི་བླ་མའི་བདུན་ཟད་པ་ཡང་བར་ཆད་གཅིག་པ་ཡིན་ཏེ་
བར་ཆད་ནི་ཕྱིར་མི་འོང་གི་འབྲས་བུ་ལ་གེགས་བྱེད་པའི་གཙོ་བོ་ཡིན་ལ་དེ་
ཡང་དགུ་པ་ཉིད་ཡིན་པའི་ཕྱིར་རོ་ཞེས་ཀྱང་འཆད་དོ།།།བར་ཆད་གཅིག་པ་
P112b འདི་ནི་བདུན་པ་དང་བརྒྱད་པ་སྤངས་པའི་ཚེ་དེ་ལ་དགུ་པ་སྤངས་ནས་ཕྱིར་
མི་འོང་དུ་འགྱུར་བ་མ་ཡིན་གྱི་ཚེ་འཕོས་ནས་དགུ་པ་སྤངས་ཕྱིར་མི་འོང་
མངོན་དུ་བྱས་ཏེ་རྗེན་དེ་ཉིད་ལ་སྐྱང་འདས་མངོན་དུ་བྱེད་པས་ན་ཕྱིར་མི་
འོང་ལ་ཉོན་མོངས་པ་གཅིག་གིས་བར་ཆོད་སྐྱང་འདས་ལ་ཚེ་གཅིག་གིས་
ཆོད་པ་ཞེས་བྱའོ།།ཉོན་མོངས་དགུ་པས་ཕྱིར་མི་འོང་ཚེ་དེ་ལ་འཐོབ་པ་ལ་

---

[95]/ D M] om. / P | [96]spang pas D M] spang bas P

---

[46]AK, vi.35c-d, Pruden, 964, Śāstrī, 946, Pradhan, 357: *kṣīṇaṣaṣṭaprakārastu sakṛdāgāmyasau punaḥ* /

Having consumed the sixth aspect, one is a Once-returner (*Sakṛdāgāmin*).[46]

One who abides in the result of Once-returner that makes effort to abandon the seventh up to the ninth [afflictions] abides having distinction in that result and is synonymous with the Non-returner enterer.

The abider who has distinction in the result of Once-returner, that which is called an *Ekavīcika*, who is such a one like this? One who has distinction as an abider in the result of Once-returner attains the result of Non-returner by abandoning the seventh and eighth desire
D294 realm afflictions and is obstructed by a single affliction and obstructed by a single life for obtaining *nirvāṇa*. The *Abhidharmakośa* states:

> Exhausting the seventh and eighth fault, destined for one life is the *Ekavīcika*, who is also an enterer to the third [fruition].[47]

Regarding that [distinctive Once-returner]," if exhausting the eighth affliction, [one] is both destined for one life and a single interval and if exhausting the seventh [affliction], [one] is destined for one life and also two intervals" some [Ābhidhārmikas] assert.

But someone [, my lama,] explains that, "exhausting the seventh [affliction] also has a single interval and an interval is the chief hindrance to the result of Non-returner because that is itself also the ninth [affliction]." This *Ekavīcika* will not become a Non-returner having abandoned the ninth at that time of abandoning the seventh and eighth. However, abandoning the ninth having died actualizes [the result of] Non-returner and by actualizing *nirvāṇa* in that very embodiment itself, one is obstructed by a single affliction for [the result of] Non-returner and obstructed by one life for *nirvāṇa*. The Non-returner is unable to be obstructed for attainment in that life by the ninth affliction. Is [the *Ekavīcika*'s abandonment] similar, for

---

[47]AK, vi.36a-c, Pruden, 964, Śāstrī, 946, Pradhan, 358: *kṣiṇasaptāṣṭadoṣāṃśa ekajamaikavīcikaḥ tṛtīyapratipannaśca* /

བར་ཆད་མི་ནུས་དེ།དཔེར་ན་རིགས་སྐྱེས་ལྔ་བ་སྤྱངས་ན་དྲུག་པ་ཡང་གདོན་
མི་ཟ་བར་སྤོང་བ་བཞིན་ཞེ་ན་མ་ཡིན་ཏེ།།[97]ཁམས་ལས་འདའ་མི་འདའི་ཁྱད་
པར་སྔར་བཤད་པའི་ཕྱིར་རོ།།དེ་ལྟར་ཡང།ཇི་སྐད་དུ་མཛོད་འགྲེལ་ལས།
ཇི་ལྟར་ན་འདི་ནི་རྣམ་པ་གཅིག་གིས་འབྲས་བུ་ལ་གེགས་བྱེད་པར་
D 295 ནུས་ཞེ་ན།ཁམས་ལས་མི་འདའ་བའི་ཕྱིར་རོ།།

ཞེས་གསུངས་པས་སོ།།དེ་[98]ལྟར་ན་བར་ཆད་གཅིག་པ་མཛོད་འགྲེལ་
གྱི་འགྲེལ་བཤད་དུ་འགྲོ་བ་གང་དུ་སྐྱེ་མི་འབྱུང་ལ།ཀུན་ལས་བཏུས་སུ།

> བར་ཆད་གཅིག་པ་གང་ཞེ་ན།ལན་ཅིག་ཕྱིར་འོང་བ་ལྷ་རྣམས་ཀྱི་
> [99]ནང་ཉིད་དུ་གང་སྡུག་བསྔལ་གྱི་ཐ་མ་འཐོབ་པའོ།།ཞེས་འབྱུང་
> བས། །འདོད་ལྷའི་རྟེན་ལ་མྱང་འདས་ཐོབ་པར་གསལ་ལོ།།ཇི་སྐད་
> དུ།མཛོད་ལས།

> རྣམ་པ་དྲུག་པ་ཟད་གྱུར་པ།།དེ་ནི་ལན་ཅིག་ཕྱིར་འོང་བ།
> །ཞེས་འབྲས་བུ་ཙམ་ལ་གནས་པའི་ཐད་དུ་འགྲེལ་པར་

> ལྷ་དག་གི་ནང་དུ་སོང་ནས་མིའི་འཇིག་རྟེན་དུ་ལན་ཅིག་ཕྱིར་འོང་
> བའི་ཕྱིར་ལན་ཅིག་ཕྱིར་འོང་བ་སྟེ་དེ་ཕན་ཆད་སྐྱེ་བ་མེད་པའི་ཕྱིར་

ཞེས་གསུངས་པ་ནི།[100]ཕྱིར་འོང་འབྲས་གནས་ཙམ་པོ་དེས་སྐྱེ་བ་གཉིས་
1313 ལེན་པའི་ཤེས་བྱེད་[101]དུ་མི་སྣང་བས་ཕྱིར་འོང་འབྲས་གནས་ཙམ་པོ་ལ་སྐྱེ་
བའི་ཁྱད་པར་མ་སྨོས་སོ།།འོ་ན་ཅི་ཞེ་ན།ལྷ་དང་མི་གཉིས་ཁར་[102]སྐྱེ་བའི་ཕྱིར་
P113a འོང་ཡོད་ཀྱང་དེ་ལན་ཅིག་ཕྱིར་འོང་མ་ཡིན་པར་མི་འགྱུར་ཏེ།འགྲོ་བ་གཅིག་
དུ་ལན་ཅིག་ལས་མི་འོང་བའི་ཕྱིར་སྙམ་དུ་བསམ་པའོ།

།ཁ་ཅིག་ཕྱིར་འོང་ཡིན་ན་འདོད་པར་ལན་ཅིག་འོང་བས་ཁྱབ་ཅེས་པ་
ནི་རང་གི་མཚན་ཉིད་སྟོན་པར་བྱེད་པ་སྟེ།དེ་ལྟ་ན་ཕྱིར་འོང་གི་རྟེན་ལ་ཕྱིར་

---

97 // D M] om. / / P | 98 de D M] da P | 99 kyi D M] gyi P | 100 / D M] om. / P | 101 byed D M] byang P | 102 gnyis khar D M] gnyis kar P

---

48 AKBh, Pruden, 964, Śāstrī, 947: *kathamasyaikaḥ prakāraḥ phalaṃ vighnayituṃ śaknoti dhāvatikramāt* / Differs in wording from Tsong kha pa.

example, to when a lineage-born abandons the fifth affliction, undoubtedly also abandons the sixth [affliction]? It is not because of the previously explained distinction of either passing or not passing over from the [desire] realm. Regarding this, the *Abhidharmakośabhāṣya* states:

In what manner is this [state] able to be hindranced to the result [of Non-returner] by one aspect [of the defilements]? This is because of having to pass over to the [form] realm. [48]

D295 Accordingly, the *Ekavīcika* does not appear to be born in the upper transmigrations in the *Abhidharmakośabhāṣyavyākhyā* of the *Abhidharmakośa*. The *Abhidharmasamuccaya* says:

> Who is the *Ekavīcika*? A Once-returner who, just among the gods, attains the end of suffering.[49]

Through stating this, [the *Ekavīcika*] evidently attains *nirvāṇa* in the embodiment of a desire realm deity. The *Abhidharmakośa* states:

> Exhausting the sixth aspect, that one is a Once-returner.[50]

Thus, in the *Abhidharmakośabhāṣya* regarding the abider in the mere result, it is taught that,

> ...having gone among the gods, returning one time in the world of humans is the Once-returner who has no further rebirth.[51]

Since the proof of taking two rebirths does not appear, the distinction of rebirth does not apply for the mere abider in the fruit of Once-returner. Well then, what about that? Although it is a Once-returner who is reborn as both a god and human, that one will return back one time, as it is thought, because of not coming back more than a single time in a single transmigration.

Someone says: "If it is an Once-returner, it is pervaded by coming back one time in the desire realm." This demonstrates our own definition and likewise, it will not be possible to attain the result of

---

[49]AS, Rahula, 155, Pradhan, 90.8: *ekavīcikaḥ katamaḥ / sakṛdāgāmī deveṣveva yo duḥkhasyāntamo anuprāpnoti /* | [50] AK vi.35c-d, Pruden, 964, Śāstrī, 946: *kṣīṇaṣaṣṭaprakārastu sakṛdāgāmyasau punaḥ /* | [51]AKBh, Pruden, 964, Śāstrī, 946: *devān gatvā sakṛnmanuṣyalokāgamanāt sakṛdāgāmī pareṇa janmābhāvāt /*

མི་འོང་ཐོབ་པ་མི་སྲིད་པ་ཉིད་དུ་འགྱུར་རོ།

ཕྱིར་འོང་བར་ཆད་གཅིག་པ་སྟེ[103]།།ཉོན་མོངས་བདུན་ནམ་བརྒྱད་
སྤངས་ཤིང་།།ཚེ་འཕོས་འདོད་ལྷའི་རྟེན་དག་ལ།།མྱང་འདས་མངོན་
དུ་བྱེད་པར་བསྟན།

D 296 །ཅེས་བྱ་བ་ནི་བསྡུ་བའི་ཚིགས་སུ་བཅད་པའོ།།ལན་ཅིག་ཕྱིར་ཕྱིར་འོང་
བའི་འབྲས་བུ་ལ་གནས་པའི་རྣམ་པར་བཞག་པ་བཤད་ཟིན་ཏོ།།
།།ཕྱིར་མི་འོང་བའི་འབྲས་བུ་ལ་ཞུགས་པ་གང་ཞེ་ན། སྔར་བཤད་པའི་
ཕྱིར་འོང་འབྲས་གནས་དེ་ཉིད་བདུན་པ་ནས་དགུ་པའི་བར་སྤོང་བའི་སྦྱོར་
བ་ཅན་ནོ།།དེ་ལྟར་ཡང་མཛོད་ལས།

ཉེས་ཆ་བདུན་དང་བརྒྱད་ཟད་པ།ཚེ་གཅིག་བར་ཆད་གཅིག་པ་
དང་།།གསུམ་པ་ལ་ནི་ཞུགས་པའང་ཡིན།

།ཞེས་གང་གསུངས་པའོ།།ཕྱིར་མི་འོང་བའི་འབྲས་བུ་ལ་གནས་པ་གང་
ཞེ་ན།བཅུ་དྲུག་པའི་རྟོགས་པ་ཐོབ་ཅིང་འདོད་པའི་སྒོམ་[104]སྤངས་དགུ་པ་
སྤངས་པའི་ཐེག་དམན་སློབ་པའོ།།འདི་ཡང་ཁམས་གོང་མའི་ཉོན་མོངས་
སྤོང་བའི་སྦྱོར་བ་ལ་མི་གནས་པ་ན་འབྲས་བུ་ཙམ་ལ་གནས་པ་ཡིན་
ལ།[105]བསམ་གཏན་དང་པོའི་ཉོན་མོངས་དང་པོ་[106]ནས་སྲིད་རྩེ་དགུ་པའི་
བར་སྤོང་བའི་སྦྱོར་བ་ལ་གནས་པའི་ཚེ་འབྲས་བུ་ཁྱད་པར་ཅན་ལ་གནས་པ་
དང་།[107]དགྲ་བཅོམ་ཞུགས་པ་གཞི་གཅིག་པ་ཅན་ཡིན་ནོ།།གཞན་ཡང་འདི་ལ་
གཟུགས་སུ་ཉེ་བར་འགྲོ་བ་དང་།[108]གཟུགས་མེད་དུ་ཉེ་བར་འགྲོ་བ་མཐོང་
1314 ཆོས་ཞི་དང་།ལུས་མངོན་བྱེད་དེ་རྣམ་པ་བཞིར་ཡང་འགྱུར་རོ།།འདི་དག་
|P113b འབྲས་བུ་ཁྱད་པར་ཅན་ལ་འཇོག་པར་འདོད་པ་ནི་ཡོད་མོད་འོན་ཀྱང་འདི་
དག་ངེས་པར་སྒོམ་[109]སྤང་ལྷག་མ་སྤོང་བའི་སྦྱོར་བ་ཅན་ཡིན་པ་ལ་ཤེས་
པར་བྱེད་པ་མི་སྣང་ངོ།

།གཟུགས་སུ་ཉེ་བར་འགྲོ་བ་གང་ཞེ་ན།འདོད་པའི་རྟེན་ཅན་གྱི་ཕྱིར་མི་
D 297 འོང་གང་གཟུགས་ཁམས་སུ་ངེས་པར་སྐྱེ་བ་བླངས་ནས་མྱང་འདས་འཐོབ་

[103] ste M] de D P | [104] sgom M] bsgom D P | [105] / D M] om. / P | [106] dang po D M] dngo P | [107] / D M] om. / P | [108] / D M] om. / P | [109] sgom M] bsgom D P

Non-returner in the embodiment of a Oncer-retuner. In a condensed verse:

> That *Ekavīcika* Once-returner, abandoning the seventh and eighth affliction, is indicated to actualize *nirvāṇa* in the
D296 embodiments of desire realm gods when dieing.

That finishes the discussion setting forth the abider in the result of Once-returner.

Who is the enterer to the result of Non-returner? That same abider in the result of Once-returner formerly explained who applies himself to abandoning from the seventh to ninth [afflictions]. Accordingly, from the *Abhidharmakośa*:

> Exhausting the seventh and eighth fault, destined for one life is the *Ekavīcika*, who is also an enterer to the third fruition." [52]

Who is the abider in the result of Non-returner? The lesser vehicle trainee who, attaining realization of the sixteenth moment, abandons the ninth affliction to be abandoned by the path of cultivation in the desire realm. Regarding this, if one does not apply oneself to abandoning the afflictions of the upper realm one is an abider in the mere [Non-returner] result and at the time of applying oneself to abandoning, from the afflictions of the first concentration up to the ninth affliction of the peak of existence, one is an abider in the distinctive [Non-returner] result and possesses the single foundation for entering to the state of Arhat. Moreover, this [distinctive Non-returner] also has four aspects: a transmigrator in the form realm (*rūpopaga*), transmigrator in the formless realm (*arūpopaga*), one who achieves emancipation in the present life (*dṛṣṭadharmaśrama*), and a bodily witness (*kāyasākṣī*). These are classified as distinctive results. However, these do not appear to be proven to have the definite application of abandoning the remaining [afflictions] to be abandoned by the path of cultivation.

Who is the transmigrator in the form realm (*rūpopaga*)? The
D297 Non-returner who possesses a desire realm embodiment that attains

---

[52] AK, vi.36c, Pruden, 964, Śāstrī, 946: *kṣinasaptāṣṭadoṣāṃśa ekajanmaikavīcikaḥ tṛtīyapratipannaśca /*

པའོ།།དེ་ཡང་གཟུགས་ཁམས་ཀྱི་སྐྱེ་སྲིད་དུ་ཉིང་མཚམས་སྦྱོར་མི་དགོས་ཏེ་བར་དོར་འདའ་བ་ལ་ཐལ་ཆེས་པར་འགྱུར་བའི་ཕྱིར་རོ།།གཟུགས་ཁམས་ཀྱི་རྟེན་ལ་འདའ་བ་ཡང་མི་དགོས་ཏེ་སྲིད་རྩེ་མཐར་ཐུག་འགྲོ་ལ་ཐལ་བར་འགྱུར་བའི་ཕྱིར་རོ།།འོད་ཁ་ཅིག་གང་དག་གཟུགས་ཁམས་ཀྱི་སྐྱེ་སྲིད་དང་བར་སྲིད་དུ་ཉིང་མཚམས་སྦྱར་ཟིན་པ་རྣམས་ཀྱང་གཟུགས་ཀྱི་ཉེར་འགྲོར་འདོད་པ་ནི་བསྟན་བཅོས་ཀྱི་དགོངས་པ་[110]ཕྲ་མོ་རང་གི་བློ་གྲོས་ཀྱི་འཇུག་པ་རྫིང་པོས་མ་ཕྱིད་པ་ཡིན་ནོ།།དེ་ཡང་སྐབས་ཇི་ལྟ་བ་བཞིན་དུ་བཤད་པར་བྱའོ།

།གཟུགས་སུ་ཉེ་བར་འགྲོ་བ་དེ་ལ་ཡང་བར་དོར་འདའ་བ་དང་།སྐྱེས་ནས་འདའ་བ་དང་།[111]གོང་དུ་འཕོ་བ་སྟེ་གསུམ་དུ་འགྱུར་རོ།།བར་མ་དོར་འདའ་བ་གང་ཞེ་ན།གཟུགས་སུ་ཉེ་བར་འགྲོ་བ་གང་གཟུགས་ཁམས་ཀྱི་ཚངས་ཆེན་གྱི་བར་དོ་མ་གཏོགས་པ་བར་དོ་བཅུ་དྲུག་གང་རུང་དུ་ཉིང་མཚམས་སྦྱོར་བའི་རྟེན་དེ་ཉིད་ལ་མྱ་ངན་ལས་འདས་པ་འཐོབ་པའོ།།དེ་ལ་ཡང་མྱུར་བ་དང་།[112]མྱུར་བ་མ་ཡིན་པ་དང་།[113]ཡུན་རིང་མོ་ཞིག་ནས་འདའ་བ་རྣམ་པ་གསུམ་མོ།།དེ་དག་ཀྱང་རིམ་པ་[114]བཞིན་དུ་བར་དོར་སྐྱེས་མ་ཐག་དང་། ཚེ་དཀྱིལ་དང་།[115]ཚེ་གཞུག་ལ་འདའ་བ་གསུམ་ཡིན་ཏེ།ཇི་སྐད་དུ་མཛོད་འགྲེལ་ལས།

། རེ་ཞིག་བར་མ་དོར་ཡོངས་སུ་མྱ་ངན་ལས་འདའ་བ་ནི་དཔེ་
D 298 གསུམ་གྱིས་མྱུར་བ་དང་།[116] མྱུར་བ་མ་ཡིན་པ་དང་།ཡུན་རིང་མོ་
P114a [117]ཞིག་ནས་ཡོངས་སུ་མྱ་ངན་ལས་འདའ་བའི་ཕྱིར་རོ།

།ཞེས་གང་གསུངས་པའོ།།དཔེ་གསུམ་ཡང་གང་ཞེ་ན།ཞོགས་མའི་མེ་
1315 སྟག་གྲུབ་མ་ཐག་འཆི་བ་དང་།ལྕགས་མགར་གྱི་ཐོ་བས་ལྕགས་བརྡུངས་པའི་
མེ་སྟག་གནམ་དུ་ཡར་བ་ཕྱིར་ལྡོག་ཁར་འཆི་བ་དང་།ལྕགས་ཀྱི་ཚྭ་ཚྭ་[118]གནམ་
དུ་ཡར་བ་ཕྱིར་ལོག་ནས་ས་ལ་མ་ལྷུང་ཙམ་དུ་འཆི་བ་གསུམ་རིམ་པ་
བཞིན།[119]བར་དོར་འདའ་བ་གསུམ་གྱི་དཔེར་སྐྱེས་བུ་དམ་པའི་འགྲོ་བ་བདུན་

---

[110]dgongs pa M P] dgengs pa D | [111] / D M] om. / P | [112] / D M] om. / P | [113] / D M] om. / P | [114]rim pa D M] rims pa P | [115] / D M] om. / P | [116] / D M] om. / P | [117]ring mo D M] rung mo P | [118]tshwa tshwa M] tsha tsha D P | [119] / D M] om. / P

nirvāṇa having definitely taken rebirth in the form realm. A connection (*mtshoms sbyor, sandhāna*) in that very rebirth existence itself of the form realm is not necessary because of the absence of connection for the *Antarāparinirvāyin*. Also it is not necessary to achieve *nirvāṇa* in a form realm embodiment because of the consequence for the *Bhavāgraparama*. Some Tibetans assert, although the connections to take rebirth in the form realm or in an intermediate state existence are finished, a transmigrator to the form realm; the subtle thought of the *śāstra* is not distinguished by the coarse application of one's own thoughts. Therefore, [this] section should be explained just how it is.

> The transmigrators in the form realm are three: the *Antarāparinirvāyin*, *Upapadyaparinirvāyin*, and *Ūrdhvasrotas*. Who is the *Antarāparinirvāyin*? [This] is one who goes in the form realm attaining *nirvāṇa* in that embodiment itself which is connected to whatever suitable of the sixteen intermediate states, not counting the intermediate state of the *Mahābrahma* heaven of the form realm. Also for that, there are three aspects: those who obtain *nirvāṇa* quickly, not quickly, and after a long time. Those are also three gradually attaining *nirvāṇa* immediately born in the intermediate state, in the middle time of the intermediate state, and at the end of period of the intermediate state. The *Abhidharmakośabhāṣya* states:

Briefly, the *Antarāparinirvāyin* is by three illustrations:
One who attains *nirvāṇa* quickly, not quickly, and after a
long time.[53]

What are these three illustrations? In the manner of three stages: like a spark of hay that is immediately extinguished, like a spark of iron stricken by the hammer of an iron smith that ascends up towards the sky and is extinguished, and like a flaming iron spark, having turned up towards the sky, is extinguished before hitting the ground, the examples of the *Antarāparinirvāyin*s which occur in the *Sūtra*

---

[53] AKBh, Pruden, 970, Śāstrī, 954: *antarāparinirvāyiṇastāvadāśvanāśucira - parinirvāṇāt dṛṣṭāntatrayeṇa /*

བསྟན་པའི་མདོར་འབྱུང་ངོ།།སློབ་དཔོན་ཐོགས་མེད་ཀྱི་བཞེད་པས་བར་དོ་འདའ་བ་གསུམ་དུ་འཇོག་པའི་ཚུལ་ནི།[120]དང་པོ་བར་དོ་གྲུབ་པ་དང་མཉམ་དུ་ལམ་མངོན་དུ་བྱས་ནས་སྤང་བྱ་ལྷག་མ་སྤངས་ཏེ་མྱང་འདས་ཐོབ་པ་དང།བར་སྲིད་གྲུབ་ཅིང་སྐྱེ་སྲིད་དུ་འགྲོ་བའི་འདོད་པ་མ་བྱུང་ཙམ་དང།བར་སྲིད་གྲུབ་ནས་སྐྱེས་གནས་སུ་བགྲོད་པར་འདོད་པ་ན་ལམ་མངོན་དུ་བྱས་ནས་ཏེ་མྱང་འདས་ཐོབ་པར་བྱེད་ལ་དེ་དག་གཟུགས་ཁམས་ཀྱི་ལྷ་གནས་སུ་དངོས་སུ་སྐྱེ་བའི་ཉོན་མོངས་སྤངས་ཀྱང་བར་སྲིད་འགྲུབ་པའི་ཉོན་མོངས་མ་སྤངས་པས་བར་དོར་སྐྱེ་བར་བཞེད་དེ།ཀུན་ལས་བཏུས་སུ།

བར་མ་དོར་ཡོངས་སུ་མྱ་ངན་ལས་འདའ་བ་གང་ཞེ་ན།སྐྱེ་བའི་
ཀུན་ཏུ་སྦྱོར་བ་ནི་སྤངས་ལ་མངོན་པར་འགྲུབ་པའི་ཀུན་ཏུ་སྦྱོར་བ་
ནི་མ་སྤངས་ཏེ།བར་མ་དོའི་སྲིད་པ་མངོན་པར་འགྲུབ་པ་ན་གང་
ལམ་མངོན་དུ་བྱས་ནས་སྡུག་བསྔལ་གྱི་ཐ་མ་འཐོབ་པ་དང།བར་མ་
D 299 དོའི་[121]སྲིད་པ་མངོན་པར་གྲུབ་པ་སྐྱེ་བའི་སྲིད་པར་འགྲོ་བར་མི་
སེམས་པ་ཉིད་ན་གང་ལམ་མངོན་དུ་བྱས་ནས་སྡུག་བསྔལ་གྱི་ཐ་མ་
འཐོབ་པ་དང།མངོན་པར་བསམས་ནས་སྐྱེ་བའི་སྲིད་པ་ལ་མངོན་
པར་འཇུག་སྟེ།སྐྱེ་བའི་སྲིད་པ་ནི་མ་ཐོབ་པ་ན་གང་ལམ་མངོན་དུ་

[120] / D M] om. / P | [121] bar ma do'i D M] bar mdo'i P

[54] Tsong kha pa draws these illustrations from Yaśomitra's AKV on AK,vi.38. The Sankskrit on that section is: *āśuparinirvāyī anāśuparinirvāyī ciraparinirvāyī ca dṛṣṭāntatrayeṇa yojayitavyāḥ / tadyathā parīttaḥ śakalikāgnirabhinirvatamāna eva nirvāthāt evaṃ prathamo ya āśuparinirvāyī / tadyathā 'yogudānāṃ vāyasphālānāṃ vā dīptāgnisaṃprataptānām ayoghanena hanyamānānām ayaḥprapāṭikotpatantyeva*

showing the Seven Transmigrations of Holy Individuals.[54] The method of positing the three aspects of the *Antarāparinirvāyin* by the explanation of the Ācārya Asaṅga is as follows: first, actualizing a path which achieves the intermediate state, one abandons the remaining abandonments and attains *nirvāṇa*, or one achieves an intermediate existence and the desire of transmigrating into a rebirth merely does not occur, and one abandons the remaining abandonments and attains *nirvāṇa*; or, having achieved an intermediate state existence, one actualizes the path when there is desire to pass through an abode of rebirth then attains *nirvāṇa*; these [*Antarāparinirvāyin*s], although abandoning the afflictions of actual birth in the god abodes of the form realm, since they do not abandon the afflictions of achieving the intermediate state existence take rebirth in the intermediate state. The *Abhidharmasamuccaya* states:

> Who is the person that attains *nirvāṇa* in the intermediate existence? This is a person who, abandoning the fetters of birth but not abandoning the fetters of coming into existence, when progressing toward the intermediate existence, having actualized the path, attains the end of suffering; or one who, progressing in the intermediate existence, while thinking to transmigrate in the existence of rebirth, actualizes the path and attains the end of suffering; or one who, having reflected (*abhisaṃcetayitva*), does not yet arrive at the existence of rebirth, actualizes the path

nirvāyāt evaṃ dvitīyo'nāśuparinirvāyī / tadyathā'yogudānāmiti pūrvavadyāvadaḥprapāṭikotplutya pṛthivyāmapatitaiva nirvāyāt evaṃ tṛtīyo yaścaraparinirvāyī / etacca sūtraṃ vistareṇa purastāllikhatamiti na punarlikhyate / Yaśomitra quotes the whole *Saptasatpuruṣagatī sūtra* as proof for the existence of the intermediate state on AK, iii.12, Śāstrī, 411-413. These same illustrations of the *Antarāparinirvāyīn* are also mentioned in Asaṅga's *Śrāvakabhūmi* with slightly different wording. See also A. Wayman, "The Intermediate-State Dispute in Buddhism," *Buddhist Studies in honour of I.B. Horner* (1974) and P. Masefield, *Divine Revelation in Pali Buddhism* (1986), 109-116. The Sanskrit of this *sūtra* compares with the Pāli of *Aṅguttara nikāya* IV.70, this comparison has been studied by L. de la Vallee Poussin in "Pali and Sanskrit," *Journal of the Royal Asiatic Society*, 1906, 446-451.

P114b བྱས་ནས་སྡུག་བསྔལ་གྱི་མཐའ་མ་འཐོབ་པའོ།

ཞེས་གང་གསུངས་པའོ།།སྐྱེས་ནས་འདའ་བ་གང་ཞེ་ན།གཟུགས་སུ་ཉེ་
བར་འགྲོ་བ་གང་གཟུགས་ཁམས་ཀྱི་ལྷ་གནས་བཅུ་དྲུག་གང་ཡང་རུང་བར་
དང་པོར་སྐྱེས་པའི་རྟེན་དེ་ཉིད་ལ་མྱ་ངན་ལས་འདའ་བའོ།།འདི་ལ་ཡང་
སྐྱེས་པ་ཙམ་ནས་འདའ་བ་དང།མངོན་པར་འདུ་བྱེད་པ་མེད་པར་
1316 དང།མངོན་པར་འདུ་བྱེད་པ་དང་བཅས་ནས་ཡོངས་སུ་མྱ་ངན་ལས་འདའ་
བ་གསུམ་དུ་འགྱུར་ལ།དེ་དག་གི་ཁྱད་པར་[122]ཡང་རིམ་པ་ལྟར་འགྲེལ་བཤད་
དུ།

> དེ་ལྟར་མངོན་པར་བརྩོན་པ་ལ་སོགས་པ་ཐ་དད་པའི་ཕྱིར་ཡོངས་སུ་མྱ་ངན་ལས་འདའ་བའི་ཁྱད་པར་བཤད་པ་ཡིན་ཏེ།སྐྱེས་ནས་ཡོངས་སུ་མྱ་ངན་ལས་འདའ་བ་ལ་ནི་མངོན་པར་བརྩོན་པ་དང།ལམ་ངང་[123]གིས་འབྱུང་བ་གཉིས་ཀ་ཡོད་དོ།།མངོན་པར་འདུ་བྱེད་པ་དང་བཅས་པས་ཡོངས་སུ་མྱ་ངན་ལས་འདའ་བ་ལ་ནི་མངོན་པར་བརྩོན་པ་ཡོད་ཀྱི་འདི་ལ་ལམ་ངང་[124]གིས་འབྱུང་བ་ནི་མེད་དོ།།མངོན་པར་འདུ་བྱེད་པ་མེད་པར་ཡོངས་སུ་མྱ་ངན་ལས་འདའ་བ་ལ་ནི་གཉིས་ཀ་ཡང་མེད་དེ་མངོན་པར་བརྩོན་པ་ཡང་མེད་ལ་ལམ་ངང་གིས་[125]འབྱུང་བ་ཡང་མེད་དོ།

D 300 །ཞེས་དེ་གསུམ་གྱི་ཁྱད་པར་དང་པོ་རིམ་[126]ཀྱང་བྱེད་བཅས་སྔོན་ལ་བསྟན་ནས་བྱེད་མེད་ཕྱིས་སྟོན་པ་ནི་བྱེ་བྲག་ཏུ་སྨྲ་བའི་ཕྱོགས་ཡིན་པས་སངས་རྒྱས་གཉིས་པས་ལུགས་དེ་བརྗོད་ནས་དེ་ལྟར་གྲག་གོ་ཞེས་མ་རངས་པ་མཛད་ནས།རང་གི་ལུགས་ནི་འགྲེལ་པར

[122] khyad par D M] khyad bar P | [123] ngang D M] dang P | [124] ngang D M] dang P | [125] ngang gis D M] dang gi P | [126] rim D M] rims P

[55] AS, Rahula, 155, Pradhan, 90: *antarāparinirvāyī katamaḥ / upapattisaṃyojane prahīṇe abhidnivṛttisaṃyojane aprahīṇe antarābhavamabhinrvarttayanneva yo*

and obtains the end of suffering.[55]

Who is the *Upapadyaparinirvāyin*? A transmigrator in the form realm who, in that very first embodiment itself in whatever suitable sixteen abodes of form realm gods attains *nirvāṇa.* This [*Upapadyaparinirvāyin*] has three [divisions] from the one who obtains *nirvāṇa* through mere rebirth, one who achieves without effort, and one who achieves with effort. The distinctions of these are sequentially explained in the *Abhidharmakośabhāṣyavyākhā*:

> Accordingly because of differences in exertion, etc. the distinction of *parinirvāṇa* is explained. The *Upapadyaparinirvāyin* has both arisen by the spontaneous path[56] and exertion. For the *Sābhisaṃskāraparinirvāyin* it is with effort for this [one] does not arise by the spontaneous path. For the *Anabhisaṃskāraparnirvāyin* there is not both, neither exertion nor arising by the spontaneous path.[57]

However, for the succession and distinction of the three, since it
D300 is the opinion of the *Vaibhāṣika*s that the previous [*Upapadyaparinirvāyin*] has effort and the latter is without effort, the Second Buddha [Vasubandhu] having expressed that system, accordingly being dissatisfied with such talk [proclaimed] our own system in the *Abhidharmakośabhāṣya*:

---

mārgaṃ saṃmukhīkṛtya duḥkhasyāntamanuprāpnoti abhinirvṛtto vā antarābhave upapattibhavagamanāya cetayannevayo mārgaṃ saṃmukhīkṛtya duḥkhasyāntamanuprāpnoti / abhisaṃcetayitvā vā upapattibhavamabhisaṃprasthitaḥ bhavānupapatticchandaṃ yo mārgaṃ saṃmukhīkṛtya duḥkhasyāntamanuprāpnoti /

[56] Yaśomitra glosses "*vāhī mārga*" in *Abhidharmakośabhāṣyavyākhā* with: *kathaṃ mārgo vāhī/ vinābhisaṃskāreṇa sammukhībhāvāt /*

[57]AKV, Śāstrī, 950: *adevamabhiyogādinānātvāt parinrivāṇaviśeṣa ukto bhavati / upapadyaparinirvāyiṇo hyubhayamasti abhiyogaśca vāhī camārga iti / sābhisaṃskāraparinirvāyiṇo 'bhiyogo 'sti na tvasya vāhī mārgaḥ anabhisaṃskāraparinirvāyiṇastṛbhayamapi nāsti nābhiyogaḥ na ca vāhī mārga iti /*

མདོ་ལས་ནི་མངོན་པར་འདུ་བྱེད་པ་མེད་པར་ཡོངས་སུ་མྱ་ངན་
ལས་འདའ་བ་སྔར་འབྱུང་བས་དེ་ཁོ་ན་བཞིན་དུ་ལམ་ངང་གིས་
འབྱུང་བ་དང་།ངང་གིས་འབྱུང་བ་མ་ཡིན་པ་དག་ནི་འབད་པ་མེད་
P115a དང་།འབད་པས་[127]འཐོབ་པའི་སྒོ་ནས་མངོན་པར་འདུ་བྱེད་པ་མེད་
པ་དང་།མངོན་པར་འདུ་བྱེད་པས་བསྒྲུབ་པར་བྱ་བ་ཡིན་པའི་ཕྱིར་
རོ།།སྐྱེས་ནས་ཡོངས་སུ་མྱ་ངན་ལས་འདའ་བ་ནི་ལམ་ཆེས་ངང་
གིས་འབྱུང་བ་དང་།།ཆེས་ཆེ་བ་དང་།ཕྲ་རྒྱས་ཆེས་ཆུང་བ་ཡིན་ནོ་

ཞེས་བར་དོར་འདའ་བ་གསུམ་དང་།སྐྱེས་ནས་འདའ་བ་གསུམ་
དང་།[128]གོང་དུ་འཕོ་བ་སྟེ་སྐྱེས་བུ་དམ་པའི་འགྲོ་བ་བདུན་བསྟན་པའི་མདོ་
ལས།འདུ་བྱེད་མེད་པར་འདའ་བ་བྱེད་བཅས་ཀྱིས་འདའ་བའི་སྔོན་ལ་འབྱུང་
བས་གོ་རིམ་ནི་མདོ་དེའི་ལུགས་ཁོ་ན་བཞིན་ཡིན་ལ།[129]ཁྱད་པར་ཡང་འབད་
པ་དྲག་པོ་ལ་མ་བལྟོས་པར་ལམ་ངང་གིས་འབྱུང་བ་བྱེད་མེད།[130]དེ་ལས་
1317 བཟློག་པ་བྱེད་བཅས་སོ།།འོ་ན་བྱེད་མེད་དང་སྐྱེས་ཙམ་ནས་འདའ་བ་ལ་
ཁྱད་པར་ཅི་སྙམ་ན།སྐྱེས་ཙམ་ནས་འདའ་བ་ལ་ནི་ལམ་ཆེས་ངང་གིས་འབྱུང་
བ་དང་།ཕྲ་བྱ་ཆེས་ཆུང་ལ་བྱེད་མེད་བྱེད་བཅས་རྣམས་དེ་ལྟ་མིན་པའི་ཕྱིར་
རོ་ཞེས་པའོ།།དེ་ལྟར་དུ་ཀུན་ལས་བཏུས་སུ་ཡང་འབྱུང་སྟེ[131]།

D 301 སྐྱེས་ནས་ཡོངས་སུ་མྱ་ངན་ལས་འདའ་བ་གང་ཞེ་ན།གཉིས་ཀར་
ཀུན་དུ་སྦྱོར་བ་མ་སྤངས་པ་གཟུགས་ཀྱི་ཁམས་སུ་སྐྱེས་པ་ཙམ་གྱིས་
གང་ལམ་མངོན་དུ་བྱས་ནས་སྡུག་བསྔལ་གྱི་ཐ་མ་འཐོབ་པའོ།

།མངོན་པར་འདུ་བྱེད་པ་མེད་པར་ཡོངས་སུ་མྱ་ངན་ལས་འདའ་བ་
གང་ཞེ་ན།གང་སྐྱེས་ནས་མངོན་པར་འདུ་བྱེད་པ་མེད་པར་ལམ་
མངོན་དུ་བྱས་ནས་སྡུག་བསྔལ་གྱི་ཐ་མ་འཐོབ་པའོ།

127 'bad pas D M] 'pad pas P | 128 / D M] om. / P | 129 / D M] om. / P | 130 / D M] om. / P | 131 ste D M] te P

58 AKBh, Pk ṅu 026a2-4, Pruden, 967, Śāstrī, 950: *sūtre tvanabhisaṃskāraparinirvāyī pūrvaṃ paṭyate tathaiva yujyate vāhyavāhimārgayoranabhisaṃskārasādhyatvādyatnayatnaprāptitaḥ upapadyparinirvāyiṇastu vāhitaro 'dhimātrataraśca mārgaḥ mṛdutarāścānuśayā iti /*

59 AS, Rahula, 156, Pradhan, 90: *upapadyaparinirvāyī katamaḥ / ubhayasaṃyojane*

> From the *sūtra*, [the Non-returner] who obtains *parinirvāṇa* without effort (*abhisaṃskāra*) arises before [the Non-returner who obtains *nirvāṇa* with effort]. Just like this it is arranged. Their path arise and do not arise spontaneously because it is caused to achieve without effort and with effort through the means of obtaining without effort and with effort. For the *Upapadyaparinirvāyin* the path is even more spontaneous, even stronger, and the *anuśaya*s are even weaker.[58]

From the *Sūtra showing the Seven Transmigrations of Holy Individuals* there are three *Antāraparinirvāyin*s, three *Upapadyaparinirvāyin*s, and the *Ūrdhvaṃsrotas*. It is just the system of that *sūtra*, the succession by first arising in liberation by the one who actualizes *nirvāṇa* without effort (*Anabhisaṃskāraparinirvāyin*) and the distinction which is just the opposite from that, without arising by a spontaneous path, attending to fierce effort. Well then, what is considered the distinction between one who achieves *nirvāṇa* from mere birth and one who achieves without effort? The *Upapadyaparinirvāyin*s arise by a more spontaneous path and the abandonments are weaker and those who achieve without effort are
D301 not like that. The *Abhidharmasamuccaya* states:

> Who is the person that attains *parinirvāṇa* having been born (*Upapadyaparinirvāyin*)? That is one who, not abandoning the two types of fetters [of birth and coming into existence], by mere birth in the realm of form, attains the end of suffering having actualized the path.[59]

> Who is the person that attains *parinirvāṇa* without effort (*Anabhisaṃskāraparinirvāyin*)? One who, having been born, actualizes the path without effort and attains the end suffering.[60]

---

aprahīne rūpadhātāvupapannamātra eva yo mārgaṃ saṃmukhīkṛtya duḥkhasyāntamanuprāpnoti /

60 ibid. *anabhisaṃskāraparinirvāyī katamaḥ / upapannaḥ anabhisaṃskāreṇa yo mārgaṃ saṃmukhīkṛtya duḥkhasyāntamanuprāpnoti /*

་།མངོན་པར་འདུ་བྱེད་པ་དང་བཅས་པས་ཡོངས་སུ་མྱ་ངན་ལས་
འདའ་པ་གང་ཞེ་ན།གང་སྐྱེས་ནས་མངོན་པར་འདུ་བྱེད་པས་ལམ་
མངོན་དུ་བྱས་ཏེ་[132]སྡུག་བསྔལ་གྱི་ཐ་མ་འཐོབ་པའོ།

།ཞེས་[133]གོ་རིམ་[134]དང་དེ་གསུམ་གྱི་ཁྱད་པར་ཡང་སྐུ་མཆེད་དགོངས་
P115b པ་གཅིག་ཏུ་འདུག་གོ།དེས་ན་དེ་ཁོ་ན་ལྟར་རིགས་པ་ཡིན་ཏེ་བྱེད་མེད་དང་
བྱེད་བཅས་ནི་གང་ཟག་དེ་དག་མྱ་ངན་ལས་འདའ་བའི་ཚུལ་བསྟན་པ་ལ་
མངོན་པར་འདུ་བྱེད་པ་ཆེན་པོ་ལ་མ་ལྟོས་པར་ལམ་རྒྱུད་ལ་འབྱུང་བ་ནི་མྱ་
ངན་ལས་འདའ་བ་མྱུར་བར་བྱ་དགོས་པའི་ཕྱིར་རོ།།དེའི་ཕྱིར་གང་ཡང་
མངོན་པར་རྟོགས་པའི་རྒྱན་[135]དུ།

བྱེད་དང་བྱེད་མིན་འོག་མིན་འགྲོ།

།[136]ཞེས་གསུངས་པ་དེ་ནི་སློབ་སྦྱོར་གྱི་ངོར་[137]མཛད་པ་ཙམ་དུ་ཁོངས་
དུ་ཆུད་པར་བྱའོ[138]།

།འདིར་མངོན་པ་བ་ཁ་ཅིག་ན་རེ།[139]སྡུག་ཀུན་དང་ལམ་བདེན་ལ་
དམིགས་པའི་ལམ་གྱིས་མྱང་འདས་འཐོབ་པར་བྱེད་པ་ནི་འདུ་བྱེད་དང་
བཅས་པས་འདའ་བ་ཡིན་ཏེ།རྒྱུ་རྐྱེན་གྱིས་འདུས་བྱས་ལ་དམིགས་པའི་ལམ་
D 302 གྱིས་འདའ་བའི་ཕྱིར་རོ།།འགོག་བདེན་ལ་དམིགས་པའི་ལམ་གྱིས་འདའ་བ་
ནི་འདུ་བྱེད་མེད་པས་འདའ་བ་ཡིན་ཏེ།རྒྱུ་རྐྱེན་གྱིས་འདུས་མ་བྱས་ལ་
1318 དམིགས་པའི་ལམ་གྱིས་འདའ་བའི་ཕྱིར་རོ།།ཞེས་པ་ནི་རིགས་པ་མ་ཡིན་ཏེ་དེ་
ལྟར་ན་བར་དོར་འདའ་བ་རྣམས་ལ་ཡང་ཐལ་བར་འགྱུར་ཏེ།དེ་དག་ཀྱང་
བདེན་པ་བཞི་ལ་དམིགས་པའི་ལམ་གྱིས་འདའ་བའི་ཕྱིར་རོ།།དེ་སྐད་
དུ།མཛོད་འགྲེལ་ལས།

---

[132]om. / D M] insert / P | [133]zhes D M] zhas P | [134]rim D M] rims P | [135]rgyan D M] brgyan P | [136]/ D M] om. / P | [137]ngor D M] dor P | [138]khongs du chud par bya'o D M] yongs su chung bar bya'o P | [139]/ D M] om. / P

---

[61] ibid. *abhisaṃskāraparinirvāyī katamaḥ / upanno ` bhisaṃskareṇa yo mārgaṃ saṃmukhīkṛtya duḥkhasyāntamanuprāpnoti /*

[62] AA, i.23c-d :....*utpadya kāra akāra akaniṣṭagāḥ /* "those who are born, who are with

> Who is the person that attains *parinirvāṇa* with effort (*Sābhisaṃskāraparinirvāyin*)? One who, having been born, actualizes the path with effort and attains the end suffering.[61]

Thus for the succession and the distinction of the three, the brothers (Vasubandhu and Asaṅga) have a single intention. Therefore, accordingly only that is the lineage: [one] without accomplishment and [then one] with accomplishment. These individuals, in demonstrating the manner of achieving *nirvāṇa*, arise in the [mental] continuum the path through not relying on great accomplishment because of the purpose to achieve *nirvāṇa* quickly. Because of that, it is taught "those with effort and without effort, those who go to Akaniṣṭha" in the *Abhisamayālaṃkāra*.[62] One should put into understanding up to the original of the verse.

Here an *Ābhidhārmika* says: "the cause to attain *nirvāṇa* by the path whose object is the truths of suffering, arising, and path is the one liberated by effort, because one attains *nirvāṇa* by the path who object is conditioned by cause and condition. One who is liberated by the
D302 path whose object is the truth of cessation is the one who is liberated without effort, because one attains *nirvāṇa* by a path whose object is unconditioned by cause and condition."[63][This] is not correct, for if it is in this way there will also be consequences for the *Antarāparinirvāyin* because even these [Non-returners] achieve *nirvāṇa* through the path who object is the four [Noble] truths. As the *Abhidharmakośabhāṣya* states:

---

effort, without effort, those who go to Akaniṣṭha [heaven]". Edition of Stcherbatsky and Obermiller, 1992: 8,1992, Dutt 1934: xxvii, Conze,1957:31.

[63] Tsong kha pa draws this opponents remarks from the AKV, Śāstrī, 950: *saṃskṛtaṃ saṃskāra ityeko'rthaḥ/ evamasaṃskṛtam asaṃskāra iti / saṃskārālambanena mārgeṇa duḥkhasamudayamārgālambanena mārgeṇa yaḥ kleśān prajahāti sa sābhisaṃskāraparinirvāyī / yo'saṃskārālambanena nirodhālambanena so'nabhisaṃskāraparinirvāyīti /* "Conditioned states are synonymous with conditionings. Likewise unconditioned states are non-conditionings. One who abandons by way of the path whose object is [the truths of] suffering, production, and path, [abandons] by a path who object is conditioned, that is one who achieves Nirvāṇa with activity. One who [abandons] by a path whose object is [the truth of] cessation, [abandons by a path] whose object is without conditioned states, that is one who achieves Nirvāṇa without activity."

གཞན་ དག་ ན་ རེ་ འདུས་ བྱས་ དང་ འདུས་ མ་ བྱས་ ལ་ དམིགས་ པའི་ ལམ་ གྱིས་ ཡོངས་ སུ་ མྱ་ ངན་ ལས་ འདའ་ བའི་ ཕྱིར་ རོ།།ཞེས་ ཟེར་ རོ།།དེ་ ནི་ མི་ རུང་ སྟེ་ ཧ་ ཅང་ ཐལ་ བར་ འགྱུར་ བའི་ ཕྱིར་ རོ།།ཞེས་ འབྱུང་བའི་ཕྱིར་རོ།

།ཞེས་འབྱུང་ངོ།།ཅི་འདི་དག་གི་མྱ་ངན་ལས་འདའ་བ་དེ་མྱང་འདས་རྣམ་པ་གཉིས་ལས་གང་ཞིག་ཡིན་ཞེ་ན།།ཁ་ཅིག་ནི་སྐྱེས་ཙམ་ནས་འདའ་བ་ནི་ཕུང་པོ་ལྷག་མེད་ཀྱི་མྱ་ངན་ལས་འདའ་བ་ཡིན་ནོ་ཞེས་འདོད་དོ།།དེ་ནི་རིགས་པ་མ་ཡིན་ཏེ་སྐྱེས་ནས་འདའ་བ་འདི་ཚེ་མ་རྫོགས་པར་ནི་འཆི་བ་མ་
P116a ཡིན་ལ་སྐྱེས་ཙམ་ནས་མྱ་ངན་ལས་འདའ་བ་མངོན་དུ་བྱེད་པས་ན་སྐྱེས་ཙམ་ནས་འཆི་བ་ཡང་མ་ཡིན་པའི་ཕྱིར་རོ།།དེས་ན་ཚེ་མ་རྫོགས་པར་འཆི་ན་ཚེ་འདོར་བ་ལ་དབང་ཡོད་དགོས་ན་ཡོད་པ་ཡང་མ་ཡིན་ཏེ།[140]ཚེ་འདོར་བ་ལ་དབང་བ་ནི་རབ་མཐའི་བསམ་གཏན་གྱི་མཐུས་ཡིན་ལ།[141]དེ་ནི་གླིང་གསུམ་གྱི་སྐྱེས་པ་དང་བུད་མེད་ཀྱི་རྟེན་ཁོ་ན་ལ་ཡོད་པའི་ཕྱིར་རོ།།དེ་བས་ན་སྐྱེས་ནས་འདའ་བ་ནི་ལྷག་བཅས་ཀྱི་མྱང་འདས་ཡིན་ལ་བར་དོར་འདའ་བ་ནི་ལྷག་མེད་ཡིན་ནོ།

D 303 །འོ་ན་བར་དོར་འདའ། བ་ཡང་ཚེ་འདོར་བ་ལ་དབང་མེད་པ་མ་ཡིན་ནམ་ཞེ་ན།[142]བདེན་ཏེ་འོན་ཀྱང་བར་དོར་འཆི་བ་ནི་ཚེ་མ་རྫོགས་པར་འཆི་བ་ཁོ་ན་ཡིན་ཏེ།[143]བར་སྲིད་དང་[144]སྐྱེ་སྲིད་གཉིས་འཕེན་བྱེད་ཀྱི་ལས་གཅིག་

140/ D M] om. / P | 141/ D M] om. / P | 142/ D M] om. / P | 143/ D M] om. / P | 144om. / D M] insert / P

64 AKBh, Pradhan, 359, Pruden, 967, Śāstrī, 950: *saṃskṛta-asaṃskṛtālambanamārganirvāṇādityapare tattu na atiprasaṅgāt /*

65 *myang 'das rnam pa gnyis* is *phung po'i lhag ma dang bcas pa dang phung po'i lhag ma med pa'i mya ngan las 'das pa = sopadhiśeṣa* ("with remnant or residue") and *nirupadhiśeṣa* ("without remnant or residue")-nirvāṇa. Tsong kha pa gives a brief analysis of Nirvāṇa among the four schools of tenets (*siddhānta*) in his *Gser phreng*, pp.53.18 57.16(1970). He gives a concise definition of these two types in regards to śrāvakas: d*es na nyon mongs pa ma lus par spangs kyang phung po'i rgyun ma log pa dang / phung po'i rgyun chad pa.../* " Therefore, [Nirvāṇa with remnant] is a state when all afflictions without exception have been abandoned but the continuity of the [psycho-physical] aggregates has not yet stopped and [Nirvāṇa without remnant] is

> Others say, [they are different] because of attaining *nirvāṇa* by the path whose object is conditioned and unconditioned. That is not suitable because the consequences are excessive.[64]

Which one from the two types of *nirvāṇa*[65] is that *nirvāṇa* of these? Someone asserts: "the *Upapadyaparinirvāyin* attains a *nirvāṇa* without remnant (*nirupadhiśeṣa*)." That [assertion] is not correct and this *Upapadyaparinirvāyin* does not complete a life, since through the activity for *nirvāṇa* from mere rebirth there is not death, because there is not death from mere rebirth. Therefore, it is necessary to have the power for abandoning life if a life's death is not complete. [The *Upapadyaparinirvāyin*] does not have this because the power to abandon life is the force of *prāntakoṭicaturthadhyāna*[66] and only the embodiment of an individual of the three continents (*dvīpa*) or a woman has that. In this way, the *Upapadyaparinirvāyin* has a *nirvāṇa* with remnant (*sopadhiśeṣa*) and the *Antarāparinirvāyin* has a *nirvāṇa* without remnant (*nirupadhiśeṣa*).[67]

Well then, notwithstanding whether one asks if it is true that the
D303 *Antarāparinirvāyin* is without the power to abandon life or not, death in the intermediate state is only a death in an uncompleted life because it (i.e., the intermediate state) is cast by a single karma which puts forth an intermediate state existence and two rebirth existences.

---

when the continuity of the [psycho-physical] aggregates comes to an end." Cf. Obermiller, "Nirvāṇa according to the Tibetan Tradition," *Indian Historical Quarterly*, 1934, 211-257. For the definition among the ancient schools see *Itivuttaka*, Vaggo II, Sutta 7.44, PTS 38-39. *Prasannapadā* (Poussin,1900), 519.7-13, 520.1-3, Poussin, Nirvāṇa 171-180, *Documents d'Abhidharma* in BEFEO, 1930, 24-28.

[66] See AK.vii.41a-c.

[67] For this discussion Tsong kha pa is relying on Yaśomitra's comments on AKBh, vi.37a-c, AKV, Śāstrī, 949: *...naitadevam so'pi nirupadhiṣaparinirvāṇeti kasmāt/ āyurutsargāvaśitvāt/ āyuṣa utsarge tasyāvaśitvā/ kasmāt punarasyātrāvaśitvam/ yatprāntakoṭika-caturthadhyānalābhina āyurutsargaviśitvam tacca prāntakoṭikaṃ dhyānaṃ manuṣyeṣveva triṣu dvīpeṣūtpādyate/ sa ca rūpadhātūpapanna iti kimantarāparinirvāyiṇo'styāyurutsargavaśitvam/ yata evamasau nirupadhiśeṣaparinirvāṇena parinirvāti tasyāpi vasitvaṃ nāsti/ antarābhavāvasthānāya tu tādṛśaṃ karma nāsti yādṛśamupapadyaparinirvāyiṇa iti ato'ntarāparinirvāyī śīghraṃ parinirvāti / upapadyaparinirvāyī tu yāvadāyuḥ sthitvā parinirvātītyupapadyaparinirvāyyeva sopadhiśeṣanirvāṇena parinirvātītyucyate/*

གིས་འཕངས་པའི་ཕྱིར་རོ།།དེས་ན་བར་དོར་འདའ་ནི་ཉོན་མོངས་མ་ལུས་པར་སྤངས་མ་ཐག་ཏུ་ཚེའི་འདུ་བྱེད་གཏོང་བས་ལྷག་མེད་དུ་འདའ་ལ།[145]སྐྱེ་གནས་སུ་ཉིང་མཚམས་སྦྱོར་བ་རྣམས་ནི་ཉོན་མོངས་མ་ལུས་པར་སྤངས་པའི་ལྷག་བཅས་སྟོན་ལ་ཐོབ་ནས་ནམ་དེ་ཚེའི་དུས་བྱས་པ་དང་ལྷག་མེད་དུ་འདའ་བ་ཡིན་ཏེ།ཅི་སྐད་དུ།མཛོད་འགྲེལ་ལས།

1319 སྐྱེས་ནས་ཡོངས་སུ་མྱ་ངན་ལས་འདའ་བ་ནི་སྐྱེས་པ་ཙམ་ལས་མི་
འཆི་བར་ཕུང་པོ་ལྷག་མ་དང་བཅས་པའི་ཡོངས་སུ་མྱ་ངན་ལས་
འདའ་བ་སྟེ།མངོན་པར་བརྩོན་པ་དང་ལམ་ངང་གིས་འབྱུང་བའི་
ཕྱིར་རོ།།གཞན་དག་ན་རེ་དེ་ཡང་ཕུང་པོ་ལྷག་མ་མེད་པས་
སོ།།ཞེས་ཟེར་རོ།།མ་ཡིན་ཏེ་ཚེ་འདོར་བ་ལ་དབང་མེད་པའི་ཕྱིར་རོ།

།ཞེས་གང་གསུངས་པའོ།།གང་དུ་འཕོ་བ་གང་ཞེ་ན།གཟུགས་སུ་ཉེ་བར་
འགྲོ་བ་གང་གཟུགས་ཁམས་སུ་དང་པོར་སྐྱེས་པའི་རྟེན་ལ་མྱང་འདས་མི་
P116b འཐོབ་པར་གོང་དུ་འཕོས་ཏེ་འདའ་བ་ཡིན་ཏེ།[146]ཇི་སྐད་དུ།མཛོད་འགྲེལ་
ལས།

གོང་དུ་འགྲོ་བ་[147]ནི་གང་དུ་སྐྱེས་པ་དེ་ཉིད་དུ་ཡོངས་སུ་མྱ་ངན་ལས་མི་འདའ་བར་གང་དུ་འགྲོ་བ་གང་ཡིན་པ་སྟེ[148]།

ཞེས་གང་གསུངས་པའོ།།གཟུགས་ཅན་གྱི་[149]ཁམས་ན་གོང་དུ་འགྲོ་བ་
D 304 མཐར་ཐུག་པ་ནི་འོག་མིན་ཡིན་ལ།གཟུགས་མེད་ཀྱི་བགྲོད་པ་མཐར་ཐུག་པ་
ནི་སྲིད་རྩེ་ཡིན་པའི་ཕྱིར།གོང་འཕོ་ལ་ཡང་འོག་མིན་གྱི་མཐར་ཐུག་པར་འགྲོ་
བ་དང་།སྲིད་རྩེའི་མཐར་ཐུག་པར་འགྲོ་བ་གཉིས་སོ།།འོག་མིན་གྱི་མཐར་ཐུག་
པར་འགྲོ་བ་གང་ཞེ་ན།གོང་དུ་འཕོ་བ་གང་འོག་མིན་གྱི་རྟེན་ལ་མྱང་འདས་
འཐོབ་པའི་རིགས་ཅན་ནོ།།དེ་ལ་ཡང་འཕར་བ་དང་།ཕྱེད་དུ་འཕར་བ་
དང་།གནས་ཐམས་ཅད་དུ་འཆི་འཕོ་ཞིང་འཕར་བ་རྣམ་པ་གསུམ་མོ།

།འཕར་བ་གང་ཞེ་ན།འོག་མིན་གྱི་མཐར་ཐུག་པར་འགྲོ་བ་གང་ཚངས་རིས་སུ་སྐྱེས་ནས་གནས་གཞན་བར་པ་ཐམས་ཅད་བོར་ནས་འོག་མིན་གྱི་

[145]/ D M] om. / P | [146]/ D M] om. / P | [147]'gro ba D M] 'pho ba P | [148]ste D M] te P | [149]kyi D M] gyis P

Therefore, the *Antarāparinirvāyin* has connections in that very abiding rebirth for *nirvāṇa* without remnant since releasing from the conditionings of life immediately abandons all afflictions without exception or, otherwise, having obtained previously a [*nirvāṇa*] with remnant which abandons all afflictions without exception at that time of death has a *nirvāṇa* without remnant. The *Abhidharmakośabhāṣya* states:

> The *Upapadyaparinirvāyin* attains *nirvāṇa* with remnant (*sopadhiśeṣa*) since not dying from mere birth and because of arising by the spontaneous path and exertion. Others say that [one] obtains *nirvāṇa* without remnant. That is not because [this *Anagāmin*] does not have the power to abandon life.[68]

Who is the *Ūrdhvaṃsrotas*? One who goes in the form realm, not attaining *nirvāṇa* in the embodiment of first rebirth in the form realm but going higher to upper [realms] obtains *nirvāṇa*. The *Abhidharmakośabhāṣya* states:

> The *Ūrdhvaṃsrotas* does not attain *nirvāṇa* where he is reborn but goes higher.[69]

If it is an *Ūrdhvaṃsrotas* who goes to the limit of the realm of form it is an *Akaniṣṭhaga* and if traveling up to the edge of the
D304 formless realm it is a *Bhavāgraparamaga*. [Therefore,] the *Ūrdhvaṃsrotas* is [divided into two]: the transmigrator up to the limit of *Akaniṣṭha* heaven and the transmigrator up to the peak of existence. Who is the transmigrator up to the limit of *Akaniṣṭha* heaven? That is the *Ūrdhvaṃsrotas* who possesses the lineage of attaining *nirvāṇa* in an embodiment of *Akaniṣṭha* heaven. For that there are three types: the jumper (*pluta*), half-jumper (*ardhapluta*), and the jumper who dies in all places (*sarvasthānacyuta*).

Who is the jumper (*pluta*)? One who is a transmigrator to the limit of *Akaniṣṭha* heaven possessing the lineage of suitably shifting to

---

[68] AKBh, Pruden, 966, Śāstrī, 948-949: *upapadyaparinirvāyī ya upapannamātro na cirāt parinirvātyabhiyuktavāhimārgatvāt sopadhiśeṣanirvāṇena / so 'pi nirūpadhiśeṣanirvāṇenetyapare na āyurūtsargāvaśitvāt* / | [69] AKBh, Pruden, 967, Śāstrī, 951: *ūrdhvasrotā yasyordhvaṃ gatirna tatraiva parinirvāṇaṃ yatropapannaḥ* /

རྟེན་ལ་འདར་ཅུང་བའི་རིགས་ཅན་ནོ།།ཕྱིད་དུ་འཕར་བ་གང་ཞེ་ན།འོག་མིན་གྱི་མཐར་ཐུག་པར་འགྲོ་བ་གང་ཚངས་རིས་སུ་སྐྱེས་དེ་ནས་ཤི་འཕོས་ཏེ་བར་པ་རྣམས་པོར་ནས་གནས་གཙང་མ་དང་པོ་གསུམ་གང་ཅུང་དུ་སྐྱེས་དེ་ནས་ཀྱང་བར་པ་རྣམས་དོར་ཏེ། འོག་མིན་དུ་འདའ་བའི་རིགས་ཅན་ནོ།གནས་ཐམས་ཅད་དུ་འཕར་བ་གང་ཞེ་ན[150]།[151]འོག་མིན་གྱི་མཐར་ཐུག་པར་འགྲོ་བ་གང་ཚངས་ཆེན་མ་གཏོགས་པ་གནས་གཞན་ཐམས་ཅད་དུ་བརྒྱུད་ནས་འོག་མིན་གྱི་རྟེན་ལ་འདའ་བའི་རིགས་ཅན་ནོ།།དེ་ལྟར་ཡང་ཛཻ་སྐད་དུ།མཛོད་འགྲེལ་ལས།

> དེ་ལ་འཕར་བ་ཞེས་བྱ་བ་ནི།འདིར་བསམ་གཏན་རྣམས་སྤེལ་ནས་
> བསམ་གཏན་དང་པོའི་རོ་མྱངས་ཏེ་བསམ་གཏན་གསུམ་ལས་
> ཡོངས་སུ་ཉམས་པ་ཚངས་རིས་པ་དག་གི་ནང་དུ་སྐྱེས་ནས་སྔོན་
> P117a གོམས་པའི་དབང་གིས་བསམ་གཏན་བཞི་པ་སྤེལ[152]ཏེ་དེ་ནས་ཤི་
> D 305 འཕོས་ནས་འོག་མིན་པ་དག་གི་ནང་དུ་སྐྱེ་བ་གང་ཡིན་པ་སྟེ་དེ་ནི་
> བར་དུ་མི་འགྲོ་བས་ན་འཕར་བ་ཞེས་བྱའོ།།ཕྱིད་དུ་འཕར་བ་ཞེས་
> བྱ་བ་ནི་དེ་ནས་གནས་གཙང་མ་[153]རྣམས་སུ་སྐྱེས་ལ་བར་ནས་
> གནས་གཞན་འགའ་ཙམ་ཡང་བརྒལ་ཏེ་འགོ་[154]མིན་དུ་འཇུག་པ་
> གང་ཡིན་པའོ།།འཕགས་པ་ནི་ཚངས་པ་ཆེན་པོ་དག་གི་ནང་དུ་མི་
> སྐྱེ་སྟེ།ལྟ་བའི་གནས་ཡིན་པའི་ཕྱིར་དང་།གཙོ་བོ་གཅིག་ཏུ་ཟད་པའི་
> ཕྱིར་རོ།གནས་ཐམས་ཅད་དུ་འཆི་འཕོ་བ་ནི།གནས་གཞན་ཐམས་
> ཅད་དུ་འཕོ་ཞིང་འོག་མིན་དུ་འཇུག་པ་གང་ཡིན་པའོ།

།ཞེས་གང་གསུངས་པ་ཡིན་ནོ།།འདིར་འཕར་བ་གསུམ་གྱིས་དང་པོར་འདོད་པའི་རྟེན་ལ་གནས་གཙང་མར་སྐྱེ་བའི་རྒྱུ་བསམ་གཏན་བཞི་པ་སྤེལ་མར་བསྒོམས་པ་[155]ཡིན་ལ་དེ་ལས་མ་ཉམས་ན་འདི་ནས་ཤི་འཕོས་ཏེ་གནས་གཙང་མ་ཁོ་ནར་སྐྱེ་བ་ཡིན་ཡང་བསམ་གཏན་དང་པོའི་སྙོམས་འཇུག་ལ་

[150]zhe na D M] zhen P | [151]/ D M] om. / P | [152]spel D M] spal P | [153]gtsang ma D M] gcad ma P | [154]'go D M] 'og P | [155]bsgoms pa M] bsgom pa D P

[70] AKBh, Pruden, 968, Śāstrī, 951-952: *tatra pluto nāma ya iha dhyānāni vyavakīrya*

an embodiment of *Akaniṣṭha* heaven jumping over all other abodes having been born in *Brahmakāyika* heaven. Who is the half-jumper (*ardhapluta*)? One who is a transmigrator up to the limit of *Akaniṣṭha*, having died, jumps over all intermediate heavens from *Brahmakāyika* heaven up to the interval for rebirth in the first three suitable *Śūddhāvasas* realms. Then, casting out the intermediate realms possesses the lineage of attaining *nirvāṇa* in *Akaniṣṭha* heaven. Who is that jumper which dies in all abodes (*sarvasthānacyuta*)? One who is a transmigrator to the limit of *Akaniṣṭha* heaven who, having transmigrated in all other abodes not counting *Mahābrahma* heaven, possesses the lineage of attaining *nirvāṇa* in an embodiment of *Akaniṣṭha* heaven. The *Abhidharmakośabhāṣya* states:

> One called a jumper has alternated concentrations down here, has a taste of the first concentration and falls from the three (higher) concentrations having been born among the *Brahmakāyika*s. There, by the power of previous enthusiasm alternates the fourth concentration and from there, having died is reborn among the *Akaniṣṭha*s. Since one does not transmigrate in [any of the fourteen] heavens in between, one is called a Jumper. One called a Half-jumper passes over any one place from birth in the *Śuddhāvāsas* heavens and enters the *Akaniṣṭha*s. An *Āryan* is not reborn among the *Mahābrahmas* because it is a place of [wrong] view and because of having one leader. One who dies in all abodes transmigrates in all other abodes and then enters into *Akaniṣṭha* heaven.[70]

Here, the three jumpers: first for a desire realm embodiment, the cause of rebirth in the *Śuddhāvāsas* heavens is the cultivation alternating the fourth concentration. If backsliding from that [concentration], having died here, although one is reborn only in the

---

dhyānatrayāt parihīṇaḥ prathamaṃ dhyānamāsvādya brahmakāyikeṣūpapannaḥ pūrvābhyāsavaśccaturthaṃ dhyānaṃ vyavakīrya tasmāt pracyuto 'kaniṣṭeṣūpapadyate/ eṣa hi madhyānimajjanāt plutaḥ / arhapluto nāma yastataḥ śuddhāvāseṣūpapadya madhyādekamapi sthānāntaraṃ vilaṅdhyākaniṣṭān praviśati / mahābrahmasvāryo nopapadyate dṛṣṭisthānatvād ekanāyakatvācceti / sarvacyuto nāma yaḥ sarvāṇi sthānāntarāṇi saṃcaryākaniṣṭān praviśati /

སྲིད་པས་རོ་མྱངས་པའི་མཐུས། བསམ་གཏན་ཕྱི་མ་གསུམ་ལས་ཉམས་ཏེ། དེ་ནས་འདི་ནས་ཚེ་འཕོས་པ་དང་ཚངས་རིས་སུ་སྐྱེས་དེར་སྔོན་འདོད་པའི་རྟེན་ལ་སྤེལ་བསྒོམ་གོམས་པའི་མཐུས་བསམ་གཏན་བཞི་པ་སྤེལ་མར་བསྒོམས་ནས་གནས་གཙང་དུ་སྐྱེ་བར་བྱེད་པ་ནི་འཕར་བ་དང་པོ་གཉིས་ཡིན་ལ། འཕར་བ་གསུམ་པ་ནི་ཚངས་རིས་ནས་འབྲས་བུ་ཆེ་བའི་བར་འོག་མ་འོག་མའི་རྟེན་ལ་གོང་མ་གོང་མའི་སྙོམས་འཇུག་བསྐྱེད་ནས་ས་གོང་མ་རྣམས་སུ་སྐྱེ་ཞིང། འབྲས་བུ་ཆེ་བའི་རྟེན་ལ་སྤེལ་བསྒོམ་བསྐྱེད་[156]ནས་གནས་
D 306 གཙང་རྣམས་སུ་རིམ་[157]གྱིས་སྐྱེ་བའོ།

1321 །འོ་ན་སྤེལ་མ་བསྒོམ་པ་ཞེས་བྱ་བ་དེ། [158]རྟེན་ཇི་ལྟ་བུས་ཏིང་ངེ་འཛིན་
P117b གང་འདྲ་བ་ཞིག་བསྒོམ་པ་ཡིན་ཞེ་ན།རྟེན་ནི་ཕྱིར་མི་འོང་དང་[159]དགྲ་བཅོམ་པ་གཉིས་ཀའི་ཆ་ལུགས་རྣམ་གྲོལ་གྱིས་བསྒོམ་སྟེ། བསམ་གཏན་ཟག་མེད་དང་སྤེལ་དགོས་པས་འཕགས་པས་བསྒོམ་དགོས་ལ་རྒྱུན་ཞུགས་དང་ཕྱིར་འོང་རྣམས་ཀྱིས་བསྒོམ་མི་ནུས་ཏེ། དེ་དག་གིས་བསམ་གཏན་གྱི་དངོས་གཞི་མ་ཐོབ་པའི་ཕྱིར་རོ།། དེ་ཡང་དང་པོར་འདོད་པའི་རྟེན་ལ་བསྒོམ་ཞིང་ཕྱིས་ནི་གཟུགས་ཁམས་ཀྱི་རྟེན་ལ་བསྒོམས་ཏེ། ཇི་སྐད་དུ། མཛོད་འགྲེལ་ལས།

> དང་པོར་འདོད་པའི་ཁམས་སུ་གླིང་གསུམ་དག་ཏུ་སྤེལ་བར་བྱེད་ལ་ཕྱིས་ནི་ཡོངས་སུ་ཉམས་པས་གཟུགས་ཀྱི་ཁམས་སུ་སྤེལ་བར་བྱེད་དོ་

ཞེས་སོ།། དང་པོར་གང་སྤེལ་ན་བསམ་གཏན་བཞི་པ་ཁོ་ན་སྤེལ་ཏེ། [160]བསམ་གཏན་དེ་ནི་ཞི་ལྷག་ཆ་མཉམ་པས་ལམ་སྣ་བ་རྣམས་ཀྱི་མཆོག་ཡིན་པའི་ཕྱིར་དང་ཏིང་ངེ་འཛིན་ཐམས་ཅད་ཀྱི་ནང་ནས་ལས་སུ་རུང་ཤོས་ཡིན་པའི་ཕྱིར་རོ།། ཕྱིས་ནི་བསམ་གཏན་གཞན་རྣམས་དང་ཡང་སྤེལ་བར་བྱེད་དེ[161]། ཇི་[162]སྐད་དུ། མཛོད་འགྲེལ་ལས།

> དེ་ལྟར་བསམ་གཏན་བཞི་པ་སྤེལ་ནས་དེའི་སྟོབས་ཀྱིས་གཞན་

---

[156] bskyed D M] bskyad P | [157] rim D M] rims P | [158] / D M] om. / P | [159] om. / D M] insert / P | [160] / D M] om. / P | [161] de D M] ste P | [162] ji D M] ci P

Śuddhāvāsas, through the force of experiencing the taste of existence in the absorption of the first concentration, one backslides from the three upper concentrations. Then, having died from this [life] and reborn in *Brahmakāyika* heaven, there, through the force of previous familiarization with alternating cultivations in a desire realm embodiment, cultivates alternation of the fourth concentration causing one to be reborn in the *Śuddhāvāsas* heavens. This applies for the first two jumpers. The third jumper from *Brahmakāyika* heaven up to the *Bṛhatphala* heaven, having produced in lower embodiments higher and higher absorptions is reborn in upper states of existence, and in a *Bṛhatphala* heaven embodiment, having generated alternating cultivation, is gradually reborn in the *Śuddhāvāsas* heavens.

D306 Well then, in regards to this "alternating cultivations" what sort of embodiment cultivates such a unique meditative stabilization? That is cultivated by the Non-returner and liberated in two ways (*Ubhayatogbhāgavimutka*) Arhat embodiments and since it is necessary to alternate with uncontaminated concentration, the cultivation necessary for a Noble Being (*āryan*) is unable to be cultivated by the Stream-enterer and Once-returner because they do not attain an actual concentration. Also, one first cultivates in a desire realm embodiment and then later cultivates in a form realm embodiment. The *Abhidharmakośabhāṣya* states:

> First, alternating in the three continents in the desire realm; later, since falling away [one] makes alternation in the form realm.[71]

The first who alternates, alternates only the fourth concentration and it is that concentration, since equalizing quiescence (*śamatha*) and special insight (*vipaśyanā*) is the best of the easy paths and is the most suitable from among all meditative stabilizations. The later makes alternation with other concentrations. The *Abhidharmakośabhāṣya* states:

> Accordingly, having thus alternated the fourth concentration, by the force of this alternation, [a

[71] AKBh, Pruden, 976, Śāstrī, 961: *kāmadhātau triṣu dvīpeṣu prathamaṃ vyavakīryate paścāt parihīṇena rūpadhātau /*

དག་ཀྱང་སྤྱེལ་བར་བྱེད་དེ་
ཞེས་དང་། མཛོད་ལས།

དང་པོར་བཞི་པ་སྤྱེལ་བར་བྱེད།།[163]ཅེས་སོ།

།ཇི་[164]ལྟར་བྱས་པས་སྤྱེལ་བར་བྱེད་ཅེ་ན།།[165]འདི་ལ་སྤྱེལ་བའི་སྦྱོར་བ་
[166]དང།གྲུབ་པའི་དུས་གཉིས་སུ་འགྱུར་རོ།།དེ་ལ་སྦྱོར་བ་ནི་ཇི་[167]སྐད་
དུ།མཛོད་འགྲེལ་དུ་[168]
D 307 འདི་ལྟར་སྤྱེལ་བར་བྱེད་དེ་དགྲ་བཅོམ་པའམ་ཕྱིར་མི་འོང་བ་ཡང་
ཙང་ཟག་པ་མེད་པའི་བསམ་གཏན་བཞི་པ་རྒྱུན་དང་ལྡན་པ་སྙོམས་པར་
འཇུག་ཅིང་དེ་ལས་ལངས་ནས་དེ་ཉིད་ཟག་པ་དང་བཅས་པ་རྒྱུན་དང་ལྡན་
པ་ལ་སྙོམས་པར་འཇུག་ལ།ཡང་ཟག་པ་མེད་པ་ལ་སྙོམས་པར་འཇུག་སྟེ་དེ་
བཞིན་དུ་རྒྱུན་ཕྲི་ནས་གང་གི་ཚེ་སྐད་ཅིག་མ་[169]གཉིས་ཀྱི་ཟག་པ་མེད་པ་ལ་
P118a སྙོམས་པར་འཇུག་ཅིང་སྐད་ཅིག་མ་གཉིས་ཟག་པ་དང་བཅས་པ་ལ་སྙོམས་
པར་འཇུག་གོ།ཞེས་གྲགས་ཏེ་[170]འདི་ནི་སྤྱེལ་པའི་སྦྱོར་བ་ཡིན་ལོ་

1322 ཞེས་གསུངས་པའོ།།གྲུབ་པའི་དུས་ཀྱང་ཇི་[171]སྐད་དུ།མཛོད་འགྲེལ་
ལས།

བྱེ་བྲག་ཏུ་སྨྲ་བ་རྣམས་ན་རེ།གང་གི་ཚེ་ཟག་པ་མེད་པའི་སྐད་ཅིག་
མའི་མཇུག་ཐོགས་སུ་ཟག་པ་དང་བཅས་པ་མངོན་སུམ་དུ་བྱེད་
ཅིང་ཟག་པ་དང་བཅས་པའི་མཇུག་ཐོགས་སུ་ཡང་ཟག་པ་མེད་པ་
མངོན་སུམ་དུ་བྱེད་ལ་དེ་ལྟར་ན་ཟག་པ་དང་བཅས་པའི་སྐད་ཅིག་
མ་དང་ཟག་པ་མེད་པ་དག་དུ་[172]བསྲེས་པས་སྤྱེལ་བ་གྲུབ་པ་ཡིན་
ཏེ་

[163]/ / D M] om. / / P | [164]ji D M] ci P | [165]/ D M] om. / P | [166]sbyor ba D M] sngor ba P | [167]ji D M] ci P | [168]du D M] de P | [169]cig ma D M] cigs P | [170]grags te D P] grag ste M | [171]ji D M] ci P | [172]du D M] tu P

[72] AKBh, Pruden, 976, Śāstrī, 960-961: *evaṃ caturthaṃ dhyānaṃ vyavakīrya tadbalenānyānyapi vyavakīryante /*

[73] AK,vi.42a, Pruden, 975, Śāstrī, 960: *ākīryate caturthaṃ prāk /*

> Noble Being] also alternates the other concentrations.[72]

The *Abhidharmakośa* says:

> First, one alternates the fourth [concentration].[73]

What is alternated by doing this? For this there are two: the application of alternating and the time of achieving. For that, the application, is stated in the *Abhidharmakośabhāṣya*:

> In this manner, one causes to alternate, whatever suitable Arhat or Non-returner enters into absorption possessing in the mental continuum the fourth uncontaminated concentration, having left from that, enters into absorption possessing in the mental continuum the contaminated of the same [fourth concentration] and also enters into the absorption for the uncontaminated and likewise by such diminishes in the mental continuum the absorption to the uncontaminated for two moments and the absorption to the contaminated for two moments. This enumerates the application of alternating.[74]

Also the time of achieving as taught in the *Abhidharmakośabhāṣya*:

> The *Vaibhāṣikas* say: when, after taking up a moment of an uncontaminated, one makes the chief aim the contaminated, and after taking up a moment of the contaminated one makes as the chief aim the uncontaminated and accordingly by mixing a moment of the contaminated and uncontaminated thoughts alternation is achieved.[75]

---

[74] AKBh, Pruden, 975, Śāstrī, 960: *evaṃ ca punaḥ vyavakīryate arhannanāgāmī vā pravāhayuktamanāsravaṃ caturthaṃ dhyānaṃ samāpadyate tasmādvyutthāya pravāhayuktaṃ tadeva sāsravaṃ samāpadyate punaścānāsravam / evaṃ pravāhāprahāṇena yadā kila dvau kṣaṇāvanāsravau samāpadyate dvau sāsravau punaścānāsravau ayaṃ vyavakiraṇasya prayogaḥ /*

[75] AKBh, Pruden, 975-976, Śāstrī, 960: *yadā tvanāsravasya kṣaṇasyānantaraṃ sammukhīkaroti sāsravasyānāravam / evaṃ sāsravasya kṣaṇasyānāsravābhyāṃ miśraṇāt vyavakiraṇaṃ niṣpannaṃ bhavatīti vaibhāṣikāḥ /*

ཞེས་གསུངས་སོ།།དེ་ལྟར་ན་ལུགས་དེ་ནི་བྱེ་བྲག་ཏུ་སྨྲ་བའི་ལུགས་ཡིན་
པས་གྲག་དང་པོ་ཞེས་མ་རངས་པ་མཛད་ནས་སློབ་དཔོན་རང་གི་ལུགས་ནི་
ཇི་སྐད་དུ།མཛོད་འགྲེལ་ལས།

> སངས་རྒྱས་མ་གཏོགས་པས་སྐད་ཅིག་མ་སྤྱེལ་བར་མི་ནུས་ཏེ་དེའི་
> ཕྱིར་རྒྱུན་ཆགས་གསུམ་ལ་ཅི་སྲིད་འདོད་པར་སྐོམས་པར་འཇུག་
> པའི་སྒོ་ནས་ཇོགས་པ་ཡིན་ནོ་

ཞེས་བྱ་བར་ལྟའོ།།ཞེས་གྲུབ་པའི་ཚད་ཀྱང་རྒྱུན་ལྔན་གསུམ་ལ་འཇུག་
D 308 པ་ཡིན་ཞེས་གསུངས་པ་ཉིད་འཐད་ཕྱོགས་སུ་གཟུང་ངོ།
ཅིའི་ཕྱིར་སྤྱེལ་མ་བསྒོམ་ཞེ་ནཱ།ཕྱིར་མི་འོང་དབང་རྣོན་རྣམས་ནི་
གནས་གཙང་མར་སྐྱེ་བའི་ཆེད་དང།མཐོང་ཆོས་ལ་བདེ་བར་གནས་པའི་
ཆེད་དུ་བསྒོམ་མོ།།ཕྱིར་མི་འོང་དབང་རྟུལ་རྣམས་ནི་དགོས་པ་གོང་མར་སྐྱེ་
བ་[173]དང་ཉོན་མོངས་ཐག་བསྲིངས་པའི་སྒོ་ནས་མི་ཉམས་པར་བྱ་བའི་ཕྱིར་
རོ།།དགྲ་བཅོམ་པ་དབང་པོ་རྣོ་རྟུལ་རྣམས་ནི་རིམ་པ་ལྟར་མཐོང་ཆོས་ལ་
བདེ་བར་གནས་པའི་ཆེད་དང།ཉོན་མོངས་པས་འཇིགས་ནས་ཉམས་པ་
སྤངས་པའི་ཆེད་དུ་བསྒོམ་ཞེས་བྱེ་བྲག་ཏུ་སྨྲ་བ་འདོད་ཀྱང་དགྲ་བཅོམ་པའི་
P118b རྣམ་གྲོལ་མི་གཡོ་བས་ཉམས་མི་སྲིད་དེ་དེའི་ཆེད་དུ་བསྒོམ་མི་དགོས་སོ།།ཇི་
ལྟར་ཡང་མཛོད་ལས།

> སྐྱེས་དང་གནས་པར་བྱ་ཕྱིར་དང།།ཉོན་མོངས་པས་ནི་འཇིགས་
> ཕྱིར་ཡང།

།ཞེས་སོ།།དེ་ལྟར་ན་འབྲས་བུ་གནས་གཙང་མའི་སྐྱེ་བ་ལྟར་ངེས་
ཏེ།དེའི་རྒྱུ་སྤྱེལ་མར་བསྒོམ་པ་ལྔ་ངེས་པའི་ཕྱིར་ཏེ།མཛོད་ལས།

---

[173] skye ba D M] skya ba P

Accordingly, for that system the Āchārya [Vasubandhu] was dissatisfied with such talk, since it is the system of the *Vaibhāṣikas*; our own system as spoken from the *Abhidharmakośabhāṣya*:

> With the exception of a Buddha, it is impossible to alternate [thoughts] in a single moment, because of that, [alternation of concentrations] is achieved by means of entering, for as long as one wants into three continuous [concentrations].[76]

The view spoken above is the measure of achievement and to teach as entering for three continuous [concentration] is itself an
D308 agreeable opinion to hold.

For what purpose is alternating concentrations cultivated? The Non-returners with sharp faculties cultivates for the sake of birth in the *Śuddhāvāsas* heavens and for the sake of abiding in bliss for this life. Alternating concentrations are necessary for Non-returners with weak faculties so that they may not backslide from keeping afflictions distant and backslide from taking rebirth in the upper realms. Even though *Vaibhāṣikas* accept that Arhats with sharp faculties cultivate for the sake of abiding in bliss for this life and those with weak faculties cultivate for the sake of abandoning backsliding through fear of the afflictions, the immovable liberation of an Arhat does not backslide and it is not necessary to cultivate alternating cultivations for that purpose. The *Abhidharmkośa* states:

> Because of abiding [in bliss] and birth [in the *Śuddhāvāsas* heavens] and through fear of the afflictions.[77]

Along these lines, the result, rebirth in the *Śuddhāvāsas* heavens, is ascertained to be fivefold because the cause of that rebirth, alternating cultivations, is ascertained as fivefold. The *Abhidharmkośa* states:

---

[76]AKBh, Pk ṅu 029a.2, Poussin, 222, Pruden, 976, Śāstrī, 961: *aśakyaṃ tu kṣaṇavyavakiraṇamanyatra buddhāt ata icchātaḥ pravāhatrayasamāpattito niṣpannaṃ bhavati* (*iti paśyāmaḥ*) /

[77]AK,vi.42c-d, Pruden, 976, Śāstrī, 961: *upapattivihārāryaṃ kleśabhīrūtayāpi ca* /

དེ་ནི་རྣམ་པ་ལྔ་ཡི་ཕྱིར།།གནས་གཙང་སྐྱེ་བ་ལྔ་པོ་ན།

1323 །ཞེས་གསུངས་པའོ།།སྤེལ་མར་བསྒོམ་པ་ལྔ་གང་ཞེ་ན།ཇི་[174]སྐད་
དུ།མཛོད་འགྲེལ་ལས་

སྤེལ་མར་བསྒོམ་པ་དེ་ནི་ཆུང་ངུ་དང་།འབྲིང་དང་།ཆེན་པོ་དང་།ཤིན་
ཏུ་ཆེ་བ་དང་།ཆེས་ཤིན་ཏུ་ཆེ་བའི་བྱེ་བྲག་གིས་རྣམས་པ་[175]ལྔ་ཡིན་
ཏེ་

ཞེས་པའོ།།ཆུང་ངུ་ལ་སོགས་པ་དེ་ལྟ་བུ་ཞིག་སྤེལ་ཞེ་ན།ཇི་[176]སྐད་
དུ།མཛོད་འགྲེལ་ལས།

དང་པོ་ནི་ཟག་པ་མེད་པ་དང་།ཟག་པ་དང་བཅས་པ་དང་།ཟག་པ་
D 309 མེད་པ་དང་།སེམས་གསུམ་མངོན་དུ་བྱེད་དོ།།གཉིས་པ་ལ་ནི་དྲུག་
གོ།གསུམ་པ་ལ་ནི་དགུའོ།།བཞི་པ་ལ་ནི་བཅུ་གཉིས་སོ།།ལྔ་པ་ལ་ནི་
བཅོ་ལྔ་སྟེ་དེ་དག་གི་འབྲས་བུ་ནི་གྲངས་བཞིན་དུ་གནས་གཙང་མ་
ལྔ་ཡིན་ལ་དེ་ཡང་ཟག་པ་དང་བཅས་པ་གང་ཡིན་པ་དེའི་དབང་
གིས་དེ་དག་ཏུ་སྐྱེའོ།

།ཞེས་གསུངས་པའོ།།དོན་འདི་ལ་གངས་ཅན་གྱི་ཆོས་མངོན་པ་བ་།སྔར་
ཐང་བ་བསམས་པ་ཟངས།ཁ་ཅིག་གཉིས་པ་མན་ཆད་ལ་སྤེལ་བའི་ཚུལ་ནི་
ཟག་མེད་གཉིས་ཟག་བཅས་གཉིས་ཡང་ཟག་མེད་གཉིས་བྱས་པས་དྲུག་
སྤེལ།ཟག་མེད་གསུམ་ཟག་བཅས་གསུམ་ཡང་ཟག་མེད་གསུམ་བྱས་པས་དགུ་
སྤེལ་སོགས་སུ་འདོད་པ་ནི་བཞིན་གྱི་གཉེར་མ་ལྟར་འགྲིག་པ་[177]ལྟར་སྣང་
ཡང་བསྟན་བཅོས་མཛད་པ་པོའི་བཞེད་པ་མ་ཡིན་ཏེ།འདི་ལྟར་སློབ་དཔོན་
P119a གྱིས།གསུམ་སྤེལ་ལ་ཟག་མེད་གཅིག་ཟག་བཅས་གཅིག་[178]ཟག་མེད་གཅིག་སྟེ་
གསུམ་སྤེལ་ལུགས་བསྟན་ནས་འོག་མ་རྣམས་ལ་ཡང་སྤེལ་ལུགས་དེ་པོ་ན་
སྦྱར་བར་དགོངས་ནས་གྲངས་ཙམ་སྨོས་ལ།[179]འགྲེལ་བཤད་དུའང་།

[174]ji D M] ci P | [175]rnams pa D M] rnam pa P | [176]ji D M] ci P | [177]’grig pa D M] ’grag pa P | [178]om. / D M] insert / P | [179]/ D M] om. / P

> There are only five [types] of rebirth in the *Śuddhāvāsas* heavens because of five types of this [alternating concentrations].[78]

What are the five cultivations for alternation? The *Abhidharmakośabhāṣya* says:

> The cultivation for alternation is fivefold: weak, moderate, strong, stronger, and strongest.[79]

What is the alternation in the five, weak and so forth? The *Abhidharmakośabhāṣya* states:

> In the first one actualizes three thoughts, contaminated, uncontaminated, and contaminated; in the second six thoughts; in the third nine thoughts; in the fourth twelve thoughts; in the fifth fifteen thoughts. In enumerating the results of these are the five *Śuddhāvāsas* heaven [rebirths]. They are produced by the power of contaminated moments in the cultivations. [80]

For this meaning, some Tibetan *Ābhidhārmika*s [, those from *sNar-thang*,] say the method of alternating for the lower two are six alternations by making two uncontaminated, two contaminated, and two uncontaminated [thoughts]; the nine alternations by making three uncontaminated, three contaminated, and three uncontaminated, etc. This assertion appears about as suitable as a frowning face. It is not the view of the *śāstra* writers. So Ācārya [Vasubandhu] for three alternations [states] one uncontaminated, one contaminated, and one uncontaminated; having taught the method alternating three, [he] merely enumerates with the intention to apply only that method for the upper alternations. The *Abhidharmakośabhāṣyavyākhyā* says:

---

[78] AK, vi. 43a-b, Pruden, 976, Śāstrī, 961: *tat pāñcavidhyāt pañcaiva śuddhāvāsopapattayaḥ* / | [79] AKBh, Pruden, 977, Śāstrī, 961: *sā hi vyavakīrṇabhāvanā pañcaprakārā mṛdumadhyādhimātrataratamabhedāt* /

[80] AKBh on AK,vi.43a-b, Pruden, 977, Śāstrī, 961-962, Pradhan, 363: *prathamāyāṃ trīṇicittāni sammukhīkriyante anāsravam sāsravam anāsravaṃ ca / dvitīyāyāṃ ṣaṭ tṛtīyāyaṃ nava caturtthāṃ dvādaśa / pañcamyāṃ pañcadaśa tāsāṃ yathāsaṃkhyaṃ pañca śuddhāvāsāḥ phalam / yattatra sāsravaṃ tadvaśāt teṣūpapattiḥ* /

གཉིས་པ་ལ་ནི་དྲུག་གོ་ཞེས་བྱ་བ་ནི་ཟག་པ་མེད་པ་དང།ཟག་པ་
དང་བཅས་པ་དང།ཟག་པ་མེད་པ་ཞེས་བྱ་བ་གསུམ་དང་ཡང་ཟག
པ་མེད་པ་དང།ཟག་པ་དང་བཅས་པ་དང།ཟག་པ་མེད་པ་ཞེས་བྱ་
བ་གསུམ་སྟེ་དྲུག་ཡིན་ནོ།གསུམ་པ་ལ་ནི་དགུའོ།[180]།བཞི་པ་ལ་ནི་
བཅུ་གཉིས་སོ།།[181]ལྔ་པ་ལ་ནི་བཅོ་ལྔ་སྟེ་ཞེས་བྱ་བ་ལ་ཡང་དེ་ཁོ་ན་
D 310 བཞིན་སྦྱར་བར་བྱའོ་

1324 ཞེས་གསུངས་པའི་ཕྱིར་རོ།།སྤྱེལ་ལུགས་དེ་ལྟར་ཡིན་ན་གསུམ་སྤྱེལ་
ནུས་པས་ལྷག་མ་ཐམས་ཅད་ཀྱང་སྤྱེལ་ནུས་པར་འགྱུར་ཏེ།དང་པོའི་སྤྱེལ་
ལུགས་དེ་ལས་གཞན་མེད་པའི་ཕྱིར་རོ་ཞེ་ན་སྐྱོན་མེད་དེ།དཀྱུས་ཐོགས་རེ་ལ་
གསུམ་སྤྱེལ་ནུས་ཀྱི་དྲུག་མ་ཡིན་པ་དང།དྲུག་སྤྱེལ་ནུས་ཀྱི་དགུ་སྤྱེལ་མི་ནུས་
པ་ལྟ་བུའི་སྒོ་ནས་སྤྱེལ་བསྒོམ་རྣམས་སོ་སོར་འཛོག་པའི་ཕྱིར་ཏེ།ཇི་[182]སྐད་
དུ།རྒྱལ་པོ་སྲས་ཀྱིས།

།་སེམས་གསུམ་ཞེས་བྱ་བ་ནི་གང་ཟག་དེ་ལ་ནུས་པ་དེ་ཙམ་ཞིག
ཡོད་པ་སྟེ།དེ་བཞིན་དུ་འོག་མ་རྣམས་ལ་ཡང་བརྗོད་པར་བྱའོ།

།ཞེས་འབྱུང་ངོ།།འོག་མིན་གྱི་མཐར་ཐུག་པར་འགྲོ་བ་བཤད་ཟིན་ཏོ།།
།།སྲིད་པའི་རྩེ་མོའི་མཐར་ཐུག་པར་འགྲོ་བ་གང་ཞེ་ན།གོང་དུ་འཕོ་བ་
གང་ཚངས་རིས་ནས་ཚང་ཆེན་མ་གཏོགས་པ་འབྲས་བུ་ཆེ་བའི་བར་ཐམས་
ཅད་དུ་བརྒྱུད་ཅིང་དེ་ནས་གཟུགས་མེད་བཞིར་རིམ་[183]གྱིས་སོང་ནས་མཐར་
སྲིད་རྩེའི་རྟེན་ལ་འདའ་བའི་རིགས་ཅན་ཏེ།འགྲེལ་པར

གོང་དུ་འཕོ་བ་བསམ་གཏན་མ་སྤྱེལ་བ་ནི་སྲིད་པའི་རྩེ་མོའི་མཐར་
P119b ཐུག་པ་ཡིན་ཏེ་དེ་ནི་སྙོམས་པར་འཇུག་པ་གཞན་རྣམས་རོ་མྱང་
བར་བྱེད་ཅིང་གནས་གཞན་ཐམས་ཅད་དུ་སྐྱེ་ལ་གནས་གཙང་མ
རྣམས་སུ་མི་འཇུག་པ་ཁོ་ནར་གཟུགས་མེད་པར་སྐྱེ་བའི་རིམ་

[180]/ D M] om. / P | [181]// D M] om. // P | [182]ji D M] ci P | [183]rim D M] rims P

> Saying 'in the second six [thoughts]' the three are thus uncontaminated, contaminated, and uncontaminated and again uncontaminated, contaminated, and uncontaminated thus are the six [thoughts]. It is just this application likewise for 'in the third nine, in the fourth twelve, in the fifth fifteen.' [81]

D310 If it is that method of alternating, because [one] is able to alternate three one will by able to alternate also all the remaining because there is not other than that method of alternating the first. Why is it without fault? With regard to length, the alternating cultivations are individually posited by means of the ability to alternate three but not six or the ability to alternate six but not the ability to alternate nine. Jinaputra [Yaśomitra] states:

> 'three thoughts' is said for such a person as long as one is able and likewise declared for those above [three].[82]

This finishes the explanation of the transmigrator to the limits of *Akaniṣṭha* heaven.

Who is the transmigrator to the limit of the Peak of Existence (*bhavāgraparamaga*)? An *Ūrdhvaṃsrotas* who, from *Brahmakāyika* heaven, not counting *Mahābrahma* heaven, is connected in all [heavens] up to the *Bṛhatphala* heaven, from that, having gone gradually in the four formless [realms], possesses the lineage of attaining *nirvāṇa* in an embodiment of the Peak of Existence (*Bhavāgra*). From the *Abhidharmakośabhāṣya:*

> The *Ūrdhvaṃsrotas* who does not alternate concentration reaches the limit of the Peak of Existence. Caused to taste the other absorptions [one] is reborn in all other abodes but does not enter only the *Śuddhāvāsas*; successively born in the

---

[81] AKV, Śāstrī, 961-962: *'dvitīyāyāṃ ṣaditi' anāsravaṃ sāsravamanāsravamiti trīṇi punaranāsravaṃ sāsravamanāsravamityaparāṇi trīṇīti ṣad bhavanti evameva ca tṛīyāyāṃ nava caturtthāṃ dvādaśa pañcamyāṃ pañcadaśeti yojyam /*

[82] AKV, Śāstrī, 961: (*prathamāyāṃ*) *trīṇi cittānīti tasya pudgalasya tāvatī śaktirityevamupariṣṭādapi vaktavyam /*

[184]གྱིས་སྲིད་པའི་རྩེ་མོར་སོང་སྟེ་ཡོངས་སུ་མྱ་ངན་ལས་འདའོ་

ཞེས་གསུངས་པའོ། །འཕར་བ་གསུམ་དང་འདི་བཞི་ངེས་པར་འོག་མིན་
D 311 དང་སྲིད་རྩེར་འགྲོ་མི་དགོས་པ་ནི་གོང་དུ་ལན་བདུན་པའི་སྐབས་སུ་འགྲེལ་
པའི་ལུང་དྲངས་པ་ལས་ཤེས་པར་བྱའོ། ། །འདི་ལ་ཁ་ཅིག་འཕར་གསུམ་ངེས་
པར་འགྲོ་ཕྱིར་འོག་མིན་དུ་མཐར་ཐུག་འགྲོ་ལ་འོག་མིན་དུ་འགྲོ་བའི་ངེས་མ་
[185]མེད་ཅེས་པ་ནི་མི་འཐད་པར་རྟོགས་ཏེ། འཕར་གསུམ་འགྲོ་ལས་གཞན་པའི་
འོག་མིན་འགྲོ་ནི་མཁས་པའི་གཞུང་ལུགས་གང་ལས་ཀྱང་མི་འབྱུང་བའི་ཕྱིར་
རོ། །དེ་ལྟར་ན་མངོན་པ་མཛོད་དུ[186]། འོག་མིན་དུ་འགྲོ་བ་ལ་འཕར་བ་གསུམ་
1325 གྱི་རྣམ་གཞག་མཛད་ལ། མངོན་པ་ཀུན་ལས་བཏུས་ལས་ནི།

གོང་དུ་འཕོ་བ་གང་ཞེ་ན། གང་གཟུགས་ཀྱི་ཁམས་སུ་ས་ནས་སར་སྐྱེ་ཞིང་འོག་མིན་གྱི་བར་དུ་ཞུགས་ནས་དེར་ལམ་མངོན་དུ་བྱས་ཏེ་སྡུག་བསྔལ་གྱི་ཐ་མ་འཐོབ་པའོ། །ལ་ལ་ནི་སྲིད་པའི་རྩེ་མོའི་བར་དུ་སོང་ནས་ལམ་མངོན་དུ་བྱས་ཏེ་[187]སྡུག་བསྔལ་གྱི་ཐ་མ་འཐོབ་པའོ།

།ཞེས་སྲིད་རྩེར་འགྲོ་དང་འོག་མིན་འགྲོ་ལ་ཡང་འཕར་བ་གསུམ་པ་ལས་འཕར་བ་དང་པོ་གཉིས་ཀྱི་རྣམ་གཞག་མ་མཛད་པར་སྣང་བའི་དགོངས་པ་ནི་བརྟག་དཀའ་བར་འདུག་སྟེ། འདི་ལྟར་ཤུགས་ཀྱིས་གོ་བས་མ་སློས་པ་ནི་མ་ཡིན་ཏེ། གཟུགས་ཀྱི་ས་ཐམས་ཅད་དུ་སྐྱེ་བ་བསྟན་པས་འཕར་བ་དང་པོ་གཉིས་གོ་བ་ལ་ནུས་པ་མེད་པའི་ཕྱིར་དང༌། བར་དོ་འདའ་བ་གསུམ་ལ་ཡང་གང་རུང་གཅིག་[188]སྟོན་པར་ཐལ་བའི་ཕྱིར་རོ། །ཆོས་མངོན་

[184]rim D M] rims P | [185]nges ma D M] ngas pa P | [186]du D M] pu P | [187]om. / D M] insert / P | [188]gcig D M] cig P

[83]AKBh, Pruden, 969, Śāstrī, 952: *avyavakīrṇadhyāna ūrdhvaṃsrotā bhavāgraniṣṭtobhavati sa hi samāpattyantarāṇyāsvādayan sarvasthānāntareṣūpapadyāpraviśyaiva śuddhāvāsānārūpyakramotpattito bhavāgraṃ gatvā parinirvāti /*

[84] Supra, folio 274.4, AKBh, Pk ṅu 26b.7-8, Pruden, 969, Śāstrī, 953: *antarāpi tu*

> formless realms [one] goes to the Peak of Existence and actualizes *nirvāṇa*.[83]

The three jumpers and this fourth one do not necessarily transmigrate to *Bhavāgra* or to *Akaniṣṭha*, one should understand this from the cited scripture of the commentary in the above section on the
D311 seven-timer.[84] Regarding this, someone says, "the three jumpers do definitely transmigrate to *Akaniṣṭha* heaven, but generally the transmigrator to the limit of *Akaniṣṭha* does not definitely transmigrate to *Akaniṣṭha* heaven." This is not correctly understood because a transmigrator to *Akaniṣṭha* heaven other than the three kinds of Jumper transmigrators does not at all occur from whichever master's textual system. Along these lines, the *Abhidharmakośa* gives a presentation of three jumpers for the transmigrator up to *Akaniṣṭha* and the *Abhidharmasamuccaya* states:

> Who is the *Ūrdhvaṃsrotas*? One who, being born enters the domain of *Akaniṣṭha* heaven, having passed through the various levels in the form realm, and there actualizes the path and attains the end of suffering. Some also, having gone up to the Peak of Existence, actualize the path and attain the end of suffering.[85]

Thus the purport of the passage does not appear to construe the presentation of *Bhavāgraparamaga* and *Akaniṣṭhaga* with the first two jumpers among the three jumpers. This is difficult to examine and cannot be understood implicitly because there is not the ability to understand the first two jumpers because the text indicates rebirth in all levels of the form realm and because of the consequence of showing one as suitable for whichever three *Antarāparinirvāyin*s. One

---

parinirvāṇamūrdhvasrotaso yujyamānaṃ paśyāmaḥ / akaniṣṭabhavāgraparamatvaṃ tu pareṇa gatyabhāvād / yathā saptakṛtvaḥ paramatvaṃ srotaāpannasyeti / "in the period for those *ū*rdhvaṃsrotas also we view as suitable for *nirvāṇa* because the transmigrators to Akaniṣṭha heaven and the Peak of Existence are without transmigrating [necessarily] up to those [realms]. For example, as like the Saptakṛtvaparamaḥ Stream-enterer."

[85] AS, Rahula, 156, Pradhan, 90: *ūrddhvaṃsrotāḥ katamaḥ / upapanno rūpāvacarāṇāṃ bhūmau bhūmau yāvadakaniṣṭagān praviśya tatrānāsravamārgaṃ saṃmukhīkṛtya duḥkhasyāntamanuprāpoti / puna kaṣcid yāvad bhavāgragān mārgaṃ saṃmukhīkṛtya duḥkhasyāntamanuprāpnoti /*

P120a པའི་མདོ་ཁུངས་མ་རྣམས་ནས་འདི་དག་མ་གསུངས་ལ་བྱེ་བྲག་ཏུ་སྨྲ་བའི་
རང་བཟོ་ཡིན་པའི་ཕྱིར་ཞེས་ཀྱང་སྨྲ་མི་ནུས་ཏེ།མངོན་པར་རྟོགས་པའི་རྒྱན་
D 312 དུ་ཡང་འཕར་བ་གསུམ་མི་གསུངས་པར་འགྱུར་བའི་ཡང་ཕྱིར་རོ།མངོན་
རྟོགས་རྒྱན་དུ་གསུངས་པ་དེ་[189]གཞན་དྲང་བའི་ཆེད་ཡིན་པས་མི་མཚུངས་
པ་ཡང་མ་ཡིན་ཏེ།དེ་ལྟར་ཡིན་ན་རྒྱན་དུ་དུས་གསུམ་རྫས་སུ་གྲུབ་པ་ལ་
སོགས་པའི་རྣམ་གཞག་དང།ལམ་རྒྱུད་ལ་བསྐྱེད་ཚུལ་གྱི་རྣམ་གཞག་རྣམས་
ཀྱང་བྱེ་བྲག་ཏུ་སྨྲ་བ་དང་སྒོ་བསྟུན་པར་འགྱུར་བའི་ཕྱིར་རོ།།དེས་ན་བྱེ་བྲག་
ཏུ་སྨྲ་བ་རྣམས་ནི་སྐྱེས་བུ་དམ་པའི་འགྲོ་བ་བདུན་བསྟན་པའི་མདོ་ལས་གོང་
དུ་འཕོ་བ་གཅིག་ཏུ་བགྲངས་པ་[190]ནི།མཛོད་ལས།

གོང་འཕོ་བ་མ་ཕྱེ་བར།།དམ་པའི་འགྲོ་བ་བདུན་དུ་འདོད།

།ཅེས་འདོད་ལ།སློབ་དཔོན་ཐོགས་མེད་ནི་མདོ་དེ་ལས་གོང་འཕོ་ལ་
འཕར་བ་རྣམས་ཀྱི་རྣམ་གཞག་མ་མཛད་པའི་རྗེས་སུ་འབྲང་བ་ཡིན་ནམ་
སྙམ་སྟེ་འདི་ནི་ཤེས་ལྡན་དག་གིས་དཔྱད་དགོས་པ་ཞིག་གོ །དེ་[191]ནི་འདི་
དཔྱད་དེ་ཅི་གཟུགས་སུ་ཉེར་འགྲོ་ཐམས་ཅད་འདོད་པའི་རྟེན་ཅན་ནོ་ཞེས་
1326 ཁྱོད་ཀྱི་སྨྲས་པ་མི་འཐད་དེ།[192]བར་དོར་འདའ་བ་ལ་ཉིས་སྟོང་ལྔ་བརྒྱ་དགུ་
བཅུ་རྩ་གཉིས་སུ་འབྱེད་པ་ནི།མཛོད་འགྲེལ་ལས།

དེ་དག་ཉིད་སའི་བྱེ་བྲག་གིས་[193]བཞིའོ[194]།
།ཞེས་དང།[195]

གནས་གཞན་གྱི་བྱེ་བྲག་གིས་བཅུ་དྲུག་གོ

།[196]ཞེས་བསམ་གཏན་བཞིའི་བར་དོར་འདའ་བ་བཞི་དང།ཚངས་ཆེན་
མ་གཏོགས་པའི་བར་དོར་འདའ་བ་བཅུ་དྲུག་གསུངས་པའི་ཕྱིར་རོ་ཞེ་ན་
ཉེས་པ་མེད་དེ།[197]འདོད་པའི་རྟེན་ཅན་གྱི་ཕྱིར་མི་འོང་བར་དོར་འདའ་བ་དེ་
ལ་བསམ་གཏན་དང་པོའི་བར་དོར་འདའ་བ་ལ་སོགས་པ་བཞི།[198]ཚངས་

---

[189] de D M] da P | [190] bsgrangs pa D M] dgrangs pa P | [191] de D M] da P | [192] om. / D M] insert / P | [193] gis M P] gi D | [194] bzhi'o M P] gzhi'o D | [195] / D M] om. / P | [196] / D M] om. / P | [197] / D M] om. / P | [198] / D M] om. / P

is also not able to say that it is the work of the *Vaibhāṣika*s in not
stating these from the source *sūtra*s of the Abhidharma because in the
D312 *Abhisamayālaṃkāra* the three jumpers are also are not mentioned.
That which is taught in the *Abhisamayālaṃkāra* is similar on account of drawing from other sources and it is in this way, because in the [*Abhisamaya*]*alaṃkāra* even the presentation of those who say the three times substantially exist, etc. and the presentations of the manner to generate the path in the mental continuum agree with the *Vaibhāṣika*s method. Therefore, the *Vaibhāṣika*s enumerate a single *Ūrdhvaṃsrotas* from the *sūtra* that discusses seven transmigrations of holy individuals. The *Abhidharmakośa* states:

> In not distinguishing the *Ūrdhvaṃsrotas* there are seven transmigrations of the holy.[86]

Ācārya Asaṅga is a follower of the arrangement of the jumpers and *Ūrdhvaṃsrotas* from the intention of that *sūtra*. Those possessing understanding should examine this.

Now, examining this, it is wrong for you to say "all transmigrators in the form realm possess an embodiment of the desire realm," for the *Antāraparinirvāyin* is categorized into two thousand five hundred and ninety two. The *Abhidharmakośabhāṣya* states:

> These themselves are four by the division of ground.[87]
>
> and
>
> Sixteen by division of other abodes.[88]

Thus how can there be a fault because there are four *Antarāparinirvāyin*s of the four concentrations (*dhyāna*s) and sixteen *Antarāparinirvāyin*s of the [form realms] not including *Mahābrahma*? The Non-returner *Antarāparinirvāyin* who possesses a desire realm embodiment conveys the meaning of the four *Antāparinirvāyin* of the

[86] AK vi.40b, Pruden 972, Śāstrī, 956, Gokhale, 94(vi.41d): *ūrdhvaṃsroturabhedana sapta sadgatayomataḥ /*

[87] AKBh on AK,vi.43c-d, Pk ṅu 029b8, Pruden, 979, Śāstrī, 363: *bhūmibhedāccatvāraḥ* / Delhi edition (1975) reads *gzhi*, "basis" which I have corrected to *bzhi*, "four" to agree with canonical and Tsong kha pa (f.120a6) Peking edition: *de dag nyid sa'i bye brag gi bzhi'o /* |

[88] AKBh on AK,vi.43c-d, Pk nyu 029b8, Pruden, 979, Śāstrī, 363: *sthānāntarabhedāt ṣoḍaśa /*

D 313 རིས་ལ་སོགས་པའི་བར་དོར་སྐྱེས་ནས་འདའ་བ་བཅུ་དྲུག་ཅེས་པའི་དོན་
ཡིན་གྱི།[199]

P120b གཟུགས་ཁམས་ཀྱི་བར་སྲིད་དུ་ཉིང་མཚམས་སྦྱོར་ཟིན་པ་རྣམས་དང་
སྐྱེ་སྲིད་དུ་ཉིང་མཚམས་སྦྱོར་ཟིན་པ་རྣམས་ཉེར་འགྲོའི་བར་དོ་དང་སྐྱེས་
ནས་འདའ་བ་དང་གོང་འཕོར་མི་འདོད་དོ།།དེ་ལྟ་མ་ཡིན་ན།མཛོད་ལས།

> གསུམ་ལ་རྣམ་གསུམ་ཕྱེ་ནས་ནི།།གཟུགས་སུ་ཉེ་བར་འགྲོ་བ་
> དགུར།།བཤད་དོ་དེ་དག་ཁྱད་པར་རྣམས།།ལས་དབང་ཉོན་མོངས་
> བྱེ་བྲག་ལས།

།ཞེས་བར་དོར་འདའ་བ་གསུམ་མངོན་པར་འགྲུབ་པའི་ལས་ཅན་
དང་།སྐྱེས་ནས་འདའ་བ་གསུམ་སྐྱེས་ནས་སྦྱོང་འགྱུར་དང་།འཕར་བ་གསུམ་
ལན་གྲངས་གཞན་ལ་སྦྱོང་འགྱུར་གྱི་ལས་ཅན་དུ་གསུངས་པ་རྣམས་མི་རིགས་
པར་འགྱུར་ཏེ།བར་སྲིད་གྲུབ་ཟིན་པ་དེ་ད་གཟོད་བར་[200]སྲིད་འགྲུབ་པ་མི་
སྲིད་པའི་ཕྱིར་དང་།གཟུགས་ཁམས་སུ་སྐྱེས་ཟིན་པའི་སྐྱེས་ནས་འདའ་བ་དེ་
ཡང་སྲིད་ལེན་མི་སྲིད་པའི་ཕྱིར་དང་།ཁམས་གོང་དུ་སྐྱེས་ཟིན་གྱི་འཕར་བ་
དང་པོ་དེས་སྐྱེ་བ་གཉིས་ལེན་མི་སྲིད་པའི་ཕྱིར་རོ།།གཞན་ཡང་ཀུན་ལས་
བཏུས་སུ།བར་དོར་འདའ་བ་དེ་སྐྱེ་སྲིད་འགྲུབ་པའི་ཀུན་སྦྱོར་ཟད་ཅིང་བར་
སྲིད་འགྲུབ་པའི་ཀུན་སྦྱོར་མ་ཟད་པར་བསྟན་པ་དང་།སྐྱེས་[201]ནས་འདའ་བ་
དེ་ཀུན་སྦྱོར་གཉིས་ཀ་མ་ཟད་པར་བསྟན་པ་ཡང་མི་འཐད་པར་འགྱུར་
1327 ཏེ།གཟུགས་ཀྱི་བར་སྲིད་དང་སྐྱེ་སྲིད་དུ་ཉིང་མཚམས་སྦྱོར་ཟིན་པའི་ཕྱིར་མི་
D 314 འོང་རྣམས་ནི་རིམ་པ་ལྟར་ལྟར་ད་གཟོད་བར་[202]སྲིད་འགྲུབ་པ་དང་སྐྱེ་སྲིད་
འགྲུབ་པའི་ཀུན་སྦྱོར་ཟད་པའི་ཕྱིར་ཏེ།དེ་དག་ཚེ་དེ་ལ་མྱ་ངན་ལས་འདའ་
བའི་ཕྱིར་དང་།ཁམས་གོང་མར་སྐྱེས་ཟིན་པའི་ཕྱིར་མི་འོང་རྣམས་ལ་གཟུགས་
སུ་ཉེར་འགྲོ་དང་།གཟུགས་མེད་ཉེར་འགྲོའི་སྒྲའི་དོན་ཡང་མེད་པའི་ཕྱིར་རོ།

---

[199] / D M] om. / P | [200] gzod bar D M] bzong bar P | [201] skyes D M] skya P | [202] gzod bar D M] bzod bar P

first concentration, etc. and there are sixteen in the intermediate state of *Brahmakāyika* heaven and so forth.

D313 However, the bonds to take rebirth in an intermediate state of the form realm and the bonds to take a rebirth-existence are not asserted for the *Antarāparinirvāyin*, *Upapadyaparinirvāyin*, or *Ūrdhvaṃsrotas* who transmigrates [in the form realm]. So if that is not the case, [then the statements] from the *Abhidharmakośa* that,

> "it is taught as nine transmigrators in the form realm, through dividing three aspects among the three, their differences from divisions of karmas, faculties, and afflictions,"[89]

regarding the three *Antāparinirvāyin* who possess the karma of coming into being (*abhinirvṛttikarma*), the three *Upapadyaparinirvāyin*s who have karma which will experience rebirth (*upapadyavedanīyakarma*), and the three jumpers taught to possess karma which will be experienced at another time (*aparaparyāyavedanīyakarma*) will not be correct and because that which established an intermediate existence will not possibly achieve an intermediate existence, and the *Upapadyaparinirvāyin* who is bonded to rebirth in the form realm also is not possible to take an existence, and the first jumper who is bonded to take rebirth in the upper realms is not possible to take two rebirths. Moreover, in the *Abhidharmasamuccaya*, the *Antarāparinirvāyin* that is shown to exhaust the fetters of coming into rebirth but not the fetters of coming into existence and that *Upapadyparinirvāyin* who is shown to exhaust both fetters will also be incorrect and the Non-returners who are bonded to take a rebirth existence and intermediate state existence of
D314 the form realm, now successively because of exhausting the fetters of coming into an intermediate state existence and coming into a rebirth existence, those at that time actualize *nirvāṇa* and the Non-returners who are bonded by rebirth in the upper realms will not even have the meaning of the word transmigrator in the form realm and transmigrator in the formless realm.

[89] AK, vi.39a-d, Pruden, 970-971, Śāstrī, 953, 955: *punastriṃstrividhān kṛtvā nava rūpopagāḥ smṛtāḥ tadviśeṣaḥ punaḥ karmakleśendriyaviseṣataḥ* /

།ཅི་བར་དོར་འདའ་བ་ནི་ཕྱིར་མི་འོང་ཁོ་ན་ལ་ཡོད་དམ་འོན་ཏེ་ཕྱིར་
P121a འོང་དང་རྒྱུན་ཞུགས་ལ་ཡང་ཡོད་ཅེ་ན།ཕྱིར་འོང་དང་རྒྱུན་ཞུགས་ལ་ནི་བར་
དོར་འདའ་བ་མེད་དོ།།དེ་ཅིའི་ཕྱིར་ཞེ་ན།ལམ་ལ་ཆེས་རིང་དུ་འདྲིས་པར་མ་
བྱས་པ་དང་།ཉོན་མོངས་པ་རྣམས་ཆེས་ཆུང་བ་མ་ཡིན་པའི་ཕྱིར་རོ།ཞེས་པ་
ནི་སློབ་དཔོན་གྱི་ལན་ནོ།།།རྒྱུན་ཞུགས་དང་ཕྱིར་འོང་འདིས་ནི་འདོད་པའི་
ཉོན་མོངས་མི་དགེ་བ་དང་།ཁམས་གོང་གི་ཉོན་མོངས་སྒྲིབ་ལ་ལུང་མ་བསྟན་
རྣམས་སྤང་དགོས་པས་སྤང་བྱ་མང་བ་དང་།རྒྱུན་ཞུགས་ཀྱིས་[203]ནི་འབྲས་བུ་
གསུམ་དང་།ཕྱིར་འོང་གིས་འབྲས་བུ་གཉིས་ཐོབ་པར་བྱ་དགོས་པས་ཐོབ་བྱ་
མང་བ་དང་།གཉིས་ཀས་ཀྱང་ཁམས་གསུམ་ཆར་ལས་འདའ་བར་བྱ་དགོས་
པའི་འདའ་བར་བྱ་བ་མང་པོ་ཡོད་པས་ན་དེ་རྣམས་སྲིད་པ་བར་མ་དུས་
ཐུང་ངུར་གནས་པ་དེ་དག་གིས་བྱ་མི་ནུས་ཤིང་[204]ཕྱིར་མི་འོང་ནི་སྤང་བྱ་
ཐོབ་བྱ་[205]འདའ་བར་བྱ་བ་རྣམས་ཉུང་བའི་ཕྱིར་རོ་ཞེས་པ་ནི་བྱེ་བྲག་ཏུ་སྨྲ་
བ་རྣམས་ཀྱི་ལན་ཡིན་ཏེ།འགྲེལ་བར་ཡང་

ཅིའི་ཕྱིར་སློབ་པ་འདོད་ཆགས་དང་མ་བྲལ་བར་མ་དོར་ཡོངས་སུ་
མྱ་ངན་ལས་འདའ་བར་མི་འགྱུར་ཞེ་ན།[206]ལམ་མ་འདྲིས་པ་ལས་
D 315 མངོན་སུམ་དུ་མི་འགྱུར་བའི་ཕྱིར་དང་།ཕྲ་རྒྱས་རྣམས་ཤིན་ཏུ་ཆུང་
བ་མ་ཡིན་པའི་ཕྱིར་རོ།།བྱེ་བྲག་ཏུ་སྨྲ་བ་རྣམས་ན་རེ།འདོད་པའི་
ཁམས་ལས་འདའ་བར་དཀའ་བའི་ཕྱིར་ཏེ་ཉོན་མོངས་པ་མི་དགེ་
བ་དང་ལུང་དུ་མ་བསྟན་པ་སྤངས་པ་དང་།དགེ་སྦྱོང་གི་ཚུལ་གྱི་
འབྲས་བུ་གཉིས་སམ་གསུམ་འཐོབ་པ་དང་།།ཁམས་གསུམ་ལས་
1328 ཡང་དག་པར་འདའ་བ་དང་[207]མང་པོའི་ཞིག་བྱ་དགོས་ལ་དེ་ཡང་
སྲིད་པ་བར་མ་ལ་གནས་པས་བྱ་བར་མི་ནུས་སོ་ཞེས་ཟེར་རོ།

།ཞེས་སོ།།[208]།དེ་ལྟར་བྱས་ན་ཆེས་ཉུང་ངུར་ཡང་འགྱུར་རོ་ཞེས་པའི་

---

[203]kyis D M] kyi P | [204]shing D M] cing P | [205]thob bya D M] tho bya P | [206]/ D M] om. / P | [207]om. / D M] insert / P | [208]/ / D M] om. / / P

Is the *Antāraparinirvāyin* only a Non-returner or is it also a Stream-enterer and Once-returner? The Stream-enterer and Once-returner results do not have an *Antāraparinirvāyin*. Why is that? Ācārya [Vasubandhu] replies, "Because of not being accustomed for very long on the path and not having less afflictions." The reply of the *Vaibhāṣika*s is "because the Stream-enterer and Once-returner have the non-virtuous affliction of the desire realm and they have many abandonments since it is necessary to abandon the obscurational afflictions of the upper realms not demonstrated in the scripture, and [they have] many results to acquire since it is necessary for the Stream-enterer to attain three results and the Once-returner to attain two results, and since both have many [realms] to pass over that are necessary in passing over the three realms; these realms are unable to be made by them because [they] abide in the intermediate state for a short time and because a Non-returner has fewer abandonments, [results] to obtain, and [realms] to pass over." The *Abhidharmakośabhāṣya* states:

> Why will trainers separated from attachment not become one who achieves parinirvāṇa in the intermediate state (*antarāparinirvāyin*)? Since one has not yet mastered the path, one will not actualize it and because the latent defilements are not extremely weak. The *Vaibhāṣika*s say: because it is difficult to pass over the realm of desire, to abandon unvirtuous afflictions not demonstrated in scripture, the necessity to acquire two or three results of the religious life (*śrāmaṇyaphala*), and to pass over the three realms; and one who abides in an intermediate state is unable to that.[90]

When construed in this way, it appears to be mistaken to take the statement "the [*anuśaya*s] will be extremely weak" in the

[90] AKBh on AK, vi.41c-d, Pk ṅu 028a.6-028b.3, Śāstrī, 959: *atha kasmādavītarāgaḥ śaikṣo nāntarāye parinirvāyī bhavati / mārgasyājitatvādasummukhībhāvataḥ anuśayānāṃ ca nātimandatvāt. duḥsamatikrāmatvāt kāmadhātoriti vaibhāṣikāḥ / bahu hyanena kartavyaṃ bhavati akuśalāvyākṛtakleśaprahāṇam dvitriśrāmaṇyaphalaprāptiḥ tridhātusamatikramaśca / taccāntarābhavastho na śaktaḥ kartumiti /*

འགྲེལ་བཤད་དུ། སྐྱེ་བ་འདིའམ་སྲིད་པ་བར་མ་དོར་མྱ་ངན་ལས་འདའ་ཞེས་
P121b གསུང་པ་ནོར་བར་མངོན་ནོ། །བར་མ་དོར་འདའ་བ་ལ་ནི་ཉིས་སྟོང་ལྔ་བརྒྱ་
གོ་གཉིས་སུ་ཅི་ལྟར་བྱས་པས་འགྱུར་ཞེ་ན། སྔར་བཤད་པ་ལྟར་བར་མ་དོར་
འདའ་བ་ལ་གཟུགས་ཀྱི་བར་མ་དོ་[209]བཅུ་དྲུག་ཏུ་འདའ་བ་ཡོད་པས། [210]དེ་
ལ་རིགས་དང་འདོད་ཆགས་དང་བྲལ་བ་དང་[211]དབང་པོའི་སྒོ་ནས་ཕྱེ་བས་
དེ་ལྟར་འགྱུར་ཏེ། འདི་ལྟར་རིགས་ནི་དྲུག་སྟེ། ཉམས་པའི་ཆོས་ཅན་
དང་། བདག་གསོད་པའི་དང་། རྗེས་སུ་བསྲུངས་པའི་དང་། གནས་པ་ལས་མི་
བསྐྱོད་པའི་དང་། རྟོགས་པའི་འོས་སུ་གྱུར་པའི་དང་། མི་འཁྲུགས་པའི་ཆོས་ཅན་
གྱི་རིགས་སོ། །དེ་ལ་བར་དོ་གཅིག་ནའང་རིགས་དྲུག་ཡོད་དེ། དེ་ཡང་འདོད་
ཆགས་དང་བྲལ་བའི་སྒོ་ནས་[212]ཕྱེ་བ་དང་རིགས་ཀྱིས་ཕྱེ་བ་གཉིས་བསྒོམས་
ན་བརྒྱད་བརྒྱ་དང་རེ་བཞིར་འགྱུར་ཏེ། བསམ་གཏན་དང་པོའི་བར་དོར་
D 316 འདའ་བ་རིགས་དྲུག་པོའི་རེ་རེར་བསམ་གཏན་དང་པོའི་སྒོམ་སྤངས་དགུ་པོ་
གཏན་མ་སྤངས་པའི་འཆིང་བ་ཀུན་ལྡན་གཅིག་ནས་སྒོམ་[213]སྤང་བརྒྱད་པ་
སྤངས་པའི་བར་རྣམ་པ་[214]དགུ་དང་། དེ་བཞིན་དུ་བསམ་གཏན་ཕྱི་མ་གསུམ་
ལའང་དགུ་དགུ་སྟེ་དགུ་དྲུག་ལྔ་བཅུ་ང་བཞི། །ང་བཞི་པ་བཅུ་དྲུག་ནི་བརྒྱད་
བརྒྱ་རེ་བཞིར་འགྱུར་རོ། །དེ་ལ་དབང་པོ་རྣོ་འབྲིང་རྟུལ་གསུམ་དུ་བྱས་པས་
བརྒྱད་བརྒྱ་རེ་བཞི་པ་སུམ་འགྱུར་ནི་ཉིས་སྟོང་ལྔ་བརྒྱ་གོ་གཉིས་སོ། །རང་གི་
གནས་ཀྱི་རྣམ་པ་དགུ་ལས་འདོད་ཆགས་དང་བྲལ་བ་ནི་གོང་མ་གོང་མའི་
འཆིང་བ་ཀུན་ལྡན་ཡིན་པས་འོག་མའི་ཆགས་བྲལ་ལ་མི་བགྲང་ངོ། །དེ་ལྟར་དུ་
སྐྱེས་ནས་འདའ་བ་གསུམ་དང་། འཕར་བ་ཐ་མ་[215]གསུམ་དང་བཞི་ལ་ཡང་

---

[209] bar ma do D M] bar mdo P | [210] / D M] om. / P | [211] om. / D M] insert / P | [212] om. / D M] insert / P | [213] sgom M] bsgom D P | [214] rnam pa D M] rna pa P | [215] tha ma M] mtha’ ma D P

Abhidharmakośabhāṣyavyākhyā to say, "one attains *nirvāṇa* in the intermediate state in this rebirth or existence."[91]

How will the *Antāraparinirvāyin* be counted as two thousand five hundred ninety-two? As is previously explained, the *Antāraparinirvāyin* passes through sixteen intermediate states of the form realm and that will be divided according by means of lineage (*gotra*), detachment (*vairāgya*), and faculty (*indriya*).

Regarding this, the lineage is of six types: the lineages of the *Parihāṇadharman* ('one who can fall away'), *Cetānadharman* ('one who can put an end to his existence'), *Anurakṣaṇadharman* ('one who can protect himself'), *Sthitākampya* ('one who cherishes deliverance'), *Prativedhanādharman* ('one who can penetrate at will'), and an *Akopyadharman* 'one who is immovable'). In one intermediate state are six lineages. Also, if combining the two, the divisions through the means of separated from attachment and the divisions by lineage, there will be eight hundred sixty-four. In each of the six lineages, the *Antāraparinirvāyin* of the first concentration, from the one bound by all bonds in not abandoning the nine obstacles
D316 to be removed by the paths of cultivation of the first concentration up
to the one abandoning the eight abandonments to be removed by the path of cultivation will have nine aspects, likewise for the three later concentrations there is nine and nine times six groups makes fifty-four. Fifty-four [times the number of states of existence,] sixteen, will make eight hundred sixty-four. By dividing into three faculties–dull (*mṛdu*), moderate (*madhya*), and sharp (*adhimātra*), three times eight hundred sixty-four makes two thousand five hundred and ninety-two. [One who is] detached from the ninth aspect of ones owns state of existence, since it possesses all the bindings of the higher [state of existence], is not counted as separated from the attachment of the lower [abode]. Since it is also counted in this way for the three *Upapadyparinirvāyin*s, and the fourth, the *Ūrdhvaṃsrotas*, there will

[91] AKV, Śāstrī, 959: (AKBh) *anuśyānāṃ ca nātimandatvāt / yasmāccānuśayāstasya nātimandāḥ ato nāntarāparinirvāyī bhavatītyayamācāryasya parihāraḥ /*

བརྩིས་པས་ཕྱིར་མི་འོང་ཁྲི་ཉིས་སྟོང་དགུ་བརྒྱ་དྲུག་ཅུར་འགྱུར་རོ།

1329 གཟུགས་སུ་ཉེར་འགྲོ་རྣམ་པ་བཅུ།།འདོད་པའི་རྟེན་ལ་ཕྱེ་བ་
P122a དང་།།གནས་གཙང་སྐྱེ་རྒྱུ་སྤེལ་སྒོམ་ལྔ།།མཁས་པའི་དགོངས་པ་ཇི་
[216]བཞིན་བཤད།

།ཅེས་བྱ་བ་ནི་བསྡུ་བའི་ཚིགས་སུ་བཅད་པའོ།།གཟུགས་ཀྱི་ཉེ་བར་འགྲོ་བ་བཤད་ཟིན་ཏོ།།

།།གཟུགས་མེད་དུ་ཉེ་བར་འགྲོ་བ་གང་ཞེ་ན།ཕྱིར་མི་འོང་གང་གཟུགས་ཁམས་སུ་མི་འཇུག་པར་གཟུགས་མེད་དུ་སྐྱེས་ནས་འདའ་བའོ།།འདི་ལ་སྐྱེས་ནས་དང་།[217]འདུ་བྱེད་མེད་པར་དང་།འདུ་བྱེད་དང་བཅས་ཏེ་འདའ་བ་དང་།གོང་དུ་འཕོ་བ་བཞི་ཡོད་ལ་དེ་དག་གི་དོན་ནི་གཟུགས་སུ་ཉེར་འགྲོའི་སྐབས་བཞིན་དུ་རིགས་པར་བྱའོ།།འདིའི་གོང་འཕོ་ལ་ཡང་འཕར་བ་གསུམ་
D 317 རྩེ་བའི་རྒྱངས་པ་ཡོད་མོད།

།ཕར་ཕྱིན་པ་འགའ་ཞིག།འདི་འདྲ་བའི་རྣམ་གཞག་མཁས་པའི་གཞུང་ལས་ཆ་ཙམ་ཡང་མི་འབྱུང་ལ་རིགས་པས་ཀྱང་མི་འཐོབ་སྟེ་ཕྱིད་འཕར་རྩེ་བའི་གནས་མེད་པའི་ཕྱིར་རོ།།།དེ་ལྟར་གོང་དུ་སྨས་པ་[218]ལྟར་གྱི་དབྱེ་བ་ཙམ་ཞིག་འཐད་དེ།འགྲེལ་པར་

ཕྱིར་མི་འོང་བ་གཞན་ནི་གཟུགས་མེད་པར་ཉེ་བར་འགྲོ་བས་ཏེ།གཟུགས་ཀྱི་འདོད་ཆགས་རྣམས་དང་བྲལ་བ་འདི་ནས་ཤི་འཕོས་ནས་གཟུགས་མེད་པ་དག་གི་ནང་དུ་སྐྱེ་བ་གང་ཡིན་པའོ།།དེ་

[216] ji D M] ci P | [217] / D M] om. / P | [218] smas pa M P] smos pa D

[92] Tsong kha adapts this method of counting from AKBh on AK,vi.43c-d with categorical details from AKV. Canonical Tibetan is Pk ṅu 029b8-030a4. Śāstrī, 964-965: *antarāparinirvāyiṇas trayo mṛdumadhyādhimātendriyamedāt / bhūmibhedāccatvāraḥ / parihāṇadharmādigotrabhedāt ṣaṭ / sthānāntarabhedāt ṣodaśa / bhūmivairāgyabhedāt ṣaṭtriṃśat / rūpadhātau sakalabandhano yāvaccaturthadhyānāṣṭaprakāravītaragaḥ sthānāntaragotra-vairāgyendriyabhedād*

be twelve thousand nine hundred sixty Non-returners.[92] In a condensed verse:

> The transmigrator in the realm of form has ten aspects, divisions in the desire realm embodiment and the five alternating cultivations causing rebirth in the *Śuddhāvāsas*, explained according to the intention of the masters.

This finishes the transmigrator in the realm of form explanation.

Who is the transmigrator in the formless realm (*arūpyaga*)? This is a Non-returner who, not entering the form realm, achieves *nirvāṇa* in a rebirth within the formless realm. There arè four–one who achieves *nirvāṇa* in the formless realm through birth (*Upapadyparinirvāyin*), with effort (*sābhisaṃskāraparinirvāyin*), without effort (*anabhisaṃskāraparnirvāyin*), and one who goes higher (*ūrdhvaṃsrotas*). The meaning of these should be understood in a similar manner to those in the section concerning the transmigrators in the form realm.

There is an erroneous way of counting the *Ūrdhvaṃsrotas* like this to have three jumpers [according to some *Prajñāpāramitā*
D317 scholars] even though the texts of scholars, even a mere portion, does not have a presentation like this and even by reasoning one cannot attain such [a enumeraton] because there is not a state of [formless realm] existence in which to count the half-jumper. In this way, only the divisions that are given above are correct. The *Abhidharmakośabhāṣya* states:

> There is another Non-returner, a transmigrator in the formless realm. Separated from the passions of the form realm, and dying here, one is born among the formless realms. Also [this Non-returner] has four

---

dvānavatīni pañcaviṃśatiḥ śatāni / kathaṃ kṛtvā / ekasmin sthāne ṣaṭ gotrāṇi gotre gotre nava pudgalāḥ sakalabandhano yāvadaṣṭaprakāravītarāgaḥ svasmāt sthānāt ṣaṇṇavakāni catuṣpañcāśat ṣodaśa catuṣpañcāśatkāni catuḥṣaṣṭānyaṣṭau śatāni/ indriyabhedāt punastriguṇa ityevaṃ kṛtvā yo hyadhare dhyāne navaprakāravītarāgaḥ sa uttare sakalabandhana uktaḥ samagaṇanārtham / yathāntarāparinirvāyiṇa evaṃ yāvadūtdhvasrotasa ityabhisamasya sarve catvāriṃśadūnāni trayodaśasahasrāṇyanāgāminām bhavanti /

[219]ཡང་སྐྱེས་ནས་ཡོངས་སུ་མྱ་ངན་ལས་འདས་པ་ལ་སོགས་པའི་བྱེ་
བྲག་གིས་རྣམ་པ་བཞི་སྟེ།

ཞེས་སོ།།གཟུགས་མེད་ཉེར་འགྲོ་བཤད་ཟིན་ཏོ།།།།
མཐོང་བའི་ཆོས་ལ་ཞི་བ་འཐོབ་པ་གང་ཞེ་ན།ཕྱིར་མི་འོང་གང་དེ་ཐོབ་པའི་རྟེན་ལ་འདའ་བ་སྟེ།མཛོད་དུ།

གཞན་ནི་འདི་ལ་མྱ་ངན་འདའ།

།ཞེས་སོ།།འོན་ཀྱང་རྒྱུན་ཞུགས་དང་ཕྱིར་འོང་དང་པོ་ཐོབ་པའི་རྟེན་ལ་དགྲ་བཅོམ་པ་ཐོབ་པ་རྣམས་ཀྱང་མཐོང་ཆོས་ཞིར་འཇོག་པ་ལ་མི་རིགས་པ་མེད་དོ།།

།ལུས་ཀྱིས་[220]མངོན་དུ་བྱེད་པ་གང་ཞེ་ན།ཀུན་ལས་བཏུས་སུ།[221]

ལུས་ཀྱིས་མངོན་སུམ་དུ་བྱེད་པ་གང་ཞེ་ན།གང་སློབ་པ་རྣམ་པར་
P122b ཐར་པ་བརྒྱད་ལ་བསམ་གཏན་པའོ།

།ཞེས་ འབྱུང་ བ་ ལྟར་ ཕྱིར་ མི་ འོང་ རྣམ་ ཐར་ བརྒྱད་ ལ་ སྙོམས་ པར་
[222]འཇུག་ནུས་པའོ།།དེ་ལྟར་ན་ཕྱིར་མི་འོང་གི་དབྱེ་བ་འདི་དག་ཀྱང་འདོད་
པར་ཚེ་[223]ཡོངས་སུ་གྱུར་པའི་ཕྱིར་མི་འོང་ལ་མི་རུང་བ་ཡིན་ཏེ།འདོད་པར་
D 318 ཚེ་ཡོངས་སུ་གྱུར་པ་ནི་ཁམས་གོང་མར་འགྲོ་མི་སྲིད་པའི་ཕྱིར་ཏེ།འགྲེལ་བར་

ཅི་ཕྱིར་མི་འོང་བ་ཚེ་ཡོངས་སུ་གྱུར་པ་ལ་ཡང་དབྱེ་བ་འདི་ཡོད་དམ་ཞེ་ ན་ མེད་ དེ།འདི་ ལྟར་ མཛོད་ ལས།འདོད་ པར་ ཚེ་ ཡོངས་ གྱུར་ པའི་འཕགས།།ཁམས་གཞན་དུ་ནི་འགྲོ་བ་མེད།།འདོད་པའི་ཁམས་སུ་ཚེ་ཡོངས་སུ་གྱུར་པའི་འཕགས་པ་ནི་ཁམས་གཞན་དུ་འགྲོ་བ་མེད་དེ།[224]ཚེ་དེ་ཉིད་ལ་ཕྱིར་

[219]de D M] da P | [220]lus kyis M] lus kyi D P | [221]/ D M] om. / P | [222]snyoms pa D M] snyems P | [223]tshe D M] che P | [224]/ D M] om. / P

> aspects, by divisions of the *Upapadyaparinirāyin* and so forth.[93]

The presentation of the transmigrator in the formless realm is finished.

Who is one that attains peace in this existence (*dṛṣṭadharmaparinirvāyin*)? One who attains *nirvāṇa* in the embodiment that attains the Non-returner state. The *Abhidharmakośa* states:

> Another, who obtains *nirvāṇa* here. [94]

However, it is reasonable to posit as a *Dṛṣṭadharmaparinirvāyin* those attaining Arhatship in an embodiment which first attains the result of Stream-enterer or One-returner.

Who is one that is a bodily witness? The *Abhidharmasamuccaya* states:

> Who is the bodily witness? One who in the course of training concentrates on the eight liberations. [95]

Thus it appears to be a Non-returner who is able to enter into absorption on the eight liberations. In this way, although there are these divisions of the Non-returner, they are not suitable for a Non-returner who has terminated rebirth in the desire realm because for the one who has terminated rebirth in the desire realm transmigration in
D318 the upper realms is not possible. The *Abhidharmakośabhāṣya* states:

> Are these divisions also for a Non-returner who has terminated rebirth or not? The *Abhidharmakośa* states:
>
> The Noble being (*ārya*) who terminates rebirth (*parāvṛttajanma*) in the desire realm does not transmigrate to another realm. The Noble being who terminates other rebirths in the desire realm does not transmigrate to another realm because in that birth

---

[93] AKBh, Pruden, 969-970, Śāstrī, 953: *anya ārūpyago 'nāgāmī yo rūpavītarāga itaścyutvārūpyeṣūpapadyate sa punaścaturvidhāḥ upapadyādiparinirvāyibhedāt* / [94]AK, vi.38d, Pruden, 970, Śāstrī (38c), 952: *iho nirvāyako'paraḥ* / | [95] AS, Rahula, 150, Pradhan, 88: *kāyasākṣī katamaḥ / śaikṣaḥ aṣṭavimokṣadhāyī yaḥ pudgalaḥ* /

མི་འོང་བའི་འབྲས་བུ་ཐོབ་ནས་ཡོངས་སུ་མྱ་ངན་ལས་འདའ་བའི་ཕྱིར་ཞེས་སོ།།

།།འདོད་པར་ཚེ་ཡོངས་སུ་གྱུར་པའི་དོན་ཡང་འགྲེལ་བཤད་དུ།

ཕྱིར་མི་འོང་བ་ཚེ་ཡོངས་སུ་གྱུར་པ་ནི་གང་ཞིག་ཚེ་དང་པོ་ལ་རྒྱུན་དུ་ཞུགས་པའི་འབྲས་བུའམ་ལན་ཅིག་ཕྱིར་འོང་བའི་འབྲས་བུ་ཐོབ་ནས་ཚེ་གཉིས་པ་ལ་ཕྱིར་མི་འོང་བར་[225]གྱུར་པ་ཡིན་ནོ།

ཞེས་པ་ལྟར་འབྲས་བུ་དང་པོ་གཉིས་གང་རུང་ཐོབ་ནས་ཤི་བའི་ཚེ་ཕྱི་མ་ལ་ཕྱིར་མི་འོང་ཐོབ་པ་ཞིག་[226]ཡིན་ལ།[227]དེ་ཡང་རྟེན་དེ་ལ་མྱ་ངན་ལས་འདའ་བར་གསུངས་པས་ན་རིགས་ནས་རིགས་སྐྱེ་འདོད་པར་ཚེ་ཡོངས་གྱུར་དུ་སྨྲ་བ་ལ་གནོད་པ་ཡིན་ནོ།།དེ་ལྟར་ན་འདོད་པར་ཚེ་ཡོངས་གྱུར་གྱི་ཕྱིར་མི་འོང་གི་དོན་དེ་ལྟ་བུ་ཡིན་ལ།སྤྱིར་འདོད་ཁམས་སུ་ཚེ་ཡོངས་སུ་གྱུར་པའི་འཕགས་པ་ནི་འཕགས་ཆོས་ཚེ་གཉིས་སུ་བསྟེན་པ།ཚེ་དེ་ལ་འདའ་བ་ཞིག་[228]དགོས་པར་གསལ་ལོ།ཁམས་གཞན་དུ་མི་འགྲོ་བ་ལ་ཚེ་གྱུར་ཙམ་མི་སྨོས་པར་འདོད་པར་ཞེས་ཁྱད་པར་སྨོས་པ་ཅི་[229]ཞེ་ན།འགྲེལ་པར་

P123a གཟུགས་ཀྱི་ཁམས་སུ་ཚེ་ཡོངས་སུ་གྱུར་པ་ནི་གལ་ཏེ་ན་གསུགས་མེད་
D 319 པའི་ཁམས་དག་ཏུ་ཡང་འཇུག་སྟེ་གོང་དུ་འཕོ་བ་སྲིད་པའི་རྩེ་མོའི་མཐར་
ཐུག་པར་འགྲོ་བ་གང་ཡིན་པའོ།

1331 །ཞེས་པ་ལྟར་ཡིན་ནོ།།དེ་ལྟར་ན་བརྒྱ་བྱིན་རྒྱུན་ཞུགས་ཡིན་པ་དེས་བདག་ཚེ་འཕོས་ནས་མིར་སྐྱེས་པའི་རྟེན་ལ་མྱང་འདས་མ་ཐོབ་པར་འཆི་བའི་ཐ་མར་དགྲ་བཅོམ་པ་མ་ཐོབ་པའི་ཉམས་པས་ཡོངས་སུ་ཉམས་ན་འོག་མིན་དུ་སྐྱེ་བར་ཤོག་ཅེས་སྟོན་པའི་དྲུང་དུ་སྨོན་ལམ་འདེབས་པ་མི་རིགས་ཏེ།འདོད་པར་འཕགས་ཆོས་ཚེ་གཉིས་སུ་བསྟེན་པའི་ཚེ་གྱུར་ཡིན་ཡང་

225 phyir mi 'ong bar M] phyir mi 'ongs ba D P | 226 zhig M] gcig D P | 227 / D M] om. / P | 228 zhig D M] cig P | 229 ci D M] ca P

96 AKBh, Pruden, 973, Śāstrī, 958: *kim puna parivṛttajanmano 'pyanāgāmina eṣa bhedo 'sti / yasmāt (AK, vi.41a b): na parāvṛttajanmāryaḥ kāme dhātvantaropagaḥ / kāmadhātau parāvṛttajanmāntara āryo na dhātvantaraṃ gacchati / anāgāmiphalaṃ prāpya tatraiva janmani parinirvāṇāt / rūpadhātau tu parāvṛttajanmā kadācidārūpyān praviśati /*

itself, having attained the result of Non-returner, one achieves *parinirvāṇa*.[96]

The meaning of one who terminates rebirth in the desire realm as stated in the *Abhidharmakośabhāṣyavyākhyā*:

> A Non-returner who terminates rebirth is one that in the first birth, having attained the result of Stream-enterer or the result of Once-returner, in the second birth becomes a Non-returner. [97]

Accordingly, having attained whichever of the first two results, at the latter time of death one attains the state of Non-returner and furthermore, since the text states that one attains *nirvāṇa* in that embodiment, it is detrimental to say that a lineage-born (*kulaṃkula*) is one who attains that life in the desire realm. In this way, such like this is the meaning of the Non-returner who terminates rebirth in the desire realm. Generally, the Noble being (*ārya*) who terminates rebirth in the desire realm relies for two lives on the quality of Nobility (*āryadharma*). It is clearly necessary to attain *nirvāṇa* in that life.

What particular expression is used for one who "does not to transmigrate to other realms but is not said to be matured only in the present life"? The *Abhidharmakośabhāṣya* states:

> [The Noble being] who terminates rebirth in the realm of form, sometimes enters to the formless realms and then becomes one who goes higher transmigrating to the Peak of Existence (*Bhavāgraparama ūrdhvaṃsrotas*). [98]

So then, Śakra is a Stream-enterer, by that, "I, having died here, in an embodiment reborn among humans not obtaining *nirvāṇa* at the end of death, if falling by the practice which does not obtain Arhat, I shall be reborn in Akaniṣṭha heaven." Thus it is not suitable to supplicate this inspirational prayer in front of the Teacher because although Śakra terminates rebirth through relying in two lives on the

---

[97] AKV, Śāstrī, 958: *parivṛttajanmānāgāmīyaḥ prathame janmani strotāpattiphalaṃ sakṛdāgāmiphalaṃ vā prāpya dvitīye janmanyanāgāmī bhavati. /*

[98]AKBh, Pruden, 973, Śāstrī, 958: *rūpadhātau tu parāvṛttajanmā kadācidārūpyān praviśati. ya ūrdhvasrota bhavāgraparamaḥ /*

[230]གཟུགས་ཁམས་སུ་འཇུག་པ་ཡང་བསྟན་པའི་ཕྱིར་རོ།

།གལ་ཏེ་ཅི་ཐག་ཏུ་སླ་བ་ཁྱོད་བརྒྱ་བྱིན་གྱིས་ཆོས་མངོན་པ་མི་ཤེས་པས་སྨོན་ལམ་དེ་ལྟར་བཏབ་ཟེར་ན།[231]དེ་ཡང་མི་འཐད་དེ།[232]དེ་ལྟར་ཡིན་ན་སྟོན་པས་དེ་སྐད་མ་སྨྲ་ཞེས་འགོག་རིགས་པ་ལས་མ་བཀག་པའི་ཕྱིར་ཞེ་ན།།འདི་ལ་ཅི་ཐག་ཏུ་སླ་བས་ནི།བརྒྱ་བྱིན་འདོད་པའི་ཕྱུག་བསྡུལ་སྤྱངབར་འདོད་ནས་དེ་སྐད་སྨྲས་པས་དེ་དགའི་བར་བྱ་བའི་ཕྱིར་མ་བཀག་ཅེས་འདོད་དེ།འགྲེལ་པར

འོ་ན་བརྒྱ་བྱིན་གྱིས།དབྱངས་དང་བཅས་པའི་བརྒྱ་བྱིན་གྱི་མདོ་ལས།འདི་ནས་ཤི་འཕོས་མིར་གྱུར་རྟེན་ལ་མི་འདའ་ཡིས།།བདག་ནི་ཐ་མར་ཉམས་ན་ལྷ་གང་འོག་མིན་ཞེས།།རྣམ་པ་གྲགས་པ་དེར་ནི་སྐྱེ་བར་འགྱུར་བར་ཤོག།ཅེས་གང་སྨྲས་པ་ཇི་[233]ལྟ་བུ་ཞེ་ན།ཅི་ཐག་ཏུ་སླ་བ་རྣམས་ན་རེ།[234]ཆོས་མངོན་པ་མངོན་པར་མི་ཤེས་པའི་ཕྱིར་ཏེ།ཡང་དག་པར་དགའ་བར་བྱ་བའི་ཕྱིར་བཅོམ་ལྡན་འདས་ཀྱིས་ཀྱང་མ་བགག་[235]གོ་ཞེས་ཟེར་རོ།

D 320 །ཞེས་འབྱུང་ལ།ཁ་ཆེའི་སློབ་དཔོན་འདུས་པ་བཟང་པོའི་ལན་ནི་འགྲེལ་བཤད་དུ།

།སློབ་དཔོན་འདུས་བཟང་[236]ན་རེ།[237]འཆི་འཕོ་བའི་རྒྱུ་མཚན་ཅན་
P123b གྱི་སྐྱེ་བའི་སྡུག་བསྔལ་གྱིས་ཡིད་འབྱུང་བ་ནི་ཡང་དག་པར་དགའ་
བར་བྱ་བ་ཡིན་པའི་ཕྱིར་རོ་ཞེས་ཟེར་རོ།

།ཞེས་བརྒྱ་བྱིན་ཡང་ཡང་ཆེ་འཕོས་ནས་སྐྱེ་བ་ལེན་པ་ལ་ཡིད་འབྱུང་སྐྱེས་ལ་དེའི་ཡིད་མི་གསད་པའི་ཕྱིར་སྟོན་པས་མ་བཀག་ཅེས་ལན་འདེབས་མོད་འོན་ཀྱང་འཐད་ཕྱོགས་མ་ཡིན་པར་མངོན་ཏེ།སློབ་དཔོན་གྱིས་ཀྱང་རྩོད་པ་[238]དེའི་ལན་ལ་ཅི་ཐག་ཏུ་སླ་བ་རྣམས་འདི་སྐད་ཟེར་ཞེས་པ་ཙམ་ལས་མ་
1332 [239]གསུངས་པ་དང།བརྒྱ་བྱིན་གྱིས་མངོན་པ་མི་ཤེས་པར་དེ་སྐད་སྨྲས་ན་སྟོན

[230]yang M] kyang D P | [231]/ D M] om. / P | [232]/ D M] om. / P | [233]ji D M] ci P | [234]/ D M] om. / P | [235]bgag M] bkag D P | [236]bzang M] bzangs D P | [237]/ D M] om. / P | [238]rtsod pa D M] brtsod pa P | [239]ma D M] om. P

quality of Nobility (*āryadharma*) in the desire realm, Śakra also is shown to enter into the form realm.

If it is the case, the *Vaibhāṣika* says Śakra supplicates accordingly the inspirational prayer since not knowing the Abhidharma. That is incorrect, if it is this way, why did the Teacher (i.e., the Buddha) not correct Śakra other than not giving a response? On this point, the *Vaibhāṣika*s assert "Śakra is not corrected since through his expression he is encouraged to abandon the suffering of desire." The *Abhidharmakośabhāṣya* states:

> (From the *Sūtra of Śakra having a soft voice*, dieing here reborn among humans by not obtaining *nirvāṇa* in that embodiment) Śakra, 'I, if falling at the end, may I be reborn there among the well known called Akaniṣṭha.' Why does he say thus? The *Vaibhāṣika*s answer: Śakra expresses himself thus, because of not knowing the Abhidharma, and if not corrected by the Bhagavān, it is with the intention of encouraging him.[99]

D320 The reply of the Kasmiri teacher Saṃghabhadra in the *Abhidharmakośabhāṣyavyākhyā*:

> Ācārya Saṃghabhadra replies 'the intention of encouraging him' is to frighten (*wid 'byung ba, udvigna*) him with the suffering of birth which is the efficient cause of death.[100]

Thus, on account of not concealing Śakra's thought of producing fright in taking rebirth through repeated death, the Teacher does not correct him although the given reply appears not to be an agreeable opinion. The Ācārya although disputing, does not state from his speech a reply to the *Vaibhāṣika*s and Śakra if saying such in not knowing the Abhidharma, the Teacher understands as obstructed and

---

[99] AKBh, Pk028a.3-5, Pruden, 973, Śāstrī, 958: *yattarhi śakreṇoktam ye te devā akaniṣṭā iti viśrutāḥ ante me hīyamānasya tatropapattirbhaviṣyati abhidharmalakṣaṇānabhijñatvāditi vaibhāṣikāḥ / bhagavatāpi anivāraṇam saṃharṣaṇīyatvāt iti /*

[100] AKV, Śāstrī, 958: *cyutinimittopapattiduḥkhodvignasya saṃharṣaṇīyatvādity-ācāryasaṅghabhadraḥ /*

པས་དགག་པར་རིགས་ཏེ་བརྒྱ་བྱིན་དགའ་བ་ཙམ་གྱི་ཕྱིར་སྟོན་པའི་གསུང་
རབ་དང་འགལ་བའི་རྣམ་གཞག་བྱེད་པ་ཡལ་བར་འདོར་མི་རིགས་པའི་ཕྱིར་
དང༌།བརྒྱ་བྱིན་ལ་ཡང་འདོད་པར་ཚེ་འགྱུར་ཁམས་གཞན་དུ་སྐྱེ་མི་དགོས་པར་
ཚེ་དེ་ལ་འདའ་བར་བསྟན་པས་དགའ་བར་ཡང་འགྱུར་བའི་ཕྱིར་རོ།།སྔར་
འདོད་པར་ཚེ་འགྱུར་ཁམས་གཞན་དུ་མི་འགྲོ་བ་དང༌།།ཚེ་དེ་ལ་འདའ་བར་
བསྟན་པ་དང་འགལ་བར་བསམས་[240]ནས།བྱེ་བྲག་ཏུ་སྨྲ་བའི་ལུགས་བཞག
པའི་ཕྱིར་རོ།།དེས་ན་མངོན་པར་འདོད་པར་ཚེ་འགྱུར་ཁམས་གཞན་དུ་མི་འགྲོ་
བར་གསུངས་པ་ཕལ་ཆེ་བ་ལ་དགོངས་སམ་སྙམ་སྟེ་དཔྱད་དོ།

།ཕྱིར་མི་འོང་བའི་འབྲས་བུ་ཁྱད་པར་ཅན་ལ་གནས་པ་རྣམས་བཤད་
ཟིན་ཏོ།།།།

D 321 དགྲ་བཅོམ་པའི་འབྲས་བུ་ལ་གནས་པ་གང་ཞེ་ན།གང་སྲིད་རྩེའི་ཉོན་
མོངས་དགུ་པ་མ་ལུས་པར་སྤངས་པའི་ཐེག་དམན་པ་སྟེ།ཀུན་ལས་བཏུས་སུ།

> དགྲ་བཅོམ་པ་གང་ཞེ་ན།།[241]སྲིད་པའི་རྩེ་མོའི་ཉོན་མོངས་པ་རྣམས་
> ཀྱི་རྣམ་པ་དགུ་པ་སྤངས་པའི་ལམ་ལ་གནས་པའི་གང་ཟག་གོ།

།ཞེས་སོ།།འདིར་དགྲ་བཅོམ་པའི་འབྲས་བུ་ལ་ཞུགས་པ་མི་འཆད་པ་ནི་
ཕྱིར་མི་འོང་འབྲས་གནས་ཁྱད་པར་ཅན་གྱི་སྐབས་སུ་བཤད་ཟིན་པར་བལྟའོ།

P124a །དགྲ་བཅོམ་པ་དེ་ལ་ཡང་སྤང་བྱ་སྤངས་པའི་སྒོ་ནས་ཤེས་རབ་ཀྱིས་
རྣམ་པར་གྲོལ་བ་དང༌།གཉིས་ཀའི་ཆ་ལས་རྣམ་པར་གྲོལ་བ་གཉིས་སུ་འགྱུར་
ཞིང༌།[242]མཐོང་ཆོས་ལ་བདེ་བར་གནས་པ་ལས་ཉམས་པ་དང་མི་ཉམས་པའི་
ཚུལ་གྱིསནི་ཉམས་པ་དང༌།འཆི་བར་སེམས་པའི་དང༌།རྗེས་སུ་བསྲུངས་པའི་
དང༌།།གནས་པ་ལ་མི་བསྐྱོད་པའི་དང༌།རབ་ཏུ་རྟོགས་པའི་འོས་སུ་གྱུར་པའི་
དང༌།མི་འཁྲུགས་པའི་ཆོས་ཅན་ཏེ་[243]དྲུག་ཏུ་ཡང་འགྱུར་ལ།དབང་པོའི་བྱེ་
བྲག་གིས་ནི་དུས་དང་སྦྱོར་བ་དང་དུས་དང་མི་སྦྱོར་བའི་དགྲ་བཅོམ་པ་
གཉིས་སུའང་འགྱུར་རོ།

1333 །དེ་ལ་དགྲ་བཅོམ་པ་གང་རྣམ་ཐར་བརྒྱད་ལ་སྙོམས་པར་འཇུག་མི་
ནུས་པ་ནི་ཤེས་རབ་ཀྱིས་རྣམ་པར་གྲོལ་བ་ཞེས་བྱ་སྟེ།བདག་མེད་རྟོགས་པའི་
ཤེས་རབ་ཀྱིས་ཉོན་སྒྲིབ་ལས་གྲོལ་ཀྱི་སྙོམས་འཇུག་གི་སྒྲིབ་པ་མ་སྤངས་པའི་

[240] bsams M] bsam D P | [241] / / D M] om. / / P | [242] / D M] om. / P | [243] te D M] de P

because of merely encouraging Śakra by showing to obtain *nirvāṇa* in that life, [Śakra] is not necessarily born in other realms, [he] is reborn in the desire realm. The former does not transmigrate in other realms and terminates rebirth within the desire realm and it is thought to be contradictory to teach that this one attains *nirvāṇa* in that life because of the system posited by the *Vaibhāṣikas*. Therefore, the Abhidharma mostly teaches [the Non-returner] who terminates rebirth in the desire realm to not transmigrate in other realms is the intention or thought to be investigated.

The presentation of the abiders in the distinctive result of Non-returner is finished.

Who is the abider in the result of Arhat? This is lesser vehicle person who totally abandons all nine afflictions of the Peak of Existence. The *Abhidharmasamuccaya* states:

> Who is the Arhat? This is the person who abides in the path of abandoning the nine aspects of afflictions of the Peak of Existence.[101]

Here, the enterer to the result of Arhat is not counted, since that explanation was considered finished in the section on the distinctive abider in the result of Non-returner.

There are two types of Arhats if classified according to abandoning obstacles, the *Prajñāvimukta* and the *Ubhayatobhāgavimukta*, and six types if according to the whether or not they fall away from abiding in bliss in the present life: the *Parihāṇadharman*, *Cetanādharman*, *Anurakṣaṇādharman*, *Sthitākampya*, *Prativedhanādharman*, and *Akopyadharman*. There are two classifications according to faculty: the occasionally delivered Arhat (*samayavimukta*) and the not occasionally delivered Arhat (*asamayavimukta*).

Regarding this, the Arhat who is not able to enter the absorption on the eight liberations is called *Prajñāvimukta* ("liberated by wisdom") because he does not abandon the obstacles to entering absorption but rather abandons the obscurational afflictions by the

[101] AS, Rahula, p. 154, #13, Pradhan, 89-90: *arhan katamaḥ/ bhāvāgrikasya navamasya kleśaprakārasya prahāṇamārge yaḥ pudgalaḥ/*

ཕྱིར་རོ།།རྣམ་ཐར་བརྒྱད་ལ་འཇུག་ནུས་པ་ནི་གཉིས་ཀའི་ཆ་ལས་རྣམ་གྲོལ་
ཡིན་ཏེ[244]།[245]ཉོན་སྒྲིབ་དང་སྙོམ་འཇུག་གི་སྒྲིབ་པ་གཉིས་ཆར་ལས་གྲོལ་བའི་
D 322 ཕྱིར་རོ།།།དེ་ལྟར་ཡང་ཀུན་ལས་བཏུས་སུ།[246]

> ཤེས་རབ་ཀྱིས་རྣམ་པར་གྲོལ་བ་གང་ཞེ་ན།གང་ཟག་པ་ཟད་པ་སྟེ་རྣམ་པར་ཐར་པ་བརྒྱད་ལ་བསམ་གཏན་པ་ནི་མ་ཡིན་པའོ།
>
> །གཉིས་ཀའི་ཆ་ལས་རྣམ་པར་གྲོལ་བ་གང་ཞེ་ན། གང་ཟག་པ་ཟད་པ་དང་བཅས་པ་རྣམ་པར་ཐར་པ་བརྒྱད་ལ་ཡང་བསམ་གཏན་པའི་གང་ཟག་གོ།

ཞེས་དང།མཛོད་ལས་ཀྱང་དེ་དང་མཐུན་པར།

འགོག་ཐོབ་གཉིས་ཀ་ལས་རྣམ་གྲོལ།།ཤེས་རབ་ཀྱིས་ནི་ཅིག་ཤོས་སོ།
།ཞེས་གང་གསུངས་པའོ།།དེ་ལྟར་མཁས་པ་དག་ལ་ནི་དགྲ་བཅོམ་པ་
དེ་གཉིས་ཀྱི་ཐ་སྙད་དེ་ལྟར་གྲགས་[247]མོད་གང་ཡང་ཤེས་རབ་ཀྲུང་བའི་ཆ་
ལས་རྣམ་གྲོལ་དང་ཞེས་བརྗོད་བ་དེ་དག།ཕར་ཕྱིན་པ་དང་སྔ་རབས་ལ་
P124b འགའ་ཞིག།ནི་ཁོ་བོ་ཅག་[248]ལ་འདི་དག་གི་དོན་ཤེས་པ་ལྟ་ཅི་སྨོས་མིང་ཙམ་
ཡང་འཆད་རྒྱུ་མེད་དོ་ཞེས་གསལ་བར་སྒྲོག་པ་ཡིན་ཏེ།[249]།ཤེས་རབ་སྦྱངས་
པའི་འཕགས་པ་དགྲ་བཅོམ་པ་དེ་འདྲ་བ་དེ་ནི་ཤིན་ཏུ་ངོ་མཚར་བ་ཞིག་
གོ།ཤེས་རབ་དང་ཏིང་ངེ་འཛིན་གྱི་སྟོབས་ཀྱིས་ཉོན་མོངས་དང་སྙོམས་འཇུག་
གི་སྒྲིབ་པ་གཉིས་ཆར་ལས་གྲོལ་བ་མིན་པར་ཤེས་རབ་ཀྱིས་ཉོན་མོངས་ཀྲུང་
བའི་ཆ་ལས་གྲོལ་བ་ལ་ཤེས་རབ་ལས་གྲོལ་བ་ཞེས་མཁས་པར་རློམ་པ་དག་
ཀྱང་བརྗོད་སྦྱོར་ན།ཀྱི་ཧུད་རྒྱལ་བའི་གསུང་རབ་འཕྲེད་པ་པོ་རྣམས་ནི་འདི་
འདྲ་བར་གྱུར་ཏོ།

[244] te D M] de P | [245] / D M] om. / P | [246] / D M] om. / P | [247] grags M] grag D P | [248] cag D M] ceg P | [249] / D M] om. / P

wisdom which cognizes selflessness. Those able to enter in the absorption for the eight liberations are *Ubhayatobhāgavimukta* because they are liberated from both the obscuration of entering
D322 absorption and the obscurations of the afflictions. The *Abhidharmasamuccaya* says:

> Who is the person liberated by means of wisdom (*prajñāvimukta*)? One who exhausts the impurities but does not concentrate on the eight liberations.[102]

> Who is the person liberated by two means (*ubhayatobhāgavimukta*)? One who exhausts the impurities and also concentrates on the eight liberations.[103]

This is also concordant with the definition from the *Abhidharmakośa*:

> One who possesses extinction is liberated by both;
> the other is liberated by wisdom.[104]

Along these lines, for some scholars the conventional terms for these two Arhats are mere talk. Those [, some previous *Prajñāpāramitā* scholars,] apply the name "liberated through nothing but the portion of wisdom" and we understand their meaning through the expression "looking at only the name without explaining the cause" and that an Arhat Ārya who abandons by only wisdom is especially surprising. When those proud in scholarship apply the term stating, "the *Prajñāvimukta* (i.e, the Arhat liberated by wisdom) is liberated from only the afflictions by wisdom, it is not liberated from either the obscurations of entering absorption or the afflictions by the power of meditative stabilization and wisdom," we say, "*Kyi hud*! Those who investigate the scriptures of the Victor will be such like this!"

---

[102] AS, Rahula, 151, #4, Pradhan, 88: *prajñāvimuktaḥ katamaḥ/ kṣīṇāsravo notvaṣṭavimokṣadhyāyī yaḥ pudgalaḥ /*

[103] AS, Rahula, 151, #4: *ubhayatobhāgavimuktaḥ katamaḥ/ kṣīṇāsravo`ṣṭavimokṣadhyāyī yaḥ pudgalaḥ/*

[104] AK, vi.64a-b, Pruden, 1018, Śāstrī, 1011: *nirodhalābhyubhayatovimuktaḥ prajñayetaraḥ /*

།ཉམས་པའི་ཆོས་ཅན་གང་ཞེ་ན།འདི་ལ་དགྲ་བཅོམ་པ་དང་པོ་ལྷ་ཁ་
[250]དབང་པོ་[251]རྟུལ་པོར་[252]བྱུང་མེད་ལ།འོན་ཀྱང་འཇིག་རྟེན་པའི་བསམ་
D 323 གཏན་གྱི་ཏིང་ངེ་འཛིན་གྱིས་ཚེ་འདི་ལ་ལུས་སེམས་བདེ་བར་གནས་པའི་རྒྱུ་
|1334 ལས་ཉམས་མི་ཉམས་ཀྱི་སྒོ་ནས་མཚན་ཉིད་ཐད་དད་པར་འགྱུར་ཏེ།[253]

འདི་ལྟར་དགྲ་བཅོམ་དབང་པོ་རྟུལ་པོ་[254]འདོད་ཡིན་གྱིས་དབྱེན་བཅོས་རུང་མ་བཅོས་རུང་ངེས་པར་བསམ་གཏན་ལས་ཉམས་པ་དང།འདོད་ཡིན་གྱིས་སྨྱོས་སམ་མ་སྨྱོས་ཀྱང་རང་གིས་རང་མི་གསོད་ན་ངེས་པར་ཉམས་ལ་གསོད་ན་གཏན་མི་ཉམས་པ་དང།འདོད་ཡིན་ལ་སེམས་བསྲུངས་ན་མི་ཉམས་ལ་ཆེད་ཆེར་མ་བསྲུངས་ན་ཉམས་པ་དང།འདོད་ཡོན་ལས་བསྲུངསསམ་མ་བ་སྲུངས་ཀྱང་ཉམས་མི་སྲིད་ལ་དབང་པོ་རྟུལ་པོ་ལས་རྣོན་པོར་འཕོ་མི་སྲིད་པ་དང།།ཉམས་མི་སྲིད་ཅིང་དབང་པོ་འཕོ་བའི་སྐལ་བ་ཅན་རྣམས་རིམ་པ་ལྟར་ཉམས་པའི་ཆོས་ཅན་ནས་རྟོགས་པའི་འོས་སུ་གྱུར་པའི་ཆོས་ཅན་གྱི་བར་རྣམས་ཡིན་ཏེ།ཀུན་ལས་བཏུས་སོ།

ཉམས་པའི་ཆོས་ཅན་གང་ཞེ་ན།[255]གང་དབང་པོ་རྟུལ་པོ་སྨྱོས་ཀྱང་
རུང་མ་སྨྱོས་ཀྱང་རུང་མཐོང་བའི་ཆོས་ལ་བདེ་བར་གནས་པ་ལས་
P125a ཡོངས་སུ་ཉམས་པར་འགྱུར་བའི་སྐལ་བ་ཅན་ནོ།།བདག་གསོད་
པའི་ཆོས་ཅན་གང་ཞེ་ན།གང་དབང་པོ་རྟུལ་པོ་སྨྱོས་ཀྱང་རུང་མ་
སྨྱོས་ཀྱང་རུང་བདག་མི་གསོད་ན་མཐོང་བའི་ཆོས་ལ་བདེ་བར་
གནས་པ་ལས་ཡོངས་སུ་ཉམས་པར་འགྱུར་བའི་སྐལ་བ་ཅན་ཡིན་
ལ་གསོད་ན་སྐལ་བ་ཅན་མ་ཡིན་པའོ།།རྗེས་སུ་བསྲུངས་པའི་ཆོས་
ཅན་གང་ཞེ་ན།གང་དབང་པོ་རྟུལ་པོ་སྨྱོས་ན་མཐོང་བའི་ཆོས་ལ་
D 324 བདེ་བར་གནས་པ་ལས་ཉམས་པའི་སྐལ་བ་ཅན་ཡིན་ལ་མ་སྨྱོས་ན་
མ་ཡིན་པའོ།།གནས་པ་ལས་མི་བསྐྱོད་པ་གང་ཞེ་ན།གང་དབང་པོ་
རྟུལ་པོ་སྨྱོས་ཀྱང་རུང་མ་སྨྱོས་ཀྱང་རུང་མཐོང་བའི་ཆོས་ལ་བདེ་

[250]kha M] ka D P | [251]dbang po M P] dbang pa D | [252]rtul por D M] brtul por P | [253]/ D M] om. / P | [254]rtul po M] brtul po D P | [255]/ D M] om. / P

Who is the *Parihāṇadharman*? Regarding this, the first five
D 323 Arhats are without distinction, having dull faculties. Notwithstanding, the characteristic is to be classified by the means of not backsliding or backsliding from the cause of abiding in bliss of body and mind in this life by the meditative stabilization of mundane concentration.

Accordingly, a dull facultied Arhat, when differentiated by gratification of the senses, artificially or unartificially, definitely backslides from concentration; whether experiencing or not experiencing sensual gratification, if not slaying the self by oneself, [the Arhat] backslides and if slaying [the self by oneself, the Arhat] does not continuously backslide; if protecting the mind from sensual gratification [an Arhat] does not backslide and if not increasingly protecting, [an Arhat] backslides; although protecting or not protecting from sensual gratification, [there is an Arhat for whom] it is not possible to backslide and not change from dull to sharp faculties; and there are those who do not backslide and possess the fortune of changing faculties; successively these are [the Arhats] from the *Parihāṇadharman* up to the *Prativedhanādharman*. The *Abhidharmasamuccaya* states:

> Who is the *Parihāṇadharman*? This is a person who, having dull faculties, distracted or not distracted, reflective or not, who possesses the fortune that will fall away from abiding in bliss for this life.
>
> Who is the *Cetanādharma*? This is a person who, having dull faculties distracted or not, reflective or not, if not slaying the self possesses the fortune that will be falling from abiding in bliss for this life; if slaying the self, does not have such fortune.
>
> Who is the *Anurakṣaṇādharma*? This is a person who, having dull faculties, if distracted possesses the fortune of falling from abiding in bliss for the present life and if not distracted does not.
>
> Who is the *Sthitākampya* Arhat? This is a person who, having dull faculties, distracted or not, reflective or not, does not possess the fortune falling

བར་གནས་པ་ལས་ཡོངས་སུ་ཉམས་པའི་སྐལ་བ་ཅན་མ་ཡིན་ལ་དབང་པོ་རྣམས་སྦྱོང་བའི་སྐལ་བ་ཅན་ཡང་མ་ཡིན་པའོ།།རབ་ཏུ་རྟོགས་པའི་འོས་སུ་གྱུར་པ་གང་ཞེ་ན།གང་དབང་པོ་རྟུལ་པོ་སྨྱོས་ཀྱང་རུང་མ་སྨྱོས་ཀྱང་རུང་མཐོང་བའི་ཆོས་ལ་བདེ་བར་གནས་པ་ལས་ཡོངས་སུ་ཉམས་པའི་སྐལ་བ་ཅན་མ་ཡིན་ལ་དབང་པོ་རྣམས་སྦྱོང་བའི་སྐལ་བ་ཅན་ནི་ཡིན་པའོ།

།ཞེས་སོ།[256]།མི་འཁྲུགས་པའི་ཆོས་ཅན་ཡང།དེ་ཉིས་ལས

།མི་འཁྲུགས་པའི་ཆོས་ཅན་གང་ཞེ་ན།གང་རང་བཞིན་གྱིས་དབང་པོ་རྣོན་པོས་ཏེ།སྨྱོས་ཀྱང་རུང་མ་སྨྱོས་ཀྱང་རུང་མཐོང་བའི་ཆོས་ལ་བདེ་བར་གནས་པ་ལས་[257]ཡོངས་སུ་ཉམས་པའི་སྐལ་བ་ཅན་ནི་མ་ཡིན་པའོ།

།ཞེས་དབང་པོའི་སྒོ་ནས་ཁྱད་པར་དུ་བྱས་སོ།།།དོན་འདི་ལ་ཕྱི་ མག་ཏུ་སྨྲ་བ་རྣམས་ནི་འདི་ལྟར་འདོད་དེ།དགྲ་བཅོམ་པ་དྲུག་པོ་དེ་ལ་དབང་པོ་དང།རིགས་དང།སྦྱོར་བའི་ཁྱད་པར་དང།གང་ཞིག་གང་ལས་ཉམས་པའི་སྒོ་ནས་མཚན་ཉིད་ཐ་དད་པར་འཆད་དོ།

P125b །དབང་པོའི་ཁྱད་པར་གྱིས་ཇི[258]་ལྟ་བུ་ཞེ་ན།དང་པོ་ལྔ་ནི་དད་མོས་སྔོན་དུ་སོང་བ་དང་དབང་རྟུལ་ཡིན་ལ།[259]་དྲུག་པ་ནི་མཐོང་བས་ཐོབ་པ་སྔོན་དུ་བཏང་བ་དབང་རྣོན་ཡིན་ཏེ།མཛོད་ལས

།དགྲ་བཅོམ་དྲུག་འདོད་དེ་དག་ལས།།ལྔ་ནི་དད་པས་མོས་ལས་སྐྱེས།།དེ་དག་རྣམ་གྲོལ་དུས་དང་སྦྱོར།།མི་གཡོའི་ཆོས་ཅན་མི་གཡོ་

[256] yin pa'o / / zhes so D M] yin pa'i ches so P | [257] om. / D M] insert / P | [258] ji M] ci D P | [259] / D M] om. / P

[105] AS, Rahula, 157, Pradhan, 91: *parihāṇadharmā arhan katamaḥ/ mṛdvindriyaprakṛtiko vikṣipto vā avikṣpto cetayitvā vā acetayitvā vā dṛṣṭadharmasukha vihārāt parihāṇameti / cetanādharmā arhan katamaḥ. mṛdvindriyaprakṛtiko vikṣipto vā avikṣipto vā acetayitvā dṛṣṭadharmasukhavihārāt parihāṇameti cetayitvā na*

from abiding in bliss for the present life and also does not possess the fortune of training his faculties.

> Who is the *Prativedhanādharman*? This is a person who, having dull faculties, distracted or not, reflective or not, does not possess the fortune of falling from abiding in bliss for the present life and does possess the fortune of training his faculties. [105]

Also the *Akopyadharman*, as stated in the same text:

> Who is the *Akopyadharman*? This is one who has by nature sharp faculties, distracted or not, reflective or not, does not possess the fortune of falling from abiding in bliss for the present life.[106]

Thus they are distinguished by means of faculty. For this meaning the *Vaibhāṣika*s accordingly assert that those six Arhat's characteristics are separately explained by means of backsliding from whichever among the distinctions of faculty, lineage, and application.

In what manner is the peculiarity of faculty? The first five have gone previously as one who aspires by faith (i.e., *śraddhādhimukta*) and have dull faculties and the sixth has gone previously as one who attains by seeing (i.e. *dṛṣṭīprāpta*) and thus has sharp faculties. The *Abhidharmakośa* states:

> Among these accepted six Arhats: five arise from those who aspire by faith (i.e., *śraddhādhimukta*). Their deliverance is occasional. The Immovable One (*akopyadharman*) is immovable. Therefore he

---

parihāṇameti. anurakṣaṇādharmā arhan katamaḥ/ mṛdvindriyaprakṛtiko vikṣipto dṛṣṭadharmasukhavihārāt parihāṇameti avikṣipto na parihāṇameti / sthitākampya arhan katamaḥ/ mṛdvindriyaprakṛtiko vikṣipto vā avikṣipto vā dṛṣṭadharmasukhavihārāt na parihāṇameti nāpi indriyāṇyuttāpayati / prativedhanādharmā arhan katamaḥ / mṛdvindriyaprakṛtiko vikṣipto vā avikṣipto vā dṛṣṭadharmasukhavihārāt na parihāṇameti kevalamindriyāṇyuttāpayati /

[106]AS, Rahula, 158, Pradhan, 91: *akopyadharmā arhan katamaḥ/ tīkṣṇendriyaprakṛtiko vikṣipto vā avikṣpto cetayitvā vā acetayitvā na dṛṣṭadharmasukhavihārāt parihāṇameti /*

D 325 བ།།དེ་ཕྱིར་དེ་དུས་མི་སྦྱོར་གྲོལ།།དེ་ནི་མཐོང་ཐོབ་རྒྱུ་ལས་བྱུང་།

།ཞེས་སོ།།[260]རིགས་ཀྱི་ཁྱད་པར་གྱིས་ཇི་ལྟ་བུ་ཞེ་ན།འདི་ལ་དང་པོ་ནས་དེའི་རིགས་སུ་གནས་པ་དང་།དང་པོ་ནས་དེའི་རིགས་མ་ཡིན་ཡང་ཕྱིས་གང་ཟག་དེའི་རིགས་སུ་སོང་བ་གཉིས་སོ།

།དེ་ལ་དང་པོ་ནི་གང་ཟག་དྲུག་ཆར་ལ་ཡོད་ལ།གཉིས་པ་ནི་ཕྱི་མ་ལྔ་ལ་ཡོད་དེ།དཔེར་ན་ཉམས་པའི་ཆོས་ཅན་གྱིས་དབང་པོ་སྦྱངས་པས་བདག་གསོད་པའི་ཆོས་ཅན་གྱི་རིགས་སུ་གྱུར་པ་ལྟ་བུའོ།།ཉམས་པའི་ཆོས་ཅན་ལས་རིགས་དམན་པ་མེད་པས་དེ་ལ་འོག་མའི་རིགས་སྦྱངས་པ་ལས་ཕྱིས་རིགས་འཕོས་པ་མེད་དེ།མཛོད་ལས།

ཁ་ཅིག་དང་པོ་ནས་དེའི་རིགས།།ཁ་ཅིག་སྦྱང་པ་ལས་གྱུར་ཏོ།

།ཞེས་སོ།།སྦྱོར་བའི་ཁྱད་པར་གྱིས་ཇི་[261]ལྟ་བུ་ཞེ་ན།མཛོད་འགྲེལ་ལས།

1336 །དང་པོ་གཉིས་ནི་སྟོན་སློབ་པའི་གནས་སྐབས་ཁོ་ན་ནི་རྒྱུན་དུ་སྦྱོར་བ་དང་།གུས་པར་སྦྱོར་བ་མེད་པ་ཡིན་ནོ[262]།།གསུམ་པ་ནི་རྒྱུན་དུ་སྦྱོར་བ་པ་ཡིན་ནོ།།བཞི་པ་ནི་གུས་པར་སྦྱོར་བ་པ་ཡིན་ནོ།།ལྔ་པ་ནི་གཉིས་ཁར་[263]སྦྱོར་བ་པ་ཡིན་ལ་དབང་པོ་རྟུལ་པོ་[264]ཡིན་ནོ།།དྲུག་པ་ནི་གཉིས་ཁར་[265]སྦྱོར་བ་པ་དང་དབང་པོ་རྣོན་པོ་ཡིན་ནོ།

།ཞེས་འབྱུང་བ་ལྟར་ཡིན་ལ།གུས་སྦྱོར་ནི་རྒྱུན་ཆད་[266]མེད་པའི་བརྩོན་འགྲུས་དྲག་པོ་ཡིན་ཞིང་།[267]རྒྱུན་སྦྱོར་ནི་རྩོལ་བ་དྲག་པོ་མེད་པའི་བརྩོན་འགྲུས་རྒྱུན་ཆགས་པའོ།

P126a །གང་ཞིག་གང་ལས་ཉམས་པའི་ཚུལ་ཡང་ཇི་[268]ལྟ་བུ་ཞེ་ན།དེ་ལྟར་དྲུག་པོ་དེ་ལས་གང་ཞིག་ཉམས་ན་དང་པོ་ལྔ་ཉམས་པར་འགྱུར་རོ།།གང་

---

260 / / D M] om. / / P | 261 ji M] ci D P | 262 no D M] na P | 263 khar M] kar D P | 264 rtul po M] brtul po D P | 265 khar M] kar D P | 266 chad D M] chags P | 267 / D M] om. / P | 268 ji M] ci D P

---

107 AK, vi.56a-57b, Pruden, 999-1000, Pradhan, 372-373, Śāstrī, 989: *ṣadarhanto mataḥ teṣāṃ pañca śraddhādhimuktijāḥ / vimuktiḥ sāmayikyeṣāṃ akopyākopyadharmaṇaḥ*

> is not occasionally delivered. That one has been one
> who attains by seeing (i.e. *dṛṣṭīprāpta*).[107]

In what manner is the peculiarity of lineage? For this there are two, the individual who abides in a particular lineage from the beginning and the individual who although not in a particular lineage from the beginning does so later.

For that, the first is the sixth type of individual. The second is for the later five. For example, it is like the way that a *Parihāṇadharman*, by purifying his faculties, comes to be one in the *Cetanādharman* lineage. Since there is not a lineage lower than the *Parihāṇadharman*, one does not change into this lineage later from purifying a lower lineage. The *Abhidharmkośa* states:

> Some have the lineage from the very beginning; some become [part of the lineage] from purification.[108]

In what manner is the particularity of application? The *Abhidharmakośabhāṣya* states:

> The first two, in the previous period of training, are without continuous application and intense application; the third has application continually, the fourth has application intensely, the fifth has both applications but has weak faculties, and the sixth has both applications and sharp faculties.[109]

Intense application is fierce effort without continual engagement and continuous application is uninterrupted effort that is without without fierce diligence.

Of what sort is the manner of backsliding from whichever [type of Arhat]? Accordingly, whichever one from among those six backslides, it will be among the first five that will backslide. Backsliding from whichever one, [one also backslides] from both

---

ato'samyamukto'sau dṛṣṭiprāptānvayaśca saḥ/ |

[108] AK, vi.57c-d, Pruden, 1001, Pradhan, 373, Śāstrī, 990: *tadgotrā āditaḥ kecitkeciduttāpanāgatāḥ /*

[109] AKBh on vi.57c-d, Pruden, 1002, Pradhan, 374, Śāstrī, 991: *prathamau dvau pūrvameva śaikṣāvasthāyāṃ sātatyasatkṛtyaprayogavikalau/ tṛtīyaḥ sātatyaprayogī / caturthaḥ satkṛtyaprayogī. pañcama ubhayathāprayogī mṛdvindriyastu / ṣaṣṭa ubhayathāprayogī tīkṣṇendriyaśca /*

D 326 ཞིག་ལས་ཉམས་ན་འབྲས་བུ་དང་རིགས་གཉིས་ལས་ཏེ།དེ་ཡང་རིགས་དང་
པོ་དང་འབྲས་བུ་དང་པོ་གཉིས་ལས་ནི་མི་ཉམས་སོ།།དེ་ལ་རིགས་དང་པོ་ནི་
བཤད་ཟིན་ཏོ།

།འབྲས་བུ་དང་པོ་ནི་འབྲས་བུ་མཐར་གྱིས་འཐོབ་པའི་ལྟར་ན་རྒྱུན་
ཞུགས་ཡིན་ལ།[269]འབྲས་བུ་ཐོད་རྒལ་བ་ལྟར་ན་ཕྱིར་འོང་དང་ཕྱིར་མི་འོང་
གཉིས་ཀྱི་[270]འབྲས་བུ་དང་པོར་འགྱུར་བས་འབྲས་བུ་ཐོད་རྒལ་བས་ཐོབ་པའི་
དགྲ་བཅོམ་པ་ནི་འབྲས་བུ་ལས་ཉམས་སྲིད་ཀྱང་འབྲས་བུ་དང་པོ་གསུམ་
ལས་ཉམས་མི་སྲིད་དེ།[271]།དེ་དག་གི་སྤངས་པ་དེ་བྱིས་ལམ་དང་འདས་ལམ་
གཉིས་ཆར་གྱིས་བརྟན་པར་བྱས་པའི་ཕྱིར་རོ།།རིམ་[272]གྱིས་པ་ནི་ཁམས་གོང་
མའི་ཉོན་མོངས་རྒྱུད་ལ་སྐྱེས་པས་དགྲ་བཅོམ་ལས་ཉམས་ཏེ་ཕྱིར་མི་འོང་དུ་
སོང་།འདོད་པའི་ཉོན་མོངས་བདུན་པ་ཡན་ཆད་སྐྱེས་པས་ཕྱིར་འོང་དུ་
སོང་།དྲུག་པ་མན་ཆད་སྐྱེས་པས་རྒྱུན་ཞུགས་སུ་སོང་བ་ཡོད་ཀྱང་རྒྱུན་ཞུགས་
ལས་ནི་ཐོས་རྒལ་བ་དང་གཉིས་ཆར་ཉམས་མི་སྲིད་ཏེ།[273]མཐོང་སྤང་རྣམས་
ཀུན་བཏགས་པའི་[274]བདག་ལྟའི་རྩ་བ་ཡིན་ལ་འཕགས་པས་ཀུན་བཏགས་
པའི་[275]བདག་མེད་པར་མངོན་སུམ་གྱིས་རྟོགས་པས་ན་བདག་ལྟ་གཞི་མེད་
ཀྱི་ཉོན་མོངས་རྣམས་མི་སྐྱེ་བའི་ཕྱིར་རྒྱུན་ཞུགས་ཀྱི་སྤངས་པ་མི་ལྡོག་གོ

1337 །སྒོམ་སྤང་གི་[276]གཞི་ཆགས་པའི་ཡུལ་སྡུག་པ་དང་ཁོན་ཁོའི་ཡུལ་མི་
སྡུག་པ་ལྟ་བུ་ནི་དངོས་པོ་[277]ལ་གནས་པས་དེ་དག་ལ་དམིགས་པའི་ཉོན་
མོངས་སྐྱེ་བས་སྒོམ་སྤང་སྤངས་པ་ནི་ལྡོག་གོ།རིགས་ལས་ཉམས་པ་ལ་ནི་བྱེ་
P126b བྲག་འདི་ཡོད་དེ།[278]ཉམས་པའི་ཆོས་ཅན་ལ་རིགས་གོང་མར་འཕོ་བ་ཡོད་
D 327 ཀྱང་འོག་མར་ཉམས་པ་མེད་དེ་དེ་ལས་རིགས་དམན་པ་མེད་པའི་ཕྱིར་
རོ།།རིགས་དང་པོ་ལས་མི་ཉམས་པའི་རྒྱུ་མཚན་ཡང་དང་པོ་ནས་ཉིད་ཀྱིས་
རིགས་དེ་སློབ་ལམ་དང་མི་སློབ་ལམ་གཉིས་ཀའི་སྐབས་སུ་ཡུན་རིང་དུ་
འདྲིས་པས་བརྟན་པར་གྱུར་པའི་ཕྱིར་རོ།།ཕྱིས་དགྲ་བཅོམ་ཐོབ་ནས་ཉམས་
པའི་ཆོས་ཅན་གྱིས་དབང་པོ་སྦྱངས་ཏེ་འཆི་བར་སེམས་པར་གྱུར་པ་ལྟ་བུའི་
རིགས་ནི་ལམ་གཉིས་ཀྱིས་བརྟན་པ་མེད་པའི་ཕྱིར་རོ།།གང་ཞིག་གང་ལས་

---

[269] / D M] om. / P | [270] kyi D M] kyis P | [271] / D M] om. / P | [272] rim D M] rims P | [273] / D M] om. / P | [274] kun btags pa'i M] kun brtags pa'i D P | [275] kun btags pa'i M] kun brtags pa'i D P | [276] gi D M] kyi P | [277] dngos po D M] ddos po P | [278] / D M] om. / P

D326 lineage and result. Furthermore, one does not backslide from the first lineage and the first two results. In this way, the explanation of the first lineage is finished.

The first result, if attained by gradual progress, is a Stream-enterer; along these lines, since for the fruition skippers, the two results of Once-returner and Non-returner will be the first result, the result of Arhat that is attained by those skipping fruitions, although it is possible to backslide from that result, is it is not possible to backslide from the first three results because the abandonment of those first three fruitions is made firm by both the childish path (i.e., mundane) and the supermundane path. The gradual progressor backslides from the result of Arhat and turns into a Non-returner by producing in the continuum the upper realm afflictions. [The Arhat] turns into a Once-returner by producing afflictions of desire realm above the seventh. One turns into a Stream-enterer by producing the lower six [desire realm afflictions]. Although is not possible to backslide from the Stream-enterer and both [fruition] skippers, since the obstacles to be abandoned by the path of seeing are the root of the [false] view of an imputed self and the Āryan, because of directly cognizing the selflessness of that imputation, does not produce the afflictions of the baseless [false] view of the self, the abandonments of the Stream-enterer are therefore irreversible.

The basis of the obstacles to be removed by the path of cultivation are the pleasing object of desire and the disagreeable object of anger, through generating afflictions which are perceived on things by abiding on objects like that, the abandoned obstacles to be removed by the path of cultivation return.

For backsliding from the lineage, there is this division: the lineage of the Parihāṇadharman does transfer into upper lineages but does not backslide into lower lineages because there is not a lower
D327 lineage than that. Further, the reason for not backsliding from the first lineage is because that lineage from the first is firm in being accustomed for a long time in the period of both the path of training and the path of no more training. Later, having obtained [the result of] Arhat, the *Parihāṇadharman* purifies his faculties and comes into the lineage of the *Cetānadharman* because of not being firm in both paths.

ཉམས་པའི་ཚུལ་དེ་ལྟར་ཡང་མཛོད་དུ།

བཞི་ནི་རིགས་ལས་ལྷ་འབྲས་ལས།།ཉམས་འགྱུར་དང་པོ་ལས་མ་ཡིན།

།ཞེས་གང་གསུངས་པའོ།།དང་པོ་ལས་མ་ཡིན་གྱི་འགྲེལ་བཤད་དུ།

འབྲས་བུ་དང་པོ་རྒྱུན་ཞུགས་ཁོ་ནར་མ་མཛད་པར་ཕྱིར་འོང་ཕྱིར་མི་འོང་ལ་ཡང་བཤད་པ་ནི་སྐབས་དེའི་འགྲེལ་པར་གསལ་ཁ་མེད་ཀྱང་འཐད་པར་རྟོགས་ཏེ།གནས་གཉིས་པར་ཐོད་རྒལ་བའི་ཕྱིར་འོང་དང་ཕྱིར་མི་འོང་ལས་ཉམས་པ་མི་སྲིད་པར་གསུངས་པ་དང་[279]གནས་དྲུག་པར་ཡང།གལ་ཏེ་འབྲས་བུ་དང་པོ་ཐོབ་པའི་ཕྱིར་རོ་ཞེ་ན་ནི།ཕལ་ཆེར་ལས་འདོད་ཆགས་དང་བྲལ་བ་དང་འདོད་པ་ལས་འདོད་ཆགས་དང་བྲལ་བ་ཡང་ཡིན་པར་འགྱུར་རོ།

།ཞེས་གསུངས་པ་རྣམས་དང་ལེགས་པར་གྲུང་འགྲིག་པའི་ཕྱིར་རོ།།དེ་ལྟར་ཡང་མཛོད་འགྲེལ་ལས།[280]

ཡོངས་སུ་ཉམས་པའི་ཆོས་ཅན་ནི་རྣམ་པ་གསུམ་ཡིན་ཏེ།[281]དེའི་སོ་ན་གནས་བཞིན་དུ་ཡོངས་སུ་མྱ་ངན་ལས་འདའ་བའམ།།དབང་པོ་
D 328 འཕོ་བའམ།།[282]ཡོངས་སུ་ཉམས་ན་སློབ་པ་ཉིད་དུ་འགྱུར་བའོ།།འཆི་བར་སེམས་པའི་ཆོས་ཅན་ནི་བཞི་སྟེ།གསུམ་པོ་དེ་དག་ཉིད་དང།ཡོངས་སུ་ཉམས་པའི་ཆོས་ཅན་གྱི་རིགས་སུ་སྣར་འོངས་

[279] om. / D M] insert / P | [280] / D M] om. / P | [281] / D M] om. / P | [282] / / D M] om. / / P

The manner of backsliding from where for whichever one is stated in the *Abhidharmakośa*:

> Four backslide from family, five backslide from result, but not the first result.[110]

[One] does not [backslide] from the first [result] but the *Abhidharmakośabhāṣyvyākhyā* states:

> The first result is construed only as a Stream-enterer but it can also be explained for the Once-returner or Non-returner, [this] is understood as correct although not clearly mentioned in the *Abhidharmakośabhāṣya* of that section. The second chapter [of the *Kośabhāṣya*] teaches that is not possible to backslide from the skipper Once-returner or Non-returner and also the sixth chapter [of the *Kośabhāṣya*] explains: If that is the case, what will be the first result that is attained? That one will be either a *Bhūyovītarāga* (i.e., one separated from attachment for the most part) or a *Kāmavītarāga* (i.e., one separated from attachment from the desire realm).[111]

These teachings are eloquently just right. The *Abhidharmakośabhāṣya* states:

> The *Parihāṇadharman* is of three aspects: attaining *nirvāṇa* by staying in his family, or changing faculties, or by backsliding and becoming a *Śaikṣa*. With respect to the *Cetanādharman* four cases are possible: three as above or backsliding and becoming a *Parihāṇadharman*. Likewise for the

---

[110] AK, vi.58a-b, Pruden, 1003, Śāstrī, 992: *gotrāccaturṇāṃ pañcānāṃ phalāddhāniḥ na pūrvakāt /*

[111] AKBh, Śāstrī, 994:*yasmāt srotaāpattiphalaṃ yadi prāpyate 'vaśyaṃ prathamaṃ bhavati / sakṛdāgāmyanāgāmiphale tu kadācittu prathame bhavataḥ yadi bhūyovītarāgakāmavītarāgayoḥ / kadācidaprathame yadyānupūrvikasya / (tatra yadyat phalaṃ prathamaṃ bhavati srotaāpattiphalaṃ sakṛdāgāmiphalam anāgāmiphalaṃ vā na tasmāt parihīyate) /*

P127a པའོ།།དེ་ བཞིན་ དུ་ གཞན་ གསུམ་ ལ་ ཡང་ རེ་ རེ་ བསྐྱེད་ དེ་ རོ་ རིམ་
|1338 བཞིན་ དུ་ རྣམ་ པ་ ལྔ་ དང་ དྲུག་ དང་ བདུན་ ཡིན་ པར་ རིག་ པར་
[283]བྱའོ།

།ཞེས་པ་ལྟར་དབྱེ་བ་བྱེད་ལ།ཡང་དེ་ཉིད་ལས་

> ཡོངས་ སུ་ ཉམས་ པའི་ ཆོས་ ཅན་ ཡང་ གནོད་ མི་ ཟ་ བར་ ཡོངས་ སུ་ ཉམས་པ་འགྱུར་བའི་ཆོས་ཅན་མ་ཡིན་ལ་རྟོགས་པའི་སྐལ་བ་ཅན་ གྱི་ བར་ དུ་ ཡང་ རྟོགས་ པར་ འགྱུར་ བ་ མ་ ཡིན་ གྱི་ སྲིད་ པའི་ ཕྱིར་ དེ་ སྐད་ཅེས་བཤད་དོ།།དེ་ལྟར་བྱས་ན་ཁམས་གསུམ་ཆར་ན་ཡང་དགྲ་ བཅོམ་པ་དྲུག་ཡོད་པར་ཏང་ངོ།

།ཞེས་ པ་ བྱེ་ བྲག་ ཏུ་ སྨྲ་ བའི་ འདོད་ པའོ།།དེའི་ འཕོས་ ཉིད་ ནས།[284]གང་ དག་ གནོད་ མི་ ཟ་ བར་ ཡོངས་ སུ་ ཉམས་ པར་ འགྱུར་ བ་ ནས།།མངོན་ པར་ རྟོགས་པའི་བར་དུ་འགྱུར་བ་དེ་དག་གི་ལྟར་ན་འདོད་པའི་ཁམས་ན་ནི་དྲུག་ གོ།གཟུགས་དང་གཟུགས་མེད་པའི་ཁམས་ན་ནི་གནས་པ་ལས་མི་བསྐྱོད་པ་ དང་མི་གཡོ་བའི་ཆོས་ཅན་གཉིས་ཏེ།དེ་ཉིད་ན་ཡོངས་སུ་ཉམས་པ་དང་།འཆི་ བར་སེམས་པ་དང་།དབང་པོ་འཕོ་བ་མེད་པའི་ཕྱིར་རོ།ཞེས་བཤད་པ་ནི་ཀུན་ ལས་ བཏུས་ དང་ མཐུན་ ཏེ།[285]ཉམས་ པའི་ ཆོས་ ཅན་ ལ་ སོགས་ པ་ ངེས་ པ་ ཅན་ དུ་འདོད་པའི་ཕྱིར་རོ།།འདིར་བྱེ་བྲག་ཏུ་སྨྲ་བ་དགྲ་བཅོམ་པ་ལས་ཉམས་པར་ འདོད་པ་ཤེས་བྱེད་གང་མཐོང་ནས་འདོད་ཅེ་ན།མདོ་ལས་

> རྐྱེན་ལྔ་[286]དང་རྒྱུ་ལྔས་དུས་ཀྱིས་རྣམ་པར་གྲོལ་བའི་དགྲ་བཅོམ་པ་
> D 329 ཡོངས་ སུ་ ཉམས་ པར་ འགྱུར་ རོ།།ང་ གང་ ཞེ་ ན།[287]ལས་ ཀྱི་ མཐའ་ ལ་
> ཞུགས་ པ་ ཡིན།[288]སྨྲ་ བ་ ཞུགས་ པ་ ཡིན།ཇོད་ པ་ ལ་ ཞུགས་ པ་ ཡིན།རིང་ དུ་ རྒྱུ་ བའི་ སྐྱོར་ བ་ དང་ ལྡན་ པ་ ཡིན།ནད་ ཀྱི་ རྣམ་ པས་ ཡུན་རིང་པོ་ནས་ཐེབས་པ་ཡིན།

ཞེས་གསུངས་པ་དང་།ཡང་མདོ་ལས།

[283]rig par D M] rigs par P | [284]/ D M] om. / P | [285]/ D M] om. / P | [286]om. / D M] insert / P | [287]/ D M] om. / P | [288]/ D M] om. / P

[112] AKBh, Pk037a.7-037b.1, Pruden, 1004, Śāstrī, 994: *parihāṇadharmaṇastrayaḥ prakārā bhavanti tadavasthasya parinirvāṇam indriyasaḥcāraḥ parihāya vā śaikṣatvam / cetanādharmaṇaścatvāraḥ eta eva trayaḥ parihāṇadharma*

> three others born in each one successively five, six,
> or seven aspects should be known.[112]

Thus accordingly are the divisions construed and also from the very same text:

> The *Parihāṇadharman* does not necessarily fall away up to also the *Prativedhanādharman* not necessarily penetrating, but because of existing they are called as such. If done accordingly also it is suitable to have six Arhats in the three realms.[113]

The above is the assertion of the *Vaibhāṣika*s. If according to them, from this procedure, necessarily from the *Parihāṇadharman* up to the *Prativedhanādharman*, there will be six in the realm of desire. In the form and formless realm the *Sthitākampya* and the *Akopyadharman* are the two because these very realms are without backsliding, volitional thought, and [the ability to] change faculties.

[This] explanation is concordant with the *Abhidharmasamuccaya* because it is accepted as definite for the *Parihāṇadharman*, and so forth. Here, what scriptural proof do the *Vaibhāṣika*s accept to assert backsliding from the state of Arhat? From the *sūtra*:

> By five causes or five conditions the Arhat who is occasionally liberated will be caused to backslide. What are the five? Extending the limit of karma occurs, extending the speech occurs, extending in effort occurs, possessing the application of a cause for a long time, and touched for a long time by the aspect of sickness.[114]

---

gotrapratyāgamanaṃ ca. evamanyeṣāṃ trayāṇāmekaikaprakāravṛddhyā yathākramaṃ pañca ṣaṭ sapta prakārā veditavyāḥ/ | [113] AKBh, Pk036b.7-8, Pruden, 1002, Śāstrī, 991: *nacāvśyaṃ parihāṇadharmā parihīyate nāpi yāvat prativedhanābhavyaḥ pratividhati / sambhavaṃ tu pratyevamucyate evaṃ ca kṛtvā dhātutraye `pi ṣadarhanto yujyante /*

[114] AKV, Śāstrī, 991: *pañca hetavaḥ pañca pratyayaḥ samayavimuktasyārhataḥ parihāṇāya saṃvartante / katame pañca / karmāntaprasṛto bhavati bhāṣyaprasṛto bhavati adhikaraṇaprasṛto bhavati dīrghacārikāyomanuyukto bhavati dīrgheṇa ca rogajātena spṛṣṭo bhavati /*

དེ་ནས་བཅོམ་ལྡན་འདས་ཀྱིས་ཚེ་དང་ལྡན་པ་ཀུན་དགའ་བོ་ལ་
P127b བཀའ་སྩལ་པ།ཀུན་དགའ་བོ་དགྲ་བཅོམ་པ་ལ་ཡང་ཉེད་པ་
དང།བཀུར་སྟིས་བར་ཆད་བྱེད་པ་ཡིན་པར་ང་སྨྲའོ།།ཚེ་དང་ལྡན་
པ་ཀུན་དགའ་བོས་གསོལ་པ།བཅོམ་ལྡན་འདས་ཅིའི་སླད་དུ་འདི་
1339 སྐད་ཅེས་ཀུན་དགའ་བོ་དགྲ་བཅོམ་པ་ལ་ཡང་ཉེད་པ་དང།བཀུར་
སྟིས་བར་ཆད་བྱེ་པ་ཡིན་པར་ང་སྨྲའོ།།ཞེས་གསུངས།[289]བཅོམ་ལྡན་
འདས་ཀྱིས་བཀའ་སྩལ་པ།ཀུན་དགའ་བོ་མ་ཐོབ་པ་ཐོབ་པར་བྱ་བ་
དང།མ་རྟོགས་པ་རྟོགས་པར་བྱ་བ་དང།མངོན་སུམ་དུ་མ་བྱས་པ་
མངོན་སུམ་དུ་བྱ་བ་ལ་བར་ཆད་བྱེད་པ་ནི་མ་ཡིན་པ་ཉིད་
དོ།།འོན་ཀྱང་འདིས་ལྷག་པའི་སེམས་ལས་བྱུང་བ་མཐོང་བའི་ཆོས་
ལ་བདེ་བར་གནས་པ་བཞི་པོ་ཐོབ་པ་གང་དག་ཡིན་པ་དེ་གང་
ཡང་རུང་བ་ཞིག་ལས་འདི་ཡོངས་སུ་ཉམས་པར་འགྱུར་བར་ང་སྨྲ
སྟེ།དེ་ཡང་འདྲིས་པར་གནས་པ་ཡིན་ནོ།།གཅིག་ཏུ་མ་འདྲེས་པར་
བག་ཡོད་པ་བརྩོན་པ་པར་གནས་པ་འདིས་སེམས་ཀྱི་རྣམ་པར་
གྲོལ་བ་ལུས་ཀྱིས་མངོན་སུམ་དུ་བྱས་པ་གང་ཡིན་པ་དེ་ལས་ནི་
རྣམ་གྲངས་གང་གིས་ཀྱང་ཡོངས་སུ་ཉམས་པར་འགྱུར་བར་ང་མི་
སྨྲའོ།།ཀུན་དགའ་བོ་དེ་ལྟ་བས་ན་ཁྱོད་ཀྱིས་འདི་ལྟར་བསླབ་པར་
D 330 བྱ་སྟེ་ཉེད་པ་དང་བཀུར་སྟི་གང་ཡིན་པ་དེ་ཟིལ་གྱིས་མནན་པར་
བྱའོ།ཉེད་པ་དང་བཀུར་སྟི་བྱུང་བ་ལ་སེམས་ཀུན་ནས་དཀྲིས་ཏེ་མི་
འདུག་པ་དེ་ལྟར་ཀུན་དགའ་བོ་ཁྱོད་ཀྱིས་བསླབ་པར་བྱའོ།
།ཞེས་འབྱུང་བ་དེ་ལས་མི་གཡོ་བ་ལ་ཉམས་པ་གཏན་མེད་ཅེས་ཁྱད་
པར་དུ་སྨོས་པས་དུས་སྦྱོར་གྱི་དགྲ་བཅོམ་པ་ལས་ཉམས་པར་བསྟན་ཏོ།།ཡང་

[289] / D M] om. / P

[115] AKV, Śāstrī, 997: *yatra bhagavānāyuṣmantamānandamāmantrayate sma arhato*

Also from the *sūtra*:

> Thereupon, the Bhagavān said to the Venerable Ānanda, "Ānanda, I say the Arhat is also interrupted by fame and fortune." The Venerable Ānanda supplicated, "Bhagavān, why do you say, 'Ānanda, I say the Arhat is interrupted by fame and fortune'?" Then the Bhagavān said, "Ānanda, obtaining or not obtaining, cognizing or not cognizing, realizing or not realizing, interruption is not that itself. But by this, some who attain the four abodes in bliss for the present life arising from superior intellect, now anyone who is characterized with this may backslide I say. Also that is mixed abiding. One who manifests physically the liberation of mind by that diligent abiding, conscientious to not mix together, through this manner, I do not say will backslide. Ānanda, by such, you should train accordingly and fame and fortune, however brilliant it is, should be overcome. Do not sit and be ensnared through all thoughts arising from fame and fortune. In this manner, Ānanda, you should train." [115]

Thus by that particular statement that "backsliding is entirely not possible for the immovable," indicates that the occasionally [delivered] Arhat can backslide. Also from the *sūtra*, the Venerable

---

'pyahamānanda lābhasatkāramantarāyakaraṃ vadāmīti / āyuṣmān ānanda āha tat kasmād bhagavānevamāha arhato 'pyahamānanda lābhasatkāramantarāvakaraṃ vadāmīti / bhagavānāha "na haivānanda aprāptasya prāptaye anadhigatasyādhigamāya asākṣātkṛtasya sākṣātkriyāyaiḥ api tu ye nena catvāra ādhicaitasikā dṛṣṭadharmasukhavihārā adhigatāḥ tato 'hamasyānyatamasmāt parihāṇim vadāmi/ taccākīrṇasya viharataḥ/ yā tvanenaikākināvyapakṛṣṭenāpramattenātāpinā prahitātmanā viharatā akopyā cetāvimuktiḥ kāyena sājñātkṛtā tato `syāhaṃ na kenacit paryāyeṇa parihāṇi vadāmi / tasmāt tarhyānandaivaṃ te śikṣitavyam yallābhasatkāramabhibhaviṣyamāno na cātyantairlābhasatkārakaiścittaṃ paryādāya sthāsyati / evaṃ te ānanda śikṣitavyam/ See also Pruden 1006, 1074, *Saṃyutta*, ii.239.

མདོ་ལས།ཚེ་དང་ལྡན་པ་གནག་ཚོགས་ཅན་དགྲ་བཅོམ་པ་ཡིན་པ་ཉམས་
པར་གསུངས་པ་དང།ཡང་སོལ་བའི་ཕུང་པོ་ལྟ་བུའི་མདོ་ལས་

> འཕགས་པ་ཉན་ཐོས་ཐོས་པ་དང་ལྡན་པ་དེ་ལྟར་སྤྱོད་པ་དེ་ལྟར་
> P128a གནས་པ་དེ་བརྒྱ་ལ་རེ་འགའ་ཞིག་དྲན་པ་ཉམས་པ་ལས་སྡིག་པ་
> མི་དགེ་བའི་རྣམ་པར་རྟོག་པ་དག་སྐྱེ་བར་འགྱུར་རོ།

།ཞེས་གསུངས་པས་ཀྱང་དགྲ་བཅོམ་ལས་ཉམས་པར་བསྟན་ཏོ།།གལ་
ཏེ་ཉན་ཐོས་འཕགས་པ་མི་དགེ་བའི་སེམས་སྐྱེས་པ་དེ་སློབ་པ་ནི་མ་ཡིན་
ཏེ།མདོ་དེ་ཉིད་ལས་གང་དག་དེའི་དབང་དུ་མཛད་ནས་ཡུན་རིང་པོ་ནས་
སེམས་དབེན་པ་ལ་གཞོལ་བ་ཡིན་ཞེས་བྱ་བ་ནས་མྱ་ངན་ལས་འདའ་བ་ལ་
འབབ་པ་ཡིན་ཞེས་པའི་བར་དུ་གསུངས་ཤིང[290]།[291]མདོ་གཞན་ལས་དེ་དག་
དགྲ་བཅོམ་པའི་སྐོབས་སུ་གསུངས་ཏེ།མདོ་ལས།

> བཙུན་པ་དགེ་སློང་དགྲ་བཅོམ་པ་ཟག་པ་ཟད་པའི་སྐོབས་དུ་ཞིག་
> མཆིས།ཤཱ་རིའི་བུ་དགེ་སློང་དགྲ་བཅོམ་པའི་སྐོབས་ནི་བརྒྱད་དེ།

།ཡུན་རིང་པོ་ནས་ཞེས་པ་ནས་འབབ་པ་ཡིན་ཞེས་པའི་བར་དང།ཟག་
པའི་གནས་ལྟ་བུའི་ཆོས་ཐམས་ཅད་ལས་ནི་བསིལ་བར་གྱུར་ཅིང་བསིལ་བར་
D 331 གྱུ་པ་ཞེས་དགྲ་བཅོམ་པར་གསུངས་པའི་ཕྱིར་རོ།།ཞེས་མདོ་སྡེ་དེ་དག་ཤེས་
བྱེད་དུ་དྲངས་ནས་དགྲ་བཅོམ་པ་ལས་ཉམས་པ་ཡོད་པར་དམ་འཆའོ།།དོན་
འདི་ལ་མཛོད་འགྲེལ་དུ་མདོ་སྡེ་པ་རྣམས་ན་རེ།[292]དགྲ་བཅོམ་པ་ཉིད་ལས་
ཀྱང་ཡོངས་སུ་ཉམས་པ་མེད་དོ།།ཞེས་ཟེར་ཏེ་འདི་ཉིད་རིགས་པ་ཡིན་ནོ་ཇི་
[293]ལྟར་ཁོང་དུ་ཆུད་ཅེ་ན།ལུང་དང་རིགས་པས་སོ་ཞེས་སངས་རྒྱས་གཉིས་པ་
ཡང་མདོ་སྡེ་པའི་ལུགས་བཟུང་ནས་ནས་བྱེ་བྲག་ཏུ་སྨྲ་བའི་ལོག་རྟོག་སུ་

[290] shing D M] cing P | [291] / D M] om. / P | [292] / D M] om. / P | [293] ji M] ci D P

[116] Pk 039a.1, "gautika", Śāstrī, p.999 note #3, also "bhautika", *Index to Abhidharmakośa*, L.V.P., VI. p.262, Pruden, p.1008., 1075, #367, Gautika is a good example of the *cetanādharman* class of Arhat, pali "Godhika", see also *Saṃyutta*, i.120; *Commentary on the Dhammapada*, 55. | [117] AKBh, Pk039b.5-6, Pruden, 1009, Śāstrī, 1001: *aṅgārakarṣūpamaṃ tarhi parihāryam yatredanuktam 'yasya khalu śrutavata*

Gautika,[116] who is an Arhat, is taught as backsliding. The *Aṅgārakarṣūpama sūtra* states:

> An *Ārya Śrāvaka* who is learned, performs accordingly, abiding in this way, sometimes, from the loss of mindfulness, produces perceptions of unvirtuous polluted [thoughts].[117]

This teaching demonstrates backsliding from the state of Arhat. If that is the case, the *Ārya Śrāvaka* who produces unvirtuous thoughts is not a *Śaikṣa*. From this very same *sūtra*, construeing one's faculty in stating, "for a long time, his mind diligent for separation" up to "turned towards *nirvāṇa*,"[118] indicates in another *sūtra* the powers of an Arhat. From the *sūtra*:

> How many powers are there of the Reverend Arhat monk who cuts off the impurities? Śariputra, the powers of the Arhat monk are eight.[119]

Statements [in that *sūtra*] from "for a long time" up to "towards *nirvāṇa*" and "he will be cool, purged from all dharmas which are like
D331 the abode of impurity," indicates an Arhat. Quoting the principles from these *sūtra*s proposes there to be a backsliding [from the state of Arhat]. For this meaning, in the *Abhidharmakośabhāṣya*[120] the *Sautrāntika*s say that one can no longer fall from the quality of an Arhat and the reasons why it is to be pressed upon the mind. Thus, by "scripture and reasoning" the Second Buddha [Vasubandhu] following the system of the *Sautrāntika* refutes the wrong view of the

---

āryaśrāvakasyaivaṃ carata evaṃ viharataḥ kadācita karhicit smṛtisampramoṣādutpadyante pāpakā akuśalā vitarkāḥ / | [118] AKBh, Pk039b.6-7, Pruden 1009, Śāstrī 1001-1002: *sa hi tatrārhanneva jñāpita 'dīrgharātra vivekanimnacittamucyate yāvannirvāṇaprāgbhāram /*

[119] The full *sūtra* quote is found in the AKV, Śāstrī, 1002: *kati bhadantārhato bhikṣoḥ kṣīṇāsravasya balāni / aṣṭau śariputrārhato bhikṣordīrgharātraṃ vivekanimnaṃ cittaṃ yāvannirvāṇaprāgbhāram. aṅgārakarṣūpamāscānena kāmā dṛṣṭvā bhavanti yathāsya kāmān jānataḥ kāmān paśyato yaḥ kāmeṣu kāmaccandaḥ kāmasnehaḥ vistareṇa yāvatkāmādhyavasānam tatrāsya cittaṃ na paryādāya tiṣṭati /....sarvairāsravasthānīyairdharmaiḥ śītībhūtaṃ vāntībhūtam /* cf.SN, iv.189,190 AN, iv.224.

[120] AKBh, Pruden , 1006, Śāstrī, 996: *arhattvādapi nāsti parihāṇiriti sautrāntikāḥ. eṣa eva ca nyāyaḥ / kathamidaṃ gamyate āgamād yuktitaśca /*

འཕྲིན་པར་མཛད་དོ།།འདིར་འགྲེལ་བཤད་དུ་ཀྱང་ཞེས་བྱ་བའི་སྒྲས་ནི་

> མཐོང་བས་སྤང་བར་བྱ་བ་སྤངས་པས་ཡོངས་སུ་ཉམས་པ་མེད་པ་
> འབའ་ཞིག་ཏུ་མ་ཟད་ཀྱི་དགྲ་བཅོམ་པ་ཉིད་ལས་ཀྱང་ཡོངས་སུ་
> ཉམས་པ་མེད་དོ་ཞེས་སྟོན་པར་བྱེད་དོ།།དང་པོ་མ་ཡིན་ལན་ཅིག
> ཕྱིར་འོང་བ་དང་ཕྱིར་མི་འོང་བའི་འབྲས་བུ་ལས་ནི་ཡོངས་སུ་
> ཉམས་པ་སྲིད་དེ།དེ་ནི་འཇིག་རྟེན་པའི་ལམ་གྱིས་ཐོབ་པ་སྲིད་པའི་
> ཕྱིར་རོ།།སྙམ་དུ་བསམས་པ་ཡིན་ནོ།[294]

།ཞེས་སངས་རྒྱས་གཉིས་པའི་ཡང་བཞེད་པས་འབྲས་བུ་དང་པོ་དང་
ཐ་མ་གཉིས་ངེས་པར་འཇིག་རྟེན་ལས་འདས་པའི་ལམ་ཁོ་ནས་འཐོབ་པ་མི་
ཉམས་ལ།[295]འབྲས་བུ་བར་པ་གཉིས་ནི་འཕགས་པས་འཇིག་རྟེན་པའི་ལམ་
གྱིས་ཀྱང་ཐོབ་པར་བྱེད་ལས་དེ་གཉིས་ལས་ཉམས་པ་སྲིད་དེ།[296]འཇིག་རྟེན་
པའི་ལམ་གྱིས་སྤངས་པ་ནི་ལྡོག་པ་སྲིད་པའི་ཕྱིར་རོ།།ཞེས་བསྟན་ཏོ།།དོན་དེ་
1341 ནི་མཁས་པ་རྣམས་ཀྱི་གཙུག་གི་ནོར་བུ་དཔལ་ལྡན་ཆོས་ཀྱི་གྲགས་པ་ཡང་
བཤེད་པར་མངོན་ཏེ།རྣམ་འགྲེལ་དུ

> །དེ་ཉིད་དང་བརྟན་དང།[297]།མ་ལུས་ཁྱད་པར་མཁྱེན་པར་
D 332 འགྱུབ།།གཤེགས་པ་རྟོགས་པའི་དོན་ཕྱིར་ཏེ།།དེ་ཕྱིར་ཕྱི་རོལ་པ་དང་
> སློབ།།མི་སློབ་ལས་ལྷག

ཅེས་ཐུབ་པའི་རྟོགས་པ་དེ་[298]དེ་ཁོ་ན་ཉིད་མཁྱེན་པ་དང།མཁྱེན་པ་
བརྟན་པ་དང།མ་ལུས་པ་མཁྱེན་པས་རིམ་པ་ལྟར་ཕྱི་རོལ་པ་དང་སློབ་པ་
དང་མི་སློབ་པ་ལས་ལྷག་ཅེས་པ་ལྟར།

> སྡུག་བསྔལ་བརྟེན་མིན་ཕྱིར་ལེགས་ཡིན།
> །ཞེས་དང།

[294]/ D M] om. / P | [295]/ D M] om. / P | [296]/ D M] om. / P | [297]/ D M] om. / P |
[298]om. / D M] insert / P

[121] AKV, Śāstrī, 996: *na kevalaṃ darśanaheyaprahāṇānnāsti parihāṇaḥ arhattvādipi nāsti parihāṇirityapiśabena darśayati aprathamabhyāṃ tu sakṛdāgāmyanāgāmi*

Vaibhāṣikas. Here is also the statement given in the *Abhidharmakośabhāṣyavyākhyā*:

> Not only is there no backsliding by abandoning that to be abandoned by the path of seeing, but there is also no backsliding from [the result of] Arhat itself. Not [from] the first [result], but there is backsliding from the result of Once-returner and Non-returner because those attainments can occur by a mundane path. That is the intended meaning.[121]

The Second Buddha [Vasubandhu] explains that both the first and last result do not backslide since they are definitely obtained only through a supermundane path and that it is possible to backslide from the two middle fruitions since an Āryan may obtain [them] by a mundane path. The abandonment by a mundane path is therefore reversible. The crowned jewel of scholars, glorious Dharmakīrti, also explains this meaning. In the *Pramāṇavārttika*, that realization of the
D332 Muni is:

> knowledge established distinctively as real, firm and complete, going is for the sake of realization, and therefore [the Muni is] superior to outsiders, trainees, and those beyond training.[122]

> [The Buddha's realization] is said to be successively superior to outsiders, trainers, and those beyond training since [he has] knowledge of reality, firm knowledge, and knowledge that is complete. In this way,

> because [the Buddha's abandonment] is not a basis of suffering it is good.... " and "because [the

---

phalābhyāṃ parihāṇiḥ sambhavati. laukikena mārgeṇa tatprāptisambhavādityabhiprāyaḥ /

[122] *Pramāṇavārttika, pramāṇasiddhi*, verse 280d according to Steinkellner's *Verse-Index of Dharmakīrti's Works* (Vienna, 1967). In Vetter's *Der Buddha und Seine Lehre in Dharmakīrtis Pramāṇavārttika* (Vienna, 1984) occurs as 280b-d, 169:*...tattvasthirāśeṣaviśeṣa-jñānasādhanam. bodhārthatvād gamer bāhyaśaikṣāśaikṣādhikas tataḥ /*

བདག་ལྟའི་ས་བོན་སྤངས་པའི་ཕྱིར།།སླར་མི་གཤེགས་པ་ཉིད་ཡིན་ནོ།།ཞེས་དང་།གོམས་ཕྱིར་མ་ལུས་སྤངས་པ་ཡིན།

།ཞེས་ཐུབ་པའི་སྤངས་པ་ལེགས་པར་སྤངས་པ་དང་།སླར་མི་ལྡོག་པར་སྤངས་པ་དང་།མ་ལུས་པར་སྤངས་པའི་སྤང་བ་ཁྱད་པར་གསུམ་ལྡན་ཏེ་རིམ་པ་ལྟར་ཕྱིར་རོལ་པ་དང་སློབ་པ་དང་མི་སློབ་པ་ལས་ལྷག་པར་བསྟན་པར་དགོངས་པ་བརྟགས་ནས་ཤིང[299]།[300]སློབ་པའི་སྤངས་པ་སླར་མི་ལྡོག་ན་མི་ལྡོག་པར་སྤངས་པས་སློབ་ལ་ལས་ཁྱད་པར་དུ་གྱུར་པར་བསྒྲུབ་མི་ནུས་པའི་ཕྱིར་རོ།

P129a །དེ་ལྟར་འཕགས་པ་སློབ་པའི་སྤངས་པ་ལྡོག་སྲིད་པར་མཁས་པ་གཉིས་མཐུན་ཡང་ལྡོག་པའི་རྒྱུ་མཚན་མི་འདྲ་སྟེ།ཆོས[301]མངོན་པའི་ལུགས་བཤད་ཟིན་ལ།[302]རིགས་པའི་དབང་ཕྱུག་ནི་ཉོན་མོངས་པ་སྤངས་པ་སླར་རྒྱུད་ལ་མ་སྐྱེས་ན་སྤངས་པ་མི་ལྡོག་ཅིང་ཉོན་མོངས་པ་ཡང་བདག་ལྟའི་རྒྱུ་ཅན་ཡིན་པས་ཇི་སྲིད་བདག་འཛིན་དྲུངས་མ་ཕྱུང་བ་དེ་སྲིད་དུ་ཉོན་མོངས་པ་རྣམས་འཇུག་པས་ན་སློབ་པ་རྣམས་ལ་བདག་འཛིན་དྲུངས་ཕྱུང་བ་མེད་པའི་ཕྱིར་རོ་སྙམ་དུ་དགོངས་སོ།

།འོ་ན་དགྲ་བཅོམ་པ་ལས་མི་ཉམས་པ་ལ་ལུང་གང་ཡོད་པ་ཡིན་ཞེ་
D 333 ན།མདོ་ལས།

དགེ་སློང་དག་འཕགས་པའི་ཤེས་རབ་ཀྱིསསྤངས་པ་གང་ཡིན་པ་དེ་ནི་སྤངས་པ་ཡིན་ནོ།

།ཞེས་དེ་འདྲ་བའི་སྤངས་པ་དེ་སླར་ཉོན་མོངས་མི་སྐྱེ་བས་སྤངས་ངེས་སུ་གསུངས་པ་དང་།སློབ་པ་ལ་བག་ཡོད་པ་ལ་བག་ཡོད་པར་བྱའོ་ཞེས་གསུངས་ཀྱི་དགྲ།འོ་ན་དགྲ་བཅོམ་པ་ལས་མི་ཉམས་པ་ལ་ལུང་གང་ཡོད་པ་

[299]shing D M] cing P | [300]/ D M] om. / P | [301]chos D M] ches P | [302]/ D M] om. / P

[123] This is a combination of sections of verse of the *Pramāṇavārttika*, *pramāṇasiddhi* chapter verses 139-142a in Vetter's *Der Buddha und Seine Lehre in Dharmakīrtis Pramāṇavārttika* (Vienna, 1984). The bold print is Tsong kha pa's reference: (139) *hetoḥ prahāṇaṃ triguṇaṃ sugatatvam aniśrayāt duḥkhasya śastaṃ nairātmyadṛṣṭes*

> Buddha's abandonment] abandons the seed of the view of self it is irreversible..." and "it is complete abandonment because of being accustomed."[123]

Thus the Muni's abandonment has the three distinctions of abandoning well, abandonment that is irreversible, and abandonment that is complete. In this succession [one] is able to designate the intention to demonstrate [the Muni's] superiority over outsiders (*bāhya*), [Buddhist] trainees (*śaikṣa*), and [those Buddhists] beyond training (*aśaikṣa*), because if the abandonment of a trainee was irreversible then [the Buddha] would be unable to be established as distinct from a trainee.

In this way, although the two masters [Vasubandhu and Dharmakīrti] are concordant in stating that the abandonment of the Noble trainee (*ārya śaikṣa*) is possible to reverse, [their] reason for reversibility is dissimilar. The system of the *Ābhidhārmika* has already been explained and for the king of reasoning Dharmakīrti: when abandoned afflictions are not generated in the [mental] continuum again, abandonment is irreversible and since afflictions possess as a cause the view of self (*ātmadarśana*), as long as [one] does not dig out the root of grasping at the self, for that long the afflictions are entered into and therefore *śaikṣas* do not dig out the root of grasping at the self. That is the intention.

Well then, what scripture is [cited] for the non-backsliding from
D333 the state of Arhat? A *sūtra* states:

> In this way Monks, abandonment is abandonment by Āryan wisdom.[124]

Thus the abandonment like that is spoken as certain abandonment since it does not produce the afflictions again and it is also indicated that "the *śaikṣa* should cultivate vigilance"[125] but [the

---

tad yuktito 'pi va (140) *punarāvṛttir ity uktau janmadoṣasamudbhavau ātmadarśanabījasya hānād apunarāgamaḥ* (141) *tadbhūtabhinnātmatayā śeṣam akleśanirjvaram kāyavāgbuddhivaiguṇyaṃ mārgoktyapaṭutā 'pi vā* (142a) *aśeṣahānam abhyāsād...*" | [124] AKBh, Pk038b.4, Pruden, 1006, L.V.P, Śāstrī, 996: *taddhi bhikṣavaḥ prahīṇaṃ yadāryaprajñayā prahīṇam /* cf. SN ii.50(*Kalārasutta*). The first and last result can only be obtained by the pure path(= *āryaprajñā*), AK, vi.45c.

[125] AKBh, Pk038b.4, Pruden, 1006, Śāstrī, 997: *śaikṣasya cāpramādakaraṇīye 'pramādakaraṇīyaṃ pravedayāmi / ityuktam nārhataḥ /* cf. SN, iv.25

ཡིན་ཞེ་ན།མདོ་ལས།དགེ་སློང་དག་འཕགས་པའི་ཤེས་རབ་ཀྱི་སྦྱངས་པ་གང་
ཡིན་པ་དེ་ནི་སྦྱངས་པ་ཡིན་ནོ།།ཞེས་དེ་འདྲ་བའི་སྦྱངས་པ་དེ་སྐད་ཉོན་
མོངས་མི་སྐྱེ་བས་སྦྱངས་ངེས་སུ་གསུངས་པ་དང།སློབ་པ་ལ་བག་ཡོད་པ་ལ་
1342 བག་ཡོད་པར་བྱའོ་ཞེས་གསུངས་ཀྱི་དགྲ་བཅོམ་པ་ལ་བག་ཡོད་པར་
བྱའོ།།ཞེས་མི་གསུངས་པ་དང།[303]ཆོས་མངོན་པ་ལས་ཀྱང་གནས་གསུམ་གྱིས་
འདོད་པའི་འདོད་ཆགས་ཀྱི་ཕྲ་རྒྱས་སྐྱེ་བ་འགྱུར་ཏེ།[304]འདོད་པའི་འདོད་
ཆགས་ཀྱི་ཕྲ་རྒྱས་མ་སྤངས་ཤིང་ཡོངས་སུ་མ་ཤེས་པ་ཡིན།འདོད་པའི་འདོད་
ཆགས་ཀྱིས་ཀུན་ནས་དཀྲིས་པར་འགྱུར་བའི་ཆོས་རྣམས་སྣང་བར་གྱུར་པ་
ཡིན།།དེ་ལ་ཡང་ཚུལ་བཞིན་མ་ཡིན་པའི་ཡིད་ལ་བྱེད་པ་ཡིན་ཞེས་ཉོན་
མོངས་སྐྱེ་བ་ལ་རྒྱུ་རྐྱེན་གསུམ་ཚོགས་དགོས་པར་གསུངས་ལ།དགྲ་བཅོམ་
པས་ཕྲ་རྒྱས་མ་ལུས་པར་སྤངས་པས་ན་སྐྱེ་བ་རྒྱུ་མ་ཚང་ངོ།།རིགས་པ་ཇི་ལྟ་
བུ་ཞེ་ན།གལ་ཏེ་དགྲ་བཅོམ་པ་དེ་ལ་ཉོན་མོངས་གཏན་མི་སྐྱེ་བའི་གཉེན་པོ་
སྐྱེས་ན་ཇི་ལྟར་ཉམས་པ་ཡིན།འོན་ཏེ་མ་སྐྱེས་ན་ཉོན་མོངས་ཀྱི་ས་བོན་
P129b རྩད[305]་ནས་མ་བཏོན་ན་ཅི་ལྟར་ཟག་ཟད་ཡིན།ཟག་ཟད་མིན་ན་ཡང་དགྲ་
བཅོམ་པར་ཇི་[306]ལྟར་འགྱུར།དེས་ན་དགྲ་བཅོམ་པ་ལས་ཉམས་པ་ནི་མེད་པ་
ཡིན་ནོ།

།འོ་ན་བྱེ་བྲག་ཏུ་སྨྲ་བས་དྲངས་པའི་མདོ་དེ་དག་གི་དགོངས་པ་གང་
ཞེ་ན།འདིར་དགྲ་བཅོམ་པ་ཉམས་པ་ནི་དུས་སྦྱོར་ཡིན་ལ།དེ་གང་ལས་ཉམས་
ན་བསམ་གཏན་བཞི་པའི་ཏིང་ནེ་འཛིན་ལས་ཉམས་པ་མདོའི་དོན་ཡིན་
D 334 ནོ།།མདོ་གཉིས་པ་ལས་ཀྱང་ལྷག་པའི་སེམས་ལས་བྱུང་པའི་བསམ་གཏན་
བཞི་ལས་ཉམས་ཞེས་འབྱུང་བ་དང་སེམས་རྣམ་གྲོལ་ལས་གཏན་མི་ཉམས་
པར་གསུངས་པས་ན་མདོའི་དོན་དེ་ལྟ་བུ་ཡིན་ནོ།

།མདོ་གསུམ་པའི་དོན་ཡང་གནག་ཚོགས་ཅན་ཡང་ཉམས་ནས་ལྡེབས་
པ་ནི་དེ་དགྲ་བཅོམ་པ་ལས་ཡང་ཡང་ཉམས་ནས་ལྡེབས་པ་མིན་ནོ།།འོ་ན་ཅི་
ཞེ་ན།གནག་ཙོགས་ཅན་སློབ་པའི་ཚེ་བསམ་གཏན་གྱི་རོ་མྱངས་པ་
དང།དབང་པོ་རྟུལ་བའི་ཕྱིར་བསམ་གཏན་ལས་ཡང་ཡང་ཉམས་པ་

[303]/ D M] om. / P | [304]/ D M] om. / P | [305]rtsad M] brtsad D P | [306]ji D M] ci P

[126] AKBh, Pk039b.2-3, Pruden, 1008-1009, L.V.P, 262, Śāstrī, 1001-1002: *abhidharme 'pi coktam "tribhiḥ sthānaiḥ kāmarāgānuśayasyotpādo bhavati kāmarāgānuśayo*

Bhagavān] did not say for the Arhat to cultivate viligance. The Abhidharma gives three causes that will generate the latent defilements of desire within the desire realm: the latent defilement (*anuśaya*) of sensual desire has not been completely known and has not been abandoned, the dharmas appear favorable to the increase of sensual desire, and there is erroneous judgement.[126] It indicates as necessary the collection of these three causes and conditions for the generation of afflictions. The Arhat, by abandoning all latent defilements without exception, does not complete the causes of generating. What is the reason for such like that? If it is the case, in that Arhat, since it produces the antidotes that do not generate the seed of afflictions, how can it backslide? Well then, if not producing, if not throwing out having eradicated the seed of afflictions, how can there be one who exhausts (*kṣīṇa*) the vices (*āsrava*) and if [one is] not a *kṣīṇāsrava*, how will one be an Arhat? Since by that [reason], there is no backsliding from the state of Arhat.[127]

Well then, what is the [actual] intention of those *sūtra*s drawn out by the *Vaibhāṣika*s? Here, a backsliding Arhat is an occasionally liberated [Arhat], and if backsliding, the meaning of the *sūtra* is to backslide from the meditative stabilization of the fourth concentration.

When the second *sūtra* (see 329.4) says, "backsliding from the
D334 four concentrations which arise from superior intellect" the meaning of the *sūtra* is that the mind does not at all backslide from deliverance.

Also the meaning of the third *sūtra*, Gautika kills himself having repeatedly backslided, he does not kill himself having repeatedly backslided from the state of Arhat. Well then, why is that? Gautika, having the taste of concentration at the time of training, because of

---

prahīṇo bhavatyaparijñātaḥ kāmarāgaparyavasthānīyāśca dharmā ābhāsagatā bhavanti tatra cāyoniśo manaskāraḥ / see also *Abhidharmakośa* V.34.

[127] Tsong kha pa has paraphrased this section from AKBh, Pk039b.3-4, Pruden, 1009, Śāstrī, 1001: *kathaṃ yuktiḥ yadi tāvadarhatastadrūpaḥ pratipakṣa utpanno yena kleśā atyantamanutpattidharmatāmāpannāḥ kathaṃ punaḥ parihīyate* / *atha notpannaḥ kathaṃ kṣīṇāsravo bhavati* / *atyantamanapoddhṛtāyāṃ tadbījadharmatāyāmakṣīṇāsravo vā punaḥ kathamarhan bhavatītyevaṃ yuktiḥ* /

དང།ཡིད་ཆད་ནས་རང་ལ་མཚོན་བསྣུན་ནས་འཆི་གའི་[307]ཚེ་དགྲ་བཅོམ་པ་
ཐོབ་ནས་མྱ་ངན་ལས་འདས་པ་ཡིན་ནོ།
1343 །མདོ་བཞི་པའི་དོན་ཡང་སློབ་པའི་དབང་དུ་མཛད་ནས་གསུངས་པ་
ཡིན་ནོ།།འོ་ན་དགྲ་བཅོམ་པའི་སྟོབས་དེ་ལ་ཡོད་པར་བཤད་པའི་སེམས་
དབེན་པ་ལ་སོགས་པ་གསུངས་པ་མ་ཡིན་ནམ་ཞེ་ན།གཉིས་པ་མེད་དེ་ཡུན་
རིང་པོ་ནས་སེམས་དབེན་པ་ལ་གཞོལ་བ་སོགས་ནི་སློབ་པ་ལ་ཡང་ཡོད་
ལ།དགྲ་བཅོམ་པའི་དེ་ནི་ཤིན་ཏུ་ཕུལ་དུ་བྱུང་བས་ཁྱད་པར་ཡོད་དོ།།

དགྲ་བཅོམ་སྤངས་པ་ཟློག་ཅེས་པའི།།ཕྱི་ཐག་སྟ་བའི་ངན་རྟོག་
རྣམས།།སངས་རྒྱས་གཉིས་པས་ལུང་རིགས་ཀྱིས།།ཞིགས་པར་
བཀག་རྣམས་རྒྱས་པར་བཀྲལ།།མངས་ཀྱིས་དོགས་ནས་ཤེས་བྱེད་
རྣམས།།རྒྱས་པར་མ་བཀོད་རང་འགྲེལ་དང༌།།འགྲེལ་བཤད་
P130a དགོངས་པ་ཇི་ལྟ་བཞིན་དུ།།ཕྱེ་བ་ཡིན་གྱི་སོམ་ཉི་དོར།།

ཞེས་བྱ་བ་ནི་བསྡུ་བའི་ཚིགས་སུ་བཅད་པའོ།།།།དུས་དང་སྦྱོར་བ་དང་
D 335 དུས་དང་མི་སྦྱོར་བ་ཡང་གང་ཞེ་ན།།དེ་ལ་དགྲ་བཅོམ་པ་དང་པོ་ལྔ་ནི་རྣམ་
གྲོལ་སྤངས་པ་དེ་དུས་རེ་ཞིག་གི་བར་དུ་གནས་ནས་ཉམས་སྲིད་པའི་ཕྱིར་
དུས་ཀྱིས་རྣམ་པར་གྲོལ་བ་ཡིན་ལ།[308]དྲུག་པ་ནི་ཉམས་མི་སྲིད་པས་རྣམ་
གྲོལ་སྤངས་པ་དེ་དུས་འདི་ཙམ་ནས་ལྡོག་པ་མེད་པའི་ཕྱིར་གཏན་དུ་གྲོལ་
བས་ན་དུས་དང།མི་སྦྱོར་བར་རྣམ་པར་གྲོལ་བ་ཞེས་བྱ་སྟེ།མཛོད་འགྲེལ་ལས།

ཡོངས་སུ་ཉམས་པ་སྲིད་པ་དང།མི་སྲིད་པའི་སྒོ་ནས་དུས་གཞན་གྱི་
བར་དང་གཏན་དུ་རྣམ་པར་གྲོལ་བའི་ཕྱིར་དུས་ཀྱིས་[309]རྣམ་པར་
གྲོལ་བ་དང།།དུས་དང་མི་སྦྱོར་བར་རྣམ་པར་གྲོལ་བ་ཉིད་ཡིན་
ཞེས་ཏེ་དེ་ནི་བྱེ་བྲག་ཏུ་སྨྲ་བའི་འདོད་པའོ།།སློབ་དཔོན་གྱི་བཞེད་པ་

---

[307] 'chi ga'i M] 'chi kha D P | [308] / D M] om. / P | [309] kyis M] kyi D P

---

[128] Tsong kha pa draws remarks from AKBh (Pruden, 1009, 1076, f.n. #380) and AKV, Śāstrī, 1002: *tattūktam dīrgharātraṃ vivekanimnam iti tacchaikṣasyāpi sambhavati / arhatastu prakarṣeṇa bhavatīti viśeṣaḥ /*

weak faculties backslides repeatedly from concentration and from disgust stabbed himself with a dagger, at the moment of death having attained the state of Arhat, he achieved *nirvāṇa*.

Further, the meaning of the fourth *sūtra* is construed according to the faculty of the *śaikṣa*. Well then, is not a mind turned toward solitude and so forth explained as being the power of an Arhat or is it not? That is not wrong, "for a long time one's mind diligent for solitude" and so forth is for the *śaikṣa*. That quality for an Arhat has the distinction of being preeminent (Skt. *prakarṣa*).[128]

Explained in condensed verse:

> The Second Buddha [Vasubandhu] extensively explained the refutations eloquently with reasoning and scripture of the bad ideas of the *Vaibhāṣika*s who say, "the Arhat reverses abandonment." Fearing it would be too prolific; I have not extensively presented the proofs of the refutations. Have no doubt though, for I have properly explained the intentions of the *Abhidharmakośabhāṣya* and *Bhāṣyavyākhyā*.

Who is the Arhat that is occasionally delivered (*samayavimukta*)
D335 and not occasionally delivered (*asamayavimukta*)? For that, the first five Arhats because it is possible to backslide from abiding at a certain time and occasion that abandons liberation, [that Arhat] is liberated by occasion and the sixth [Arhat], since it is not possible to backslide, because of not reversing from merely this time that abandons liberation, when delivered is called one that is not occasionally delivered (*asamayavimukta*). The *Abhidharmakośabhāṣya* states:

> Because of being liberated continually or occasionally by means of it being not possible or possible to backslide, [these Arhats are] liberated not connected with occasion or liberated by occasion.[129]

Thus is the assertion of the *Vaibhāṣika*. From the same text, the description of the Ācārya [Vasubandhu]:

---

129 Pk036a.7, Pruden, 1001, Śāstrī, 989:*kālāntarātyantavimuktito vā kopyākopyadharmanoḥ samayāsamaye vimuktatvam parihāṇisambhavāsambhavataḥ* /

ནི་དེ་ཉིད་ལས།

> དགྲ་བཅོམ་པ་ཉི་ཀྱི་རྣམ་པར་གྲོལ་བ་ནི།རྟག་ཏུ་རྗེས་སུ་འབྲེལ་
> བའི་ཕྱིར་དུས་དང་མི་སྦྱོར་བ་ཡིན་པར་ཡང་མི་རུང་ལ་

ཞེས་དགྲ་བཅོམ་པའི་རྣམ་གྲོལ་སྤངས་པ་ནི་རྟག་ཏུ་དེ་ཁོ་ན་ལྟར་
གནས་པས་ཉམས་པ་མི་སྲིད་པས་དེ་ལ་དུས་ལ་ལྟོས་མི་ལྟོས་མི་རུང་ཞེས་
བཀག་ནས།[310]འོ་ན་[311]མཛོད་འགྲེལ་ལས།དུས་ཀྱིས་[312]རྣམ་པར་གྲོལ་བའི་
1344 དགྲ་བཅོམ་ཞེས་ཅི་སྐད་ཅེས་བྱ་ཞེ་ན།གང་ཞིག་དབང་པོ་རྟུལ་བའི་ཕྱིར་ཏིང་
ངེ་འཛིན་མངོན་སུམ་དུ་འགྱུར་བ་དུས་ལ་ལྟོས་པ་ཡིན་ནོ།།རྣོག་པ་ནི་དུས་
དང་མི་སྦྱོར་བར་རྣམ་པར་གྲོལ་བ་ཡིན་ནོ།།[313]ཞེས་པ་ལྟར་བསམ་གཏན་གྱི་
དངོས་གཞིའི་ཏིང་ངེ་འཛིན་མངོན་དུ་འགྱུར་བ་འཚོ་བའི་ཡོ་བྱད་དང་ལྡན་
པ་དང་།ལུས་ལ་ནད་མེད་པ་དང་།ཡུལ་མི་མཐུན་པ་མེད་པའི་དུས་ཀྱི་ཁྱད་
D 336 པར་ལ་ལྟོས་པ་དང་མི་ལྟོས་པ་གཉིས་རིམ་པ་བཞིན་དུ་དུས་སྦྱོར་དང་དུས་
|P130b མི་སྦྱོར་གྱི་དོན་ནོ།།བལྟོས་[314]པའི་དུས་ཀྱི་ཁྱད་པར་ལ་ཕྱི་ཐག་ཏུ་སྣ་བ་དང་
འདྲ་ཡང་བལྟོས་[315]ཆོས་ལ་མི་མཐུན་ཏེ།[316]ཕྱི་ཐག་ཏུ་སྣ་བ་ནི་རྣམ་གྲོལ་དགྲ་
བཅོམ་པ་ཉིད་ལ་འཆད་ཅིང་།སློབ་དཔོན་ནི་བསམ་གཏན་བཞི་པའི་ཏིང་ངེ་
འཛིན་ལ་བཞེད་པའི་ཕྱིར་རོ།།བཙུ་ལས་འཕྲོས་པ་ལས་ཀྱང་

> བསྐྱེད་པར་བྱ་བའི་ཆོས་ནི་གཅིག་སྟེ་སེམས་རྣམ་པར་གྲོལ་བ་དང་
> སྦྱོར་བ་པ་ཡིད་དུ་འོང་བ་ཡིན་ནོ།།མངོན་སུམ་དུ་བྱ་བའི་ཆོས་ནི་
> གཅིག་སྟེ་སེམས་རྣམ་པར་གྲོལ་བ་མི་གཡོ་བ་ཡིན་ནོ།

།ཞེས་གསུངས་པས་ན་ཕྱི་ཐག་ཏུ་སྣ་བའི་དེ་[317]མི་འཐད་དེ་གལ་ཏེ་
དུས་སྦྱོར་གྱི་རྣམ་གྲོལ་ནི་དགྲ་བཅོམ་པ་ཡིན་ན་མངོན་དུ་བྱ་བའི་ཆོས་སུ་
བསྟན་པ་དེ་ཡང་དགྲ་བཅོམ་པ་ཉིད་ཡིན་པས་ན་དགྲ་བཅོམ་པ་ལན་གཉིས་
སུ་བསྟན་པ་དང་།དགྲ་བཅོམ་ནི་དགྲ་བཅོམ་པས་གང་དུ་ཡང་བསྐྱེད་བྱར་མ་

---

[310] / D M] om. / P | [311] om. / D M] insert / P | [312] kyis M] kyi D P | [313] / / D M] om. / / P | [314] bltos M] ltos D P | [315] bltos M] ltos D P | [316] / D M] om. / P | [317] de M P] da D

---

[130] AKBh, Pk038b.1, Pruden, 1007, Śāstrī, 998: *arhacvavimutkistu nityānugatavānna yujyate sāmayikī* / | [131] Pruden, 1006-107.

> The liberation of the Arhat is not suitable to be occasional because it is possessed in a permanent manner.[130]

Thus with regard to abandoning the liberation of the Arhat, since it abides only in a permanent manner, it is not possible to backslide, and this refutes the question whether or not it is suitable to rely on an occasion for the [Arhat]. Well then, why does the *Abhidharmakośabhāṣya*[131] say "the Arhat who is liberated occasionally"? This is one who, because of weak faculties, directly perceives meditative stabilization relying on a certain time. The opposite is called liberation that is not connected with time and occasion. In such a sequence, of relying or not relying on the particularity of time, [the time] that will have direct meditative stabilization on the fundamental threshold of concentration, possess the provisions of life, be without sickness for the body, and not have
D336 unharmonious [meditative] objects is the meaning of being connected with time and not connected with time. For the specifics of the time that is relied upon, the *Vaibhāṣika* explain discordant qualities for reliance and the *Vaibhāṣika*'s explanation for the Arhat's liberation is itelf [discordant] because the Ācārya [Vasubandhu] explains [reliance on time and occasion] for the meditative stabilization of the fourth concentration. Also, if they state from the *Daśottara*,

> there is a single dharma which one should produce, the cherished and occasional deliverance of mind. There is a single dharma which one should actualize, the immovable liberation of mind,[132]

the *Vaibhāṣika*s are incorrect in this. If it is the case that occasional liberation is the quality of the Arhat, [the *sūtra*] should teach as a quality that should be actualized. Also, if this refers to an Arhat itself, Arhat should be indicated two times and [here, with regards to] Arhat: no part of the scripture says that the Arhat should

---

[132] AKBh, Pruden, 1008, Śāstrī, 376 : *daśottare coktam, eko dharma utpādayitavyaḥ sāmayikī kāntā cetovimuktiḥ. Eko dharmaḥ sākṣātkartavyaḥ akopyā cetovimuktiriti* / DN, iii.273 differs.

གསུངས་ལ་སྐབས་དེའི་བསྐྱེད་བྱ་དང་མངོན་དུ་བྱ་བ་གཉིས་ནི་དགྲ་བཅོམ་པའི་དབང་དུ་མཛད་པའི་ཕྱིར་རོ།སྔར་བཤད་པའི་དགྲ་བཅོམ་པ་དེ་དག་ལ་མི་སློབ་པ་དགུ་ཞེས་པའི་ཐ་སྙད་ཀྱང་མཛད་དོ།།མདོ་ལས་

> མི་སློབ་པ་དགུ་གང་ཞེ་ན།ཡོངས་སུ་ཉམས་པའི་ཆོས་ཅན་དང་ཡོངས་སུ་ཉམས་པར་མི་འགྱུར་བའི་ཆོས་ཅན་དང་།འཆི་བར་སེམས་པའི་ཆོས་ཅན་དང་།ཞེས་པ་ནས།[318]མི་གཡོ་བའི་ཆོས་ཅན་དང་ཤེས་རབ་ཀྱིས་རྣམ་པར་གྲོལ་བ་དང་གཉིས་ཀའི་ཆ་ལས་རྣམ་པར་གྲོལ་བ་སྟེ།འདི་དག་ནི་མི་སློབ་པ་དགུ་ཞེས་བྱའོ།[319]

1345 །[320]ཞེས་གང་གསུངས་པའོ།།ཁ་།བོད་རྣམས།ཅིག་དགྲ་བཅོམ་པ་རྒྱུན་
D 337 ཅན་དང་རྒྱུན་མེད་ཅེས་པའི་ཐ་སྙད་བྱེད་མོད།འོང་ཀྱང་རྒྱུན་ཡོད་མེད་ནི།ཀུན་ལས་བཏུས་ལས།འགོག་བདེན་ལ་ཤེས་རབ་ཀྱིས་རྣམ་གྲོལ་གྱི་འགོག་པ་རྒྱུན་མེད་དང་།[321]གཉིས་ཀའི་ཆ་ལས་རྣམ་གྲོལ་གྱི་རིག་པ་གསུམ་དང་མངོན་ཤེས་དྲུག་ལྡན་གྱི་འགོག་པ་རྒྱུན་བཅས་སུ་གསུངས་ཀྱི་དགྲ་བཅོམ་པ་ལ་ནི་རྣམ་གཞག་བྱས་པ་མ་མཐོང་ལ་ཅི་སྟེ་ཐ་སྙད་འདོགས་ན་ནི་ཤེས་རབ་ཀྱིས་དང་གཉིས་ཀའི་ཆ་ལས་རྣམ་གྲོལ་གྱི་རང་བཞིན་ཇི་འདྲ་བ་དེ་ལྟ་བུར་བསྙད་དོ།།དགྲ་བཅོམ་པའི་འབྲས་བུ་ལ་གནས་པ་བཤད་ཟིན་ཏོ།།

།།དེ་ལྟར་ཞུགས་གནས་བརྒྱད་བཤད་པ་དེ་དག་ནི་སྤང་བྱ་མཐར་གྱིས་སྤོང་བ་དང་།འབྲས་བུ་མཐར་གྱིས་མངོན་དུ་བྱེད་པའི་དབང་དུ་བྱས་ནས་བསྟན་གྱི་འཕགས་པའི་གང་ཟག་དེ་དག་དེ་ཁོ་ནར་ངེས་པ་ནི་མ་ཡིན་ཏེ།འདི་ལྟར་དུ་འབྲས་བུ་འཐོབ་པ་ལ་ཐོད་རྒྱལ་བ་དང་རིམ་གྱིས་པ་[322]གཉིས་དང་།སྤང་བྱ་སྤོང་བ་ལ་ཡང་མཐར་གྱིས་དང་[323]ཅིག་ཅར་དུ་སྤོང་བ་གཉིས་ཏེ་བཞིར་འགྱུར་རོ།དེ་ལ་འབྲས་བུ་ཐོད་རྒྱལ་བ་ནི་[324]སྤང་བྱ་རིམ་གྱིས་པ་[325]དང་

318/ D M] om. / P | 319/ D M] om. / P | 320/ D M] om. / P | 321/ D M] om. / P | 322rim gyis pa D M] rims kyis pa P | 323om. / D M] insert / P | 324om. / D M] insert / P | 325rim gyis pa D M] rims kyis pa P

133 Sanskrit found in the AKV, Śāstrī, 998: *navāśaikṣāḥ katame/ parihāṇadharmā*

produce the above qualities; the two [qualities] that should be actualized and produced in this section [the of *sūtra*] concern the faculties of an Arhat. These Arhats that have been earlier explained are given the name "nine *aśaikṣa*s." A *sūtra* states:

> Who are the nine *aśaikṣa*s? The *Parihāṇadharman*, *Aparihāṇadharman*, *Cetanādharman*, up to the *Akopyadharman*, *Prajñāvimukta*, and *Ubhayatobhāgavimukta*, these are called the nine *aśaikṣas*.[133]

Some [Tibetans] give the terms "ornamented and unornamented
D337 Arhat." However, as to having or not having an ornament the *Abhidharmasamuccaya* teaches[134] in [the section on] the truth of cessation (*nirodhasatya*) that the cessation of one who is liberated through wisdom (*prajñavimukta*) is without ornament and the cessation which possesses the six supernatural knowledges and the three sciences of the liberated by both ways (*ubhayatobhāgavimukta*) is ornamented but to make [this] explanation for the Arhat is not seen and if one should apply the terms, what kind of nature of the *Prajñāvimukta* ('liberated through wisdom') and *Ubhayatobhāgavimukta* ('liberated by both ways') was informed? The abider in the result of Arhat explanation is finished.

In this way, those explained as the eight abiders and enterers are indicated through the domain of actualizing by progressive fruition and abandoning by progressive abandonment, but these Noble (*āryan*) individuals are not ascertained as only that. Accordingly, in terms of attaining results there are two: those who do so gradually (*rim gyis pa*) and those who skip over (*thod rgal ba*) and in terms of abandoning defilements there are two: those who do so gradually (*mthar gyis pa*) and those who do so simultaneously (*cig car ba*), to make four. Regarding this, the fruition skipper is not contradictory with the

---

aparihāṇadharma cetanādharmā anurakṣaṇādharmā sthitākampyaḥ prativedhanābhavyaḥ akopyadharmā prajñāvimuktaḥ ubhayatobhāgavimuktaḥ ima ucyante navāśaikṣāḥ /

[134] AS, Rahula, p. 100-101, Pradhan, 63: *niralaṃkārataḥ katamat / prajñāvimuktānāmarhtāṃ yo nirodhaḥ / sālaṃkāra katamat / ubhayabhāgavimuktānāṃ traividyānāṃ ṣadabhijñānāmarhataṃ yo nirodhaḥ* / See Rahula f.n. 1-2,.100-101.

མི་འགལ་ལ།[326]འབྲས་བུ་རིམ་གྱིས་པ་ནི་སྤྱང་གྲྭ་ཅིག་ཅར་བ་དང་འགལ་བ་
ཡིན་ནོ།

།དེ་ལྟར་གང་ཟག་བཞི་པོ་འདི་ཞུགས་གནས་བརྒྱད་གང་ལ་བཞག་ཅེ་
ན།[327]འབྲས་བུ་དང་སྤྱང་གྲྭ་མཐར་གྱིས་པ་ནི་ཞུགས་གནས་བརྒྱད་ཆར་ལ་
ཡོད་ལ།འབྲས་བུ་ཐོད་རྒལ་བ་ནི་འབྲས་བུ་བར་པ་གཉིས་ཀྱི་ཞུགས་གནས་
བཞི་ཁོ་ན་ལ་བཞག་སྟེ།བཅུ་དྲུག་པ་དང་པོར་ཐོབ་པའི་ཚེ་འབྲས་བུ་སྔ་མ་
D 338 སྔོན་དུ་མ་བཏང་བར་འབྲས་བུ་ཕྱི་མ་ཐོབ་པ་དེ་འབྲས་བུ་ཐོད་རྒལ་བའི་དོན་
ཡིན་ཞིང་[328]རྒྱུན་ཞུགས་ལ་འབྲས་བུ་སྔ་མ་དོར་རྒྱུ་མེད་པའི་ཕྱིར་དང་།དགྲ་
བཅོམ་པ་བཅུ་དྲུག་པའི་ཚེ་ཐོབ་པར་མི་ནུས་ཏེ་མཐོང་ལམ་གྱི་སྔོན་དུ་སྲིད་
རྩེའི་སྒོམ་སྤང་མི་སྤོང་བ་དང་མཐོང་ལམ་གྱིས་ཀྱང་སྒོམ་སྤང་དེ་སྤང་མི་ནུས་
པའི་ཕྱིར་རོ།

1346 །དེ་ལ་སྤྱང་གྲྭ་ཅིག་ཅར་པ་[329]ནི་འབྲས་བུ་དང་པོ་དང་ཐ་མ་གཉིས་
P131b ཉིད་ལ་བཞག་སྟེ།[330]ཕྱིར་འོང་ལ་ཁམས་གོང་མའི་ཉོན་མོངས་གང་ཡང་
སྤངས་པ་མེད་པའི་ཕྱིར་དང་།འདོད་པའི་དགུ་པ་མ་སྤངས་ནི་ཕྱིར་མི་འོང་དུ་
མི་འགྱུར་ལ་དགུ་པ་སྤངས་ན་ཁམས་གསུམ་གའི་[331]དགུ་ཆར་སྤངས་པས་
དགྲ་བཅོམ་དུ་འགྱུར་བའི་ཕྱིར་རོ། །དེ་ལ་མངོན་པ་མཛོད་དུ་ནི།འབྲས་བུ་ཐོད་
རྒལ་དུ་དང་མཐར་གྱིས་མངོན་དུ་བྱེད་པ་གཉིས་བཤད་ཀྱི་ཅིག་ཅར་བ་
[332]གཏན་མི་འདོད་མོད།རྫོངས་པ་དག །སྔ་རབས་པ། ནི་མཛོད་ནས་བཤད་
པའི་བསེ་རུ་ལྟ་བུའི་རང་རྒྱལ་ཅིག་ཅར་བར་[333]འདོད་པ་ནི་ཆ་མེད་ཀྱི་[334]རྒྱུས་
གཏམ་སྨྲ་ནས་རང་གི་དེ་ཁོ་ན་ཉིད་སྔོན་པར་མཐོང་སྟེ།མཛོད་ལས་
སྤྱིར།[335]འདོད་པའི་ཁམས་ཀྱི་རྗེས་མ་ཡིན།།ཞེས་པ་ལྟར་ཁམས་གོང་གི་གཉེན་
པོར་སོང་བ་དེས་འདོད་པའི་གཉེན་པོ་བྱེད་པར་གཏན་མི་འདོད་དོ།།བྱེ་བྲག་
སྨྲ་བ་བསེ་རུ་ལྟ་བུ་ནི།མཛོད་ལས་

[326]/ D M] om. / P | [327]/ D M] om. / P | [328]zhing M] cing D P | [329]cig car pa D M] cig char pa P | [330]/ D M] om. / P | [331]ga'i D M] kha P | [332]cig car ba D M] cig char ba P | [333]cig car bar D M] cig char bar P | [334]gyi D M] kyi P | [335]/ D M] om. / P

gradual abandoner but the gradual progressor in fruitions is contradictory with the simultaneous abandoner.

Accordingly, what is established for whichever enterer and abider for these four individuals? The gradual progressor in fruitions and [gradual] abandoner may exist as one of eight enterers and abiders but the fruition skipper is established for only the four enterers and abiders among the two middle fruitions. This is due to the fact that one does not obtain a later fruition in previously letting go from a former result at the time of first obtaining the sixteenth [moment of
D338 the path of seeing], which is the meaning of fruition skipper, and the Stream-enterer does not have a reason to cast away a former fruition and the Arhat [state] is unable to be obtained at the time of the sixteenth [moment] because [one] cannot abandon the path of cultivation abandonments of the Peak of Existence previous of the path of seeing and because the path of seeing is unable to abandon those [path of] cultivation abandonments.

In this regard, the simultaneous abandoner is established as two: the first and last fruitions; [they are so defined] because [1] the Once-returner does not abandon the afflictions of the upper realms and because [2], if not abandoning the ninth [affliction] of the desire realm, [one] will not be a Non-returner and if abandoning the ninth, [one] abandons all nine [afflictions] of the three realms and then becomes an Arhat.

Regarding this, in the *Abhidharmakośa*, two are explained–those who actualize through skipping results and through gradual progression but it does not assert a system of simultaneous [abandoners]. Those [former scholars] with obscured minds who assert as the simultaneous abandoner the pratyekajina like a rhinoceros horn are seen to demonstrate their own nature through such unintelligent discourse.

In general, the *Abhidharmakośa* states "subsequent knowledge is not of the desire realm."[135]Thus, what is understood as the antidotes of the upper realms are not acceptable to construe as antidotes for the desire realm. The *Vaibhāṣika*s say as like a rhinoceros horn, from the *Abhidharmakośa*:

---

[135] AK, vii.9d, Pruden, 1098, Śāstrī, 1044: *kāmadhātostu nānvayam /*

སྔོན་དང་བསེ་རུ་བྱང་ཆུབ་པར།།བསམ་གཏན་མཐའ་བརྟེན་གཅིག
ལ་ཀུན།།དེ་ཡི་སྔོན་དུ་[336]ཐར་ཆ་མཐུན།

།ཞེས་པ་ལྟར་བསམ་གཏན་བཞི་པ་ལ་བརྟེན་ནས་སྦྱོར་ལམ་མཐོང་
D 339 ལམ་བསྒོམ་ལམ་མི་སློབ་ལམ་ཀུན་སྟན་གཅིག་ལ་བསྐྱེད་པ་ཡིན་པས་ན་སོ་སོ་
སྐྱེ་བོ་དང་དགྲ་བཅོམ་པ་གཞི་གཅིག་པ་ཞིག་[337]ཁས་ལེན་དགོས་ཏེ།འདོད་
ཉོན་དགུ་པ་མ་སྤངས་པར་བསམ་གཏན་གྱི་དངོས་གཞི་མི་ཐོབ་ལ་དེ་ཐོབ་ན་
ཁམས་གསུམ་ཆར་གྱི་དགུ་པ་སྤངས་པས་དགྲ་བཅོམ་དུ་ཐལ་བའི་ཕྱིར་
རོ།།དེའི་ཕྱིར་བསེ་རུ་ལྟ་བུ་ཡིན་ན་རིམ་པར་ཅིག་ཅར་བ་[338]ཡིན་པ་འགལ་བ་
ཡིན་ནོ།།དེས་ན་འབྲས་བུ་ཐོད་རྒལ་བའི་བཟླས་[339]དྲངས་པའི་མཐར་གྱིས་པ་ནི་
འབྲས་བུ་མཐར་གྱིས་པ་ཡིན་ཏེ།མཛོད་འགྲེལ་ལས།

རྫས་[340]སུ་ནི་རྣམ་པ་ལྔ་སྟེ་ཞུགས་པ་དང་པོ་དང་འབྲས་བུ་ལ་
གནས་པ་བཞིའོ།[341]།ཞུགས་པ་ལྷག་མ་རྣམས་ནི་འབྲས་བུ་ལ་གནས་
P132a པ་གསུམ་ལས་ཐ་མི་དད་པའི་ཕྱིར་རོ།།མཐར་གྱིས་འཐོབ་པའི་ཕྱིར་
དེ་སྐད་ཅེས་བཤད་ཀྱི་[342]

1347 ཞེས་ཞུགས་པ་ཕྱི་མ་གསུམ་འབྲས་བུ་ལ་གནས་པ་དང་པོ་གསུམ་ལས་
རྫས་ལོག་པ་མེད་པས་རྫས་ལྔར་བཞག་པ་ནི་མཐར་གྱིས་པའི་དབང་དུ་བྱས་
ཞེས་པའི་འགྲེལ་བཤད་དུ།

འབྲས་བུ་བཞི་མཐར་གྱིས་འཐོབ་པའི་ཕྱིར་ཞེས་འབྱུང་བའི་ཕྱིར་རོ།
།ཡང་འགྲེལ་པ་དེའི་འཁྲོས་ཉིད་ནས།

ཕལ་ཆེར་ལས་དང་འདོད་པ་ལས་འདོད་ཆགས་དང་བྲལ་བ་དག
ཅིག་ཡིན་ན་ནི་མཐོང་བའི་ལམ་ལ་ལན་ཅིག་ཕྱིར་འོང་བ་དང་ཕྱིར་
མི་འོང་བའི་འབྲས་བུ་ལ་ཞུགས་པ་དག་ཡིན་གྱི་རྒྱུན་དུ་ཞུགས་པ་

---

[336]de yi sngon du D M] de'i sngon du P | [337]zhig M] gcig D P | [338]cig car ba D M] cig char ba P | [339]zlas D M] bzlas P | [340]rdzas D M] rjes P | [341]/ D M] om. / P | [342]kyi M] kyis D P

> The master and one like a rhinoceros horn go as far as bodhi in one sitting, relying on the last concentration, before that the *mokṣabhāgīya*s.[136]

Therefore, since producing in a single session of meditative equipoise all, the path of preparation, path of seeing, path of cultivation, path of no more learning, having relied on the fourth
D339 concentration it is necessary to acknowledge each individual basis of the ordinary individual and the Arhat. When not obtaining the actual basis of concentration, [one] does not abandon the nine afflictions of the desire realm, and if obtaining that, it will follow as an Arhat on account of abandoning the nine parts of the three realms. Therefore, if an individual is like a rhinoceros horn (i.e., *pratyekabuddha*) it is definitely contradictory to be a simultaneous abandoner. Consequently, one that gradually progresses who may be interpreted as a fruition skipper is [actually] a gradual progressor in results. The *Abhidharmakośabhāṣya* states:

> In actuality there are five aspects, the first enterer and four abiders in a result because the remaining enterers are not differentiated fromthe three abiders in the result. It is explained in this manner because of attainment by gradual progression.[137]

Thus, the three latter enterers, without being substantially opposite from the first three abiders in the result, are in substance set forth as five, construed through the domain of gradual progression. The *Abhidharmakośabhāṣyavyākhyā* states:

> ...because of obtaining gradually the four results.[138]

Further, from the details of that commentary:

> The *bhūyovītarāga*'s and *kāmavītarāga*'s are, in the path of seeing, enterers to the result of Once-

[136] AK, vi.24.a-c, Pruden,p.941-942, Pk018a.7, 018b.2, Śāstrī, 920-921: *ābodeḥ sarvamekatra dhyānāntye śāstṛkhadgayoḥ prāktebhyo mokṣabhāgīyam /*

[137] AKBh, Pk031b.5-6, Pruden, p.985, Śāstrī, 963: *dravyatastu pañca / prathamaḥ pratipannakaḥ catvāraśca phalasthāḥ śeṣāṇāṃ pratipannakānāṃ triphalasthāvyatirekāt. anupūrvādhigamaṃ pratyevamucyate /*

[138] AKV, Śāstrī, 963:*anupūrveṇa catuḥphalaprāptiṃ* (*pratyucyate dravyata pañceti*)/

དང་ལན་ཅིག་ཕྱིར་འོང་བ་དག་ཀྱང་མ་ཡིན་ནོ།[343]

།ཞེས་རིམ་གྱིས་པའི་[344]ལུགས་སྔར་བཤད་པ་ལྟར་ཡིན་གྱི།[345]ཐོད་རྒལ་
བ་ཡིན་ན་འབྲས་བུ་ཕྱི་མ་ལ་ཞུགས་པ་འབྲས་བུ་སྔ་མ་ལ་གནས་པ་ཡིན་པའི་
D 340 ངེས་པ་མེད་དེ།[346]ཐོད་རྒལ་བའི་ཕྱིར་འོང་ལ་ཞུགས་པ་དང༌།ཕྱིར་མི་འོང་
ཞུགས་པ་རིམ་པ་བཞིན་རྒྱུན་ཞུགས་དང་ཕྱིར་འོང་མིན་ནོ།།ཞེས་[347]གསུངས་
པའི་འགྲེལ་བཤད་དུ།[348]

> དེ་ལྟ་ཡིན་ན་ནི་རྫས་སུ་རྒྱུན་དུ་ཞུགས་པ་དང༌།ལན་ཅིག་ཕྱིར་འོང་བ་དང་ཕྱིར་མི་འོང་བའི་འབྲས་བུ་ལ་ཞུགས་པ་གསུམ་དང༌།འབྲས་བུ་ལ་གནས་པ་བཞི་སྟེ་བདུན་དུ་འགྱུར་གྱི།[349]དགྲ་བཅོམ་པ་ཉིད་ཀྱི་འབྲས་བུ་ལ་ཞུགས་པ་གཅིག་པུ་ཕྱིར་མི་འོང་བའི་འབྲས་བུ་ལས་ཐ་མི་དད་དོ་ཞེས་བྱ་བར་ཁོང་དུ་ཆུད་པར་བྱའོ།

།ཞེས་མཛོད་པའི་དགོངས་པར་བསམས་ནས་ཆགས་བྲལ་སྔོན་སོང་ལ་རྫས་བདུན་གྱི་རྣམ་གཞག་ཀྱང་ཡོད་དོ།།ཞེས་ཕྱོགས་བཅུར་སྒྲོགས་པའི་མཁས་པ་ཆོས་མངོན་པའི་དོན་ལྟ་བ་ལ་བློ་གྲོས་ཀྱི་མིག་དང་ལྡན་པ་དག་སྣང་སོད།

P132b དེ་ལྟར་བཞག་པར་ནུས་པ་མ་ཡིན་ཏེ།འགྲེལ་བཤད་ཀྱི་དགོངས་པ་ནི་
མཐར་གྱིས་པ་ལ་རྫས་ལྔ་དང༌།ཐོད་རྒལ་བའི་ཞུགས་པ་གཉིས་འབྲས་གནས་
ལས་རྫས་ལོག་པར་བཞག་པ་དེ་ལྟ་ཡིན་ཏེ་དེ་ལྟར་ཕྱུས་ན་ཞུགས་གནས་ཀྱི་
གང་ཟག་དེ་དག་རྫས་བདུན་དུ་འགྱུར་ཏེ་[350]མཐར་གྱིས་པའི་སྐབས་སུ་ཞུགས་
པ་དང་པོ་གཅིག་པུ་དང་ཐོས་རྒལ་བའི་ཞུགས་པ་གཉིས་ཏེ་འབྲས་བུ་དང་པོ་
1348 གསུམ་ལ་ཞུགས་པའི་གང་ཟག་གསུམ་དང༌།འབྲས་གནས་བཞི་དང་བདུན་དུ་
འགྱུར་བའི་ཕྱིར་རོ།།དགྲ་བཅོམ་པ་ལ་ཞུགས་པ་ནི་མཐར་གྱིས་པ་ཁོ་ནའི་ཡིན་
ལ་འབྲས་བུ་གཞན་ཡང་སྔོན་དུ་བཏང་བས་ན་དེ་ཕྱིར་མི་འོང་ལས་ཐ་མི་
དད་ཅེས་པའི་དོན་ཡིན་ནོ།།ཐོད་རྒལ་བའི་སྐབས་ཐམས་ཅད་དུ་ཕལ་ཆེར་

---

[343] / D M] om. / P | [344] rim gyis pa'i D M] rims kyis pa'i P | [345] / D M] om. / P | [346] / D M] om. / P | [347] / / zhes D M] ces P | [348] / D M] om. / P | [349] / D M] om. / P | [350] om. / D M] insert / P

returner and Non-returner but are not Stream-enterers or Once-returners.[139]

Thus, it is the system of gradual progression as explained earlier but if it is a fruition skipper, the enterer to the later fruit is without
D340 certainty of being an abider to the former fruit, as like the stages of the fruition skipper Once-returner enterer and Non-returner enterer who are not Stream-enterers nor Once-returners. The *Abhidharmakośabhāṣyavyākhyā* states:

> That being the case, in actuality there are seven: the three enterers to the results of Stream-enterer, Once-returner, and Non-returner and the four abiders in the result. However, one should realize that one [of the eight,] the enterer to the result of Arhat, is not different from the result of Non-returner.[140]

Reflecting on the intention of the *Abhidharmakośa*, one gone previously separated from attachment (*vītarāgapūrvin*), in substance, is also explained among the seven. Thus the scholar who calls out in the ten directions illuminates those who have an eye of intelligence for viewing the meaning of the Abhidharma.

Accordingly there is not the ability to split the intention of the *Abhidharmakośavyākhyā*–the gradual progressor in substance is five and the two fruition skipper enterers, are classified as opposite in substance from an abider in a result, so if construed accordingly, those individuals of entering and abiding will be seven. In the phase of a gradual progressor, there is a single enterer to the result and there are two fruition skipper enterers such that there are three individuals who enter into the first three fruitions along with four abiders in the result to add up to seven. The enterer to the Arhat is only a gradual progressor and furthermore, the result that is previously released is the meaning of saying undifferentiated from the Non-returner [result]. Since it occurs in all texts of Abhidharma, in all periods of the fruition

---

[139]AKBh, Pk031b.6-7, Pruden, 985, Śāstrī, 973: *bhūyaḥkāmavītarāgau tu syātāṃ darśanamārge sakṛdāgāmyanāgāmiphalapratipannakau na ca strotaāpanna sakṛdāgāmināviti.*

[140]AKV, Śāstrī, 974: *tathā ca sati dravyataḥ sapta bhavanti srotaāpattisakṛdāgāmyanāgāmiphala-pratipannakāstrayaś catvāraś ca phalasthā iti arhattvaphalapratipannaka eko'nāgāmiphalasthān na vyatirikta ity avagantavyam /*

D 341 ལས་དང་འདོད་པ་ལས་ཆགས་བྲལ་སྔོན་དུ་སོང་བ་གཉིས་ཁོ་ན་མངོན་པའི་
གཞུང་ ཐམས་ ཅད་ དུ་ འབྱུང་ བས་ དེ་ [351]ལ་ ནི་ སློབ་ དཔོན་ རྒྱལ་ པོའི་ སྲས་
གྲགས་པའི་བཤེས་གཉེན་ཆོས་མངོན་པ་རྣམ་པར་འབྱེད་པ་ལ་ཆོས་ཀྱི་སྤྱན་
ལྡན་ཆེན་པོ་ལ་འཁྲུལ་བའི་གནས་གང་ན་ཡོད་དེ།[352]དེའི་ཕྱིར་ཅིག་དེ་ལྟ་བུ་
ལ་རྣམ་[353]གཏད་པར་མི་བྱའོ།

།སྤང་བྱ་ཅིག་ཅར་བའི་[354]ཟླས་དྲངས་པའི་མཐར་གྱིས་པ་ནི་སྤང་བྱ་
མཐར་གྱིས་པ་ཡིན་པས་མཐར་གྱིས་པའི་དོན་དེ་གཉིས་སུ་ངེས་སོ།།དེའི་ཕྱིར་
གང་ །བོད་སྤྱ་ཁ་ཅིག།དག་ལམ་རིམ་གྱིས་པ་[355]ཞེས་པའི་བརྡ་འདོགས་པ་
ཡང་མཐར་གྱིས་པའི་བརྡ་སྦྱོར་འདོད་ཀྱང་བརྡའི་དོན་མ་ཤེས་པར་ཟད་དོ།

།ཐོད་རྒལ་བའི་ཕྱིར་འོང་ལ་ཞུགས་པ་གང་ཞེ་ན།སྒྱུར་འབྲས་བུར་
འཛོག་པ་ནི་མཐོང་སྤང་[356]སྤངས་པའི་སྤང་[357]པའི་སྟེང་དུ་སྒོམ་སྤང་[358]གི་
སྤངས་པ་[359]བསྒོམས་ནས་འབྲས་བུ་ཕྱི་མ་གསུམ་འཇོག་ལ།།མཐོང་སྤང་
[360]སྤངས་པ་བཅིག་པུས་ནི་རྒྱུན་ཞུགས་ཀྱི་འབྲས་བུ་ཁོ་ན་འཇོག་གོ།།དེ་ལ་
P133a མཐོང་ལམ་གྱི་སྔོན་དུ་འཇིག་རྟེན་པའི་ལམ་གྱིས་འདོད་པའི་སྒོམ་སྤང་
[361]དྲུག་པ་སྤངས་དགུ་པ་མ་སྤངས་པ་དང།རྟོགས་པ་སྐད་ཅིག་མ་དང་པོ་
བཅོ་ལྔ་ལ་གནས་པ་ན་ཕྱིར་འོང་གི་འབྲས་བུ་ལ་ཞུགས་པ་ཡིན་ཞིང་[362]དེས་
བཅུ་དྲུག་པ་ཐོབ་པ་དང་མཐོང་སྤང་[363]མ་ལུས་པར་སྤངས་པ་དང།།སྔར་གྱི་
དྲུག་པ་སྤངས་པའི་སྒོམ་སྤང་[364]གི་སྤངས་པ་བསྒོམས་པས་ཕྱིར་འོང་གི་
འབྲས་བུ་དང་པོར་ཐོབ་པ་དེ།[365]ཕྱིར་འོང་ཐོད་རྒལ་བ་སྟེ།[366]རྒྱུན་ཞུགས་ཀྱི་
འབྲས་བུ་མ་ཐོབ་པར་ཕྱིར་འོང་ཐོབ་པའི་ཕྱིར་རོ།།ཐོད་རྒལ་བའི་ཕྱིར་མི་འོང་
D 342 ལ་ཞུགས་པ་གང་ཞེ་ན།མཐོང་ལམ་གྱི་སྔོན་དུ་བྱིས་ལམ་གྱིས་འདོད་ཉོན་དགུ་
1349 པ་ངེས་པར་སྤངས་པ་བསམ་གཏན་དང་པོ་ནས་ཅི་ཡང་མེད་པ་ཕྱིན་ལ་
ཆགས་པ་དང་མ་བྲལ་ཡང་རུང་བྲལ་ཡང་རུང་དེ་ལྟ་བུ་དེ་མཐོང་ལམ་དང་
པོ་བཅོ་ལྔ་ལ་གནས་པ་ན་ཕྱིར་མི་འོང་ལ་ཞུགས་པ་ཡིན་ནོ།།དེ་ལྟ་བུ་དེས་

[351]de D M] da P | [352]/ D M] om. / P | [353]rnam M] rna D P | [354] cig car ba'i D M] cig char ba'i P | [355]rim gyis pa D M] rims kyis pa P | [356]spang M] spangs D P | [357]spang M] spangs D P | [358]spang M] spangs D P | [359]spangs pa D M] spang ba ba p | [360]spang M] spangs D P | [361]sgom spang M] bsgom spangs D P | [362]zhing M] cing D P | [363]spang M] spangs D P | [364]spang M] spangs D P | [365]/ D M] om. / P | [366]/ D M] om. / P

skipper, that [there are] only two–those separated from attachment to a great extent (*bhūyovītarāga*) and those who come along previously
D341 separated from [desire-realm] attachment (*kāmavītarāga*), in this regard, the Ācārya Jinaputra Yaśomitra, having the great eye of dharma for analyzing the Abhidharma, wherever a mistaken point exists, one should not fix their ears upon such words like that.

Since the gradual progressor that may be interpreted as an instantaneous abandoner is [really] a gradual abandoner the meaning of gradual progressor is ascertained as twofold. Therefore, some previous Tibetans also impute the term "stages of the path progressor"[141] even though applying the term of gradual progressor is accepted, the meaning of the term is not completely understood.

Who is the enterer to the Once-returner fruition skipper? Generally, when placed in a result, through abandoning the path of cultivation obstacles together with abandoning path of seeing obstacles, one is placed among the three later results and if abandoning a single path of seeing obstacle one is placed only in the result of Stream-enterer.

For that, abandoning six, but not abandoning nine, abandonments of the path of cultivation of the desire realm by a mundane path previous of the path of seeing and abiding in the first fifteen moments of realization is an enterer to the Once-returner result. That individual, by obtaining the sixteenth [moment] and abandoning all abandonments of the path of seeing together with abandoning the sixth obstacle of the path of cultivation, will first attain the result of Once-returner. The fruition skipper Once-returner does not attain the result of Stream-enterer because of attaining the [result of] Once-returner.

D342 Who is the enterer to the Non-returner fruition skipper? Abandoning definitely the nine afflictions of the desire realm by the child's path previous of the path of seeing, suitably or not suitably separated from attachment from the first concentration up to the realm of nothingness, like that, that individual, if abiding on the first fifteen [moments] of the path of seeing, is an enterer to the Non-returner [fruit]. Likewise, that individual, if obtaining the sixteenth moment

[141] Compare with Tsong kha pa's comments in the *Gser phreng* (1970: 225.9).

བཅུ་དྲུག་པ་ཐོབ་པ་ན་སྔར་ལྟར་སྤྱངས་པ་བསྒོམས་པས་ཕྱིར་མི་འོང་ཡིན་ནོ། །དེ་དག་གི་ཤེས་བྱེད་ཀྱང་མཛོད་ལས།

གཉིས་པ་ལ། །དགུ་པ་ཙུན་ཆད་ཟད་པ་ཡིན། །འདོད་པའམ་ཡང་ན་
གོང་མ་ལ། །ཆགས་བྲལ་གསུམ་པ་ལ་ཞུགས་པ། །གང་ཞིག་གང་ལ་
ཞུགས་པ་ཡི། ། །བཅུ་དྲུག་པ་ལ་དེ་འབྲས་གནས།

།ཞེས་གང་གསུང་པའོ། །འདིར་མཁས་པ་སྔ་མ་རྣམས་རྒྱུན་ཞུགས་ལ་ཡང་ཆགས་བྲལ་སྔོན་སོང་འདོད་པ་དང་། །ཀུན་ལས་བཏུས་ལས།

འདོད་པ་ལ་འདོད་ཆགས་དང་མ་བྲལ་བ་ནི་ཡང་དག་པ་ཉིད་དུ་
ངེས་པར་གྱུར་པ་ལ་ཞུགས་ནས་རྒྱུན་དུ་ཞུགས་པར་འགྱུར་རོ། །ཐལ་
ཆེར་ལས་འདོད་ཆགས་དང་བྲལ་བ་ནི་ཡང་དག་པ་ཉིད་དུ་ངེས་
པར་གྱུར་པ་ལ་ཞུགས་ནས་ལན[367]ཅིག་ཕྱིར་འོང་བར་འགྱུར་
P133b རོ། །འདོད་པ་ལས་འདོད་ཆགས་དང་བྲལ་བ་ནི་ཡང་དག་པ་ཉིད་
དུ་ངེས་པར་གྱུར་པ་ལ་ཞུགས་ན་ཕྱིར་མི་འོང་བར་འགྱུར་རོ།[368]

།ཞེས་པའི་དོན་དུ་བསམས་ནས་ཞུགས་པ་དང་པོ་དང་ཐོད་རྒལ་བའི་འབྲས་བུ་བར་པ་གཉིས་ལ་ཞུགས་པ་རིམ་པ་བཞིན་དུ་རྒྱུན་ཞུགས་དང་ཕྱིར་འོང་ཡིན་ཅེས་འདོད་པ་ཡང་འཐད་པར་མ་མཐོང་སྟེ་རྒྱུན་ཞུགས་ལ་མཐོང་
D 343 ལམ་གྱི་སྔར་འདོད་ཉོན་གཅིག་ནས་ལྔའི་བར་སྤྱངས་པ་སྔོན་དུ་སོང་བ་ཡོད་མོད།

འོང་ཀྱང་དེ་ཙམ་གྱིས་ཆགས་བྲལ་སྔོན་སོང་དུ་མི་འགྱུར་གྱི་འབྲས་བུ་གང་དང་གང་གི་ཐུན་མོང་མ་ཡིན་པའི་སྤང་བྱ་དེ་ཉིད་སྤངས་པ་སྔོན་དུ་འགྲོ་དགོས་ཤིང་།[369]རྒྱུན་ཞུགས་ཀྱི་སྤང་བྱའི་གཙོ་བོ་མཐོང་སྤང་ཡིན་ལ། དེ་ལ་སྲིད་རྩེའི་ས་པའི་མཐོང་སྤང་ཀྱང་ཡོད་པས་དེ་བྱིས་ལམ་གྱིས་སྤོང་མི་ནུས་པའི་ཕྱིར་རོ། །དེ་ལྟ་མ་ཡིན་ན་དགྲ་བཅོམ་པ་ལ་ཡང་ཆགས་བྲལ་སྔོན་སོང་

[367] lan D M] lam P | [368] / D M] om. / P | [369] / D M] om. / P

[142] AK, vi.30b-31a-b, Pruden, .953-954, Śāstrī, 934: *dvitīye `rvāṅnavakṣayāt / kāmād viraktāvūrdhvaṃ vā tṛtīyapratīpannakau / sodaśe tu phalasthau tau yatra yaḥ pratipannakaḥ /*

together with abandonment like the former [enterer], will be a Non-returner. The scriptural proof of these is stated in the *Abhidharmakośa*:

> They are enterers for the second [result] until exhausting the ninth [affliction]. They are enterers to the third [result] through detachment with respect to the desire realm or higher realms. In the sixteenth moment, one becomes an abider in the result for which he was entering.[142]

Here, former scholars also assert one previously separated from attachment for the Stream-enterer. The *Abhidharmasamuccaya* states:

> A person who is not separated from attachment in the desire realm entering into the certitude of perfection will be a Stream-enterer. A person who is separated from attachment for the most part entering into the certitude of perfection will be a Once-returner. A person who is separated from attachment from the desire realm, entering into the certitude of perfection will be a Non-returner. [143]

Having reflected on the meaning of this, the first enterer and the enterer to the two middle skipper fruitions, in stages are asserted as being the "Stream-enterer, Once-returner, and Non-returner," [and this] is not seen as correct.

The Stream-enterer goes previously abandoning from one to
D343 five desire realm afflictions in the former path of seeing but, by merely that, the result that has not gone previously separated from attachment must go previously abandoning that very defilement which is not harmonious with the upper realms and the principal of that to be abandoned of the Stream-enterer is the abandonments of the path of seeing. For that, since it is also the Peak of Existence level abandonments of the path of seeing, those are unable to be abandoned

---

[143] AS, Rahula, p.152, Pradhan, 89: *darśanamārgaḥ samyaktvaniyāmāvakrāntiḥ / dharmābhi(samaye) pi saḥ / kāmeṣvavītarāgaḥ pudgalaḥ samyaktvaniyāmamavakrāman srotaāpanno bhavati yad bhūyo vītarāgaḥ samyaktvaniyāmamavakrāman sakṛdāgāmī bhavati / kāmebhyo vītarāgaḥ samyaktvaniyāmamavakrāmannanāgāmī bhavati /*

1350 འདོད་དགོས་ཏེ།[370]དགྲ་བཅོམ་པ་ལ་གེགས་སུ་གྱུར་པའི་སྤང་བྱ་འགའ་ཞིག་
མཐོང་ལམ་གྱི་སྔོན་དུ་ཡང་སྤངས་པ་ཡོད་པའི་ཕྱིར་རོ།།ཀུན་ལས་བཏུས་ཀྱི་
ལུང་གི་དོན་ཡང་དེ་མ་ཡིན་ནོ།།འོ་ན་ཅི་ཞེ་ན།ལུང་དེའི་གོང་དུ་རྒྱུན་དུ་
ཞུགས་པ་གང་ཞེ་ན།གང་མཐོང་བའི་ལམ་གྱི་སེམས་ཀྱི་སྐད་ཅིག་མ་བཅུ་དྲུག་
པ་ལ་གནས་པའི་གང་ཟག་གོ།མཐོང་བའི་ལམ་ནི་ཡང་དག་པ་ཉིད་དུ་ངེས་
པར་[371]གྱུར་པ་ལ་ཞུགས་པ་སྟེ།ཞེས་བཅུ་དྲུག་པ་ལ་གནས་པ་དེ་རྒྱུན་ཞུགས་
སུ་བཤད་པ་ན་སེམས་བཅུ་དྲུག་པ་ལ་དང་པོར་འབྲས་བུ་ཐོབ་པ་ཐམས་ཅད་
རྒྱུན་ཞུགས་ཡིན་ནམ་སྙམ་པ་ལ།[372]འདོད་པའི་ཉོན་མོངས་གཏན་མ་སྤངས་
པ་ཞིག་མཐོང་ལམ་ལ་ཞུགས་ནས་བཅུ་དྲུག་པ་ཐོབ་པ་ན་རྒྱུན་ཞུགས་
དང་།[373]དེ་བཞིན་དུ་འདོད་པའི་ཉོན་མོངས་ཕལ་ཆེ་བ་དྲུག་པ་མན་ཆད་ཙམ་
སྤངས་པ་དང་།འདོད་པའི་དགུ་པ་རིལ་གྱིས་སྤངས་པ་མཐོང་ལམ་ལ་ཞུགས་
P134a ནས་བཅུ་དྲུག་པ་ནམ་ཐོབ་པའི་ཚེ་རིམ་པ་བཞིན་ཕྱིར་འོང་དང་ཕྱིར་མི་འོང་
D 344 ཡིན་ནོ་[374]ཞེས་པ་ཡིན་གྱི།།[375]བཅུ་དྲུག་པོའི་སྔོན་དུ་དེ་དག་ཡིན་ཞེས་པའི་
དོན་མིན་ཏེ།ཀུན་ལས་བཏུས་ལས།དེའི་གོང་དུ་རྒྱུན་དུ་ཞུགས་པའི་འབྲས་བུ་
མངོན་དུ་བྱ་བའི་ཕྱིར་ཞུགས་པ་དང་རྒྱུན་དུ་ཞུགས་པ་དང་དེ་བཞིན་དུ་ཕྱིར་
འོང་ཕྱིར་མི་འོང་དགྲ་བཅོམ་གསུམ་ཆར་ལ་བཤད་པའི་ཕྱིར་རོ།།

།དེ་ལྟར་སློབ་དཔོན་ཐོགས་མེད་ནི།འབྲས་བུ་དང་པོ་གསུམ་ལ་གནས་
པའི་མཐོང་ལམ་པར་ཡང་བཞེད་དེ་བཅུ་དྲུག་པ་མཐོང་ལམ་ཡིན་པའི་ཕྱིར་
རོ།།མཛོད་པ་ནི་སློབ་པ་འབྲས་གནས་ཡིན་ན་སྒོམ་ལམ་པས་ཁྱབ་པར་འདོད་
དོ།།བཅུ་དྲུག་པ་མ་ཐོབ་པར་འབྲས་བུ་མི་འཐོབ་པའི་ཕྱིར་དང་།བཅུ་དྲུག་པ་
སྒོམ་ལམ་ཡིན་པར་འདོད་པའི་ཕྱིར་རོ།།གལ་ཏེ་འབྲས་བུ་སྔ་མ་སྔོན་དུ་མ་
བཏང་བར་འབྲས་བུ་ཕྱི་མ་ཐོབ་པ་དེ་ཐོད་རྒལ་བ་ཡིན་ན་ཅིག་ཅར་བའི་
[376]དགྲ་བཅོམ་པ་ཡང་ཐོད་རྒལ་བར་འགྱུར་ཏེ།[377]ཕྱིར་མི་འོང་མ་ཐོབ་པར་
དགྲ་བཅོམ་གྱི་འབྲས་བུ་ཐོབ་པའི་ཕྱིར་རོ།ཞེ་ན།ཉེས་པས་གོས་པ་མེད་
1351 དེ།[378]འདི་ལྟར་ཁོ་བོ་ཅག་འབྲས་བུ་སྔ་མ་སྔོན་དུ་མ་བཏང་བར་འབྲས་བུ་ཕྱི་
མ་ཐོབ་ཙམ་གྱིས་[379]ཐོད་རྒལ་བར་མི་འདོད་དོ།།འོ་ན་ཅི་ཞེ་ན།སྤྱིར་རྒྱུན་
ཞུགས་ཀྱི་འབྲས་བུ་སེམས་བཅུ་དྲུག་པ་ལ་ཐོབ་པ་དེས་ཕྱིས་ལམ་བསྒོམ་སྟེ་

[370]/ D M] om. / P | [371]nges par D M] ngos par P | [372]/ D M] om. / P | [373]/ D M] om. / P | [374]om. / D M] insert / P | [375]/ / D M] om. / / P | [376]cig car ba'i D M] cig char ba'i P | [377]/ D M] om. / P | [378]/ D M] om. / P | [379]gyis M] gyi D P

by the child's path. So, if it is not, it is necessary to assert having gone previously separated from attachment also for the Arhat because then only that to be abandoned which is a hindrance for the Arhat is also abandoned previous of the path of seeing. The meaning of the pronouncement of the *Abhidharmasamuccaya* is not that. Well then, what is [the meaning]? What is the Stream-enterer in the sense of that quotation? It is the individual who abides on the sixteenth moment of thought of the path of seeing. The path of seeing, he who abides on the sixteenth thus "enters to the certitude of perfection," if explained as a Stream-enterer, all obtain the result first on the sixteenth thought, it is a Stream-enterer or for the sense does not abandon the series of desire realm afflictions, when obtaining the sixteenth having entered to the path of seeing, the Stream-enterer according to that abandons merely the lower six [defilements], if most of the desire realm afflictions at the time of obtainment or the sixteenth, having entered to the path of seeing abandons the whole nine [afflictions] of the desire [realm], gradually one is a Once-returner and Non-returner. It is thus but saying "it is those previous of the sixteenth" is not the meaning
D344 because it is explained from the *Abhidharmasamuccaya* in regards to the enterer for the sake of manifesting the result of Stream-enterer and the Stream-enterer and likewise the three parts of the Once-returner, Non-returner, and Arhat.

Accordingly, the Ācārya Asaṅga maintains that the abiders in the first three results are also in the path of seeing because the sixteenth [moment] is the path of seeing. The *Abhidharmakośa* asserts that when a trainee abides in the result that it is pervaded by the path of cultivation because if not obtaining the sixteenth [moment] one does not obtain the result and because the sixteenth [moment] is asserted as being the path of cultivation. If it is the case, that it is a fruition skipper that obtains the later results in not letting go previously a former result, the Arhat who simultaneously [abandons] also will be a fruition skipper because of obtaining the result of Arhat in not obtaining the Non-returner [result]. Why? That is without fault, accordingly, we do not assert as the fruition skipper who merely obtains later fruitions in not letting go previously former fruitions. Well then, why is that? Generally, the result of Stream-enterer, by that obtainment on the sixteenth thought, cultivates the child's path and is

དྲུག་པ་སྤངས་ནས་ཕྱིར་འོང་དགུ་པ་སྤངས་ཏེ་ཕྱིར་མི་འོང་འཐོབ་པ་ལུགས་
དང་མཐུན་པ་ལ།ཅི་ཡང་མེད་པ་ཕྱིན་གྱི་སྒོམ་སྤང་[380]ཅི་རིགས་པ་བྱིས་ལམ་
གྱིས་སྤྱོད་བ་ཡོད་པས་གང་ཟག་གི་ཁྱད་པར་འགའ་ཞིག་མཐོང་ལམ་གྱི་སྔོན་
དུ་འདོད་པའི་དྲུག་པ་དང་དགུ་པ་སྤངས་པ་དེ་དག་བཅུ་དྲུག་པ་ཐོབ་མ་
D 345 ཐག་འབྲས་བུ་བར་པ་གཉིས་འཐོབ་པས་དེ་དག་སྔར་བཤད་པ་ལྟར་གྱི་
P134b འབྲས་བུ་འཐོབ་པའི་གོ་རིམ་[381]དང་མི་[382]མཐུན་པས་ཐོད་རྒལ་བར་བཞག་
ལ།།[383]དེ་ལྟ་བུའི་སྤངས་པ་སྔོན་དུ་སོང་བ་ནི་ཅིག་ཅར་བ་[384]ལ་མེད་ན་ཏ་
ཅང་ཐལ་བ་ཅི་སྟེ་ཚོལ་དེའི་ཕྱིར་ཀླན་ཀ་དེ་ནི་གྱི་ནའོ།

།འོ་ན་ཐོད་རྒལ་བའི་ཕྱིར་འོང་འབྲས་གནས་དེས་ཕྱིས་ཕྱིར་མི་འོང་
ཐོབ་པ་ན་གང་ཟག་དེ་གང་དུ་འདོད་པར་བྱ་ཞེ་ན།འདི་།ཉ་དཔོན།འབྲས་བུ་
ཐོད་རྒལ་བ་དང་མཐར་གྱིས་པ་གང་ཡང་མིན་ཞེས་པ་དང།ཕྱིར་[385]མི་འོང་
ལ་སྔོན་ལ་བཏང་བར་བྱས་པ་ནི་ཕྱིར་འོང་ཡིན་ལ་དེ་བཏང་བས་འབྲས་བུ་
མཐར་གྱིས་པ་ཡིན་ཞེས་ཀྱང་འདོད།བདག་གི་བླ་མ་དག།པ་ཡོད་པས་གང་ལ་
དད་པའི་རྗེས་སུ་འབྲང་ངོ།།དེ་ལྟར་ན་མཇོད་ལས་ཐོད་རྒལ་བའི་སྐབས་སུ་
རྒྱུན་ཞུགས་བཤད་པ་ནི་ཞར་བྱུང་ཙམ་སྟེ་འགྲེལ་པའི་བཤད་ཟིན་གྱི་མཚམས་
སྦྱོར་དུ་ཕལ་ཆེར་ལས་དང་འདོད་པ་ལས་འདོད་ཆགས་དང་བྲལ་བའི་གང་
ཟག་རྣམས་ཀྱི་རྣམ་པར་བཞག་པ་ནི་དེ་ལྟ་བུ་ཡིན་ནོ་ཞེས་གཉིས་ཤིག་སྨོས་
པའི་ཕྱིར་རོ།

།ཐོད་རྒལ་བ་ལ་རྫས་བདུན་དང།།ཞུགས་པ་དང་པོ་རྣམ་པ་
གསུམ།།རྒྱུན་ཞུགས་སོགས་སུ་འདོད་པ་ཡི།།ངན་རྟོག་བཀག་ནས་
ཐོད་རྒལ་བའི།།འཕགས་པ་རྣམས་ཀྱིས་[386]སྤངས་རྟོགས་[387]དག་།མ་
ནོར་བཤད་ནས་བདག་གཞན་རྣམས།།མཁས་པའི་རྗེས་སུ་ཁྲིད་
ནས་ནི།།ཐུན་པའི་ངན་རྟོག་[388]བྲལ་བར་བྱས།
1352 །ཞེས་བྱ་བ་ནི་བསྡུ་བའི་ཚིགས་སུ་བཅད་པའོ།།ཐོད་རྒལ་བ་བཤད་ཟིན་
ཏོ།།།།

---

[380] spang D M] spangs P | [381] rim D M] rims P | [382] mi M] ma D P | [383] / / D M] om. / / P | [384] cig car ba D M] ci char ba P | [385] phyir D M] phyer P | [386] kyis D M] kyi P | [387] rtogs D M] rtog P | [388] rtog D M] rtogs P

harmonious with the system of obtaining the Once-returner having abandoned the sixth, the Non-returner having abandoned the ninth and the path of cultivation abandonment which goes to Nothingness realm in some measure since it is abandoned by the child's path, yet since only the superior individual, those who abandon the six or ninth [afflictions] of the desire [realm] previous of the path of seeing are those who obtain the two middle results immediately upon obtaining
D345 the sixteenth, it is unharmonious with the succession of obtaining results which are like the ones formerly explained, and to establish as a fruitition skipper, one who goes previously abandoning such like this, if it is not a simultaneous [abandoner], how can that logical absurdity be searched, therefore, that argument is pointless.

Well then, that abider who is like a Once-returner skipper, later, if obtaining Non-returner, should one assert that individual as above? This one is said (by Nya dbon) "not to be either one who goes gradually or skips fruitions" and (my *bla ma*) asserts that since the Once-returner is caused to be dropped previous to the Non-returner it is a gradual progressor, that one being a follower of faith. In this way, explaining the Stream-enterer in the period of the fruition skipper from the *Abhidharmakośa* merely occurs as an addendum and in connection with the complete explanation of the *Abhidharmakośabhāṣya*, "the presentation of the individuals who are separated for the most part and separated from attachment from the desire realm is such like this", only the two are mentioned.

> Separating from unwholesome thoughts which are foolish, from following the guidance of the Masters, I and others have explained unmistakably, the realized abandonments of the Āryas who skip fruitions, having refuted the negative thoughts that are asserted for the Stream-enterer and so forth, the first enterer has three aspects and the fruition skipper is seven in substance.

Thus is described in a condensed verse. The explanation of the fruition skipper is finished.

སྤང་བྱ་ཅིག་ཅར་[389]དུ་སྤོང་བ་གང་ཞེ་ན།ཀུན་ལས་བཏུས་ལས།

D 346 རྒྱུན་དུ་ཞུགས་པའི་གང་ཟག་ཅེས་གང་གསུངས་པ་ལ་རྒྱུན་དུ་
ཞུགས་པ་ནི་རྣམ་པ་གཉིས་ཏེ།[390]མཐར་གྱིས་པ་དང།ཅིག་ཅར་
[391]ངེས་པར་འབྱིན་པའོ།།མཐར་གྱིས་པ་ནི་ཇི་སྐད་བསྟན་པ་བཞིན་
ནོ།།ཅིག་ཅར་[392]ངེས་པར་འབྱིན་པ་ནི་གང་བདེན་པ་རྣམས་མངོན་
P135a པར་རྟོགས་པར་བྱས་ནས་མི་ལྕོགས་[393]པ་མེད་པ་ལ་བརྟེན་ཏེ་
འཇིག་རྟེན་ལས་འདས་པའི་ལམ་གྱིས་ཁམས་གསུམ་ན་སྤྱོད་པའི་
ཉོན་མོངས་པ་རྣམས་རྣམ་པས་ཅིག་ཅར་[394]སྤངས་[395]ཏེ་འདི་ནི་
རྒྱུན་དུ་ཞུགས་པའི་འབྲས་བུ་དང་དགྲ་བཅོམ་པའི་འབྲས་བུ་དང་
འབྲས་བུ་གཉིས་ལ་གདགས་སོ།།ཕལ་ཆེར་ནི་མཐོང་བའི་ཆོས་སམ་
འཆི་བའི་དུས་ཀྱི་ཚེ་ཀུན་ཤེས་པ་ཐོབ་པར་བྱེད་དོ།།གལ་ཏེ་མི་བྱེད་
ན་ཡང་དེ་སྨོན་ལམ་གྱི་སྟོབས་ཅན་ཡིན་ཏེ་སྨོན་ལམ་གྱི་དབང་
གིས་འདོད་པའི་ཁམས་ཉིད་དུ་སྐྱེས་ཏེ་[396]སངས་རྒྱས་འབྱུང་བ་
མེད་པ་ན་རང་རྒྱལ་བར་འགྱུར་རོ།

།ཞེས་གསུངས་པ་ལྟར་བཤད་དོ།།དེ་ཡང་དུས་ནམ་གྱི་ཚེནས་དང།[397]ས་གང་ལ་བརྟེན་པའི་ལམ་ཇི་ལྟ་བུས་དང།སྤང་[398]བྱ་གང་ཚུལ་ཇི་ལྟར་ཅིག་ཅར་[399]སྤོང་བ་དང།དེ་ལྟ་བུ་དེ་གང་ཟག་གང་ལ་བཞག་པ་དང།དེས་མཐར་འབྲས་བུ་མངོན་དུ་བྱེད་པའི་ཚུལ་དང་ལྷས་རིག་པར་བྱའོ།

།དུས་གང་ནས་ཅིག་ཅར་[400]སྤོང་ཞེ་ན།བདེན་པ་བཞི་མངོན་པར་རྟོགས་ཟིན་པར་བྱས་པ་བཅུ་དྲུག་པའི་ཚེ་ནས་བཟུང་སྟེ་མཐོང་ལམ་གྱི་སྔར་བྱིས་ལམ་ལ་སྤང་བྱ་ཅིག་ཅར་[401]སྤོང་བའི་ནུས་པ་མེད་པའི་ཕྱིར་དང།མཐོང་

---

[389]car D M] char P | [390]/ D M] om. / P | [391]car D M] char P | [392]car D M] char P | [393]lcogs D M] lcog P | [394]car D M] char P | [395]spangs M P] spongs D | [396]te M] de D P | [397]/ D M] om. / P | [398]spang D M] spangs P | [399]car D M] char P | [400]car D M] char P | [401]car D M] char P

---

[144] AS, Pk sems-tsam, Li, 130b.4-8, Rahula, 160, Pradhan, 92: *punaḥ khalu srotaāpannaḥ pudgalo yaduktaḥ sa dvividhaḥ / kramanairyāṇikaḥ sakṛnnairyāṇikaśca /*

Who is one that abandons simultaneously that to be abandoned? The *Abhidharmasamuccaya* states:

> For that one taught who is called the person who enters the stream, the Stream-enterer, is of two types: one who is liberated gradually and the other who is liberated simultaneously. The one who obtains gradually as taught previously. One who is liberated simultaneously, is a person which, having made the comprehension of the truth, having relied on [the liminal absorption of] that which is not-incapable, by the supermundane path, abandons simultaneously the afflictions which are committed in the three realms. Here are distinguished two [results], the result of the Stream-enterer and the result of Arhat. Ordinarily, in the present life or at the time of death, one obtains perfect knowledge itself. If it is the case that one does not do so, one possesses the power of resolution. By the power of resolution, [one] take birth just in the desire realm. If a Buddha does not appear, one will be a *Pratyekajina*.[144]

Thus it is taught accordingly. Also that, one should understand as five, (1) from the time or circumstance, (2) by such path of relying on what ground, (3) abandoning simultaneously according to what method of that to be abandoned, (4) setting forth for the individual such like that, and (5) the method of making manifest the fruit of liberation by that.

(1) What is the simultaneous abandoner from what circumstance? Holding from the moment of the sixteenth causing to finish the clear realization of the four noble truths because there is not the ability of abandoning simultaneously the defilements in the child's

---

kramanairyāṇiko yathā pūrvamuktaḥ / sakṛnnairyāṇikaḥ satyābhisamayamabhisaṃpraviṣṭaḥ aprāpta samāpattimāśritya adhigatena lokottaramargeṇa sakṛt traidhatukāvacarāt sarvakleśān prajahāti prakāraśaḥ prajahāti dvayoḥ phalayoḥ srotaāpattiphalārhatvaphalayoḥ prajñāpyate/ sa ca pudgalo bhūyo dṛṣṭe dharme maraṇakāle ājñāmārāgayati / yadi nārāgayati praṇidhānavaśena tarhi praṇidhānavaśena kāmadhātāvevopapannaḥ abuddhabhave pratyekajinobhavati /

ལམ་གྱིས་ཆེ་ཡང་སྒོམ་[402]སྤང་སྤོང་བ་མེད་པའི་ཕྱིར་རོ།
།ས་གང་ལ་བརྟེན་པའི་ལམ་ཇི་ལྟ་བུས་ཅིག་ཅར་[403]སྤོང་ཞེ་ན།ཁམས་
D 347 གསུམ་སུ་དགུ་ལས་བསམ་གཏན་དང་པོའི་ཉེར་བསྡོགས་མི་ལྟོགས་པ་མེད་
པ་ཁོ་ན་ལ་བརྟེན་པའི་འདས་ལམ་གྱིས་སྤོང་སྟེ་མི་ལྟོགས་པ་མེད་པ་ལ་མི་
1353 བརྟེན་ན་དེའི་གོང་མའི་བསམ་གཏན་རྣམས་ལ་བརྟེན་དགོས་ལ་དེ་དག་ལ་
བརྟེན་པ་ནི་མ་ཡིན་ཏེ།འདོད་པའི་དགུ་པ་མ་སྤངས་པར་བསམ་གཏན་
དངོས་གཞི་མི་ཐོབ་ཅིང་ཅིག་ཅར་[404]པས་ནི་ཁམས་གསུམ་གའི་[405]ཉོན་མོངས་
P135b ཅིག་ཅར་[406]དུ་སྤོང་[407]དགོས་པའི་ཕྱིར་རོ།།དེ་ལྟ་བས་ན་འདི་དང་རྒྱུན་ཞུགས་
དང་ཕྱིར་འོང་རྣམས་ངེས་པར་བསམ་གཏན་དང་པོའི་ཉེར་བསྡོགས་ལ་
བརྟེན་དགོས་ཏེ།འདི་འམ་གོང་མ་རྣམས་ལ་བརྟེན་ནི་དགོས་ལ་བསམ་
གཏན་གྱི་དངོས་གཞི་མ་ཐོབ་པའི་ཕྱིར་རོ།།འདས་ལམ་ཁོ་ན་དགོས་པ་ཡང་
འཇིག་རྟེན་པའི་ལམ་གྱིས་[408]སྤང་བྱ་ཅིག་ཅར་[409]སྤོང་མི་ནུས་པའི་ཕྱིར་
རོ།།འདིར་མི་ལྟོགས་མེད་པ་ནི་བསམ་གཏན་དང་པོའི་ཉེར་བསྡོགས་ཐམས་
ཅད་ལ་འདོད།མཚོན་པ་བ་ཁ་ཅིག།པ་ཡོད་ཀྱང་ཟག་མེད་ཁོ་ན་ལ་བཟུང་
སྟེ།[410]མི་ལྟོགས་མེད་ཀྱི་དོན་ནི་རང་ས་འོག་ས་གོང་ས་ཐམས་ཅད་ཀྱི་སྤང་བྱ་
སྤོང་མི་ནུས་པ་མེད་པའི་དོན་ཡིན་ལ[411]།[412]དེ་ཡང་ཟག་བཅས་ཀྱི་ཉེར་
བསྡོགས་ལ་མེད་པའི་ཕྱིར་རོ།

།འདི་ཁོ་ན་ལ་མི་ལྟོགས་པ་མེད་པ་ཞེས་པ་ཅི་ཡིན་ཞེ་ན།།མི་ལྟོགས་
མེད་ཀྱི་དོན་ནི་སྔར་བསྟན་པ་ལྟར་ཡིན་པས་འདི་ཁོ་ན་ལ་ཡིན་ཏེ།འོག་མའི་
ཉེར་བསྡོགས་རྫོགས་པར་མ་ཐོབ་པར་[413]དེའི་དངོས་གཞི་མི་འཐོབ་ཅིང་།ཉེར་
བསྡོགས་རྫོགས་པ་ན་ཡང་ས་འོག་མའི་ཉོན་མོངས་དགུ་བ་སྤངས་ཟིན་པས་
D 348 དངོས་གཞི་ས་འོག་མ་ལས་རྒྱལ་བར་མི་བྱེད་པའི་ཕྱིར་རོ།།དེ་ལ་དགོངས་
ནས་མཛོད་ལས།

བརྒྱད་ཀྱིས་[414]རང་གོང་ས་ལས་རྒྱལ།

།ཞེས་བསམ་གཏན་དང་པོའི་དངོས་གཞི་ཙམ་དང་།ཁྱད་པར་ཅན་

---

[402]sgom D M] bsgom D P | [403]cig car D M] gcig char P | [404]car D M] char P | [405]ga'i D M] kha'i P | [406]car D M] char P | [407]spong D M] slong P | [408]gyis M] D P gyi | [409]car D M] char P | [410]/ D M] om. / P | [411]la M] na D P | [412]/ D M]

path previous of the path of seeing and because also at the time of the path of seeing there is not the abandonment of the defilements removed by the path of cultivation.

(2) By such path of realizing on what ground is there simultaneous abandonment? Abandonment by the supermundane path which relies on only the not-unable preparation of the first
D347 concentration from the nine levels and three realms. If not relying on the not-unable, for those need to rely on the upper concentrations of the three realms, these are not [true] reliance. The simultaneous [abandoner] not obtaining the actual concentration in not abandoning the nine [afflictions] of the desire [realm] because the afflictions of the three realms need to be abandoned simultaneously. If by such [manner], this one, the Stream-enterers and Once-returners need to definitely rely on the preparation of the first concentration. Relying on this or the upper [ones] is necessary because of not obtaining the actual basis of concentration. Also on the supermundane path is necessary because the abandonment of the mundane path is unable to abandon simultaneously. Here, the not-incapable is asserted (by some *Ābhidhārmika*s) for all preparations of the first concentration, also, held as only uncontaminated and the meaning of not-unable if it is the meaning which is not-unable to abandon the abandonments of all one's ground, lower ground, and upper ground, that is because of being without a contaminated preparation.

For only this, why is it called "not-incapable"? The meaning of not-unable, since it is accordingly former shown it is only this and in not obtaining to complete the lower preparations, not obtaining the actual basis of that, also if completing the preparations, the actual basis since finishes to abandon the nine afflictions of the lower
D348 grounds it does not cause to conquer over the lower grounds. Having the intention for that from the *Abhidharmakośa*:

> One conquers over one's own realm and upper realms by the eight [pure paths].[145]

om. / P | [413]ma thob par D M] ma thob la / P | [414]kyis M] kyi D P

[145] AK, vi.48c-d, Pruden, 989, Shastri, 977: *āryairaṣṭābhiḥ svordhvabhūjayaḥ /*

གཉིས་བསམ་གཏན་ཕྱི་མ་གསུམ་གཟུགས་མེད་ཀྱི་དངོས་གཞི་དང་པོ་གསུམ་
གྱིས་[415]རང་ས་གོང་ས་ཙམ་ལས་རྒྱལ་བར་གསུངས་སོ།

།སྤང་བྱ་གང་ཚུལ་ཇི་ལྟར་ཅིག་ཅར་[416]སྤོང་ཞེ་ན།བརྗོད་པར་བྱ་སྟེ་
ཕྱིར་སྤང་བྱ་ལ་ནི་གཉིས་ཏེ་མཐོང་སྤང་[417]དང་སྒོམ་སྤང་ངོ[418]།།དེ་ལ་མངོན་
པ་མཛོད་པ་ནི་མཐོང་སྤང་[419]ཀྱང་རིམ་གྱིས་[420]སྤོང་བར་འདོད་དེ།[421]འདི་
1354 ལྟར་སྡུག་བསྔལ་ལ་ཆོས་བཟོད་ཆོས་ཤེས་གཉིས་ཀྱིས་འདོད་པའི་སྡུག་བསྔལ་
P136a མཐོང་སྤང་[422]སྤོང་སྡུག་བསྔལ་ལ་རྗེས་[423]བཟོད་རྗེས་ཤེས་གཉིས་ཀྱི་[424]ཁམས་
གོང་མའི་སྡུག་བསྔལ་མཐོང་སྤང་[425]སྤོང་ངོ།།དེ་བཞིན་དུ་ལྷག་མ་རྣམས་ལ་
ཡང་འདོད་པ་ཡིན་ཏེ།[426]འདོད་པ་ཁམས་ཀྱི་རྗེས་མ་ཡིན།།[427]ཞེས་པ་ལྟར་རོ།

།འོ་ན་མཛོད་ལས།[428]སྒོམ་པའི་ལམ་ལ་འགོག་པ་འམ།།ལམ་ལ་ཆོས་ཤེས་གང་ཡིན་དེ[429]།།ཁམས་གསུམ་གྱི་ནི་གཉེན་པོ་ཡིན[430]།།ཞེས་མ་བཤད་དམ་ཞེ་ན།།སྐྱོན་མེད་དེ།[431]དེ་ནི་ཤེས་པ་བཅུ་ལས་འགོག་པ་ཤེས་པ་དང་ལམ་ཤེས་པ་སྒོམ་[432]ལམ་གྱིས་བསྡུས་པ་ལ་རིགས་ཀྱི་དབང་དུ་བྱས་ནས་ཁམས་གསུམ་གྱི་གཉེན་པོར་བསྟན་གྱི་གཉེན་པོ་རྫས་གཅིག་[433]གིས་ཅིག་ཅར་[434]ཁམས་གསུམ་གྱི་ཉོན་མོངས་སྤོང་བར་གཏན་མི་འདོད་དོ།

།ཀུན་ལས་བཏུས་པ་ནི་སྡུག་བསྔལ་ལ་ཆོས་བཟོད་ཆོས་ཤེས་གཉིས་
ཀྱིས་ཁམས་གསུམ་ཆར་གྱི་སྡུག་བསྔལ་མཐོང་སྤང་[435]སྤོང་བ་སོགས་སུ་འདོད་
D 349 པས་ན་མཐོང་སྤང་[436]ནི་མཐོང་ལམ་ཐམས་ཅད་ཀྱིས་ཅིག་ཅར་[437]དུ་སྤོང་
བར་འདོད་དོ།[438]དེ་ཡང་ཁམས་གསུམ་གའི་[439]སྡུག་བསྔལ་དང་ཀུན་འབྱུང་
མཐོང་སྤང་[440]ཅིག་ཅར་[441]དུ་སྤོང་ཞེས་པ་ཡིན་གྱི་བདེན་བཞི་མཐོང་བས་

---

[415]kyis M] kyi D P | [416]car D M] char P | [417]spang D M] spangs P | [418]sgom spang ngo D M] sgom spangs so P | [419]spang D M] spangs P | [420]rim gyis D M] rims kyis P | [421]/ D M] om. / P | [422]spang D M] spangs P | [423]rjes D M] rjas P | [424]kyi D M] kyis P | [425]spang D M] spangs P | [426]/ D M] om. / P | [427]/ / D M] om. / / P | [428]/ D M] om. / P | [429]de D M] te P | [430]khams gsum gyi ni gnyen po yin M] khams gsum pa'i gnyen po yin D P | [431]/ D M] om. / P | [432]sgom M] bsgom D P | [433]gcig D M] cig P | [434]car D M] char P | [435]spang D M] spangs P |

Thus is the mere actual basis of the first concentration and the two who are superior, the three later concentrations are taught as conquering over merely ones own ground and higher sphere of the first three actual basis of the formless realms.

(3) In what manner is that to be abandoned abandoned simultaneously? That which is pronounced for abandonment generally are the two: the defilements to be abandoned by the path of seeing and the defilements to be abandoned by the path of cultivation. For that, the *Abhidharmakośa* accepts that the defilements to be abandoned by the path of seeing are abandoned gradually. Accordingly, the defilements to be abandoned by the path of seeing of the suffering of the desire realm is abandoned by the two: the dharma forbearance and dharma knowledge on the truth of suffering, the defilements to be abandoned by the path of seeing of the suffering of the upper realms is abandoned by the two: the subsequent forbearance and subsequent knowledge on the truth of suffering. Likewise, also for the remaining [truths] it is asserted, that is according thus not subsequent of the desire realm.

Well then, from the *Abhidharmakośa*, why does it not explain the cessation for the path of cultivation or the dharma knowledge on the truth of the path is the antidote of the three realms. That is without fault; it is not asserted the series to abandon the afflictions of the three realms simultaneously by a single substance the antidote which is taught as the antidote of the three realms from making the power of the lineage to condensed by the path of cultivation the path knowledge and the knowledge of cessation from the ten knowledges.

The Abhidharmasamuccaya is by asserting the abandonment and so forth the defilements to be abandoned by the path of seeing the suffering of the three realms by the two dharma forbearance and dharma knowledge on the truth of suffering, the defilements to be abandoned by the path of seeing are asserted as being abandoned
D349 simultaneously by the whole path of seeing. Also that it is said, "the defilements to be abandoned by the path of seeing, the truth of suffering and [the truth of] arising of the three realms, are abandoned

---

[436]spang D M] spangs P | [437]car D M] char P | [438]/ D M] om. / P | [439]ga'i D M] kha'i P | [440]spang D M] spangs P | [441]car D M] char P

སྤང་བར་བྱ་བ་ཐམས་ཅད་ཅིག་ཅར་[442]དུ་ནི་མ་ཡིན་ནོ།།[443]དེས་ན་སྒོམ་སྤང་
སྤང་བ་ཁོ་ན་ལ་ཅིག་ཅར་[444]དང་རིམ་གྱིས་[445]སྤོང་བ་གཉིས་སུ་འགྱུར་
རོ།།དེའི་ཕྱིར་འདོད་པའི་སྒོམ་སྤང་[446]དང་པོ་སྤོང་བ་དང་དུས་ཅིག་ཅར་[447]དུ་
ཁམས་གསུམ་གའི་[448]ཡང་དང་པོ་རྣམས་སྤོང་བ་ཡིན་ཏེ།གཞན་རྣམས་ལ་
ཡང་དེ་ལྟར་རིག་པར་བྱའོ།

།དེ་ལྟ་བུ་དེ་གང་ཟག་གང་ལ་བཞག་ཅེ་[449]ན།གཞུང་དང་འགྲེལ་པ་
གཉིས་ཀར་དགྲ་བཅོམ་དང་རྒྱུན་ཞུགས་ཀྱི་འབྲས་བུ་ལས་གཞན་མི་འབྱུང་
ཞིང།[450]ཁ་ཅིག་རྒྱུན་ཞུགས་ཞུགས་པ་དང་དགྲ་བཅོམ་ཞུགས་པའི་རྣམ་བཞག་
P136b བྱེད་དགོས་ཟེར་ནས་མཐོང་ལམ་སྐད་ཅིག་བཅོ་ལྔའི་རྫོགས་པ་ལ་གནས་པ་
བཅུ་དྲུག་པ་ཐོབ་ནས་ཅིག་ཅར་[451]སྤང་བྱ་སྤོང་བར་འགྲོ་རྒྱུ་དེ་ལ་རྒྱུན་ཞུགས་
ཞུགས་པ་དང་རྒྱུན་ཞུགས་འབྲས་གནས་ཁམས་གསུམ་གྱི་ཉོན་མོངས་དང་པོ་
1355 སྤོང་བ་ལ་བརྩོན་པ་ནས་ཁམས་གསུམ་གྱི་དགུ་པའི་བར་སྤོང་བ་ལ་བརྩོན་པ་
དགྲ་བཅོམ་ཞུགས་པར་འཆད་པ་དང།གཞན་དག་འདིའི་ཞུགས་པ་མ་བཤད་
པའི་རྒྱུ་མཚན་མཐར་གྱིས་པའི་སྐབས་སུ་སྟར་བཤད་ཟིན་པས་ཅིག་ཅར་
[452]བའི་ཞུགས་པ་ཡང་དོན་གྱིས་བཤད་ཅེས་པ་དང།ཞུགས་པ་མེད་པའི་
འབྲས་གནས་མེད་ཅེས་སྨྲ་མོད།འོན་ཀྱང་འདིའི་ཞུགས་པ་ཚོལ་བའི་ངལ་བ་
དེ་ཙམ་མི་དགོས་པར་མངོན་ཏེ་ངར་བཤད་པ་ལྟར་བཅུ་དྲུག་པ་ཐོབ་ནས་
D 350 སྤང་བྱ་དེ་ལྟར་སྤོང་བའི་ཉོན་ཐོས་ནི་ཡོད་ལ།[453]དེ་ཕྱིར་འོང་དང་ཕྱིར་མི་
འོང་གཉིས་སུ་བཞག་ཏུ་མ་བཏུབ་པས་དེ་རྒྱུན་ཞུགས་སུ་བཞག་པ་ཡིན་ཞིང་
[454]རྒྱུན་ཞུགས་ཀྱི་འབྲས་བུ་ཐོབ་པ་ནི་སྒོམ་[455]སྤང་འགའ་ཞིག་རིམ་གྱིས་
[456]དང་ཅིག་ཅར་[457]སྤོང་བ་ལ་ལྟོས་པ་མེད་པའི་ཕྱིར་ཅིག་ཅར་[458]བའི་རྒྱུན་
ཞུགས་ཞུགས་པ་བརྟགས་མི་དགོས་སོ།།གཞན་ཡང་ཀུན་བཏུས་སུ་བདེན་པ་
རྣམས་མངོན་པར་རྟོགས་པ་བྱས་ནས་ཞེས་དེ་ནས་མཚམས་བཟུང་བའི་ཕྱིར་
རོ།།དགྲ་བཅོམ་པ་ལ་ཞུགས་པ་ནི་རྣམ་གཞག་བྱས་ཀྱང་འགལ་བ་མེད་པ་
ཙམ་ཡིན་ནོ།

---

[442] car D M] char P | [443] / / D M] om. / / P | [444] car D M] char P | [445] rim gyis D M] rims kyis P | [446] sgom spang M] bsgom spang D P | [447] car D M] char P | [448] ga'i D M] kha'i P | [449] ce M] ca D; zhe P | [450] / D M] om. / P | [451] car D M] char P | [452] car D M] char P | [453] / D M] om. / P | [454] zhing M] cing D P | [455] sgom M] bsgom D P | [456] rim gyis D M] rims kyis P | [457] car D M] char P | [458] car D M] char P

simultaneously, but all that to be abandoned by seeing the four noble truths is not simultaneously [abandoned]. Therefore, only the defilements to be abandoned by the path of cultivation will be as two, abandoned simultaneously or gradually. Because of that, abandoning the first defilement abandoned by the path of cultivation abandons also the first set of the three realms simultaneously. The other [path of cultivation defilements removed simultaneously] accordingly should be understood.

(4) What is set forth for the individuals such like that? In both the text and commentary [that] does not arise other than the fruit of Stream-enterer and Arhat Someone says: from saying it necessary to make the arrangement of the Stream-enterer enterer and the Arhat enterer, abiding on the realization of the fifteenth moment of the path of seeing, for that cause the transmigrator abandons that to be abandoned simultaneously having obtained the sixteenth [moment], the Stream-enterer enterer and the abider in the Stream-enterer result, from making effort to abandon the first affliction of the three realms to making effort to abandon up to the ninth [affliction] of the three realms is explained as an arhat enterer, the reason of not explaining this enterer [for] other [results], since it finishes to explain formerly in the period of the gradual progressor, the simultaneous enterer also is explained by the meaning taught [there] and there is not an abider in the result without an enterer. However, that fatigue of searching for [this] enterer is evident as unnecessary and as like explained formerly, the *śrāvaka* who abandons accordingly that to be abandoned having
D350 obtained the sixteenth has for that since it is not convenient as setting forth as two, the Once-returner and Non-returner, that is set forth as a Stream-enterer and obtains the result of Stream-enterer, and because there is no reliance on abandoning gradually or simultaneously any of the defilements to be abandoned by the path of cultivation, it is unnecessary to examine the enterer to the simultaneous abandoner Stream-enterer. Moreover, in the *Abhidharmasamuccaya* because of holding the border from that "the noble truths having made clear realization." The enterer to arhat having set forth also is merely without contradiction.

།གང་ཟག་དེས་འབྲས་བུ་ཐོབ་པའི་ཚུལ་ཇི་ལྟ་བུ་ཞེ་ན།།འདིས་ཚེ་དེ་ལ་
ཉོན་མོངས་ཐམས་ཅད་སྤང་[459]ནས་མཐོང་ཆོས་སམ་འཆི་བའི་སྔོན་རོལ་ཡན་
ཆད་སྔོན་དུས་ཀྱི་སྲིད་པའི་ཚེའམ་འཆི་སྲིད་ཀྱི་ཚེ་དགྲ་བཅོམ་པ་ཕལ་ཆེར་
འཐོབ་ལ་གལ་ཏེ་ཚེ་དེ་ལ་ཉོན་མོངས་མ་ལུས་པར་སྤང་མ་ནུས་ན་ཤི་ནས་
ཡང་འདོད་ཁམས་སུ་སྐྱེས་ནས་དགྲ་བཅོམ་འཐོབ་ཅིང་དེ་ཡང་དེའི་ཚེ་
སངས་རྒྱས་དང་ཉན་ཐོས་མེད་པ་དང་དེ་དག་གི་བསྟན་པ་ནུབ་པ་དང་
P137a འདོམས་ན་སྲིད་པ་ཐ་མའི་ཚེ་འདོད་པར་གཞན་ལ་མ་ལྟོས་པར་བྱང་ཆུབ་
མངོན་དུ་བྱས་པའི་ཐེག་དམན་ཡིན་པའི་ཕྱིར་རང་རྒྱལ་བར་འགྱུར་རོ།།དེས་
ན་ཅིག་ཅར་[460]སྦྱོང་བའི་ཚེ་རང་རྒྱལ་མིན་ཡང་སྤངས་ནས་རང་རྒྱལ་དུ་
འགྱུར་བ་ནི་ཡོད་དོ།

།ད་ནི་འདི་དཔྱད་དེ་[461]ཅི་ཞུགས་གནས་བརྒྱད་པོ་དེ་དག་རང་རྒྱལ་ལ་
1356 ཡང་སྦྱར་རུང་ངམ་ཞེ་ན།[462]འདི་ལ་སྔ་རབས་པ་རྣམས་རང་རྒྱལ་ལ་འབྲས་བུ་
བར་མ་གཉིས་མི་འོང་ཞེས་ཟེར་ནས་འབྲས་བུ་རྣམ་གྲོལ་གྱི་ལམ་ཡང་བཅུ་
D 351 བདུན་དུ་གྲངས་ངེས་པའི་ཡིད་བརྟན་མི་རུང་བའི་རྟོག་བཟོ་མང་པོ་བྱེད་
མོད།འོང་ཀྱང་འཐད་པར་མི་རྟོག་སྟེ་འབྲས་བུ་བར་བར་པ་གཉིས་མི་རྩི་བའི་
རྒྱུ་མཚན་རང་རྒྱལ་ཅིག་ཅར་[463]བར་འཆད་པ་ནི་བཀག་ཟིན་ཏོ།

།སྤྱིར་རང་རྒྱལ་གྱི་རྣམ་གཞག་ཆེ་ལོང་ཙམ་ནི་འདི་ཡིན་ཏེ།ཀུན་ལས་བཏུས་སུ་

> ངེས་པར་འབྱེད་པའི་ཆ་དང་མཐུན་པ་སྔོན་མ་སྐྱེས་པ་བསྐྱེད་པ་དང།སྔོན་འབྲས་བུ་མ་ཐོབ་པ་ཐོབ་པ་ཡང་རུང་སྟེ་སངས་རྒྱས་འབྱུང་བ་མེད་པར་བདག་ཉིད་ཀྱིས་ལམ་མངོན་དུ་བྱས་ན་བསེ་རུ་ལྟ་བུར་གྱུར་ཏེ་གཅིག་པུར་གནས་པའམ་རང་རྒྱལ་བར་འགྱུར་ཏེ།ཚོགས་དང་སྤྱོད་པ་གང་སྟུག་བསྐལ་གྱི་མཐར་ཕྱིན་པ་འཐོབ་པའོ།

།ཞེས་པ་ལྟར་བཤད་ན་རང་རྒྱལ་ལ་ཉན་ཐོས་ཀྱི་ལམ་སྔོན་དུ་མ་བཏང་

---

[459] spang M] spangs D P | [460] car D M] char P | [461] de D M] do P | [462] / D M] om. / P | [463] car D M] char P

---

[146] AS, Rahula,146-147, Pradhan, 87 : *anutpāditpūrvanirvedhabhāgīyaḥ utpādita-pūrvanirvedhabhāgīyaḥ aprāptapūrvaphalaḥ abuddhabhave ātmanā cetanayā ārya*

(5) What is such method of obtaining the definite result by that individual? At that time by this, having abandoned all afflictions, in the present life, at the time of circumstance previous of death or at the time of death, the [state of] *arhat* [is] obtained for the most part. If it is the case at that time, if [one] is not able to abandon all afflictions without exception, having died, also having been reborn in the desire realm, if in obtaining arhatship at that time, the situation occurs that there are no Buddhas or *śrāvaka*s and their teaching has disappeared, at the time of the last [conditoned] existence, because it is the lesser vehicle which makes manifest enlightenment in not relying on others in the desire [realm], [that one] will be a *pratyekajina*. Therefore, at the time of abandoning simultaneously, [one] is not a *pratyekajina*, although after abandonment [one] will become a *pratyekajina*.

Now, [we] will examine this. Is it suitable to count this *pratyekajina* among the eight enterers and abiders? Regarding this, earlier [Tibetan] scholars who say "the *pratyekajina* does not have the two middle results", assert the [*pratyekajina*] result's paths of
D351 liberation as definitely seventeen, but these are fabricated thoughts that are untrustable. Moreover, it is not realized correctly, for [they think] the reason to not count the two middle results is that the *pratyekajina* is explained as a simultaneous abandoner, yet this has already been refuted.

In general, a merely rough establishment of the *pratyekajina* is this: when explaining from the *Abhidharmasamuccaya*,

> ...whether not generating or generating the preparatory analytical factors, whether obtaining a result previously or not, where a Buddha has not arisen, when manifesting the path by ones self one will be like a rhinoceros abiding solitarily, or one will be a *pratyekajina* obtaining the end of suffering when practicing in a group.[146]

The *pratyekajina*, either in not releasing or releasing previously from the *śrāvaka* path, has two [aspects]: first, in not generating

---

mārga-saṃmukhībhūtaḥ khadgaviṣāṇakalpaḥ ekavihārī pratyekajinaḥ varggacārī duḥkhasya-antamanuprāpnoti / Tsong kha pa's quote follows the options given by Pradhan, 87 in footnotes #5 and #6

བ་དང༌།བཏང་བ་ལ་གཉིས་ལས།དང་པོ་ནི་ཚེ་རབས་སྔ་མ་ལ་ངེས་འབྱེད་ཆ་
མཐུན་མ་བསྐྱེད་པ་བསེ་རུ་ལྟ་བུ་དང༌།གཉིས་པ་ནི་འབྲས་བུ་མ་ཐོབ་པར་
སྦྱོར་ལམ་ཙམ་སྔོན་དུ་བཏང་ནས་རང་རྒྱལ་དུ་གྱུར་པ་དང༌།རྒྱུན་ཞུགས་ཀྱི་
འབྲས་བུ་ཙམ་ཐོབ་ནས་རང་རྒྱལ་དུ་གྱུར་པ་གཉིས་སོ།།དེ་ཡང་

> སྔོན་སེ་ལྔ་བསྟེན་པའི་དྲང་སྲོང་ལྔ་བརྒྱ་དབེན་པ་ཞིག་ན་གནས་
> P137b པའི་སར་རང་རྒྱལ་གྱི་དྲུང་དུ་བསྟད་པའི་སྤྲེའུ་ཞིག་དེར་ཕྱིན་ནས་
> རང་རྒྱལ་གྱི་ལུས་ཀྱི་སྤྱོད་ལམ་དེ་སྤྲེའུ་དེས་དེ་རྣམས་ལ་བསྟན་པས་
> དེ་རྣམས་ཀྱིས་ཀྱང་དེ་ལྟར་བྱས་པས་རང་རྒྱལ་ལྔ་བརྒྱར་གྱུར་

ཅེས་འབྱུང་བས་ན་བསེ་རུ་ལྟ་བུ་གཅིག་པུར་གནས་ལ་འཕགས་པ་
དཀའ་ཐུབ་དྲག་པོས་གདུངས་པ་མ་ཡིན་པས་སོ་སྐྱེའི་ལམ་ཙམ་སྔོན་དུ་
D 352 བཏང་བའི་རང་རྒྱལ་ཡིན་ནོ།།དེ་ལ་ཕྱི་མ་གཉིས་ལ་ནི་ཚོགས་དང་གནས་པ་
ཡང་ཟེར་ལ་ཚོགས་སྤྱོད་ཆེ་ཆུང་ནི་བོད་ཀྱི་ཐ་སྙད་དུ་སྣང་ངོ།དེའི་ཕྱིར་ཕྱི་མ་
གཉིས་ལྟ་བུའི་རང་རྒྱལ་ལ་ནི་ཕྱིར་འོང་དང་ཕྱིར་མི་འོང་ཡང་ཡོད་དེ།རྒྱུན་
ཞུགས་ཙམ་ཐོབ་ནས་རང་རྒྱལ་དུ་གྱུར་ནས་དེས་འདོད་ཉོན་དྲུག་པ་སྤངས་
1357 ནས་ཕྱིར་འོང་དགུ་པ་སྤངས་ན་ཕྱིར་མི་འོང་དུ་འགྱུར་བའི་ཕྱིར་རོ།

།འོ་ན་དགེ་སྦྱོང་གི་འབྲས་བུ་བཞིར་འཛོག་པའི་རྒྱུ་མཚན་ཡང་གང་ཞེ་
ན།འདི་ལ་བྱེ་བྲག་ཏུ་སྨྲ་བ་ནི།མཛོད་ལས།

> འབྲས་བུ་བཞི་རྣམས་བཞག་པ་ནི།།རྒྱུ་ལྔ་དག་ནི་སྲིད་ཕྱིར་
> རོ།།འབྲས་ལ་སྔོན་ལམ་བཏང་བ་དང༌།།གཞན་ཐོབ་པ་དང་ཟད་
> བསྒོམས་དང༌།།ཤེས་པ་བརྒྱད་ཙན་ཐོབ་པ་དང༌།།རྣམ་པ་བཅུ་དྲུག

[147] A similar account is found in AKBh, on iii.94a-b: *parvate kila pañcaśatāni tāpasānāṃ kaṣṭāni tapāṃsi tapyante sma yāvat pratyekabuddhasahoṣitena*

preparatory analytical factors in a former time period [one] is like a rhinoceros and the second has two [aspects], having released previously only the path of preparation in not obtaining a result or having obtained only the result of Stream-enterer, one will become a *pratyekajina*. Regarding this,

> Previously, in a solitary place where five hundred *ṛṣi*s who practiced austerities with five fires abided, a monkey who had lived with a *pratyekajina* went there. That monkey then demonstrated to those [*ṛṣi*s] the physical conduct of a *pratyekajina*, and those [*ṛṣi*s], having performed accordingly, became five hundred *pratyekabuddha*s.[147]

With this occurrence, since the Noble Being who solitarily abides like a rhinoceros is not tormented with fierce effort, [this one] is a *pratyekajina* who has previously released only the ordinary
D352 individual path. For the latter two of the *pratyekajina*, saying "abiding with a group" also is also called "the greater and smaller practicing with a group", which appears to be a Tibetan term. Therefore, the *pratyekajina* which is like the latter two is also a Once-returner or Non-returner because, having obtained merely [the result of] Stream-enterer, [this one] becomes a *pratyekajina*, and then, having abandoned the sixth desire realm affliction becomes a Once-returner or, if abandoning the ninth [desire realm affliction] becomes a Non-returner.

Well then, what is the reason of positing four results of *śramaṇya*? Regarding this the *Vaibhāṣika*s [teach] from the *Abhidharmakośa*:

> Four results are established because five causes exist. In a result, there is the release of a previous path, obtaining another path, a collected cessation, obtaining the eight

markaṭenāgamya tadīryāpathasaṃsarśanāt pratyekabodhimabhisaṃbaddhā / This is a condensed and slightly different account of a legendary story that occurs in the *Divyāvadāna* (Vaidya, 1959: 216 217), specifically the *Pāṃśupradānāvadānam*. The account here given by Tsong kha pa mentions "ṛṣis" (tib. *drang srong*) and austerities with five fires (*pañcatapas*), these are mentioned in the *Divyāvadāna*, which Tsong kha pa must have emended to the AKBh version.

ཐོབ་པའོ།

།ཞེས་འབྲས་བུ་བཞིར་འཇོག་པ་ལ་ཞུགས་པའི་ལམ་སྟོན་ལ་བཏང་པ་
དང༌།།གཞན་འབྲས་བུའི་ལམ་ཐོབ་པ་དང་ཟད་པ་བསྒོམས་པ་ནི་སྤངས་པ་
[464]བསྒོམས་པ་སྟེ།དཔེར་ན་བཅུ་དྲུག་པའི་ཚེ་མཐོང་སྤང་[465]སྤངས་པ་ཐམས་
ཅད་ཀྱི་ཐོབ་པ་གཅིག་ཉིད་པ་ལྟ་བུའོ།།ཆོས་ཤེས་བཞི་རྗེས་ཤེས་བཞི་སྟེ་
བརྒྱད་ཐོབ་པ་དང།མི་རྟག་པ་ལ་སོགས་པའི་ཟག་མེད་ཀྱི་རྣམ་པ་བཅུ་དྲུག་
ཐོབ་པ་སྟེ།།ཁྱད་པར་དེ་ལྟ་ཐོབ་པ་ནི་འབྲས་བུ་བཞིར་འཇོག་པའོ་ཞེས་འདོད་
P138a དོ།།འོན་ཀྱང་སྤང་བྱ་[466]སྤངས་པའི་སྒོ་ནས་འབྲས་བུར་འཇོག་ལ་དེ་ཡང་
འབྲས་བུ་དང་པོ་ནི་མཐོང་སྤང་[467]སྤངས་པ་ཙམ་གྱིས་འཇོག་ལ།[468]སྒོམ་སྤང་
སྤངས་པའི་སྒོ་ནས་[469]འབྲས་བུ་ཕྱི་མ་གསུམ་འཇོག་སྟེ་དེ་ཡང་འདོད་པའི་
སྒོམ་སྤང་[470]སྤངས་པ་ལས་འབྲས་བུ་གཉིས་འཇོག་སྟེ་དྲུག་པ་སྤངས་པའི་
D 353 ཕྱིར་འོང་[471]དང་།དགུ་པ་སྤངས་པས་ཕྱིར་མི་འོང་དུ་འཇོག་པའི་ཕྱིར་
རོ།།ཁམས་གོངས་མའི་ཉོན་མོངས་མ་ལུས་པར་སྤངས་པས་ནི་དགྲ་བཅོམ་
པའི་འབྲས་བུར་འཇོག་གོ །

དེ་ལྟར་ན་དེ་དག་གིས་ནི་ཞུགས་པ་དང་གནས་པའི་སྐྱེས་བུ་ཆེན་པོ་
རྣམས་ཀྱི་རྣམ་པར་བཞག་པ་རྣམས་དཔྱིས་ཕྱིན་པར་བཤད་ཟིན་ཏོ།
།དེ་ལྟར་ན།ཁོ་བོས་ཞུགས་གནས་ཀྱི་སྐྱེས་བུ་རྣམས་ལས་བརྩམས་ཏེ་
བརྒྱལ་བ་དང་ལན་གྱིས་སྨྲས་ན་སྟོན་པའི་གསུང་རབ་དང་ཤིང་རྟ་ཆེན་པོ་
རྣམས་ཀྱི་བསྟན་བཅོས་ཕལ་མོ་ཆེ་བཤད་པར་ནུས་མོད།།འོན་ཀྱང་བློ་དམན་
པ་རྣམས་ཀྱིས་རྗེས་སུ་འབྲང་བར་མི་ནུས་པས་བཞག་གོ།འཕགས་པ་འདི་
1358 དག་གི་རྣམ་གཞག་ལ་ཙིག་སྐྱོན་ཆོད་པ་གཙོ་བོར་བྱས་ཏེ་མཚན་ཉིད་ཅུང་
ཟད་རེ་དང་དེའི་ཤེས་བྱེད་དུ་ལུང་ཅུང་ཟད་དྲངས་ཏེ།ཆེ་ལོང་ཙམ་ཞིག་

[464] spangs pa D M] spang P | [465] spang D M] spangs P | [466] spang bya D M] spangs bya P | [467] spang D M] spangs P | [468] / D M] om. / P | [469] om. / D M] insert / P | [470] spang D M] spangs P | [471] phyir 'ong M] phyir 'ongs D P

knowledges, and obtaining the sixteen aspects [of the four Noble Truths].[148]

One posits four results as follows: (1) there is the release from a previous path of result ; (2) obtaining the path of another result, and ;(3) a collected cessation, or collected abandonment, as in acquiring a single attainment which consists of all the abandonments to be abandoned by the path of seeing at the time of the sixteenth moment ; (4) eight knowledges to be obtained are the four dharma knowledges [on the truths of suffering, origination, cessation, path] and the four subsequent knowledges;(5) one also obtains the sixteen uncontaminated aspects, impermanence and so forth [of the four Noble Truths]. Attainment of these five distinct states are posited as the four results. However, when establishing results by means of abandoning defilements, the first result is established by merely abandoning that to be abandoned by the path of seeing and the latter three results are established by means of abandoning that to be abandoned by the path of cultivation and the two [middle] results are established from abandoning that to be abandoned of the desire realm by the path of cultivation because it is the Once-returner who
D353 abandons the sixth [desire realm defilement] and the Non-returner is established by abandoning the ninth [desire realm defilement]. The result of Arhat is established by abandoning all the afflictions without exception of the upper realms.

In this way, through these [explanations], the presentations of the great individuals who enter and abide [in the four results] comes to an end [and] is finished.

Accordingly, we would be able to explain most of the teachings of the Teacher and the *śāstra*s of the Great Charioteers in regard to the individuals who enter and abide if elaborating through question and debate. However, the feeble minded would be unable to follow the presentation. If for the presentation of these Noble Beings (*ārya*), [we were to] principally cut out the fault of [many] words, use few definitions, and quote few scriptures as proofs of these definitions,

---

[148] AK, vi. 52a-53b, LVP, 242, Pradhan, 370: *catuṣphalavyavasthā tu pañcakāraṇasaṃbhavāt / pūrvatyāgo 'nyamāgāptiḥ kṣayasaṃkalanaṃ phale/ jñānāṣṭakasya lābho'tha ṣodaśākārabhāvanā.../*

བརྩམས་ན་རྫོངས་པ་ཅིག་ལ་རྟོན་པ་[472]དག་མགུ་མོད།ཤེས་རབ་ཅན་དོན་ལ་རྟོན་པ་དག་ནི་མཐའ་དཔྱད་དེ་གསུང་རབ་ཀྱི་དོན་ཤེས་པར་འདོད་པས་དེ་དག་རྗེས་སུ་བཟུང་བ་ཕྱིར་བདག་གིས་རྒྱས་པར་བཀྲལ་ལོ།།།།

གང་ཞིག་བརྟེན་ན་ཐར་ལམ་བགྲི་བའི་གྲོགས།།གྲོགས་ཀྱི་མཆོག
གྱུར་ཞུགས་གནས་འཕགས་པའི་ཚོགས།།ཚོགས་མཆོག་དམ་པ་དགེ་
འདུན་རྣམས་ཀྱི་ཚུལ།།ཚུལ་བཞིན་མ་ནོར་གསལ་བར་བདག་གིས་
བཤད།

།རྒྱ་ཆེན་རྒྱ་མཚོ་ལྟ་བུ་ཤེས་བྱའི་གནས།།ཇི་སྙེད་[473]ཇི་བཞིན་[474]སྟོན་
པ་མངོན་པའི་ཆོས།།མ་ནོར་མ་འདྲེས་འབྱེད་པར་བྱེད་པ་ལ།།བློ་
P138b བཟང་བློ་ལ་གཞན་གྱིས་བསྒྲུན་པར་[475]དཀའ།

D 354 །གང་གསུངས་ལེགས་[476]བཤད་རྒྱ་སྐར་ཕྲེང་བ་ཡིས།།བདག་བློའི་བྱ་
ལམ་ཡངས་པ་མཛེས་བྱེད་པའི།།མཁས་མཆོག་ཆོས་ཀྱི་སྤྱན་ལྡན་
རེད་མདའ་པ།།གཞོན་ནུའི་མཚན་ཅན་གང་དེ་རྟག་ཏུ་རྒྱལ།

།གོང་འོག་མངོན་པའི་གཞུང་དང་འགྲེལ་བཤད་ལ།།རིང་དུ་འདྲིས་
ནས་མི་འཇིགས་ཐོབ་པའི་ཚེ།།གཞན་གྱིས་བསྐུལ་ཕྱིར་རང་བློ་
འཕེལ་བའི་ཕྱིར།།།བློ་གསལ་འཇུག་པའི་ཐེམ་སྐས་འདི་བྱས་སོ།

།མི་བརྟན་ཚེ་འདིའི་བདེ་ཙམ་སྒྲུབ་པའི་ཐབས།།ཟང་ཟིང་ཟས་
ལའང་ཆོག་ཤེས་མེད་གྱུར་ན།།གཏན་བདེ་སྒྲུབ་བྱེད་ནོར་མཆོག་
ཐོས་པའི་ནོར།།དེ་ལ་ཆོག་པར་འཛིན་རྣམས་བདུད་ཀྱི་[477]ཐེབས།

[472]rton pa D M] brton ba P | [473]ji snyed M] ci snyed D P | [474]ji bzhin M] ci bzhin D P | [475]bsgrun par M] bskrun par D P | [476]legs D M] lags P | [477]kyi D M] kyis P

setting out merely a rough [presentation], then dull ones who rely on words would be satisfied. Those who arc wise, that rely on the meaning, since they desire to thoroughly discuss and understand the meaning of scripture, I have extensively written [this essay] for the sake of nourishing them.

> I have clearly explained unmistakenly in an exact manner, the manner of the Saṃghas, the holy supreme assembly.
>
> The assembly of the Noble Beings who enter and abide, the supreme of friends, the friends who lead to the path of liberation for whomever relies on them.
>
> It is difficult to produce by others an awareness of the excellent mind, distinguishing unmistakenly without mixing up the *Abhidharma*, as exact and as vast as it is, an abode of the objects of knowledge, like a great extensive ocean.
>
> He who is always victorious, possessing the marks of youth, Red mda' ba who possesses the eye of dharma, a supreme master, who ornaments the spacious sky (lit. "bird's path") of my mind with a star garland of his spoken eloquence.
>
> At the time of obtaining confidence after studying for a long time the texts and commentaries of the upper and lower *Abhidharma*s, because of being urged by others and for the sake of expanding my own mind [I] wrote this *Stairway taken by the Lucid*.
>
> The means which achieves the mere happiness of this unstable life, material goods [and] things, even [they] are without satisfaction. The wealth of studying, the supreme wealth which achieves perpetual happiness, those who are satisfied with that are afflicted by Māra.

།ཤེས་ཀྱི་ཁེ་དང་རྙེད་བཀུར་འདོད་པ་རིང་དུ་དོར།།མཁས་མཁས་
གམ་དུ་རློམ་པ་སྤངས་ཏེ་དོན་ལ་སྦྱངས།།ལུང་བསྟན་བརྙེས་པའི་
མཁས་རྣམས་དགོངས་པ་རིང་ནས་རྙེད།།ཨེ་མའོ་དེ་ནི་ཐོས་ལ་
བརྩོན་བྱས་དགོས་པ་གྲུབ[478]།

།རྙེད་བཀུར་ཕྱིར་དུ་གཞན་ངོར་ཚིགས་བརྒྱུད་ཙམ་ཞིག་
འཛིན།།འཁོར་ལ་སྲིད་ནས་སྨུར་བར་སློབ་མའི་ཚོགས་མང་
སྡུད།།ཡིད་བརྟན་མེད་པར་ཁ་ཆོན་བཅད་དེ་ངན་རྟོག་
1359 འདོམས།།དེ་དག་མཐོང་ཚེ་བློ་བཟང་གྲགས་པ་ཤིན་ཏུ་སྐྱོ།

།དེ་ལྟར་བདག་གིས་འབད་ལ་མ་བཤད་མིན་པར་བཤད་ལ་
སོགས།།ཉེས་ཚོགས་མཆིས་ན་རྟུལ་བྲལ་རྣམས་དང་འཛམ་གླིང་
[479]མཁས་པའི་མཆོག།སྐུ་མཆེད་གཉིས་དང་མཁས་པའི་མཁས་པ་
ཆེན་པོ་རྒྱལ་པོའི་སྲས།།གྲགས་པའི་བཤེས་གཉེན་རྣམས་ལ་ཉོངས་
པ་འཆགས་སོ་བཟོད་པར་གསོལ།

།བདག་གིས་ལྷག་བསམ་དག་པས་འབད་པ་བགྱིས་ལས་བསྒྲུབ་པའི་
D 355 བསོད་ནམས་གང་ཞིག་ཐོབ་པ་དེས།སྲིད་ནས་སྲིད་དུ་རྒྱལ་བའི་ཆོས་ཀྱི་ཚུལ་
|P139a འཛིན་མཁས་མཆོག་རྣམས་ལ་མི་ངོམས་པའི།།མང་དུ་ཐོས་པར་བྱེད་ཅིང་
མཁས་རློམ་དོར་ཏེ་གཞན་གྱི་ལེགས་བཤད་ལྟ་བ་ལའང།ཕྲག་དོག་ཟུག་རྔུས་
བློ་གྲོས་མིག་ནི་ནམ་ཡང་སྒྲིབ་པར་མ་གྱུར་ཅིག།

ཞུགས་པ་དང་གནས་པའི་སྐྱེས་བུ་ཆེན་པོ་རྣམས་ཀྱི་རྣམ་པར་བཞག་པ་བློ་གསལ་བགྲོད་པའི་ཐེམ་སྐས་ཞེས་བྱ་བ་འདི་ནི།།བདེ་བར་གཤེགས་པའི་གསུང་རབ་ཐམས་ཅད་ལ་ཆོས་ཀྱི་སྤྱན་ལྡན་ཆེན་པོ་དཔལ་ལྡན་ས་སྐྱའི་པཎྜི་ཏ་རེད་མདའ་པ་གཞོན་ནུ་བློ་གྲོས་ཀྱི་དྲིན་ལས།ཆོས་མངོན་པའི་གཞུང་གོང་འོག་ཐམས་ཅད་ཀྱི་དོན་ལ།བློའི་སྣང་བ་ཐོབ་ཅིང་མདོ་སྡེ་དང་འདུལ་བའི་སྡེ་སྣོད་དང།གཏན་ཚིགས་རིག་པའི་ཚུལ་ལ་ཡང་སྦྱོབས་པ་དགེ་བས་རིགས་པ་

[478] grub D M] grus P | [479] 'dzam gling D M] 'jam glang P

> Caste far away the desire for profit, fame, and honor, abandon masters who are arrogant as scholars and search for the meaning. Find after a long time the thought of the scholars identified through prophecy. Hey! That person should complete the purpose by making effort through study.
>
> Grasping only streams of words as an appearance to others for the sake of fame, quickly gathering many assemblies of students through attachment to a retinue, oneself without a firm mind instructing poor understanding to others seeing these things, [I] Blo bzang grags pa am very very sad.
>
> Therefore, I made effort to explain without [leaving anything] unexplained, etc.If any faults exist, to those free from dust, the best of Jampudvīpa masters, the two brothers [Asaṅga and Vasubandhu], the great scholar of scholars Jinaputra, and Yaśomitra, I confess these faults and ask for forgiveness.

Whatever merit that was produced from making effort through
critical reflection by me, that obtainment [I dedicate so that] from
D355 existence to existence [I] may be able to study very much without
satisfaction the supreme scholars who hold the [correct] manner of the Victor's doctrine, to cast away conceited scholarship and even look to others eloquent teaching, may the eye of my mind never be obscured by the pain of jealousy.

This "Stairway taken by the Lucid, Presentation of the Great Individuals who Enter and Abide" was composed through the kindness of the Sakya paṇḍita Red mda' pa gzhon nu blo gros, illustrious one who possesses the great eye of Dharma in regard to all the great teachings of the *Tathāgatha*. [I] obtained illumination of [my] mind in regard to the meaning of all the upper and lower texts of *Abhidharma* and was able to examine what is correct and incorrect with special confidence in the methods of logical reasoning

དང།མི་རིགས་པ་རྣམ་པར་དཔྱོད་པར་ནུས་པ་ཤར་ཙོང་ཁ་པ་བློ་བཟང་གྲགས་པས་བློ་གསལ་དོན་གཉེར་དང་ལྡན་པ་འགས་བསྐུལ་བའི་ངོར་[480]ཆོག་གྲུ་ཆེན་པོ་བདེ་བ་ཅན་དུ་སྦྱར་བའོ།།།།[481]

---

[480]ngor D M] dor P | [481]manggalam D; rings nas thugs bskyed tshogs gnyis ma' la yi'i / /snyan pa'i dri pa sung chud med rtag 'babb pa / /yid 'phrog skyed tshal sku gsum po brang cher / /don gnyis gtan pa de' dpal la sgyu ma'i gar / /bgyur mkhas 'jam dbyangs mi yi zlos gar mkhan / /btsong kha pa zhes snyan pa'i rngo po che / /srid 'dir ches cher sgrog pa'i mgon de'i gsung/ zhugs gnas skyes bu'i rnam bzhag mkhas pa'i rgyan / /sngon med par du skrun pa'i byed po yi / /legs bshad smra ba'i gtam gyis 'dzin ma'i khyon / /ma lus khyab cing dga' pa'i dpal ldan pa'i / /chos srid 'byor pa mkha' ltar rgya che zhing / ches gsal [P139b] nyi zla'i dpal la 'gran bzod cing / /dbyar mtsho ji bzhin dgung du 'phel bar shog / //sarvamanggalam // P

(*pramāṇa*), and in the *piṭakas* of *Sūtra* and *Vinaya*. [This text] was written at the great college Bde-ba-can in the face of being urged on by some possessing clear mindedness searching for meaning.

Principle Indian Sources

Abhidharmakośabhāṣya by Vasubandhu. Translated and annotated by Louis de La Vallée Poussin (1971). *L'Abhidharmakośa de Vasubandhu*. Nouvelle éd. anastatique présentée par Étienne Lamotte. Bruxelles: Institut belge des Hautes études chinoises, 6 tomes. (MCB, XVI). English translation by Leo M. Pruden (1989), Volumes I to IV, Asian Humanities Press, Berkeley. Translated by Jinamitra, Dpal brtsegs. *Chos mgnon pa'i mdzod kyi bshad pa*. Pk 5591, Volume 115. Edited by P. Pradhan (1967. Reprint 1975). *Abhidharmakośabhāṣya of Vasubandhu*. Patna: K.P. Jayaswal Research Institute (Tibetan Sanskrit Works Series, Vol. VIII.). Compiled by A. Hirakawa (1973-1978). *Index to the Abhidharmakośabhāṣya*. Part I: Sanskrit-Tibetan-Chinese. Part II: Chinese-Sanskrit. Part III: Tibetan-Sanskrit. Tokyo: Daizo Shuppan, 3 volumes.

Abhidharmakośabhāṣyavyākhyā by Yaśomitra. Edited by Swami Dwarikadas Shastri (1971). *Abhidharmakośa & Bhāṣya of Ācārya Vasubandhu with Sphuṭārthā Commentary of Ācārya Yaśomitra*. Bauddha Bhāratī Series, No.5 Vārāṇasī: Bauddha Bhāratī, 4 volumes. Translated by Viśuddhisiṃha, Dpal brtsegs. *Chos mgnon pa'i mdzod kyi 'grel bshad*. Pk. 5593, Volume 116.

Abhidharmakośakārikā by Vasubandhu. Edited by V.V. Gokhale (1946). "The Text of the Abhidharmakośakārikā of Vasubandhu." Journal of the Bombay Branch, Royal Asiatic Society 22: 73-102; (1947) 23: 12. Translated by Jinamitra, Dpal brtsegs. Chos mngon pa'i mdzod kyi tshig le'ur byas pa. Pk 5590, Volume 115.

Abhidharmāmṛtarasaśāstra by Ghosaka. Translated and annotated by José van den Broeck (1977). La Saveur de L'Immortel = A-p'it-t'an Kan Lu Wei Lun: la version chinoise de l'Amṛtarasa de Ghosaka. (T. 1553). Broeck. Louvain-la-Neuve: Université catholique de Louvain, Institut orientaliste; Louvain: commandes.

Abhidharmasamuccaya of Asaṅga. Fragments edited by V.V. Gokhale (1947). "Fragments from the Abhidharmasamuccaya of Asaṅga." Journal of the Bombay Branch, Royal Asiatic Society 23: 13-38. Edited by Pralhad Pradhan (1950). Abhidharmasamuccaya. Santiniketan: Visvabharati. Translated by Jinamitra, Śīlendrabodhi, Ye she sde. Chos mngon pa kun las btus pa. Pk. 5550, Volume 112. Translated by Rahula (1971). Le Compendium de la super-doctrine (Philosophie) (Abhidharmasamuccaya) d'Asaṅga. Publications de l'École franṛaise d'Extrême-Orient, vol. LXXVIII. Paris: École franṛaise d'Extrême-Orient. Translation of Rahula (1971) by Boin-Webb (2001). Abhidharmasamuccaya. The Compendium of the Higher Teaching (Philosophy) by Asaṅga. Fremont: Asian Humanities Press.

Abhidharmasamuccayabhāṣya by Jinaputra. Edited by Nathmial Tatia (1976). Abhidharmasamuccayabhāṣya. Patna: K.P. Jayaswal Research Institute. Translated by Jinamitra, Śīlendrabodhi, Ye she sde. Chos mngon pa kun las btus pa'i bshad pa. Pk. 5554, Volume 113.

Abhisamayālaṃkāra. Edited by Th. Stcherbatsky and E. Obermiller (1929). *Abhisamayālaṃkāraprajñāpāramitopadeśaśāstrakārikā*. Leningrad. (Bibliotheca Buddhica, XXIII, fasc. 1.) Delhi: Sri Satguru Publications, 2nd edition, 1992. Translated by Go mi 'chi med, Blo ldan shes rab. *Shes rab kyi pha rol tu phyin pa'i man ngag gi bstan bcos mngon par rtogs pa'i rgyan zhes bya ba'i tshig le'ur bya pa*. Pk 5184, Voume 88. Translated by E. Conze (1954). *Abhisamayālankāra. Introduction and Translation from Original Text with Sanskrit-Tibetan Index*. Roma: Istituto Italiano per il Medio ed Estremo Oriente.

Abhisamayālaṃkārālokā Prajñāpāramitāvyākhyā by Haribhadra. Edited by U. Wogihara (1932-1935). *The Work of Haribhadra*. Tokyo: The Toyo Bunko. Edited by Giuseppe Tucci (1932). Baroda: Oriental Institute. Compiled by Ryusei Keira & Noboru Ueda (1998). *Sanskrit Word-Index to the Abhisamayālaṃkārālokā Prajñāpāramitāvyākhyā (U. Wogihara edition)*. Sankibo Press, Tokyo.

Abhisamayālaṃkāraprasphuṭapadā by Dharmamitra. Translated by Abhiyuktaka Tāraśrīmitra, Chos kyi shes rab. *Mngon par rtogs pa'i rgyan gi tshig le'ur byas pa'i 'gral bshad tshig rab tu gsal ba shes bya ba*. Pk 5194, Vol. 91.

Abhisamayālaṃkārasphuṭārthā by Haribhadra. Edited Sanskrit Manuscript by Hirofusa Amano. *Abhisamayālaṃkāra-kārikā-śāstra-vivṛti: Haribhadra's Commentary on the Abhisamayālaṃkāra-kārikā-śāstra edited for the first time from a Sanskrit Manuscript* Kyoto, Heirakuji-shoten, 2000. Translated by Vidyākaraprabha, Dpal brtsegs. *Shes rab kyi pha rol tu phyin pa'i man ngag gi bstan bcos mngon par togs pa'i rgyan ces bya ba'i 'grel pa.* Pk 5191, Volume 90. Edited by Rāmaśaṅkara Tripāṭhī. *Prajñāpāramitopadeśaśāstra Abhisamayālaṅkāravṛttiḥ Sphuṭārthā Ācāryaharibhadraviracitā*; Saṃskṛtarūpāntarakāraḥ sampādakaś ca Sāranāthah: Kendriya-Tibbati-ucca-Siksha-Samsthanam, 1977.

Dhammapada. Pāli text with English translation in John Ross Carter and M. Palihawadana (trans.) (1992) *Sacred Writings, Buddhism: The Dhammapada.* New York: Quality Paperback Book Club.

Mahāvyutpatti. Hon'yaku my'gi taishū: Bon-z'-kan-wa yon'yaku taik'. Chosakusha Sakaki Ry'zabur'. Ky'to: Shingonshū Ky'to Daigaku, Taishë 5-14, 1916-1925.

Mahāyānottaratantraśāstra. Edited by E.H. Johnston and T. Chowdhury. *The Ratnagotravibhāga Mahāyānottaratantraśāstra*, Patna: Bihar Research Society (1950). Translation by E. Obermiller. "Sublime Science of the Great Vehicle to Salvation, *Acta Orientalia*, 9 (1931): 81-306. Translation by J. Takasaki. *A Study on the Ratnagotravibhāga*, Rome: Istituto Italiano per il Medio ed Estremo Oriente (1966).

Puggalapaññatti. Edited by Richard Morris (1972). London: Luzac for the Pali Text Society. Translation by Bimala Charan Law. *Designation of Human Types (Puggalapaññatti)*, London, pub. for the Pali Text Society by Luzac & Co., 1969 [c1924].

Puggalapaññatti-atthakathā. Edited by Georg Landsberg and Mrs. Rhys Davids (1972). London: Luzac for the Pali Text Society.

Principle Indigenous Tibetan Sources

A mchog Rinpoche Blo bzan mkhyen rab rgya mtsho. "Introduction." *Lotsaba chen po'i bsdus don bzhugs so = Commentary on the Abhisamayālaṃkāra by Rnog Lotsaba Blo-ldan-'ses-rab; with an introduction by the 81st abbot of Shar-rtse Grva-tshan, 4th A-mchog Rinpoche Blo-bzan-mkhyen-rab-rgya-mtsho and David P. Jackson*. Dharamsala, H.P.: Library of Tibetan Works and Archives, 1993.

Bod rgya tshig mdzod chen mo (*The Extensive Tibetan-Chinese Dictionary*). Beijing: National Minorities Press, Mi rigs dpe skrun khang, (one volume), 1998.

Bstan pa dar rgyas, Ser Smad Mkhas grub (1493-1568). *Dge 'dun ni su'i mtha' dpyod bzhugs so*. Dge-'dun-bstan-dar-ba chen po'i gsun. Ser Smad Grwa-tshan, 1969.

Bu ston rin chen grub (1290-1364). *Bde bar gshegs pa'i bstan pa'i gsal byed chos kyi 'byun gnas gsun rab rin po che'i mdzod ces bya ba*. Translated from Tibetan by E. Obermiller. *History of Buddhism (Chos 'byung)*, Heidelberg, 1931-1932.

———. *Gsan yig. The Collected Works of Bu-ston*, part 21(La), New Delhi, 1971.

———. *Shes rab kyi pha rol tu phyin pa'i man ngag gi bstan bcos mngon par rtogs pa'i rgyan ces bya ba'i 'grel pa'i rgya cher bshad pa lung gi sne ma. The Collected of Bu-ston*, part 18 (Tsha), New Delhi, 1971.

Dkon mchog 'jigs med dbang po (1728-91). *Sa lam gyi rnam gzhag theg pa gsum gyi mdzes rgyan.* In *The Collected Works of dkon mchog 'jigs med dbang po*. New Delhi: Nga wang Gelek Demo, 1972.

Go ram pa bsod nams seng ge (1429-1489). *Zhugs gnas kyi rnam gzhag skyes bu mchog gi gsal byed.* Sa skya'i 'kah 'bum, Volume 14, Toyo bunkyo, Tokyo, 1969.

'Jam dpal rgya mtsho, Rtogs ldan, 1356-1428. *Rje btsun tsong kha pa'i rnam thar chen mo'i zur 'debs rnam thar legs bshad kun 'dus bzhugs so*. Varanasa: Legs bshad gter mdzod par khan, 1970.

mKhas grub dge legs dpal bzang po (1385-1438). *Rje btsun bla ma tsong kha pa chen po'i no mtshar rmad du byung ba'i rnam par thar pa dad pa'i 'jug ngogs zhes bya ba'i bzhugs so*. Vārānasī: K. Lhundup and Lama Samdup, 1966.

Ngag dbang bkra bshis (1678-1738). *Zhugs pa dang gnas pa'i 'phags pa'i dge 'dun gyi rnam gzhag gi mtha' dpyod skal bzang 'jug ngogs* in *dge 'dun nyi su'i mtha' dpyod; with other minor texts from the Yig-cha of Sgo-mang College*. Delhi: Kesang Thabkhes, 1980.

Nya dbon kun dga' dpal (14th century). *Bstan bcos mngon par rtogs pa'i rgyan 'grel pa dang bcas pa'i rgyas 'grel bshad sbyar yid kyi mun sel*. bKra shis 'khil ba'i chos grva edition, New Delhi, 1978.

rGyal tshab dar ma rin chen (1364-2432). *Shes rab kyi pha rol tu phyin pa'i man ngag gi bstan bcos mngon par rtogs pa'i rgyan gyi rtsa ba 'grel pa dang bcas pa'i rnam bshad snying po'i rgyan* (=*rnam bshad nying po'i rgyan*). (Sung 'bum, t. kha).

rNam gyal dbang chen (contemporary). *Dbu sems kyi lta ba dang tshad mar sgrub pa'i le'u'i snying don, mngon rtogs rgyan gyi tshig don bcas gsal bar bstan pa'i legs bshad utpala'i gru char.* Bras spung blo gsal gling dpe mdzod khan, Karanataka, 1996.

rNgog blo ldan shes rab, "rNgog lo tsā ba" (1059-1109). *Lo tsa ba chen po'i bsdus don: A Commentary on the Abhisamayālaṃkāra. Introduction by Blo bzang mkhyen rab rgya mtsho and Dr. David P. Jackson.* Library of Tibetan Works and Archives, 1993.

Rong ston shes bya kun rig (1367-1449). *Mngon par rtogs pa'i rgyan 'grel pa dan bcas pa'i dka' ba'i gnas rnam par 'byed pa zab don gnad kyi zla 'od: a detailed exegesis of the Abhisamayālaṃkāra and its commentary by Haribhadra.* Gangtok: Sherab Gyaltsen, 1979.

———. *Rong-ston on the Prajñāpāramitā philosophy of the Abhisamayālaṃkāra: his sub-commentary on Haribhadra's 'Sphñārthā'.* Edited by David P. Jackson in collaboration with Shunzo Onoda. Kyoto: 1988.

Śākya mchog ldan, Gser mdog Pan chen, (1428-1507). *Dge 'dun nyi shu'i mtha'rnam par dpyad pa'i thal 'gyur ngag gi dbang po'i mdzes rgyan zhes bya ba bzhugs so. Complete Works of Gser mdog paṇchen śākya mchog ldan*, Thimphu Bhutan, Vol. 13, 1-111, 1975.

———. *Mngon par rtogs pa'i rgyan 'grel pa don gsal ba dan bcas pa'i rnam par bshad pa shing rta'i srol gnis gcig tu bsdus pa'i lam po che zhes bya ba bzhugs so.* Lhun-grub-rtse'i-rdzon, 1969?

Se ra rje btsun Chos kyi rgyal mtshan, (1469-1546). *Bstan bcos mngon par rtogs pa'i rgyan 'grel pa dan bcas pa'i rnam bshad rnam pa gnis kyi dka' ba'i gnas gsal bar byed pa legs bshad skal bzang klu dbang gi rol mtsho zhes bya ba.* Bylakuppe: Se-ra Byes Grwa-tshan, 1980.

———. *Dge 'dun nyi su'i mtha' gcod: Rje-btsun Chos-kyi-rgyal-mtshan-dpal-bzan-po'i gsung rtsom dri ma med pa mkhas pa'i mgul rgyan zhes bya ba bzhugs so*. Sbag-sa: Se-ra Byes Grwa-tshan, 196?.

sGra sbyor bam po gnyis pa. Ishikawa, Mie, editor. *A Critical Edition of the sGra sbyor bam po gnyis pa. An Old and Basic Commentary on the Mahāvyutpatti*. Studia Tibetica, 18, Materials for Tibetan-Mongolian Dictionaries, vol. 2, Tokyo: The Toyo Bunko, 1990.

Shes rab rgya mtshan, Dol po pa, 1292-1361. *Rnam bshad mdo'i don bde blag tu rtog pa,* vol. 6, 323-882, in *The 'Dzam-thang edition of the collected works (gsung-'bum) of Kun-mkhyen Dol-po-pa Shes-rab-rgyal-mtshan.* Collected and presented by Matthew Kapstein. Delhi, India: Shedrup Books, 1992.

Tāranātha, Jo nang pa, b. 1575. Translated from the Tibetan by Lama Chimpa and A. Chattopadhyaya. Edited by D. Chattopadhyaya. *Rgya gar chos 'byung. Tāranātha's History of Buddhism in India*. Simla, Indian Institute of Advanced Study, 1970.

Tshe mchog gling Ye shes rgyal mtshan, 1713-1793. *Byang chub lam gyi rim pa'i bla ma brgyud pa'i rnam thar*. Biographies of the eminent gurus in the transmission lineages of the teachings of the graduated path: being the text of Byang chub lam gyi rim pa'i bla ma brgyud pa'i rnam par thar pa rgyal bstan mdzes pa'i rgyan mchog phul byung nor bu'i phreng ba. New Delhi: Ngawang Gelek Demo, 1970-1972.

Tsong kha pa blo bzang grags pa (1357-1419). *Dbu ma la 'jug pa'i rnam bshad dgongs pa rab gsal*. Sarnath: Gelupa Students Union, 1973.

———. *Dbu ma rtsa ba'i tshig le'ur byas pa shes rab ces bya ba'i rnam bshad rigs pa'i rgya mtsho*. Va na mtho slob dge ldan spyi las khang nas, 1975.

———. *Dge 'dun nyi su bsdus pa rjes gnang ba dang zhugs gnas bzhugs so*; fols. 593-606. Collected Works, 1977, Volume 27.

———. *Drang nges legs bshad snying po = The Essence of Eloquent Speech on the Definitive and Interpretable*. Mundgod, District North Kanara, Karnataka, India: SOKU Publication, 1991.

———. *Khams gsum chos kyi rgyal po tsong kha pa chen po'i gsung 'bum. Collected Works*. Dge ldan gsung rab mi nyams rgyun phel series 79-105, published by Ngag dbang dge legs bde mo, 1975-79.

———. *Rje rin po che blo bzang grags pa'i dpal gyi gsan yig. Khams gsum chos kyi rgyal po tsong kha pa chen po'i gsum 'bum*. Vol. Ka, pp. 233-293.

———. *Shes rab kyi pha rol tu phyin pa'i man ngag gi bstan bcos mngon par rtogs pa'i rgyan 'grel pa dang bcas pa'i rgya cher bshad pa legs bshad Golden Garland zhes bya ba bzhugs so (=Legs bshad Golden Garland)*. Volume 1, Sarnath: Lama Thuptan Jungnes, 1970. Also Collected Works, 1977, Volumes 26+27, gSung 'bum lHa sa edition, v. tsa and tsha.

———. *Yid dang kun gzhi'i dka' ba'i gnad rgya cher 'grel ba legs bshad rgya mtsho*, New Delhi, Volume 27, 1977. Introduced and translated by Gareth Sparham in collaboration with Shotaro Iida. *Ocean of Eloquence: Tsong Kha Pa's commentary on the Yogācāra Doctrine of Mind*. Albany: SUNY, 1993.

———. *Zhugs pa dang gnas pa'i skyes bu chen bo rnams kyi rnam par bshag pa blo gsal bgrod pa'i them skad zhes bya ba bzhugs so* in *The Collected Works (gsun bum) of Rje Tson-kha-pa Blo-bzan-grags-pa*. Reproduced from an example of the old Bkra-sis-lhun-po redaction from the library of Klu 'khyil Monastery of Ladhakh by Ngawang Gelek Demo. New Delhi: 1977, Volume 27.

Zhang zhung chos sbang grags pa (1404-1469). *Shes rab kyi pha rol tu phyin pa'i man ngag gi bstan bcos mngon par rtogs pa'i rgyan gyi 'grel pa don gsal ba'i rnam bshad rtogs par dka' ba'i sngang ba* (= *rtogs dka'i snang ba*). In *Collected Works of mKhas grub rje* (gSung 'bum, vol. ka)

Secondary Sources

Apple, James. 2003. "Twenty Varieties of the Saṃgha: A Typology of Noble Beings (Ārya) in Indo-Tibetan Scholasticism (Part 1)." *Journal of Indian Philosophy* 31/5: 503-592.

———. 2004. "An Assembly of Irreversible Bodhisattvas. Twenty Varieties of the Saṃgha: A Typology of Noble Beings (Ārya) in Indo-Tibetan Scholasticism (Part 2)." Journal of Indian Philosophy 32:211-279.

———. 2008. *Stairway to Nirvāṇa: A Study of the Twenty Saṃghas based on the works of Tsong-kha-pa* (State University of New York Press).

Bareau, André. 1947. "Les Sectes Bouddhiques du Petit Vehicule et Leurs Abhidharmapiṭaka." *B.E.F.E.O* 44 (1947): 1-11.

———.1954. "Trois Traités sur les Sectes Bouddhiques Attribues á Vasumitra." *Journal Asiatique*: 229-266; (1956): 167-299.

———.1955. *Les Sectes Bouddhiques du Petit Véhicule*. Saṅgon: École Francaise d'Extrême-Oricnt.

———.1957. "Les Controverses Relative á la Nature de L'Arhant dans le Bouddhisme Ancien." *Indo-Iranian Journal* 1: 241-250.

Chandra, Lokesh (ed). 1985. *Materials for a History of Tibetan Literature*. New Delhi: Sharada Rani.

Collins, Steven. 1982. *Selfless Persons: Imagery and Thought in Theravada Buddhism*. New York: Cambridge University Press, 1982.

———.1992. "Problems with Pacceka-Buddhas." *Religion* 22 (1992): 271-278.

———.1998. *Nirvāṇa and other Buddhist Felicities: Utopias of the Pali Imaginaire.* New York: Cambridge University Press, 1998.

Davidson, Ronald Mark. 1985. "Buddhist Systems of Transformation: āśraya-parivṛtti / parāvṛtti among the Yogācāra." Ph.D. dissertation, University of California, Berkeley.

De Jong, J.W. 1971. Review of Étienne Lamotte, *Traité de la Grande Vertu de Sagesse de Nāgārjuna*. III. Asia Minor 17: 105-112.

———.1979. *Buddhist Studies*, Berkeley, Calif.: Asian Humanities Press.

———.1986. Review of J. Hopkins' *Meditation on Emptiness*. JIABS 9.1: 124-128.

———.1999. Review of J. Makransky, *Buddhahood Embodied*. IIJ 42: 70-75.

Gethin, Rupert. 1992. "The Mātikās." *In the Mirror of Memory*. Edited by Janet Gyatso, 1992.

———. 1997. "Cosmology and Meditation: from the Aggañña-Sutta to the Mahāyāna." *History of Religions* 36.3 : 183-217.

———. 2001. *The Buddhist Path to Awakening, A Study of the Bodhi-Pakkhiyā Dhammā*. Oxford: Oneworld.

Gonda, Jan. 1939. "The Meaning of Word Alaṃkāra." *A Volume of Eastern and Indian Studies*, Bombay, 97-114.

Gyatso, Janet, editor. 1992. *In the Mirror of Memory: Reflections on Mindfulness and Remembrance in Indian and Tibetan Buddhism*. Albany: State University of New York Press.

Harris, Paul. 1989. "Buddhism: A Religion of Revelation After All." *Numen* 36 (1989): 256-264.

Hastings, James, editor. 1955-58. *Encyclopaedia of Religion and Ethics*. New York, Scribner's.

Hayashima, Kyosho. 1961. "Abhisamaya." Encylopedia of Buddhism 1: 104-114.

Hopkins, Paul Jeffrey.

Compassion in Tibetan Buddhism. With Kensur Lekden's Meditations of a Tantric Abbot. N.Y., U.S.A.: Snow Lion, 1980, 1985 printing.

———.*Emptiness in the Mind-Only School of Buddhism.* Berkeley: University of California Press, 1999.

———.*Meditation on Emptiness*. London: Wisdom Publications, 1983.

———. 1992. "A Tibetan Perspective on the Nature of Spiritual Experience." In Buswell and Gimello, Kuroda Institute, 225-268.

Horner, I.B. (Isaline Blew)

———.1979. *The Early Buddhist Theory of Man Perfected.* New Delhi: Oriental Books Reprint Corp.

———.1934. "The Four Ways and the Four Fruits in Pāli Buddhism." *Indian Historical Quarterly* 10 (1934): 785-796.

Hurvitz, Leon. 1967. "The Road to Buddhist Salvation as described by Vasubhadra." *Journal of the Amercian Oriental Society* 87 (1967): 434-486.

———. 1977. "Path to Salvation in the Jñāna-prasthāna." *Studies in Indo-Asian Art and Culture* 5 (1977): 77-102.

———. 1979. "Dharmaśrī on the Sixteen Degrees of Comprehension." *JIABS* 2.2 (1979): 7-30.

Jaini, Padmanabh S. 1958. "On the Theory of Two Vasubandhus." BSOAS 21: 48-53.

Jinpa, Thupten. 1997. "'Self', Persons and Madhyamaka Dialectics. A Study of Tsongkhapa's Middle Way Philosophy." Ph.D. dissertation, University of Cambridge, U.K.

———.1998. "Delineating Reason's Scope for Negation, Tsongkhapa's Contribution to Madhyamaka's Dialectical Method." *Journal of Indian Philosophy* 26: 275-308.

———.1999. "Tsongkhapa's Qualms about Early Tibetan Interpretations of Madhyamaka Philosophy." *Tibet Journal* 24.2: 3-28.

———.2000. "The Question of 'Development' in Tsongkhapa's Madhaymaka Philosophy." *Études Asiatiques* 54.1: 5-44.

Joshi, Lal Mani. 1991. "A Survey of the Conception of Bodhicitta." *Journal of Religious Studies* 3.1 : 70-79.

Kaschewsky, Rudolf. 1971. *Das Leben des lamaistischen Heiligen Tsongkhapa Blo-Bzaṅ-Grags-Pa* (1357-1419), *dargestellt und erläutert anhand seiner Biographie "Quellenort allen Glṃcks".* 2 vol. Asiatische Forschungen, Vol. 32. Wiesbaden: Harrassowitz.

Kloppenborg, Ria. 1974. *The Paccekabuddha: A Buddhist Ascetic. A Study of the Concept of the Paccekabuddha in Pāli Canonical and Commentarial Literature.* Leiden: Brill.

Kuip, Leonard W.J. van der. 1983. *Contributions to the development of Tibetan Buddhist epistemology: from the eleventh to the thirteenth century.* Wiesbaden: Steiner.

———.1985. "Apropos of a Recent Contribution to the History of Central Way Philosophy in Tibet: Tsong Khapa's Speech of Gold." *Berliner Indologische Studien* 1: 47-74.

———.1999. "Remarks on the "Person of Authority" in the Dga' ldan pa/ Dge lugs pa School of Tibetan Buddhism." JAOS 119.4: 646-672.

Kritzer, Robert. 2000. "Rūpa and the Antarābhava." JIP 28: 235-272.

Lakatos, I. 1978. "History of science and its rational reconstructions." In J. Worral and G. Currie (eds.), *Imre Lakatos, The Methodology of Scientific Research Programmes*. Philosophical Papers Vol. 1, Cambridge: Cambridge University Press, 102-138.

Lalou, Marcelle. 1953. "Les textes bouddhiques au temps du roi Khri-sroṅ-lde-bcan." *Journal Asiatique* CCCLXI: 313-353.

Lamotte, Étienne. 1944. *Le Traité de la Grande Vertu de Sagesse de Nāgārjuna.* volume 1(3-620), Louvain, 1944; volume 2 (621-1118), Louvain, 1949; volume 3 (119-1733), Louvain, 1970; volume 4(1735-2162), Louvain, 1976; voume 5 (2163-2451) Louvain-la-Neuve,1980.

La Vallée Poussin, Louis de. 1906. "Pali and Sanskrit." *Journal of the Royal Asiatic Society*: 446-51.

———. 1910a. "Bodhisattva." *Encyclopaedia of Religion and Ethics.* Edited by J. Hastings, II: 739a-753b.

———. 1910b. "Mahāyāna." *Encyclopaedia of Religion and Ethics* VIII: 330a-336b.

———. 1910c. "Pratyekabuddha." *Encylopaedia of Religion and Ethics* Edited by J. Hastings, X: 153b.

———. 1923. *L'Abhidharmakośa de Vasubandhu.* Paris: Geuthner.

———. 1925. *Nirvāṇa.* Etudes sur L'Histoire des Religions, 4. Paris: Gabriel Beauchesne.

———. 1930. "Documents d'Abhidharma 1. Textes Relatifs au Nirvāṇa et aux Asaṃskṛtas en General." *Bulletin de l'Ecole Francaise d'Extréme-Orient* 30 (1930): 1-28.

———. 1931-32. "Documents d'Abhidharma 2. La Doctrine des Refuges." *Mélanges Chinois et bouddhiques* 1 (1931-32): 65-109.

———. 1970. *Mūlamadhyamakakārikās (Mādhyamikasūtras) de Nāgārjuna, avec la Prasannapadā commentarie de Candrakīrti.* St. Petersburg: Bibliotheca Buddhica IV. Reprint Osnabrück: Biblio Verlag.

Macy, Joanna. 1976. "Perfection of Wisdom: Mother of all Buddhas" *Anima* 3.1: 74-80.

Margolis, John. 1998. "Structuralism in Literary Theory." *Routledge Encyclopedia of Philosophy.* Edited by Edward Craig, 9: 181-184.

Masefield, Peter. 1986. *Divine Revelation in Pali Buddhism*. London: Allen & Unwin.

Masuda, Jiryo. 1925. "Origin and Doctrines of Early Indian Buddhist Schools." *Asia Major* 2: 1-78.

Moriyama, Seitetsu. 1984. "The Yogācāra-mādhyamika Refutation of the Position of the Satyākāra and Alīkāra-vādins of the Yogācāra School. Part 1: A Translation of Portions of Haribhadra's *Abhisamayālaṃkārālokā Prajñāpāramitā-vyākhyā.*" *Bukkyo Daigaku Daigakuin Kenkyu Kiyo* 12: 1-58.

Mullin, Glenn H., trns. 1985. *Essence of Refined Gold: Selected Works of the Dalai Lama III, commentary by H.H. the Dalai Lama XIV*. Ithaca, N.Y., U.S.A.: Snow Lion.

Naughton, Alexander T. 1989. "The Buddhist Path to Omniscience." Ph.D. dissertation, University of Wisconsin-Madison.

———.1991. *Classic Mahāyāna Soteriology-An Annotated Translation of Chapters 1-7 of Haribhadra's Short Commentary on the Abhisamayālaṃkāra known as Sphuṭārtha* (sic), Annual Memoirs of the Otani University, Vol.9 Kyot': Shin Buddhist Comprehensive Research Institute.

Nishi, Yoshio. 1953. *Genshi bukkyo ni okerru hannya* (Prajñā in Early Buddhism) Yokohama: Okurayama bunka kagaku kenkyusho, 299-318.

Noriaki, Hakamaya. 1986. "Chibetto ni okeru Maitreya no goh' no kiseki." *Chibetto no Bukkyō to Shakai.* Edited by Yamaguchi Zuih', Tokyo (1986): 235-268.

Norman, Kenneth Roy. 1997. *A Philological Approach to Buddhism.* School of Oriental and African Studies: London.

Peri, N. 1911. "A propos de la date de Vasubandhu." *Bulletin de l'Ecole francaise d'Extrême-Orient* 11: 339-390.

Pettit, Philip. 1977. *The Concept of Structuralism: A Critical Analysis.* University of California Press, Berkeley.

Rahula, Walpola. 1962. "A Comparative Study of Dhyānas According to Theravāda, Sarvāstivāda and Mahāyāna." *Maha Bodhi*, 190-199.

Roerich, George (trans.). 1976. *Blue Annals.* Delhi: Motilal Banarsidass.

Sangpo, Khetsun. 1973-. *Biographical Dictionary of Tibet and Tibetan Buddhism.* Dharamsala, H. P.: Library of Tibetan Works and Archives.

Sharf, Robert H. 1995. "Buddhist Modernism and the Rhetoric of Meditative Experience." *Numen* 42.3: 228-283.

Sparham, Gareth. 1987. "Background Material for the First of the Seventy Topics in Maitreya-nātha's Abhisamayālaṃkāra." *JIABS*, 10.2: 139-158.

Thurman, Robert A.F. 1982. *The Life and Teachings of Tsong Khapa.* Dharmsala, India: Library of Tibetan Works and Archives.

———.1984. *Tsong Khapa's Speech of Gold in the Essence of True Eloquence*. Princeton, N.J.: Princeton University Press.

Vetter, Tilmann. 1990. *Der Buddha und seine Lehre in Dharmakīrtis Pramāṇavārttika.* Arbeitskreis fṃr Tibetische und Buddhistische Studien, Wien: Arbeitskreis fṃr Tibetische und Buddhistische Studien, Universität Wien.

Willemen, Charles, Bart Desein, and Collet Cox. 1998. *Sarvāstivāda Buddhist Scholasticism.* Handbuch der Orientalistik: Abt. 2, Indien; Bd. 11. Leiden: Brill, 1998.

Willis, Janice Dean. 1979. *On Knowing Reality: the Tattvārtha Chapter of Asaṅga's Bodhisattvabhūmi*. New York: Columbia University Press.

INDEX

A

Abhdharmakośabhāṣya 70

Abhdharmasamuccaya-bhāṣya 88

Abhidharma 12, 27–28, 32, 36, 44, 70, 84, 130, 144, 172, 186, 212, 216

Abhidharmakośa 3, 7, 13, 21, 27–28, 32, 37, 50, 56, 76, 80, 94–98, 120, 130–132, 142, 150, 154, 160, 166, 172, 182–186, 190, 194, 200, 210

Abhidharmakośabhāṣya 12, 37, 52, 56–58, 62, 76–80, 84–88, 92, 96, 102, 106, 110, 114, 120–124, 128, 132, 136, 140–146, 156, 160, 168, 176–178, 184, 196

Abhidharmakośabhāṣya-vyākhyā 48–52, 58, 66, 72, 80, 88,96, 116, 126, 134, 158, 174

Abhidharmasamuccaya 3, 12, 28, 32, 37, 50–52, 74, 92, 96, 104, 108, 130, 134, 142, 148, 152, 162, 180, 190–196, 202, 206

Abhidharmasamuccaya-bhāṣya 48, 86

Ābhidhārmika 110, 172

Abhisamayālaṃkāra 3, 7, 10–11, 13, 17, 20, 22, 25, 110, 130

abider 10, 16, 44, 54–62, 74–76, 92, 98–100, 148, 180, 186, 190, 194, 204

absorption 17, 48, 118–122, 142, 148–150, 196

Ācārya 46, 50, 68, 84–86, 92, 104, 126, 132, 146, 176, 188, 194

afflictions (kleśa) 12, 56, 62, 76–80, 84, 88–100, 104, 112, 124, 134–136, 148–150, 158, 172–174, 182–184, 190–194, 198–202, 206, 210

aggregates (skandha) 8, 112

Akaniṣṭha 10, 58, 110, 116–118, 128–130, 144

Akaniṣṭhaga 116, 130

Akopyadharman 138, 148, 154, 162, 180

alternating concentrations 108–118, 130

Anabhisaṃskāra-parinirvāyin 108

anāgāmin 11, 17

Ānanda 164–166

anāśuparinirvāyī 102

Aṅgārakarṣūpama 166

Aṅguttaranikāya 6, 12

Antarāparinirvāyin 100–104, 110, 114, 132–134

Anurakṣaṇadharman 138

Aparihāṇadharman 180

ardhapluta 116

Arhat 2, 11, 16–17, 33, 37, 42, 88, 100, 118, 124, 144, 148–152, 156–168, 192–194, 198, 202, 210

arūpyaga 140
ārya 3, 8, 15, 33, 46, 50, 60, 70, 86, 142, 172, 208, 212
aśaikṣa 7, 13, 170
Asaṅga 8, 22, 46, 50, 74, 92, 104, 110, 132, 194, 214, 218
āśuparinirvāyī 102

B
backsliding from a result 37, 124, 152, 158–160, 164–166, 170, 174–178
Bde-ba-can 24, 26–28, 31–34, 216
Bhavāgra 128
Bhavāgraparama 100, 144
Bhūyovītarāga 160
bodhicittotpāda 26
Brahmakāyika 106–108, 118, 122
Bṛhatphala 58, 108, 118
Buddha 2, 4–9, 18, 33, 42, 48, 68, 74, 90, 106, 122, 146, 168–172, 176, 198, 206
Buswell, Robert E. 9

C
Candrakīrti 17, 22
Catuḥpratisaraṇasūtra 90
Cetanādharman 148, 156, 162, 180
cetovimuktiḥ 178
ciraparinirvāyī 102
community 1, 5–6, 8, 11
concentration 14, 26, 29, 100, 116–122, 128, 132, 138, 150, 174, 178, 184, 190, 198
Conze, Edward 110
cultivation (bhāvanā 11, 13–16, 46, 52–62, 74–82, 92, 100, 118–120, 124, 138, 158, 182–184, 188–190, 194, 198–204, 210

D
darśanamārga 7, 14, 86
Daśottara 178
defilements 13–16, 46, 52, 58, 78, 92, 96, 136, 172, 180, 192, 198–204, 210
desire-realm 64, 188
Devakulaṃkula 82
Dhammapada 42, 166
Dharmakīrti 30, 170
Dharmamitra 21
dharmānusārin 46, 52
dhyānaṃ 48, 114, 118–122
Divyāvadāna 208
Dreyfus, George B.J. 9
Dṛṣṭadharmaparinirvāyin 142
dṛṣṭadharmasukhavihārā 166
dṛṣṭīprāpta 154
dṛṣṭisaṃpanna 70
Dutt, N. 110

E
Eimer, Helmut 11
ekābhisamayaḥ 42
Ekavīcika 76, 94–100
embodiment 9, 19, 64, 74, 80, 96–104, 112–120, 128, 132, 140–146
enterer (pratipannaka) 10–11, 16, 44–50, 54–56,

92–100, 148, 182–196, 204–206

F
faculties (indriya) 4, 10, 46, 52, 124, 134, 150–156, 160, 174, 178
faith (śraddhā 8, 10, 30, 46, 52–54, 154, 196
follower 52–54, 132, 196
forbearance 48, 202

G
Gautika 166, 174
Gimello, Robert M. 9
Gnam-rtse-ldeng 19
Gnas-rnying 28
Gnyal 36
Gokhale, V.V. 132
gotra 136
gradual 27, 92, 158, 182–188, 196, 204
Gsang-phu 27
Gtsang25, 27, 29

H
Half-jumper 118
Haribhadra 8, 23, 44, 50
heaven58, 66, 102, 110, 116–118, 126–132, 144
Hopkins, Paul Jeffrey 11, 50
Horner, I.B. 11, 102

I
Immovable 154
intermediate state 9, 62–66, 70–74, 102–104, 114–116, 132–138
irreversible 33, 158, 170–172

Itivuttaka 112

J
Jambudvīpa 82, 214
Jinaputra 68, 84, 90, 126, 188, 214
Jo-mo-nang 27
Jumper 118, 130

K
Ka-dam-pa (bka'-gdams-pa) 24
Kalārasutta 172
Kāmavītarāga 160, 186, 188
Karmapa 24
Kaschewsky, Rudolf 26, 31
Kāsyapīyas 68
kāyasākṣī 11, 100, 142
knowledge 5, 33, 36, 42–46, 80, 170, 184, 198, 202, 212
kramanairyāṇikaḥ 198
kṣīṇāsrava 174
Kuijp, Leonard van der 19, 27, 30, 34
Kulaṃkula 76–78, 82, 86–92

L
laukikamārga 15
Lhasa 19
lineage 13, 21–23, 50, 70, 76, 80, 94, 110, 116, 128, 136–138, 154–160, 202
lokottaramargeṇa 198

M

Mādhyamika-prāsaṅgika 50
Mādhyamika-svātantrika-yogācāra 50
Mahābrahma 66, 102, 116, 128, 132
Mahāyāna 4, 7, 25
Mahāyānasūtrālaṃkāra 26
Maitreya 19, 25
Majjhimanikāya 6
Mal-gro-lha-lung 30, 32
Mañjuśrī 19, 22
Manuṣyakulaṃkula 82
Māra 214
Mar-res-spyi-po-lhas 27
Masefield, Peter 104
May, Jacques 16, 19, 36
Mdo-smad 30
Mimaki, Katsumi 90
mind 5, 30, 33, 48, 150, 164–168, 174, 178, 212–216
Mi-nyag 24
mokṣabhāgīyas 184
mṛdvindriyaḥ 52, 238
Mullin, Glenn H. 5
mundane 15, 48, 52, 60, 80, 150, 158, 168, 188, 200

N
Nāgārjuna 22
Nāropa 26
Ngam-ring 29
Nikāya 6, 13, 42
nirvāṇa 2, 7–9, 13, 16, 58–64, 74, 82, 96–116, 128, 134, 140–146, 160, 166, 174
nītārthasūtra 90
Noble being (ārya) 1–3, 6–7, 10–15, 18, 26, 32, 38, 42, 52, 58, 66, 70, 76, 102, 110, 132–134, 162, 172, 198–202
Non-returner 2, 10–12, 16–17, 42, 62, 68, 76, 92–100, 106, 118, 132–136, 140–144, 148, 158–160, 168, 182, 186–196, 204, 208
Nothingness 194

O
Obermiller, Eugene 25, 110
obstacles 46, 52–58, 62, 74, 82, 138, 148, 158, 188
Once-returner 2, 10–13, 15–17, 42, 62, 76–78, 84, 88, 92–98, 120, 134–136, 144, 158–160, 168, 182, 186–196, 204, 208

P
Pāṃśupradānāvadāna 208
Pañcaviṃśatisāhasrikā 25
parāvṛttajanmā 142
Parihāṇadharman 1 3 6 , 148–152, 156–162, 180
parinirvāṇa 60, 66, 72, 80, 106–108, 136, 142
parivṛttajanmano 142
pluta 116
Po-ta-la 28
Poussin, Louis de la vallée 17, 44, 104, 112, 122

Pradhan, Pralhad 46, 52, 74–78, 86, 92–98, 104, 108, 112, 126, 130, 142, 148, 154–156, 180, 192, 198, 208–210
Prajñāpāramitā 3, 12, 17, 20–22, 25–29, 34, 62, 140, 150
Prajñāvimukta 148–150, 180
Pramāṇa 18, 33
Pramāṇavārttika 1 2 1 , 29–31, 33, 170
prāntakoṭicaturthadhyāna 112
Prasannapadā 17, 112
Prasphuṭapadā 21
Prativedhanādharman 138, 148, 152, 162
Pratyekabuddha 17, 48
pratyekajina 182, 206–208
prayogamārga 46
preparation 46, 52, 60, 184, 198, 208
progressor 92, 158, 182–188, 196, 204
pṛthagjana 15, 62, 64
Pruden, Leo 54–62, 66, 72, 76–80, 88, 94–102, 108, 112–128, 132–134, 140–146, 150, 156, 160, 166–168, 172–178, 184–186, 190, 200, 217
pudgala 44, 90

Q
qualities 4, 7–9, 76, 86, 178

R
Rahula, Walpola 8, 74, 92, 98, 104, 108, 130, 142, 148, 154, 180, 192, 198
realization5, 14, 22, 29, 42, 50–54, 58, 100, 170, 188, 198, 204
realm 11–17, 22, 52, 58, 64–74, 78–80, 86, 92–108, 114–120, 130–136, 140–148, 158–162, 172, 182, 188–202, 206, 210, 239
rebirth 16, 56–64, 68, 74, 78, 86, 92, 98–100, 104–106, 112–118, 124, 130–136, 140–148
result 13, 15–16, 44–64, 74–80, 92–100, 124, 142–144, 148, 158–160, 168, 172, 180–194, 198, 204–210
reversibility 172
rhinoceros 11, 182, 206
Rtse-chen 28
Ruegg, David Seyfort 20
rūpadhātau 120, 138, 142
rūpavītarāga 140
rūpopaga 100

S
Sābhisaṃskāraparinirvāyin 106
śaikṣa 7, 13, 33, 170–176
sakalabandhana 52, 138
Sakṛdāgāmin 94
sakṛnnairyāṇikaḥ 198

śamatha 120
saṃgha 1, 5–9, 11, 13, 17, 35, 42
Saṃghabhadra 146
Saṃghānusmṛtivyākhyā 8
Saṃyutta Nikāya 6, 44, 66,74, 166
Sangītisutta 6
Śāntideva 22
Saptakṛtvaparama 58
Saptasatpuruṣagatī 102
saptasthānakuśala 70
Śariputra 168
sarvacyuto 118
sarvasthānacyuta 116
Sarvāstivāda 13
Sa-skya-pa 20
sāsravaṃ 122, 126
Śāstrī, Dwarikadas 42, 48, 54–62, 66–68, 72, 76–82, 88, 94–102, 106–128, 132–146, 150, 156, 160–168, 172–180, 184–186, 190
Sautrāntika 50, 168
selflessness 44, 148, 158
seven 56–74, 130, 162, 186–188, 196
seven-footed snake 50
seven-petaled leaf 62
seven-timer 58, 62, 128
seven-times-at-the-most 56–62, 74
simultaneous 42, 54, 182–184, 194, 198, 204
skipper 160, 182–196
Skyor-mo-lung 28–29, 33
sNar-thang 126
Snye-thang 24, 26
Sopa, Geshe Lhundup 8, 11
soteriology 7–8, 28, 39
Sphuṭārthā 23
śraddhādhimukta 154
śraddhānusārin 46, 52
śrāvaka 7, 11, 13, 16, 35, 42, 204, 208
Śrāvakabhūmi 102
srota-āpanna 11, 17, 64, 76, 82, 88, 160, 198
Stairway 1, 7, 11, 17, 20, 22, 24, 31–36, 38, 40, 214
Stcherbatsky, Th. 110
Sthitākampya 138, 148, 152, 162
Stod-byang 27
Stream-enterer 2, 10–11, 15, 17, 31, 42–46, 50–64, 72–80, 92, 120, 128, 134–136, 142, 158–160, 182, 186–198, 204–208
Śuddhāvāsas 118, 124–128, 140
suffering 16, 33, 46, 74, 86, 98, 104, 108–110, 130, 146, 170, 202, 208
supermundane 15, 158, 168, 196–200

T

Tathāgata 50
Teacher 44, 144–146, 212
Theravāda 6, 10
Thurman, Robert A.F. 31, 90
tīkṣṇendriya 54
transmigrator 64–72, 76, 100, 104, 116, 128–130, 134, 140, 204

tripiṭaka 44
Triśaraṇagamanasaptati 8
truths, Nobles' Four 52, 110, 198, 202–206, 210
Tsong-kha-pa 1, 6, 9–11, 14–18, 20–31, 34, 40, 70, 78–82, 88, 94, 102–104, 122, 130, 162–166, 178, 196
Twenty Saṃghas 3, 8–9, 17–22, 25–31, 202

U
Ubhayatobhāgavimukta 148, 180
udārācāraparamparā 21
uncontaminated 8, 78–80, 120–126, 200, 210
Upapadyaparinirvāyin 102–108, 112–114, 132
Ūrdhvaṃsrotas 108, 114, 128–132, 138
ūṣmagata 48

V
Vaibhāṣika 46, 50, 64, 68, 144, 176
Vaidya, P.L. 208
vairāgya 136
Vasubandhu 22, 50, 74, 106, 110, 122, 126, 134, 168, 172, 176–178, 214, 217
Vatthūpamasutta 6
vehicle 7, 52, 94, 100, 148, 206
viṃśatiprabhedasaṃgha 3
Vimuktisena 22
Vinaya 5, 8, 19, 28–29, 33, 44, 216

W
Wayman, Alex 102

Y
Yaśomitra 90, 102, 106, 126, 188, 214
Yogācāra 17